THE MYSTERY OF
JACK OF KENT
& THE FATE OF
OWAIN GLYNDŴR

THE MYSTERY OF
JACK OF KENT
& THE FATE OF
OWAIN GLYNDŴR

ALEX GIBBON

ILLUSTRATED BY B.A. REEVES

This book was first published in 2004 by
Sutton Publishing Limited · Phoenix Mill
Thrupp · Stroud · Gloucestershire · GL5 2BU

This revised paperback edition first published in 2007

British Library Cataloguing in Publication Data
A catalogue record for this book is available from the British Library.

ISBN 978-0-7509-3320-9

Typeset in 10/12pt Iowan.
Typesetting and origination by
Sutton Publishing Limited.
Printed and bound in Great Britain by
J.H. Haynes & Co. Ltd, Sparkford.

CONTENTS

Map 1 : Wales	vi
Map 2 : The Legends of Jack of Kent	vii
Foreword	ix
Acknowledgements	xi
Abbreviations and Terminology	xiv
Preface: The Legends of Jack o' Kent	xvii
1. The Celtic Otherworld (25,000 BC–AD 43)	1
2. A Tale of Two Rivers (AD 43–800)	10
3. The Battle for Wales (800–1155)	16
4. The Legacy of the Lord Rhys (1155–1380)	27
5. Owain Glyndŵr (1380–1400)	36
6. Interregnum (1380–1400)	54
7. Uprising (1400–2)	65
8. War (1403)	86
9. Millennium (1404–5)	108
10. Turn of the Tide (1406–9)	128
11. Outlaw (1410–24)	144
12. End-Game (1413–14)	163
13. Halcyon Days (1414–15)	176
14. The Dove and the Raven (563–1415)	198
15. Jack-in-the-Box (1415)	221
16. Epiphany	237
Epilogue (1415–2004)	242
Appendix 1: The Legends' Analysis	267
Appendix 2: Addenda	298
Tables	303
Notes	314
Select Bibliography	328
Index	333

Map 1 : Wales

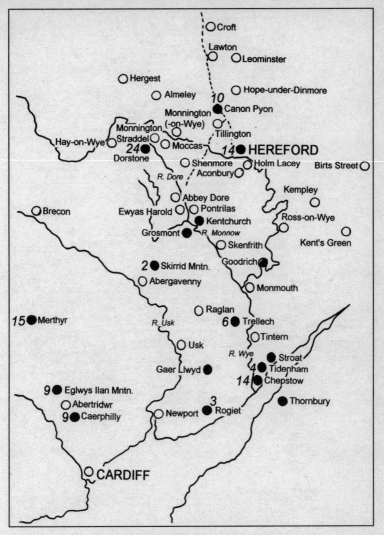

Map 2 : The Legends of Jack of Kent

In addition to the nine legends shown here (Legends 2, 3, 4, 6, 9, 10, 14, 15 and 24), another eight legends are associated with sites in the immediate vicinity of Kentchurch and Grosmont (Legends 1, 5, 12, 17, 19, 22, 23 and 25); meanwhile, another nine legends are not identified with specific sites (Legends 7, 8, 11, 13, 16, 18, 20, 21 and 26). Also shown here are sites associated with Jack of Kent but not with particular legends (e.g. Siôn Cent's Quoits' at Gaer Llwyd), and sites such as Thornbury, where the stone thrown by Jack in Legend 4 landed. It is also worth noting that some legends appear in more than one location, such as Legends 9 and 14, both of which also appear in the vicinity of Kentchurch and Grosmont in addition to those listed above.

FOREWORD

Ten years ago, while virtually living in a car, it seems that I unwittingly embarked upon a long slow journey, for loitering at the wayside of the countless miles that hurtled beneath my wheels, was a character known as Jack o' Kent.

On several occasions I was hijacked by this hitch-hiker, who explained that he was a popular figure in the Borders of Wales – although there were many who said he was a giant, or an elf. Together we frequented country inns in the Marches of Monmouthshire and Herefordshire, where 'Jack' was indeed well-known to the locals – but often he would leave before last orders, or draw his old grey cowl around him, and simply disappear, and it was then that I would hear the village elders tell stories of his dealings with the Devil. They said that long, long ago, in the untold centuries of his youth, Jack had once been much bigger – that he had left vast footprints in the landscape, and enormous boulders embedded in the fields – for as an old worthy of south Herefordshire had once famously remarked . . . ''E were always a'flingin' stones'.

Eventually, in 1996, there came a day when I tired of market-forces, and having thus arrived at a crossroads, I abandoned my vehicle beside an ancient preaching-cross – and there beneath a gnarled old oak stood Jack o' Kent – a character of myth and legend, whose colourful life-story had never been properly addressed.

Without visible means of support, I immediately conceived the ludicrous idea of collecting as many folk-tales about Jack o' Kent as I could find, and assembling the illustrated result into an A5 booklet, using a photocopier and a staple-gun. This would not only make no money whatsoever, and would thus be reprehensible in the eyes of modern society, but it would also preserve an obscure strand of its heritage which had never been collated. Jack immediately declared in favour, donned his traditional Franciscan habit, and together we set off for the nearest village pub – on foot.

What thus began as an inkling, has since become this book, and another two volumes, which are currently under construction. In the process I have been fortunate to have received the help of some of the leading experts in many fields, unfortunate to have been expertly attacked in a field by a mad horse near Stroat at winter solstice, and I can also claim (purely in scholastic terms), to have become an honorary Franciscan monk, for which reason – should this endeavour accidentally result in any money – I shall count it very carefully, with a stick, so as not to touch it. Having embarked upon this self-appointed task, '. . . to fully account for the origin and evolution of the Jack of Kent legends . . .', I have become both poorer and happier then I was when I lived in a car, and indeed somewhat hermit-like, and along the way I have also met the many remarkable people who are listed in the Acknowledgements. Regarding these, I would particularly like to extol the performance-geometer Tina Hyde (people may run), whose influence is so invariably invaluable, intelligent, inimitable, irrepressible, and endearing, Lynn Harrison, whose contribution has exceeded mere photography, Doreen Ruck, who not only fell off her bicycle near Jacky Kent's Barn and lived to tell the tale, but who, along with Sue Rice and her family, are as steeped in the history of the Monnow Valley as the very flanks of Garway Hill, the Dark Age and medieval Welsh Border peasantry, who in the most appalling times and circumstances somehow retained a sense of humour, which survives in their folklore – and of course, the elusive Mr. J. o' Kent, without whom none of this, would ever have happened.

ACKNOWLEDGEMENTS

I would particularly like to thank the following, not only for their regular help in answering my endless questions, but also for being such great company while doing so, after which I can only hope that they will be amused by my conclusions: the Scudamore family of Kentchurch; M. Paul Bryant-Quinn (of the Centre for Advanced Welsh & Celtic Studies, University of Wales, Aberystwyth); Steve Blake (of the Centre for Arthurian & Related Studies, Bangor); Doreen Ruck and Sue Rice (of the Woolhope Naturalists' Field Club, south Herefordshire).

I would also like to thank the following institutions, historians, consultants and individuals, without whose help and cooperation (often beyond the call of duty), this book would have been impossible:

The University of Wales, Aberystwyth; Cambridge University; Edinburgh University; the National Library at the University of Wales; the Library of the Museum of Welsh Life (St Fagan's); the School of Scottish Studies Sound Archive; Cambridge University Library; the Bodleian Library; Guildhall Library (London); St Paul's Cathedral Library; Hereford Cathedral Library; Gloucester Cathedral Library; Exeter Cathedral Library; the National Museum of Wales; the Museum of Welsh Life (St Fagan's); the Franciscans of Oxford Greyfriars; CADW (Welsh Historic Monuments); Cambrian Archaeology (Llandeilo); the Woolhope Naturalists' Field Club (south Herefordshire); the Welsh Watermills Society; the Offices of Westminster Abbey; the Offices of Dover Castle (Kent); the Wales Tourist Board; the English Tourist Board; the Ordnance Survey (Southampton); the National Rivers Authority; St Asaph's Cathedral; Herefordshire County

Council; Monmouthshire (Gwent) County Council; Cumbria County Council; Flintshire County Council; Cardiganshire County Council; Carmarthenshire County Council; Pembrokeshire (Dyfed) County Council; Hereford City Library; Hereford Records Office; St Helens Records Office (Worcester); Cardigan Archives Office; Monmouthshire (Gwent) County Council Library (Cwmbrân); Edinburgh Central Library; Wrexham Central Library; Cardigan Library; Gloucester Records Office; Gloucester Central Library; Bristol Reference Library; Haverfordwest Library; Carmarthen Library; Llandovery Heritage Centre; Carmarthenshire Museums; Monmouthshire Museums.

Dr Robin Gwyndaf (Museum of Welsh Life, St Fagans); Professor Dafydd Johnston (University of Wales, Swansea); Nick Walker (Museum of Welsh Life, St Fagans); Cathlin Macaulay (School of Scottish Studies Sound Archive); Tim Ayres (Courtauld Institute of Arts); Professor George Shaw (School of Scottish Studies); Joe Wisdom (St Paul's Cathedral Library); Quentin Drew (University of Wales Lampeter, Archaeology); Dianne Williams (CADW, Welsh Historic Monuments); Ray Howell (University of Wales, Newport, History/Archaeology); Joan Williams (Hereford Cathedral Library); Sue Hubbard (Herefordshire Records Office); Gerallt Nash (Welsh Watermills Society); Naomi Fields (Linsey Archaeological Services); Sian Hopcyn (Embassy Glyndw^r); Bruce Copplestone-Crow; Ron Shoesmith; Paul Remfry; Graham Spracklin (Woolhope Naturalists' Field Club); Joe Hillaby; Delphine Coleman; Roger Turvey; David Gealey; Chris Barber; Phil Pembridge; Mary Strong; David Atkins (Croft Castle); Mike Chandler (Carew Castle) Richard Davies (Mostyn Hall); Phillip Morgan; Rob Parret; Audrey Tomlin; George Marsh; Diana Cox (Kempsford Mummers); Mark and Julie Whittering; Alan Emanuel; Dr Norman McLeod; Anthony and Shirley Trinder; Tim Hayward-Monsdale; Mike Rizdale; John Chinn; Rowland of Corras; Peter Wihl; John Beatley of Pinner; Elizabeth Hackett; Christopher Feeney; Elizabeth Stone.

I would also like to thank the following, who have all made direct contributions to the book at various stages: Sue Allen; Tina Hyde;

Acknowledgements

Lynn Harrison; Tania Milne; Barry Reeves; Elizabeth Taylor; Richard and Birdy Jordan; Virgil Pomfret; Joy Storey; Rupert Clausen; Russell and Mrs James; Kevin, Nichola, Lianne, Shelley and Jacqui at AJC; Helen Richards; Andrew and Bev at the Clytha, the Evanses at the Star; Keith Ruck, Uncle Ed and the Martins; Emma and Neil; Heidi the vicar; everyone I have left out, and the many keepers of village post offices and country pubs, vicars of village churches, farmers, and memorable suppliers of mince-pies in Aber-erch, etc., who have helped with many an odd enquiry along the way – you know who you are!

Abbreviations and Terminology

b.	=	born
d.	=	died
?	=	date unknown
c.	=	circa/approximate date
b.c.	=	born circa
d.c.	=	died circa
fl.	=	floruit/was active

Loose use of the terms Celtic, Celtic-Christian Church, English, Anglo-Saxon, Norman, Stone Age, Dark Age, Medieval, etc. may be criticised by academics, but these terms are used colloquially in this book precisely for their loose-usefulness. This also applies to the 'Morrigan', a name originally given by the Irish to the dark aspect of the female deity who was well known across Europe as a death-goddess in the form of a raven. Meanwhile, the author is also aware that the invaluable adjective 'folkloric', used by so many writers, does not, according to the standard dictionary, currently exist, a lamentable omission which has lumbered those with an interest in the oral tradition of history with being inelegantly referred to as 'folklor-ists'. This therefore seems an excellent opportunity to point out that since historians are not expected to be 'history-ists', there is absolutely no reason why a student of folklore should not be at least a 'folklorian' – and preferably a 'folkloricist' (soft 'c').

LEGEND 1 : THE BRIDGE

One sunny afternoon, Jack of Kent met the Devil on the banks of the Monnow at Kentchurch, and the Devil agreed to build the bridge over the river in return for the first soul to cross it, but when the work was finished, Jack threw a loaf of bread across the bridge and the hungry village dog raced after it in hot pursuit.

Other versions
Another version sees the villagers of Kentchurch attempting to build the bridge, but the Devil causing it to fall down each night until he is placated by the offer of a soul. Meanwhile, it has also been said that the bridge had to be built and completed within a single night, otherwise it would fall down the next day, and that there was a problem with 'malign spirits' (i.e. the Devil's imps), who were removing the stones as fast as they were put in place. In some accounts a bone or a piece of meat replaces the original loaf of bread, while in another account the dog is replaced by a nocturnal tale of how Jack's shadow was first to make the crossing by moonlight.

Regarding the construction of what is still known as Jacky Kent's Bridge, Jack and the Devil are sometimes said to have brought the stones from Garway Hill, or occasionally from the Graig Mountain, and the rocks which lie in the river nearby are said to be the remains of their work.

[See also Appendix 1, p. 267.]

LEGEND 2 : THROWING STONES

One fine morning on the Skirrid Mountain near Abergavenny, Jack of Kent and the Devil had a stone-throwing competition, which Jack won. As Jack ran away, the Devil, enraged, threw three great stones after him, which landed at Trellech, near Monmouth, where they can still be seen today.

Other versions
This story is said to account for the three standing neolithic stones at Trellech near Monmouth, and also for 'the Devil's Heelmark', a landslip on the the Skirrid mountain near Abergavenny. The 'Heelmark' was allegedly created either when a stone-hurling Devil lost his footing while chasing Jack over the side of the Skirrid, or as the pair landed, having jumped from the top of the nearby Sugarloaf mountain. Alternatively, Jack jumped before throwing the stones himself in answer to the Devil's contempt of his feat. Variations are endless and one occasionally hears of them jumping the other way, or of five stones being thrown rather than three.

[See also Appendix 1, p. 269.]

THE LEGENDS OF JACK O' KENT

The tales of Jack of Kent, a handful of which are still remembered in the Borders of Wales, or are reproduced in books, turn out to consist of at least twenty-five basic legends with numerous variations, which show that Jack is a very much more substantial figure in folklore than either folkloricists or historians have previously realised.

Geographically, the stories are mainly identified with sites distributed across south Herefordshire and Monmouthshire, although Jack is also known in Gloucestershire, and there was once a substantial and overlapping tradition of Sioni Cent (the Welsh version of his name) around Merthyr Tydfil in Glamorganshire, where his exploits were still popular with schoolchildren in the early 1900s, and where a Jack o' Kent necklace was an imp upon a chain. However, while the stories are widespread, the sites associated with Jack cluster conspicuously around a particular part of the Monnow Valley near Offa's Dyke, where the boundary river is the border between England and Wales.

Here, joined by 'Jacky Kent's' Bridge (the Herefordshire version of his name), two ancient settlements face each other across the waters of the Monnow. On the Monmouthshire side ascends the historic village and castle of Grosmont ('great hill') which today lies in Wales, while on the Herefordshire side nestles the tiny hamlet of Kentchurch, which today lies in England. However, this was once the other way round.

In medieval times, the English borough of Grosmont was the most important town in the area, and a favourite haunt of the Crown, with its towering castle flanked by two adjacent fortresses at Whitecastle and Skenfrith, and attended by a cathedralesque church. Meanwhile, far below and adjacent to Kentchurch, was a sprawling settlement of bitter and oppressed Welsh peasantry who inhabited the vanished township of Llanithak in the curious zone of Archenfield, a defunct Welsh kingdom long since corralled on behalf of the English Crown by a network of Marcher lords of mainly Norman descent.

In the early 1300s, the Marcher lords of Kentchurch were the Scudamores, a Norman family whose residence in Britain pre-dated the Norman invasion, and who had propagated from their historic seat of Upton Scudamore in Wiltshire to found the manor of 'Kenschirche' in South Herefordshire in c. 1310, where they have remained to this day. Indeed, in 1840 it was a certain Colonel Scudamore of Kenchurch who, doubtless mindful of Jack of Kent, was responsible for the insertion of the 't' into what only then became Kentchurch (see Table I), so as to prevent his mail from going to nearby Kenderchurch or Kenchester. Thus, while Kentchurch may be named after Jack of Kent, our hero did not derive his name from the village.

In the early 1400s, Sir John Skydemore, Lord of 'Keynchurch' and its chapel Sancta Keyna, was a trusted officer of the Crown during the devastating conflict between King Henry IV and Owain Glyndŵr, the warrior hailed by the Welsh as the last great military leader of their nation against the Anglo-Saxon regime. The war mainly spanned the years 1400–10, and as a soldier of distinction Scudamore remained publicly loyal to the king, and was charged with the defence of various key castles in south Wales before being knighted in 1408. However, it subsequently emerged that at some point he had secretly married Glyndŵr's daughter Alice, for which he was branded a traitor, fined, and stripped of all his titles in 1433.

Furthermore, it was also rumoured at Kentchurch that Scudamore and his wife had sheltered a withered and world-weary Glyndŵr in the wake of his final defeat, and it is this allegation, supported by numerous details, combined with the fact that Kentchurch Court also appears to be the epicentre of the Jack of Kent legends, that has led many to suggest that

Owain and Jack might be one and the same. However, until now no one has ever understood the real nature of the connection between the last military hero of the Welsh nation and Jack of Kent, the hero of Border-country folklore.

As we shall see, the folkloric Jack of Kent has a great deal in common with the modern Doctor Who: a character with magical powers, who exists independently of time, and who obtains a new lease of life whenever a new actor appears to play the role. It is thus very likely that there have been a series of Jack of Kents throughout history, and a comprehensive list of suspects suggested by previous investigators will be found in Table II. However, the four main candidates who have traditionally been suggested are as follows:

Candidate 1: OWAIN GLYNDŴR (*c.* 1354–1415)

The celebrated last leader of the Welsh nation against the Anglo-Saxon oppressor. His uprising began in 1400, his extraordinary triumph lasted from 1403 to 1405, his final defeat was complete by 1410, and in 1413 he mysteriously vanished. With his outstanding credentials Owain is the most viable Jack of Kent of them all, and is the subject of this book.

Candidate 2: SION CENT (*c.* 1375–*c.* 1445)

A radical Welsh bard of notoriety and renown, whose uncompromising death-poetry reflected 'the voice of the preacher' and who flourished in the aftermath of Glyndŵr's war. Like Glyndŵr he has been linked by many authors to Lollardy, Kentchurch and the Scudamores, and it has been erroneously suggested that he is identical with the next candidate.

Candidate 3: JOHN OF KENT (Rector of Kentchurch)
(fl. 1381–90)

The priest of the Scudamores' private chapel at Kentchurch in the late 1300s, just before Glyndŵr's war (see Table III). His ecclesiastical credentials, evident residence at Kentchurch, and suggested identity with the candidate above have caused him to be viewed with great suspicion by many investigators.

Candidate 4: JOHN DE WENT (*c.* 1300–48)

The 20th Provincial Minister (Head) of the Franciscans in England, whose name means 'John of Gwent'. Possibly born at Chepstow, he presided over the Grey Franciscan Order at the peak of its corruption. He died at the onset of the Black Death and was buried at Hereford, and his Franciscan credentials thus find him clad in the grey habit traditionally associated with the folkloric Jack of Kent.

The lives of the 'pre-Glyndŵr' candidates (3 and 4), along with some of the other suspects (see Table II), here serve mainly to confirm that the tradition of Jack of Kent probably pre-dates Glyndŵr's assumption of the role by a matter of centuries. Meanwhile, Candidate 2 wrote his poetry in the wake of Glyndŵr's war, and will therefore be discussed in the Epilogue.

This leaves us with only Glyndŵr to consider, apart from one other major candidate, whose omission from the list above is caused solely by the failure of previous investigators to suggest him. This overlooked contender is the hedgerow-preacher John Ball (?–1382), the co-author with Wat Tyler of the Peasants' Revolt in 1381. As we shall see, John Ball's status as both a cleric and a rebel is highly conducive to his candidature. He is actually recorded as 'John (Mad Priest) of Kent' and his ambition was to become Wat Tyler's Archbishop of Canterbury. Furthermore, his egalitarian message was exceptionally well received by the oppressed Welsh peasantry of the south Herefordshire borders, and nineteen years later many of his former followers (whom we shall henceforth call 'Ballards') were targeted by, and signed up to, the cause of Owain Glyndŵr. This might well imply that John Ball was an important precursor in the role, whereafter the inheritance of his legacy helped to launch Glyndŵr as the ultimate Jack of Kent.

Whenever Jack and I set off across country for some nearby village inn, we would always come to Grosmont, wind down Cupid's Hill, cross the Monnow via Jacky Kent's Bridge, and babble along the riverbank until we came to the pub at the water's edge, which stands upon the Scudamore estate at

Kentchurch. With its faded whitewash and a picture of Jack beside the bar, the Bridge Inn used to boast a somewhat dilapidated charm, but today the fire blazes in the hearth and the inn sign still depicts the scene on Jacky Kent's Bridge on the glorious occasion that Jack deceived the Devil, armed only with a loaf of bread and a spirited village dog (see Legend 1).

Later, I would wander home, and spend long hours wondering who Jack really was. After all, his legendary performance upon Jacky Kent's Bridge had displayed his essential features: he was a clergyman, traditionally a Franciscan, who rejoiced in dealing with the Devil. However, such tales as 'Throwing Stones' (Legend 2) and 'The Millstone Grit' (Legend 4) showed that this was also a pastime which he had once pursued on a grand scale, in the form of a boulder-hurling giant. After much contemplation, I finally perfected two theories regarding Jack's origins – and since these theories are not mutually exclusive, and are essentially consecutive, it is possible that both are true. Furthermore, they are both working principles via which the popular term 'a Jack of Kent' might have become a catch-all phrase applicable to a whole class of individuals. First, therefore, I offer you:

THE EVERYMAN THEORY

In AD 597 St Augustine allegedly landed on the Isle of Thanet, aligned himself with the King of Kent (Cant), whose powerful overlordship then extended as far north as the Trent and as far west as Mercia, and established himself as the very first Archbishop of 'Kent-erbury' (Canterbury) – whereupon he imperiously turned his attention to the Celts.

However, by this time the Celts had already been Christian for almost 300 years, in a relaxed form amicably fused with the old pagan beliefs that had once been tolerated by the Romans in Britain. Furthermore, a purer Celtic Christianity had recently been distributed from the island of Iona to the north and west – and therefore, since the heathen Anglo-Saxons had only recently converted for reasons of political convenience, the

Celts were scarcely delighted to receive instructions in such matters from an Anglo-Saxon-allied 'Johnny-Come-Lately' like St Augustine.

Thus, having been duly rebuffed in his attempts to dictate new religious procedures to the Celtic bishops, St Augustine promptly hurled the following partisan prophecy in the direction of the Celts: 'If ye will not have peace with the brethren, ye shall have war from thine enemies, and if ye will not preach the way of life to the English, ye shall suffer the punishment of death at their hands.'

At this point it so happened that the Celtic West started to collapse, and the Celts were driven back from the River Severn and pressurised into capitulation upon the margins of modern Wales. Thus united in victory, St Augustine and the Anglo-Saxons continued to fuse their interests, and a 'hellfire and brimstone' message from Canterbury was soon delivered at spearpoint to the inhabitants of a beleaguered Wales, in the form of a two-pronged supernatural assault. First, the traditional Celtic attitude to the next world came under fire, as the dichotomy of the Christian afterlife was harshly underlined, and a terrible fate was predicted for the Celts if they did not fully abandon their old beliefs and take the absolute existence of God and the Devil very seriously indeed. Secondly, it was demanded that the Celts immediately abandon their traditional reverence for their ancestors, those mighty progenitors who were believed to send aid from beyond the grave, whose spirits haunted countless sacred stones and ancient burial sites, and who were regularly reincarnated in human form as formidable Celtic leaders. Indeed, as the invaders were doubtless keen to point out, since only Christ was empowered to return in this manner, such supernatural (and in any case arguably semi-pagan) entities were clearly not 'of God' and must therefore be demonic.

My suggestion, therefore, is that a 'Sioni Cent' is a term which may have originated among the Dark Age Welsh Border peasantry as a name applied to overbearing English clergymen from Kent, who, armed with the hellfire and brimstone message of St Augustine, had also brought with them the newly promoted and redesigned Christian Devil as a threat of enforcement. In their weakened position, the only response available to the Celtic peasantry of what would soon become the Welsh Marches, was thus to ridicule Beelzebub in precisely the manner found in 30 per cent of the (surviving) Jack of Kent legends.

In common with the Scandinavians, and other peoples of northern Europe who cherished their ancient roots, the Celts genuinely believed that their ancestors had been colossi, which is why numerous ancient British burial mounds, cromlechs and monoliths are still called 'Giants' Graves'. In commemorating these ancestors within a folk tradition, the Celts thus employed countless tales of boulder-hurling giants, who performed incredible feats of strength in a thoroughly warlike manner but who subsequently became rather smaller, and more domesticated, and developed an interest in constructive pursuits such as stone masonry and farming. This is also the pattern of the Scandinavian Trolls, many of whose adventures were adopted by the British Celts and adapted to feature their own local heroes, thus preserving memories of the early tribal leaders who had once inspired the late Neolithic era and left their megalithic marks upon the land. However, in AD 597 the overbearing clergymen from Kent had arrived and denounced all such heritage as demonic, whereafter the Anglo-Saxon agenda was to identify the ancestral Celtic giants with the Devil.

With this in mind, it is interesting to reconsider such tales as 'Throwing Stones' (Legend 2), in which the Celtic perspective can be restored simply by replacing the Devil with the original ancestral giant. The result is the simple but enormously powerful image of a mighty Celtic ancestor standing upon the Skirrid Mountain, having precipitated a landslip, and hurling three huge boulders eastwards in the direction of Trellech ('Tri-lech'), where their arrival is marked by three standing Neolithic stones.

If so, we may well infer that the Dark Age Celts knew exactly what they were doing, for if the 14-mile line from the Skirrid Mountain to the standing stones at Trellech is extended another 200 miles eastwards across Britain, the result is a direct hit upon the 25-mile-wide target of Kent in south-east England. This is surely no coincidence in view of the fact that the subject of the boulder-hurler's wrath was a folkloric Anglo-Saxon clergyman called Jack of Kent, and the fact that nobody has ever mentioned it before shows, I suspect, that folklore should be taken more seriously.

Furthermore, these three standing stones at Trellech are also occasionally known as 'Harold's Stones', and are alleged to commemorate three chieftains lost by King Harold in his battles against the Welsh before 1066. King Harold's family were, in fact, none other than the Earls of Kent – and it is therefore most interesting that an old saying in the Monnow Valley, 'As great as Jacky Kent and the Devil!', appears to mirror a more widespread popular saying that went, 'As great as the Devil and the Earl of Kent!', another that instructed, 'Go to the Devil or go to Kent!', and one which in the 1700s declared, 'As great *friends* as the Devil and the Earl of Kent!' – thus confirming the popular perception that both Jack and the Devil originally came from the same place, Kent.[1]

Under normal circumstances, therefore, the sceptical Welsh Border peasantry mainly saw the Devil as Jack's colleague rather than his adversary, both of them having come from 'Kent-erbury', and so the folkloric relationship between the two is usually just that, Jack being depicted as a clergyman 'in league' with a Devil whose power to intimidate is deliberately depleted by his portrayal as a malleable fool (Legends 1, 7, 8, 14, 23, 26) and as a loser in any kind of competition (Legends 4, 6, 10, 18). Better still from the Border Welsh point of view, by the Middle Ages a third of the male population of Britain was called John (i.e. Jack), and countless clergymen were thus actually called 'John of Kent'. By this time such men were so learned in divers sciences that they were frequently said to have sold their souls to the Devil in return for supernatural powers, and were therefore regularly accused of witchcraft.

If correct, this Everyman theory would therefore imply that long before the Middle Ages, Jack of Kent was already a well-known wizard-priest who had always been in league with the Devil. It was thus perfectly natural that the antics of this overbearing duo should feature not only boulder-hurling and mud-slinging competitions, which (as the Devil's master) Jack invariably won (Legends 4, 6, 10), but also agricultural business arrangements, in which the Devil was embarrassingly swindled (Legends 7, 14), and theological banana-skins which questioned the very basis of St Augustine's harshly polarised cosmology (Legends 1, 13, 23).

This theory, which illustrates that (like the English) the Welsh have always referred to Everyman as 'Sioni' or Jack, can thus explain Jack's geographical location, his customary clerical garb and the context of his dealings with the Devil. It also identifies the term 'Sioni Cent' as an essentially pre-medieval Border Welsh tradition, which originally reflected scepticism regarding overbearing English clergymen from Kent, and which thus comfortably embraces such early suspects as John of Kent 'Cancellarius' (see Table II) who lived during the 1200s. However, for the purposes of this book, which will paradoxically confirm none other than Owain Glyndŵr as the latest and greatest performer in the role, I also propose another theory.

THE OUTLAW THEORY

In 1321 (perhaps in the context of a Welsh Border peasantry long familiar with the concept of a wizard-priest called Sioni Cent), there occurred the famous Lancastrian Revolt, led by Thomas de Lancaster, the elder brother of Henry de Lancaster ('Wryneck'), Lord of Monmouth and the Three Castles (Skenfrith, Whitecastle and Grosmont), in the heart of the Monnow Valley. This revolt against Edward II and his hated favourites the Despensers (who were Marcher lords in the Chepstow area), thus inevitably focused upon Thomas de Lancaster's headquarters in the north and upon his brother Henry's headquarters in the Monnow Valley at Grosmont, where the Red Rose of Lancaster is said to have originated. Thus, while living in the lee of Lancaster, many local Welsh Border peasantry were keen to support such an uprising against the despised Despensers and the English Crown.

However, the revolt failed. Thomas de Lancaster was caught and beheaded the following year, and many of his supporters became outlaws in the forests and mountains of Yorkshire and Cumbria, through which passes the route from Wakefield (Yorkshire) to Kendal (Cumbria). Meanwhile, many hopes had been dashed, and amid the embers were found documents that not only compared Thomas de Lancaster with King Arthur, but which also hinted at a possible alliance between Thomas de Lancaster and Robert the Bruce of Scotland, with a view to an invasion of northern England by a Scottish army.

So it was that from a Welsh point of view the eternal dream of a Celtic alliance against the English had been thwarted yet again, and a glorious opportunity had been lost to reverse the stranglehold imposed upon Wales by Edward I. Meanwhile, Edward II remained as unpopular as ever, and as Lancaster's revolt faded into memory there were also many in England who lamented its failure. Furthermore, those outlaws who continued to survive in Yorkshire and in Cumbria proved ingenious and resourceful, and sometimes fled into Wales – and so it was that Thomas de Lancaster's revolt of 1321 became the basis of a romantic strand in literature.

One of the main heroes to emerge from this scenario seems to have been Robin Hood, apparently a certain 'Robyn Hode' of Wakefield, a Lancastrian rebel who was duly outlawed and who, just as folklore prescribes, did indeed possess an outlaw friend called 'John the Little' (whose real name was Reynold Greenleaf).

I therefore suggest, that the traditional behaviour of such rebels was essentially as follows. Once outlawed, they fled swiftly towards Kendal in south-east Cumbria, where a well-known woollen cloth was manufactured in a factory later immortalised by a weaver called John Kempe ('Jack of Kemp') of Flanders (see Table II). Here they obtained the necessary clothing for survival in the mountain forests, and promptly dyed it green, using dyer's greenwood from the adjacent region of Windermere immediately to the west. Thus camouflaged, they then vanished into the trees, clad in an outfit identified by Shakespeare in *Henry IV* as 'Kendal Green'.

However, the crucial piece of information here is that Kendal lies in the valley of the River Kent, and its name is thus derived from 'Kents-dale'. Therefore to the wider public any such outlaw was simply a 'Jack o' (the) Kent' or a 'Jack-in-the-(Kentsdale)-Green'. Furthermore, since Robin Hood's original companion was an equal partner and colleague named Little John, there was even a 'Little Jack' as a role model (see Appendix I: Legend 10).

If this theory stands, then after 1321 an outlaw in the woods might equally be referred to as 'a Robin (of the) Hood' or as 'a Jack (of the) Kent', for both meant exactly the same thing (e.g. 'John A Kent', see Table II). Indeed, the use of catch-all names for outlaws was a natural evolution, firstly because it offered anonymity to outlaws, who remained constantly on the move so as to obscure their identities, and secondly because their anonymity was traditionally respected by the peasantry, who supported and applauded outlaws as popular heroes in the face of an oppressive regime.

As a result, there existed an ever-shifting itinerant subculture of outlawry amid the trees, which comprised a full spectrum of society, from ex-baronial rebels and fallen gentlemen to ordinary criminals, all of whose interests were mingled in the common cause of anonymity and opposition to the state. Thus, whenever such a Jack of Kent was caught, it was notoriously difficult to ascertain, in the absence of either a national database or a photo-fit picture, who he really was. Invariably he would withhold his name, either because as the leader of a rebel band he sought to protect his comrades and sustain the cause for which he stood by never being seen to die, or because as a simple outlaw he was determined to protect his family and honourably maintain anonymity among thieves. Furthermore, since a name extracted by torture couldn't be relied upon, such a man would simply be referred to even by the courts as a 'Robin Hood' or a 'Jack of Kent'.

Meanwhile, there was great fun to be had at the expense of the establishment regarding this entire affair, because the 'Kendal Green' worn by such outlaws was also the uniform of the king's Foresters. These much hated and notoriously corrupt local officials, who were famous for extortion, would therefore have been open to accusations of highway robbery when they were in fact elsewhere – and in such circumstances would desperately have exclaimed 'Well, there must be a Jack o' Kent in the woods!' Indeed, as a former forester himself, Robyn Hode of Wakefield would have been particularly adept at 'impersonating a police officer' in this manner, doubtless thus relieving rich travellers of their goods relatively gently, while also having something to prove regarding the dispensing of natural justice.

Such was the unpredictable nature of the forest outlaw phenomenon that it would also have allowed the peasantry to invoke a spurious Jack o' Kent in the local woods as an excuse for actions or embezzlements which would otherwise be punishable. Meanwhile, this entire hornets' nest also raised the disturbing possibility that the man dressed in Kendal Green possessed the demonic power of pluripresence, the ability to be in two places at the same time – a forked path leading rapidly into territory where the folkloric figures of both Robin Hood and Jack o' Kent become sprite-like and elemental, like the ancient spirits of the woods, while as tribal leaders they also begin to merge with the perennial Celtic figure known today as the Oak-king or Green Man.

Finally, this theory also explains two more phenomena: first, that Jack of Kent is occasionally called Jack of Kemp in old documents (suddenly explicable by the identification of the famous weaver John Kempe with Kendal); and secondly, that while Kentchurch hosts a legend in which Jack of Kent abruptly becomes an outlaw (Legend 19), at Canon Pyon in south Herefordshire he actually shares a legend with Robin Hood (Legend 10), thus perhaps provoking T.A. Davies's reference in *c.* 1900 to Jack of Kent as 'the Robin Hood of the Wye'.

From this we might well conclude that in the Lancastrian-held region of Monmouth and the Monnow Valley, and in the adjacent areas of the southern Marches, 'a Jack o' (the) Kent' simply became the popular term for an outlaw, rather than 'a Robin Hood'! However, while the Outlaw theory can account for Jack's location in the southern Marches, through his connection with the Lancastrian territory of Henry 'Wryneck', can it also account for his customary clerical garb and for his dealings with the Devil? Regarding Jack's garb, the answer is yes, because the Franciscan Order had an exceptional reputation for harbouring outlaws, and if a forest outlaw wished to visit a town then the low-profile grey habit of a Franciscan was a popular disguise. Furthermore, in competing with the popular image of an outlaw clad in forest green, it may well be that the image of an outlaw wearing clerical garb was boosted in 1381 by the example of John Ball.

Regarding Jack's dealing with the Devil, the answer is also yes, because, as we have seen, the higher clergy at least, especially senior Franciscans, were regularly accused of being in league with the Devil, as, significantly, was a Franciscan-supported outlaw named Owain Glyndŵr.

Once persuaded, we are thus forced to address the fact that the Outlaw theory accounts just as well as the Everyman theory for all Jack's essential features. This therefore raises the issue of whether the Everyman theory is required at all, and whether Jack of Kent might simply be explained by the Outlaw theory, and by the outlaws John Ball and Owain Glyndŵr – in which case there would have been no tradition of Jack of Kent before 1321.

However, in 1595 Shakespeare's close colleague and contemporary Anthony Munday, who was a popular playwright specialising in outlaw romances and tales of Robin Hood, chose to write a play entitled *Jack A Kent, Jack A Cumber* (i.e. Cumbria), in which he seems to confirm *all* of our suspicions. Having described Jack A Kent as a powerful Welsh wizard who was already 'anciaunt of fame' and allegedly acquainted with Llywelyn the Great (d. 1240), Munday promptly exclaims, 'why how now Jack! Turned greene to Fryer's gray?' (and then vice versa), proceeds to use pluripresence as a dramatic device and portrays Jack A Cumber (Cumbria) as a Johnny-Come-Lately whose attempt to masquerade as Jack A Kent is a poor substitute for the 'anciaunt' original.

If, regarding the above, and also the putative contributions of St Augustine and King Harold, we therefore concur with Munday's assertion that Jack was already 'anciaunt' in 1595, but had recently acquired a well-known tendency to flit between 'green and grey', it is therefore plausible to suggest that *both* these theories are essentially correct, in which case Jack o' Kent's folkloric career can be summarised as follows:

In the wake of St Augustine, 'Jack of Kent' first arose among the Welsh Border peasantry during the 600s as a term for overbearing English clergymen from Kent (Kenter-bury), and thus came to refer to a wizard-priest in league with the Devil. However, as time went by the Welsh peasantry grew familiar not only with this popular clerical villain, but also with the fact that before long there were Englishmen called John of Kent living to the west of them, as well as to the east.

After 1066, Jack of Kent was thus no longer useful to the Welsh Border peasantry as a cultural weapon against Anglo-Saxons coming exclusively from the east, and he was therefore increasingly used as a weapon against the Anglo-Norman medieval Church, and especially against its ongoing propaganda effort, supported by the state, to instil a polarised and paralysing fear of the Devil into a Celtic race who had once seen the next world very differently.

The result of this was that Jack steadily became less of an enemy and more of an ally to the Welsh, as he was employed primarily to criticise the Church and to serve as an eternal reminder that the Devil was not to be taken seriously. After all, for the Welsh at that time it was important that they should remember their original heritage as 'Christians' of an older tradition, and paramount that they remember that they knew *who* had invented the medieval Devil, and Hell, and *when*, and *why*, and that they should never let their children be ruled by fear of such a terrible thing.

During the early 1300s the corruption of the clergy, and especially the Franciscan Order, was at its peak, scepticism was rife, and Jack of Kent was therefore kept busy in his business of making a fool out of the Devil and the Church, a task upon which he is engaged in a third of the surviving legends.

By 1321, Jack the wizard-priest had thus become a fully fledged hero and something of a supernatural outlaw set against the established Church, and it was at this point that Thomas de Lancaster raised his standard of revolt. The aftermath of that failure sparked the rise of the outlaw romance in popular culture, which was centred around Wakefield in Yorkshire and the valley of the River Kent in Cumbria, and as a supernatural outlaw already named Jack o' Kent, it was very natural for our hero to merge with the new 'Jack o' (the) Kent', and thus to expand his operations against the Anglo-Norman regime. Furthermore, being already a clergyman, it was also understandable that Jack's habit now became grey, since this was the traditional disguise of outlaws sheltered by the Franciscans. Thus we have neatly explained why the folkloric Jack o' Kent wears a grey cowl and is a wizard-priest-outlaw, while his latter-day colleague Robin Hood is but a simple outlaw, clad in forest green.

The year 1348 saw the nightmare of the Black Death, which almost certainly killed the head of the Franciscan Order, John de Went. This natural disaster was widely interpreted as a punishment from God for the corruption of the clergy, and was doubtless also interpreted by those peasantry who adhered to beliefs much older than Christianity as the failure of the new magic to placate the elements of the pre-Christian (Celtic) Otherworld. After the Black Death, with the population drastically reduced and the Church and State having lost credibility in tandem, the peasantry were suddenly in demand, and were able to demand higher wages – and the level of peasant militancy increased.

In 1381 the Peasants' Revolt erupted, led by Wat Tyler and John Ball, the latter being an elusive recusant and wizard-priest-outlaw known as 'John (Mad Priest) of Kent'. Meanwhile, in north Wales, a certain Welshman descended from the ancient rulers of both north and south was preparing to marry Margaret Hanmer, the daughter of a high-flying English lawyer. That Welshman was Owain Glyndŵr, of Glyndyfrdwy and Sycharth (Llansilin) on the borders of north-east Wales. His neighbours the Hanmers lived nearby, in Maelor Saesneg, a part of Flintshire embezzled by the English, and it was through Glyndŵr's involvement with the Hanmers that he soon became a student of law at the Inns of

Court in London, and thus added legal acumen to his well-known prowess as a soldier in the English army.

As a descendant of the ancient royal lineages of Wales, Owain Glyndŵr was an example of Welsh nobility, an archaic status still recognised by an English Crown which sought to absorb such individuals into the English establishment by the provision of certain privileges. These privileges remained substantial, and even resulted, as R.R. Davies (*The Revolt of Owain Glyndŵr*) observes in 'quasi-autonomous islets of Welsh rule'. However, despite such prudent generosity, the English establishment also offered a glass-ceiling above which a Welshman could never rise – and so Glyndŵr was permanently excluded from the prospect of knighthood.

In 1387, Glyndŵr effectively retired from the English army, and, perhaps inspired by his personal bard, appears to have quietly embraced his royal Welsh lineage and to have embarked upon a drastic course of action intended to achieve the liberation of his oppressed countrymen – but which in the event brought more destruction upon them than even the Black Death. His motivation to a considerable extent appears to have been genuinely inspired by the ancient Welsh (bardic) tradition of prophecy, and it is thus a fact that Glyndŵr's actions cannot be properly understood unless the language of prophecy is taken seriously, for as R.R. Davies also observes, 'Glyndŵr subscribed fully to the historical and prophetic ideology of his own propaganda', an ideology 'which was not solely the preserve of a literary coterie and its aristocratic patrons', but which 'in a vulgar and often bowdlerised form also dominated the popular oral culture of Wales'.

Such was the medium by which Owain Glyndŵr, in a form unrecorded by definition, communicated with and raised the illiterate mass of the Welsh peasantry, aided by many a minstrel with a tavern song, and with such spectacular success that for two brief but never-forgotten years the English and their army were uprooted and expelled from Wales.

Much later, finally defeated but still hailed by his core supporters as the Son of Prophecy who would eventually return, Owain Glyndŵr ultimately refused to die. Instead he deliberately disappeared, and so began the mystery of his fate.

As we mentioned earlier, there are reasons to suspect that an ageing and outlawed Glyndŵr subsequently received shelter from his daughter Alice and her husband Sir John Scudamore at Kentchurch in south Herefordshire. This trail was recently pursued by the Owain Glyndŵr Society, which in 1996 set out to ascertain the location of Owain's burial site before excavating a mound at nearby Monnington Straddel, to no avail.

Instead, it may be that it requires a Jack of Kent expert, rather than an Owain Glyndŵr expert, to inadvertently stumble upon the site of Owain's grave – but no excavations should be countenanced, either without the presence of a representative of the Romano-Celtic-Christian Church, which is what Glyndŵr would have wanted, or without putting such an issue to the people of Wales via its National Assembly, which is also what he would have wanted. Like all of us, Owain has a right to rest in peace, and it might also be pointed out that it would be refreshingly and uncharacteristically civilised of modern homo sapiens, and a credit to Wales, to decide *not* to meddle for a change, where meddling is possible.

Finally, therefore, let us embark in that spirit upon what will be a great journey, for it is time to move swiftly towards a meeting with Owain Glyndŵr himself, whose story we shall tell from an entirely new perspective. Already we have spoken much of those ancestral giants, the precursors of both Owain Glyndŵr and the folkloric Jack o' Kent, who were in fact the fallen Celtic heroes of the late Neolithic era, and it is for this reason that we must briefly pay a visit to the Stone Age.

* * *

> . . . *such worshipping of stones, there was,*
> *before the coming of good St Patrick.*
>
> (*The Book of Leinster*)

LEGEND 3 : THE DEVIL'S QUOIT

At Rogiet, near Chepstow, Our Lord and the Devil were engaged in a trial of strength upon the summit of Gray Hill. The Devil hurled a stone into the long field beyond Putcher's field, where it still stands, but Our Lord threw a bigger one into the Channel, where it formed the Denny.

Other versions
Although the story as it is told today features Our Lord in the hero's role, there are reasons to suspect (see Appendix 1), that this was originally a story of Jack of Kent, and that he was subsequently supplanted by Our Lord for Christian reasons. Meanwhile, it is also sometimes said that the standing stone at Rogiet was hurled from across the Channel by the Devil, who had experienced a fit of rage at Portishead near Bristol.
[See also Appendix 1, p.271.]

LEGEND 4 : THE MILLSTONE GRIT

Upon the heath known as Poor Man's Allotment at Tidenham Chase near Chepstow, Jack of Kent and the Devil were engaged in another stone-throwing contest. The Devil took a millstone grit, a score feet long, and hurled the stone as far as the Horse Pill over a mile away, where it lies beside the railway line at Stroat to this day. However, baring his chest, and inhaling the sharp sea breeze, Jack twirled his slab above his head before landing his stone on the other side of the Severn near Thornbury! The writer W.H. Greene provides us with a little poem which commemorates this story:

> If ever to Stroat you happen to go
> The Devil's Quoit there you'll surely see
> And beyond the river, the good folk show
> Jack's little pebble at Thornbury

[See also Appendix 1, p. 272.]

ONE

THE CELTIC OTHERWORLD
(25,000 BC–AD43)

STONE

In the Palaeolithic era the production of new life was often assumed to be a purely female procedure, and so it was believed that the entity which had given birth to the world was surely a goddess. Stone had clearly been used by the goddess in the foundation of the world, and therefore it was a sacred substance, with a mystical dimension.

Stone also offered shelter, heat and weaponry, and each evening the Palaeolithic hunter returned to his wombish cave, struck a spark to produce fire, propped a flint-headed spear against a boulder, and wondered if he would make a kill tomorrow. Soon, it occurred to him that he might ask the goddess for success, and so at night he tried to communicate with her via the medium of stone.

Cave art is therefore thought to address a supernatural realm that lies beyond the surface of the cave wall. Thus handprints seem to reach into the lithosphere, and pictures of hunted animals are superimposed, having been dispatched by ritual into the rock with the aid of rhythmic chants, trances and hallucinogens. If so, such images record the careers of early tribal seers, whose prayers were answered (for tribes which survived) either by success in hunting, or by the darkness itself – as their chants re-echoed from special caves and places such as the Hearkening Rocks near Monmouth – and thus confirmed that matter was aware of Man.

Soon, the hunter and the seer became dual roles. The hunter

became a great tribal leader, while the seer became the high priest of a cavernous church, enchanting a realm that would one day become the Otherworld of the Celts.

WATER

While stone reflected sound, water reflected the human face, confirming the existence of an Otherworld immanent within matter, and containing the analogues of everything in life. More importantly, however, it was through the water-cycle that the spirits were transported, as they permeated the mysterious 'deep' of the subterranean, sea and sky.

THE MOON

The earliest lunar calendars were engraved even as the last Neanderthals stood with their backs to the rugged coast of western Europe, where far below the precipice of *Stone* there churned the *Waters* of birth and renewal: a vast cauldron stirred by the menstrual tides of the *Moon*, a shining goddess of creation and destruction, whose unerring advance through a monthly trinity of phases – new, full and dark – determined the moment at which birth, survival or extinction would occur.

In the Neolithic era, the connection between sex and procreation was recognised, a potential threat to the goddess's omnipotence, which she immediately transcended by becoming the Virgin who had created the living world by a miraculous birth. Nevertheless, a male divine-principle, interactive with the goddess, was now in play, frequently in the form of a miraculous son, who, having sprung forth from her body (the earth), returned to the Otherworld before springing forth again and again, sometimes by an incestuous procedure.

At this time the three elements of Neolithic science, *Stone*, *Water* and the *Moon*, were brought into powerful interaction with the erection of tribal earthworks and megaliths such as those at Silbury Hill and Stonehenge. Smaller monoliths also appeared upon the hillsides as the significance of stone inspired the ritual of burial, and burial sites were marked with a head-stone into which the spirit of the deceased could be summoned to converse. Meanwhile, as the rituals surrounding the death and burial of great tribal leaders became more sophisticated, the Celtic tribes migrated from central Europe to become established in Britain under a plethora of tribal kings.

The function of a Celtic tribal king was twofold: to guarantee the harvest (domestic policy), and to produce victory in battle (foreign policy) – and as the divine son of the virgin goddess he embodied the vitality of the tribe.

While the tribe was successful, it remained entrenched within the territory it traditionally controlled, its survival facilitated by defensible high ground, enclosing fertile lowlands in which crops could be grown. Here the king reigned like a demigod in conjunction with the seers, and he was encouraged to consort with many wives.[2] However, his rule might be cut short by a horrific ending – for when the king's life was threatened by ill-health or by advancing age, his vitality was reclaimed by the tribe. Upon a four-pointed oak tree the king then underwent a voluntary sacrifice for the benefit of all, undergoing in terrible stages the Triple-Death, a ritual procedure during which his flesh was stripped from his bones, and his vitality transferred to his successor.

Afterwards, a burial site was selected, ideally upon high ground and adjacent to the tribal river boundary. Here the king was interred, and a stone tomb or cromlech constructed upon his grave – and so the stones of ancient cromlechs (or giants' graves) remained forever sacred to the Celts, because they knew that the spirits who inhabited them were the mighty ancestors of the past.[3]

From where he lay, the fallen king continued to guard the frontier and to raise the crops – for he had passed into the Otherworld and thus was immanent within matter, and within the processes of nature. As water rained upon his grave, it caused his spiritual essence to flow away, both down into the river valley, where it charged the defensive boundary river and ultimately knew the sea, and down into the fields where it 'pushed up the daisies' and the crops. In this way the king epitomised the process by which corn became flesh, springing forth from the body of the goddess (the earth), being consumed by man, who then returned to the earth, before springing forth as corn once more, and so on.

In all of this, the essential medium was water, for via the water-cycle the deceased ruler was at one with the goddess, and thus possessed omniscient knowledge of the past and future. He knew the bottomless Celtic deep of the subterranean, and also the deep of the sea ('Môr'), where the Moon appointed time and tides. He spanned the deep of the sky, and fell upon the crops as rain, he dwelt in sacred rivers and lakes; he was transported by mists which rose and fell, clinging to the mountain peaks, and he was immanent in damp air. In the deep, the king dwelt not only with the ancestors but with many other entities of the Otherworld, ranging from aspects of the goddess herself, to fairies, or elementals such as the earth-spirits or goblins who dwelt in the mines, attended old cromlechs, haunted landslip areas, or issued forth from fissures in disturbed ground.

So it was that such a crop-raising elder statesman might perish at the hands of his own people by the domestic ritual of the Triple-Death, but let us not forget the fate of a leader who, while preoccupied with foreign policy, faces imminent defeat in battle.

Like all good Celts, the beleaguered king believes his head to be the container of his soul, for this is the basis of the well-known Celtic head-cult; and so he knows that if he is slain, his comrades will try to carry him, or at least his head, away for burial. The preservation of his skull, often for consultation as an oracle through which he may speak or 'sing' prophecies, will ensure his safe passage into the Otherworld, until his subsequent return by reincarnation at a time and tide selected by the goddess. Furthermore, the opposition will be prevented from putting his head on a pole and declaring him dead. Therefore, as the enemy closes in, the king removes all apparel of his rank in case he is killed and left intact upon the battlefield, and thus he may still avoid being identified and pronounced dead, and certain sorceries will not be performed upon his skull – for it is better that he should fall incognito, and be taken by the ravens, than that the enemy should find his head, and destroy or imprison his soul.

Upon the battlefield the fallen king will lie unknown, noticed only by the carrion crows. The sleeping death of the Celts is incomplete until the flesh has left the bones, but soon the ravens will arrive and display an exceptional interest in the head, the container of the soul, and so one day the bards and seers will sing that:

> Ravens gnawed the head of Domnall Brech

and

> Ravens gnawed the head of Dyfnwal Frych

whose bodies may in any case have been protected by mail or armour.

At last the ravens will strip the flesh from the bones and carry such entrails as the liver and the lungs aloft (Legend 22). This is sky-burial,[4] another tradition dating from Neolithic times when the corpse was deliberately exposed before the bones were interred.

Warrior-kings and ravens thus became synonymous in the killing fields – both warrior-kings and ravens were the harbingers of death, and as birds of prophecy ravens shared with fallen kings an omniscient knowledge of the past and future, for they were manifestations of the dark-lunar aspect of the Celtic Trinity of Fate, a death-goddess of the 'deep', sometimes called the Morrigan, who took the form of an enormous carrion crow.

In ancient times, all carrion birds such as ravens, crows, rooks and 'jack'-daws were similarly regarded as birds of darkness, and along with the female principle, such beliefs remained potent even among the peasantry of the late Middle Ages and beyond. Today, the raven capers upon the motorway's edge in keen anticipation of road-kill, but in the past its airborne capacity for inferential reasoning would have enabled it to recognise the signs of approaching battle in the form of armies which were still several miles apart. Meanwhile, other factors also seemed to confirm the ravens' reputation for prophecy – such as their expert inspection of entrails in the aftermath of battle, which evidently enabled them to predict the occasion of future conflicts; their habit of acquiring shiny objects and storing them in their nests, which demonstrated their practice of the predictive art of scrying, as per the crystal ball or water-pool, their caw, which has a cognitive air, and the ability of domesticated ravens (particularly the jackdaw) to parrot speech. This must have startled the ancient mind, since the raven therefore shares with the cave wall, the stone cromlech and the church, an ability to echo the human voice.

The discovery of farming saw the stony goddess rapidly fleshed with soil and clad in foliage, as in her positive (full lunar) aspect she became a nurturing earth-mother or nature goddess, from whom all life sprang. In her many forms across the world she was then called fertile, green and verdant, permitting the growing of corn according to her pleasure or displeasure, and controlling the weather via her feathered agents, the birds.

Thus in Celtic Britain the Druids are found describing their headquarters on the viridian isle of Anglesey, as 'the Mother of the World', foretelling the future by the expert inspection of the entrails of sacrificed animals and humans, practising the prophetic art of augury by observing the flight-patterns of birds, turning people into ravens, continuing the grisly practice of the Triple-Death (the victim of which later became known as the Green Man or Oak-king), and presiding over the sophistication of Neolithic science known as sympathetic magic, which in domestic matters sought to please the spirits of the Otherworld, and thus maintain harmony with Mother Nature.

Finally, as high priests of an ancient religion, the Druids also aspired (like later clergy) to preserve the history and wisdom of their race, preferring not to write it down but to transmit it orally by great feats of memory in the form of magical music and verse. Combined with their prowess as prophets, and the fact that by universal consent they alone were allowed to cross the tribal boundaries of Celtic Britain, they thus laid the foundations of what would one day become the bardic tradition of 'prophecy', as later recited by wandering minstrels in Wales.

So it was that the resulting oral tradition of history sang not only of a past which alleged the descent of the British Celts from the legendary giant Brutus the Trojan (who came to Britain in c. 1200 BC), but also of the future, as determined by some truly ancient oracular methods. The tradition which ensued was known as 'Brut', and to a lute-like accompaniment it resonated with an agricultural audience who were long familiar with the sacredness of certain ancient stones in the landscape, the significance of the water-cycle, the lunar Triple Goddess, and the occult nature of ravens. All such things were religious icons not only of vast antiquity, but also of exceptional power, for they were a metaphysics which peasant folk saw confirmed and enacted by the forces of nature every day, just as surely as the rain fell, and the ravens threatened eternally to destroy their crops – and the result was a deep-seated and widespread belief-system which Christianity would one day find extremely difficult to shift.

LEGEND 5 : WHITE ROCKS

One night, Jack of Kent and the Devil were trying to build a dam, or a weir, in order to make a fishpond. They were carrying the stones in their leather aprons as they came over Garway Hill, when suddenly the cock crowed. At this, the Devil's apronstrings broke, and the stones tumbled out to form the White Rocks.

Other versions
Numerous other versions cover every permutation of the local geography. In some the two are seen trying to dam a stream on Garway Hill so as to flood a nearby valley, in others they are trying to make a fishpond on Garway Hill or Orcop Hill, but they are frequently on their way to dam the Monnow. When I was at White Rocks on Garway Hill some years ago, I discussed the story with a local lady who later sent me a postcard pointing out that according to some the stones had fallen in the same way from Jack's apron rather than the Devil's.

[See also Appendix 1, p. 273.]

LEGEND 6 : JACK STONES

At Trellech, it is said that the three standing stones were thrown from nearby Trellech Beacon, where Jack of Kent and the Devil had met and quarrelled. The Devil then challenged Jack to a throwing competition. With a deadline of midnight to complete the contest, the players threw a little further each time, and Jack won, much to the Devil's disgruntlement.

[See also Appendix 1, p. 275.]

TWO

A TALE OF TWO RIVERS
(AD 43–800)

In AD 43 the Romans arrived and soon persecuted the Druids, so as to prevent them from uniting the Celtic tribes, but the conquerors were content to tolerate the old beliefs, many of which they shared. In AD 313, after a close contest with the cult of Mithras, Christianity was selected as the official religion of Rome, and with the aid of incoming missionaries the Romans had little difficulty in impressing Christianity upon a Celtic nobility which had benefited from its membership of the Roman Empire, and a people which had no difficulty in interpreting the new religion in terms of the old.

This religious *rapprochement* was eased by the fact that the old beliefs had never been confined to the Celtic tribes, or even to Europe, and were also understood by the Romans. Indeed, the old (Neolithic) religion had been a logical first attempt at science based upon the observation of nature, and thus with countless local variations it had long since become the supernatural landscape of the ancient world. Later religions, such as those wishing to assert the supremacy of a male divine-principle, therefore had no choice but to subsume the existing symbology, and early Christianity was no exception.

For example, the story of the Flood presented in the Old Testament was merely a modification of the much older *Epic of Gilgamesh*, in which the lunar goddess Ishtar had precipitated the Flood before releasing her birds across the waters. While both texts described exactly the same 'sweet savour upon the air', in the biblical version Ishtar was deleted, Yahweh was inserted, and it was Noah who released the raven and the dove in search of dry land as the waters subsided.

This theme was therefore already familiar to such goddess-based peoples as the Celts, and the remaining quibble over the actual precipitator of the Flood was then resolved by a compromise in which an entity called 'Sophia' was temporarily inserted into early Christian theology and described as God's creative wisdom.

Nor did the British Celts have any great problem with the New Testament, which seemed designed with them in mind, for they were already familiar with the idea of a miraculous son of a virgin mother (goddess) who embodied a *trinity* of (lunar) aspects, and who was hailed in the world as a great tribal king of his people. Furthermore, they were utterly unsurprised when he declared that his flesh was bread (corn) and that his blood was wine, and they nodded sagely when it was predicted that he would eventually return for the benefit of all, on a day when the harvest would finally be reaped and gathered in. Nor were the British Celts remotely disconcerted to hear that in order to ensure this, he had undergone a voluntary sacrifice (crucifixion) on the four points of a modified tree – for this was ever the fate of the reincarnating tribal king who was later known to the Welsh as the Son of Prophecy or as the Mab Darogan – which is why, much later, they would apply this title both to Christ and to their own great leaders, including Owain Glyndŵr.

A nominal Romano-Celtic-Christian compromise thus achieved, the matter of the new religion was therefore left to rest, and the great mass of British peasantry remained close to the ground, and deeply entrenched in the old beliefs – and then the Romans departed – under attack from barbarians ranging from the Vandals, Goths and Visigoths, who swarmed across mainland Europe, to the Angles and Saxons who harried the eastern coast of Britain. 'The barbarians drive us into the sea, and the sea drives us back to the barbarians!', wailed the British scribe Gildas – as the Celts were compressed into the west.

Before long, the Anglo-Saxons controlled the eastern half of Britain and were seeking to command the Pennines. A sense of urgency then infused the Celts as it suddenly became apparent that any further incursions would see them not only pressed against the western wall of the mainland, but impaled upon the estuaries of two rivers, the Dee in the north and the Severn in the south. Therefore, as the Dark Age curtain fell, the disparate tribes were marshalled against the Anglo-Saxons by a Romano-Celtic leader named Cunedda, whose relatives and descendants would subsequently make legendary efforts to defend the Celtic territories west of the Pennines. Eventually, there came a time when this task fell to a certain Cawrdaf, King of Brycheiniog (Breconshire), who was among the very last of such leaders to maintain Celtic control west of the Pennines, and who was fully aware of a particular military imperative, dictated by geography.

In c. AD 500, Cawrdaf's powerful influence is likely to have extended eastward from Brycheiniog into Herefordshire, as well as north-eastward into Radnorshire and thence along the River Teme via Ludlow towards Worcester, where the river Severn marked the boundary of the Celtic West. Cawrdaf surely understood the overall strategic position of the 'Cymry' (brotherhood) at this time, and as the ruler of Brycheiniog and Radnorshire he was therefore undoubtedly preoccupied with a certain geographical weakness which offered a potentially catastrophic invasion-route to the Anglo-Saxon enemy, and which placed his own territories in the front line (see Map I inset). This invasion route led from the region of the Severn around Worcester, via Herefordshire and Brycheiniog into south-west Wales, and via the Tywi Valley into Carmarthenshire, and for reasons we will discuss later it was this line of attack which offered to fulfil all the westerly ambitions of the Anglo-Saxons. Only Cawrdaf stood in their way, bolstered by the interested support of the rulers of the south-western Welsh kingdom known as Deheubarth, and therefore this axis of alliance came to constitute a key defence against the Anglo-Saxons which we will henceforth call Cawrdaf's Spear – its point being at Worcester where the Teme meets the river Severn, and its haft being anchored in south-west Wales, where the rulers of Deheubarth dwelt in a region of the Tywi Valley later known as Cantref Mawr.

So it was that mighty Cawrdaf stood firm in Brycheiniog and Radnorshire, strongly supported by the rulers of Deheubarth in south-west Wales and instead, it was the northern Celts who first came under attack.

As the 500s drew to a close, the Angles of Northumbria sought to wrest Cumbria from Celtic control, but were fiercely opposed by a coalition under the leadership of King 'Urien', ruler of Rheged, a region which extended across the Dee from Flintshire into Cheshire and thence northwards into Cumbria and beyond by virtue of a string of Celtic alliances.[5] Sometimes called the Cumbrian King or King Rience of Gore, Urien was thus concerned with holding the territory west of the northern Pennines, and furthermore, he was no ordinary Dark Age king.

In addition to being an historical figure, Urien of Rheged also bestrode the Celtic Otherworld, and claimed direct family connections with the 'deep' – for it was alleged that he had married a dark goddess identified with the Morrigan.

So it was that Urien set out with confidence to crush the Angles of Northumbria in *c.* AD 590 – but the Lord of Rheged was doomed to fail – along with the incoherent cause of Celtic Britain. In his battle against the Northumbrians, Urien was upon the verge of victory when he was embroiled in a family feud and was killed as a consequence, whereafter his fragile alliance of northern kingdoms fell apart – and the estuary of the River Dee was lost.

In the early 600s, the aftermath may well have seen Urien's son 'Owein' flying southwards, accompanied by his legendary 'bodyguard of fierce ravens'; abandoning Rheged, as the Cumbrian corridor closed irrevocably behind him, and Cheshire also fell, and coming to rest in distant lands which had been held by his father in the Tywi Valley in south-west Wales. Here in Deheubarth, the 'Ravens of Rheged' are said to have held the Lordship of Is-cennen and to have founded the spectacular site of Carreg Cennen Castle – and perhaps it is true, as some people say, that Owein of Rheged is the mighty warrior who still sleeps in the Raven's Cave under the castle, awaiting a call from the Cymry.

With Cumbria and Cheshire already lost, Cawrdaf's former kingdom now surely came under massive pressure, and no doubt the Celts of Brycheiniog and Radnorshire fought desperately to hold Ludlow and Worcester, and thus to maintain their grip upon what we have called Cawrdaf's Spear. However, although they were doubtless supported at this moment by an anxious Deheubarth in the south-west, it was only a matter of time before they would finally be driven back from the River Severn and onto the borders of modern Wales marked by the River Wye between Monmouth and Chepstow – a catastrophic collapse, which had been caused by the failure of Celtic kingdoms to form coherent alliances. This is duly lamented in the *Mabinogion* ('The Dream of Rhonabwy'), wherein, in the face of a threat from 'Osla Big Knife' (King of Northumbria), none other than Owein of Rheged and his ally, a spectral King Arthur, nonchalantly indulge in a game of 'gwyddbwyll' using silver pieces upon a golden board, while fighting breaks out between Owein's 'ravens' and Arthur's 'courtiers'.

King Arthur is of course but another alleged defender of territory and a raiser of crops, a 'once and future king' interred in a dark sarcophagus of stone, upon some ancient tribal river boundary. Thus upon his death Arthur's soul is said to have 'turned into a raven' and flown away to dwell in a cave – crossing the sky as had his famous sword Excalibur en route to meet 'The Goddess of the Lake', whereupon it was said to have brilliantly reflected the Moon before vanishing at last into the deep from whence it came.

There Excalibur lay, shining among the countless artefacts which since time immemorial the Celts had hurled into shimmering waters in their efforts to influence the Otherworld[6] – for beneath the surface of the lake there dreamt the mighty chieftains of the past, and when it pleased 'The Lady' to decide that time and tides were right, as prophecy foretold, they would return.

LEGEND 7 : TOPS and BOTTOMS

One day when Jack of Kent and the Devil were walking through a field, Jack bet the Devil that if they shared the field equally he would make more profit than the Devil. Knowing in advance that the field was full of

turnips which were already below the ground, Jack asked the Devil whether he would have tops or bottoms. The Devil chose tops and so Jack had the turnips and the Devil had only the greens.

The following year the Devil tried again, this time choosing bottoms, but Jack had chosen a field which he knew was full of wheat, so he got the corn and straw, and the Devil got the roots. When it came to the threshing they repaired to the barn where they made the bet again. The Devil

chose tops so Jack set up a hurdle for the Devil to do the threshing on, and since Jack took to the barn floor (i.e. bottoms) he collected all the corn.

Other versions
In the Welsh tradition, a version is told in which the Devil had helped Siôn Cent by ploughing the field in question in a single night, in return for which he was to have the crops which were 'out of earth'. However, since the crops were potatoes, Siôn Cent kept the proceeds. The next year the arrangement was repeated, and this time the Devil chose the crops which were 'in earth', but the crop was wheat, and so Siôn Cent reaped the benefits again.

[See also Appendix 1, p. 276.]

THREE

THE BATTLE FOR WALES
(800–1155)

Celtic Britain had collapsed in an incompetent display, the Northumbrians would have stood no chance against Urien's alliance, had it not foundered upon an internecine feud. As a consequence the Cumbrian corridor to north Wales was lost, and the Celts of Strathclyde were cut off, later to be absorbed by the Northumbrians. Arthur, too, was undone, by Medrod (Mordred), who divided the Knights of the Round Table, and in the south, Devon and Cornwall were also severed by the Severn estuary from the last region of southern Britain available to the Celts – Wales.

The territory of Wales offered a natural enclave, defensible along a relatively short front, and its various small kingdoms knew that any further yielding to the Anglo-Saxons would soon deposit them either in the Otherworld or the Irish Sea. Accordingly they rallied under the surviving descendants of Cunedda, and during the 800s a united Welsh nation emerged under the leadership of Rhodri Mawr, King of Wales – just in time to see the Anglo-Saxon kingdoms collapse in the face of the Viking invasion.

Having fought both Vikings and English with the dream of restoring Celtic Britain, Rhodri Mawr died in 877, whereafter the inheritance of Wales by his sons led to the foundation of the 'Three Kingdoms' which would henceforth dominate the future of Welsh history: Gwynedd in the north, Powys in the centre and Deheubarth in the south.

In 942 the Viking tide receded as Rhodri's grandson, Hywel Dda of Deheubarth, presided over a united Wales from the family fortress of Dinefwr, at Llandeilo in Carmarthenshire. Three years later he summoned the first Welsh Assembly to meet at Whitland west of Carmarthen – and within another five years he died, having enshrined and enacted Welsh laws and customs so comprehensively that in highland areas they would not be dislodged by the English until the reign of Edward I.

In 1070 the Normans arrived upon the borders of a divided Wales which had recently known unity under a ruler of the northern kingdom of Gwynedd, whereupon the Normans chose Chester as a military base for the containment of Gwynedd, selected Shrewsbury for the future harassment of Powys, and Hereford as the headquarters for a series of immediate incursions into the south – for regarding Wales, the Norman calculation was correct, and the answer was 'geography'.

Gwynedd was impenetrably mountainous, and with the exception of Anglesey possessed few fertile lowlands. It was therefore both well defended and economically undesirable. Powys was traditionally weak. Although mountainous, it was pressurised by both Gwynedd and Deheubarth, and exposed upon the eastern Radnorshire border. However, Powys's weakness was also its defence, since any occupying force risked a two-pronged response from its neighbours.

The priority, therefore, was to invade, occupy and undermine the south, thus simultaneously removing Powys's defence and surrounding the remnants of the Welsh on two fronts. With the south-east topographically weak, the crucial key to control of Wales was therefore correctly identified as the dominant south-western kingdom of Deheubarth. In view of this strategic truth, the battle for Welsh independence becomes essentially a battle for Deheubarth, and in this brief history of the Welsh nation we too will therefore concentrate our attention upon the south.

In 1078 Deheubarth's ruler was a descendant of Hywel Dda called Rhys ap Tewdwr, whose headquarters were also at Dinefwr Castle (Llandeilo) upon the western bank of the Tywi in the commote of Cantref Mawr. Faced with the appalling might of a Norman military machine which had not merely vanquished England but which raised stone castles at a sorcerous speed, Rhys accelerated the policy of his ancestors in exercising Deheubarth's support for the weak south-eastern kingships of Gwent (Monmouthshire), Morgannwg (Glamorgan) and especially Brycheiniog (Breconshire), in a desperate attempt to block the invasion route once defended by Cawrdaf.

Until 1093 Rhys ap Tewdwr managed to preserve the integrity of Deheubarth by a combination of negotiation and resistance, but he was slain in Brycheiniog, while opposing the early stages of a Norman invasion. It was a disaster. Gwent and Morgannwg rapidly succumbed, and immediately the invaders marched west. When it was over, both Ceredigion and Dyfed were occupied and only a vestigial Deheubarth remained, diminished and isolated in its ancient heartland of the Tywi Valley.

Afterwards, Henry I of England (son of the Conqueror) sought to break the Welsh spirit by installing heavily fortified Norman settlements right across south Wales. This culminated in a vice-like military grip upon the south-western corner, Dyfed (Pembrokeshire), into which Henry injected an abrasive mixture of Norman colonists and English and Belgian traders. It was a well-laid policy, ruthlessly designed to compromise the security of Deheubarth, and thus the whole of the south, by permanent control of the territory behind it.

Henry I brooked opposition from no one, and he knew that brief demonstrations of military power were no substitute for the emplacement of infrastructure. At his command were the resources which had overwhelmed the formidable England of King Harold, and like a leopard he had placed his paw upon the throat of Wales – the south, through which the Tywi flowed like an artery in the west. Indeed, as one chronicler wearily avowed, he was 'the man with whom none may strive, save God himself – Who hath given him the dominion', and yet, unlike the English, the Welsh would not give up. Traditionally incapable of unified resistance, they were equally incapable of unified surrender.

In 1116 Rhys ap Tewdwr's son Gruffydd, who had fled to Ireland, returned, and made valiant but futile attempts to regain his homeland. After nearly two decades of struggle Gruffydd still held only the family patrimony of Caeo within the heavily wooded terrain of Cantref Mawr. Here, accompanied by two elder sons from a previous marriage, Anarawd and Cadell, Gruffydd finally settled with his new wife Gwenllian, who bore him four sons, the two eldest being Maredudd and Rhys.

Then, in December 1135, came the news that Henry I was dead. As the Scots poured into northern England, so Gwynedd rose in north Wales, and acting in accord with the princes of Snowdonia, Gruffydd and his two eldest sons broke forth from their small confinement and raged against the Normans, Belgians and English of south-west Wales.

Pitchforks and the populace flocked to support the royal family of Deheubarth, reinforced by military assistance from the north. Together they seized Cantref Mawr and crossed the River Tywi to wrest Cantref Bychan from its Norman keeper, one Walter de Clifford. At Loughor the Welsh defeated the Normans and then marched west towards the fertile lowlands of Ceredigion – the bread-basket of the south where Gruffydd's forces pursued an excoriating campaign against the Norman settlers, raping and pillaging, and slaying every Frenchman in their path until, following an encounter at Crug, the only Norman survivors were left cowering in Cardigan Castle keep.

Meanwhile, the cost of northern aid had been met by Gwenllian, for while Gruffydd was away negotiating with Gwynedd, his wife and her two infant sons had been slain by the Normans after she had led an attack upon Kidwelly. Nor did Gruffydd get to keep Ceredigion – for it was the price demanded by the northern princes for their aid – whereafter Gruffydd launched an assault upon Dyfed in an attempt to dislodge the Norman-Flemish stronghold there.

In 1137 Gruffydd died, as the struggle for the south-west went on under his three elder sons, Anarawd, who was murdered, Cadell, who died in the monastery of Strata Florida, and Maredudd, who died in 1155, whereafter the inheritance of Deheubarth fell to the sole survivor, Rhys ap Gruffydd, later to be celebrated simply as 'the Lord Rhys', and whose story is crucial to our quest.

Born in the 'Jack-land' of Caeo, young Rhys ap Gruffydd was raised in arms, fighting beside his brothers as they stormed a series of castles and engaged in a fast and furious battle against their father's former ally for the bread-basket of Ceredigion. Three years later, with Ceredigion restored and defended under Rhys's leadership, Deheubarth was briefly back in business – but even as the sunlight played upon the walls of Dinefwr, a vast storm-cloud was overwhelming the horizon. In recent years Deheubarth's cause had been assisted by a civil war in England between King Stephen and the adherents of King Henry's daughter Mathilda – but suddenly that was over, and upon the English throne sat a new monarch, every bit as formidable as Henry I – Henry II.

In 1157, treachery among the princes of mid and north Wales offered Henry II a unique opportunity to attack the hitherto inviolate kingdom of Gwynedd, and he seized it with overwhelming force. Having subdued the northern kingdom and tethered its resources to the Crown, Henry's long shadow then fell immediately upon the aspiring Deheubarth of Rhys ap Gruffydd. Utterly isolated, and with no prospect of aid or diversion, Rhys responded in the time-honoured tradition of the rulers of Deheubarth, ushering his people, 'their wives and children and all their animals into the forest-land of the Tywi', where amid this dense defence he prepared to do battle with an opponent against whom there was no hope of victory.

However, even as the populace of Deheubarth huddled amid the woods of Cantref Mawr, it transpired that the new king was a busy man, averse to wasting either time or resources, for he sent Rhys a message, offering to discuss terms.

A miserable meeting ensued at which Ceredigion, the adjacent regions of Newcastle Emlyn, and the rest of the inheritance for which Rhys and his family had fought for so long – all reverted to the English Crown – and as the Anglo-Norman families reclaimed their lands, Rhys retained only the forestland of Cantref Mawr.

Deheubarth's heir could only smoulder amid the trees as all around the settlers returned. Within twelve months the Marcher

Lord of Cantref Bychan, Walter de Clifford, had regained his lands – and he had not forgotten the past. Intent on revenge, de Clifford crossed the Tywi, slaughtered some of Rhys's men and ransacked Cantref Mawr. Rhys appealed to the King, but when this brought no redress he retaliated, crossing the river himself and invading Cantref Bychan with a substantial force – whereafter he proceeded to liberate much of Ceredigion.

Thus began a pattern of antagonism between Rhys ap Gruffydd of Deheubarth and Henry II of England, the focus of which was the ongoing and explosive feud between Rhys and his neighbour, Walter de Clifford. Whenever Henry left to attend to his affairs upon the continent, Rhys went on the offensive. Twice, in 1159 and 1163, all his efforts came to naught, and he became an outlaw in the forest of Cantref Mawr – and all the heroism of his ancestors, his parents Gruffydd and Gwenllian, his brothers Anarawd, Cadell and Maredudd, and the two infants who had not survived, must have haunted him in those dark days.

One grim evening in 1164, Rhys returned from a certain meeting to find the hated de Clifford in full possession of Cantref Mawr and busily engaged in the murder of his relatives – whereupon Deheubarth's heir and his supporters wrested back the castle of Dinefwr by force. Once again, Rhys appealed to the king to settle the feud with de Clifford and to stabilise relations with the other Marcher lords – but once again, there was no redress from the Crown.

The rain still fell, and his great sword lay silent across his knees. The Lord of Deheubarth brooded alone in the darkened hall of Dinefwr Castle, as a heavy brand of embers tumbled into ashes, and a sudden wind danced sparks into the blackness of the flue. His stare flared crimson. He knew the power for which his family had fought, knew how restlessly they slept beneath the draining earth, like the Loegr with the light in their eyes, and as night descended upon dark wings through the freezing air outside, he heard their whispered communion with the mighty ancestors of Deheubarth – the Ravens of the North . . .

The specific genealogy by which Rhys ap Gruffydd claimed descent from Urien of Rheged is uncertain, but the principle is clear enough. Rhys was descended from Rhodri Mawr, a descendant of the primordial Cunedda of Strathclyde who had married the daughter of Urien's forebear, King Coel of Rheged – whereafter the royal line had descended to Hywel Dda, and thence via the last crowned king of Celtic Britain, Cadwaladr, to Rhys. Furthermore, the reputed Dark Age Lords of Is-cennen, Urien and his son Owein, were alleged to have held lands adjacent to the Tywi Valley, including Carreg Cennen Castle near Dinefwr; and if so, their descendants might well have married into the royal line of Deheubarth. Meanwhile, Rhys's mother Gwenllian, the fallen heroine of his father's uprising, had been a daughter of the Princes of north Wales – a line that also returned to Rheged via 'Old King Coel'.

So it was, one night before the medieval hearth, that the Lord Rhys, heir of Dinefwr and Deheubarth, gathered unto himself a dark robe. He adopted the arms of Three Ravens Sable, and declared himself the corvine descendant of Urien of Rheged – a Dark Age hero of Celtic Britain.

Once again, Rhys exploded out of the woods of Cantref Mawr and seized Ceredigion. From the kingdom of the north there came applause – and all the native princes and rulers of Wales were rallied to arms. Unified at last by the carrion call of the Lord Rhys, a combined Welsh muster assembled in open defiance at Corwen near Carrog in north Wales, and there awaited the arrival of the English – for months.

Henry II was busily assembling an army of greater proportions than ever before – for this time the situation was serious. The negotiations from which Rhys had returned upon that fateful evening in 1164 had been the 'Council of Woodstock' – a meeting to which Henry had summoned all the native princes of Wales, as well as Malcolm, King of the Scots – in order to dictate the formal subordination of Wales and Scotland to the English Crown. However, one result was surely a dialogue between the Welsh princes and the Scottish king, in which Rhys's enthusiasm for his ancestry may have played its role, for in Scotland and the north of England, the battle-cry of the raven had never ceased to stir the land.

Rhys had returned that night to find Dinefwr despoiled and his trust betrayed, whereafter his reply had not only called all Wales to arms, but had simultaneously informed the Scots of the worth of England's words at Woodstock. Suddenly Henry II faced a Wales which was united, for his own efforts had made Gwynedd its undisputed leader. No longer could he play one kingdom against another, nor wait, nor dare deploy his forces south, lest the Scots descend via Strathclyde and Cumbria to conjoin with the Welsh upon the estuary of the Dee – a threat which would hurl England back into the Dark Ages. There was no option but to confront the Welsh where they were massed, at Corwen near Carrog, so ominously close to the Dee.

In 1165, after much preparation, Henry II set forth towards Corwen, confident in the belief that he had assembled a truly crushing force, sufficient to destroy the Welsh once and for all – notwithstanding that he must fight them in their mountainous terrain. However, upon entering the maze of the Berwyn mountains, the English found their logistics constricted by the difficulty of supplying vast forces via narrow passes, and their morale worn down by extended marches during which the Welsh were rarely seen. Led on, frayed and infuriated by the harassment of sharp skirmishes which always seemed to promise battle, they toiled on amid the rocks, until eventually it began to rain, and rain, and rain. It was August, and the English had never conceived of such conditions at this time of year. Drenched and freezing at night, they camped amid the peaks in misery and hunger, until, with all their efforts wasted, there was nothing left but to wend their weary way back home – and the raven's laughter echoed amid the crags, for the old beliefs were true – it was the feather ruled the weather . . .

Henry II was furious. Wracked by ignominy and expense in terms of both cash and credibility, he hauled before him the hostages he had taken in previous campaigns against the Welsh – among them one of Rhys's sons, Maredudd – and ordered that their eyes be gouged out, and with his impotence thus confirmed never again did Henry disrespect the borders of Wales.

Honoured by his countrymen, Rhys shook hands with the Prince of Gwynedd and departed the area of Corwen and Carrog, returning southward to consolidate Ceredigion and to capture Cardigan Castle, which had become a symbol of the Anglo-Norman occupation of Deheubarth.

Afterwards, the whole of Wales famously 'cast off the Norman yoke', and in 1170 the death of Gwynedd's ruler permitted Rhys to emerge as the leading prince in Wales. When Henry II sought safe passage to Ireland across the south, it was afforded by Rhys, and *rapprochement* grew, as Henry realised that in future it would be easier to work with Rhys than against him.

Two years later, Rhys was confirmed in all his conquests and appointed as the king's Justiciar, exercising nominal royal authority over all the other princes of Wales. During the seventeen years of peace which ensued, he held a grand Eisteddfod, turned the ancient ramparts of Dinefwr to stone, and further entrenched his power with the raising of another six stone castles across Deheubarth. Thereafter, Rhys extended Deheubarth's influence northwards and eastwards by marital alliances into Rhayader and Radnorshire – and having thus rebuilt as much as possible of what had once been Cawrdaf's Spear, he also strengthened Deheubarth's infrastructure by harnessing the expertise of Norman colonists and traders, some of whom may have aided him in the raising of castles. Finally, Rhys extended the legal system set in place by his ancestor Hywel Dda, and declared himself *Proprietarius Princeps Sudwallie* – 'the rightful prince of South Wales'. He had done it – from mere embers he had rekindled the kingdom of Deheubarth.

In 1189 Henry II died, leaving his heir Richard I ('Lionheart') upon the throne. Rhys had already opposed Richard's upstart ambitions, and so he knew that *rapprochement* was over. Instantly he attacked Dyfed and Gower, in a convulsive attempt to prise the Anglo-Norman grip from the south-western corner of Wales – and yet, even as he gained territory towards the coast, an older enemy arose to mire his efforts in disarray. For Rhys had many sons, including some by his wife, and it was at this moment that they squabbled and fought over their inheritance. Rhys's proud new Deheubarth suddenly faltered, threatening to disintegrate into the discord and division that had plagued Celtic leaders since time immemorial.

In 1195 Rhys was defeated in battle by his sons, and imprisoned in his own castle at Nevern, while the victors took possession of Dinefwr. Luckily the English had their own problems at this time, and failed to capitalise on Deheubarth's disarray. However, the ageing Rhys was released the following year, just as Richard I chose to celebrate his return from crusade with a raid upon the central Welsh kingdom of Powys. Whereupon, with Richard thus engaged, Rhys placed himself at the head of an army of his supporters and with typical audacity seized the castles of Carmarthen, Colwyn, Painscastle and Radnor.

It was his last great success, for a terrible 'pestilence' had arisen, and on 28 April 1197 it deprived Wales of an historic leader, an indomitable man who had claimed descent from Urien of Rheged, the Lord Rhys – 'The Raven of Dinefwr' – who from the ancient forestland of Cantref Mawr had raised the southern kingdom of Deheubarth from its ashes.

LEGEND 8 : BURDOCKS

Once, Jack of Kent challenged the Devil to mow a field of corn quicker than he could. However, on the night before the contest, Jack had planted iron spikes along the swathes the Devil was to mow, and whenever he struck another of these staves, the furious Devil was heard to mutter 'Burdocks! Burdocks!', under his breath.

Other versions
Some cite this tale, rather than a jumping competition, as the cause of the disagreement which led to the episode of 'Throwing Stones' and the creation of 'the Devil's Heelmark' (see Legend 2). Meanwhile, it is also sometimes said that the obstacles planted by Jack were in fact 'harrow tines' (the prongs of a fork or rake) and that the demoralised Devil gave up when Jack persuaded him that the corn was not worth cutting anyway.
[See also Appendix 1, p. 276.]

FOUR

THE LEGACY OF THE LORD RHYS (1155–1380)

As we have seen, the idea that the world was born by virgin birth to a lunar Triple-Goddess was the basis of an ancient belief-system which had descended from the Neolithic to the Druidic, and which had survived the onset of Christianity by remaining potent among the peasantry – but it did not stop there.

In attempting to assimilate pagan cultures such as those of the Celts, the early Roman Catholic Church had pursued a policy of superimposing Christian churches upon pagan sites, Christian festivals upon pagan celebrations, and 'Sophia' upon the ubiquitous goddess. However, 'Sophia' was suppressed in the Gnostic texts by the Emperor Constantine during the early 300s, to be replaced by a more confrontational approach whereby all supernatural powers not authorised by Yahweh were simply to be abhorred as manifestations of the 'Devil'. Nevertheless, the goddess principle persisted: dressed as 'Sophia' in 'The Vision of Boethius' in AD 524; veiled in the wake of St Augustine's visit to Britain in c. 600; swathed in secrecy after the Synod of Whitby preferred Augustine's agenda to that of Iona in AD 663; cloaked in ambiguity under the auspices of the Coptic Church, the Cathar Church, and the Order of the Knights Templar in the 1100s; and resurgent via such agencies during the days of the Lord Rhys.

At this point the Coptic Church even suggested an entity who was a combination of the three Marys (Mary the Virgin, Mary of Bethany, and Mary Magdalene), a being thus coincidental with the old lunar Triple-Goddess, and whose dark aspect was identified with Mary Magdalene. However, the response of the Roman Catholic Church to such medieval Gnosticism was both persecution and a fresh attempt to accommodate the female principle by a massive re-launch of the Virgin Mary – whose profile was promptly raised to the heights we know today.

In Wales, Rhys's old adversary Henry I had recently sought to suppress the heresy inherent in earlier traditions by censuring the old Romano-Celtic saints and incorporating St David's within the see of Canterbury. However, the consequence in the Welsh countryside was a determination to maintain the old beliefs – and while church attendance remained compulsory, the peasantry continued in the pagan superstitions of an Otherworld which they had always known.

Similarly, some years later, as the Anglo-Norman medieval Church deployed its superstructure across south Wales, I suggest that the Lord Rhys simply emulated the policy of his ancestors by accepting the new order only at a political and economic level – for it has been noted that while he was willing to do business with the secular medieval Church, he played no active role in its religious affairs (unlike the other Welsh princes) and there are other details which also suggest that the Lord Rhys was a Christian only in the Romano-Celtic sense.[7]

Rhys is known to have held a very low opinion of the corrupt Anglo-Norman Houses of Benedictines and Augustinians which had been inflicted upon Deheubarth during the periods of occupation. Instead, he chose to patronise the new Order of Cistercians, based in Burgundy and reformed by a certain Bernard of Clairvaux – a man who had quietly incorporated into Cistercianism the remnants of Romano-Celtic Christianity while also sponsoring the Knights Templar, an organisation noticeably sympathetic to the Welsh princes, and one which would eventually be brutally suppressed for pursuing a heresy related to the Celtic head cult.

The Cistercians' first foundation in Wales was at Whitland, where Hywel Dda had once held court, and having entrusted the care of his blinded son to the Welsh abbot there, Rhys proceeded to sponsor the spread of Cistercianism across Wales. From within the church of St Bridget at Rhayader (Rhaeadr Gwy) he issued a charter for the Cistercian abbey of Strata Florida in northern Ceredigion, and later supported the establishment of Cistercian abbeys at Cwm-hir, on the eastern border of mid-Wales, and at Llantarnam in Gwent, in the Valley of the Crows.

So much for the religious policy of a man who was a keen student of Dark Age bardistry, and who via Urien of Rheged had effectively claimed descent from the Morrigan. However, if we require further evidence regarding Rhys's convictions, then we might notice that St Bridget was none other than 'Brigit', a triple-aspected Celtic goddess and that during his lifetime Rhys went to some lengths to acquire a relic of Celtic Christianity with pre-Christian connotations known as the torque of St Cynog,[8] which he is said to have hidden within Dinefwr Castle. Furthermore, he founded two religious houses of his own, both of which were unusual.

In the late 1180s, Rhys founded an abbey of the French Order of Premonstratensians at Talley, just north of Dinefwr Castle, deep in the forest in his spiritual homeland of Cantref Mawr – and it is interesting that he did so in the wake of the foundation of a similar abbey at Shap Fell in the Valle Magdelene, near Penrith in Cumbria, an area often described as the spiritual homeland of Urien of Rheged. Closely associated with the Cistercians, the Premonstratensian Order had been established by Bernard of Clairvaux's personal friend St Norbert, who was allegedly instructed during a vision of the Virgin received near Amiens to found a monastery upon a miraculous site called Prémontré, translatable either as 'the meadow which was pointed out' or as 'the clearing made in the forest'. I therefore suggest that this was interpreted by the Lord Rhys as an act of feminine creativity by a Virgin-Mother who had indicated a 'sacred (Druidic) grove'.

I also suggest that Talley, the only abbey of the Pre-monstratensians in Wales, was thus established upon a similar site, in a clearing made in the forest of Cantref Mawr, in an area where the burial mounds of numerous fallen tribal kings still lie adjacent to the western bank of the Tywi – the defensive boundary river of Deheubarth. Furthermore, the proper name of Talley is Talyllychau, meaning 'The Forehead of the Two Lakes', a translation which not only commemorates Deheubarth's Irish connections,[9] but which indicates the twin lakes and the nearby proboscine ridge as two eyes and a nose – thus causing one to wonder if Talley was the place implied in the *Mabinogion* tale of 'Branwen, Daughter of Llyr', wherein the Dark Age Celtic warrior Brân (meaning 'raven') is said to have crossed the Irish Sea in the form of a mountain, with a ridge as his nose and two lakes as his eyes.[10]

At Talley therefore, I suggest that the Lord Rhys had established his Premonstratensian abbey upon a special site of ancient Celtic significance, where the membrane between this world and the Otherworld was thin, and where the twin lacustrine eyes of Brân sank deep into the spirit-realm.

Finally, just before his death at the age of sixty-five, Rhys established his second unusual foundation at Llanllŷr, in northern Ceredigion. This was a Cistercian nunnery, significantly situated in a sea-marsh close to the coast. Here amid the waters,[11] these chaste ladies would nonetheless occasionally fall inexplicably pregnant, and since they are recorded as having been the daughters of the Welsh nobility, the result of such miraculous births were always likely to be the warrior sons of the 'deep'.[12]

When the Lord Rhys died, rumours abounded that his death had been attended by the Three Fates of Greece ('the Moerae'), and the Welsh bards produced a liturgy of lamentation almost unparalleled in Welsh history:

The noble crown of Welsh honour has fallen
This is to say, Rhys is dead, the whole of Wales mourns . . .
Rhys is dead, the glory of the universe has left us . . .
Wales lives on in her grief . . .
Rhys, whom the people ever loved, . . .
The loyal standards of his legion fall.
No right hand now lifts them aloft . . .
Naught avails you now, Wales, Rhys is gone . . .

The people weep as our enemies rejoice
England stands, Wales has fallen, . . .
The dread arrow of the ruler's death strikes every heart . . .
Overwhelmed with sorrow the reins of life fall slack . . .
It does not die but moves on,
For his fair name is held ever fresh throughout the universe
Camber and King Locrinus who gained Alba [Scotland]
Are inferior in name and repute to Rhys.
Caesar and Arthur, both brave as lions in arms,
Rhys was their equal and of like mould.
Rhys was a second Alexander of like desire . . .
Let my pen grow wet with tears, its theme is grief,
Let it not lack beauty, let not the letters cease.

Such was the legacy of the Lord Rhys of Dinefwr, who, as the historian Sir J.E. Lloyd observed, had kept alive the idea of Welsh nationality in south Wales, and whose descendants were called 'The Blood of the Raven'.

The early 1200s saw the rise of Llywelyn the Great of the northern kingdom of Gwynedd, whose spectacular achievement during the reign of King John (1199–1216) was an independent Wales into which Deheubarth was subsumed. Llywelyn died peacefully as a Cistercian monk in the year 1240, but his united Wales did not survive for long. In 1282 his dominion was undone upon the death of his grandson Llywelyn the Last, who perished at the hands of the English near Cilmeri in mid-Wales, and in 1295 Edward I, who was truly 'The Hammer' of both the Welsh and the Scots, routed a brief rebellion and reversed every hard-won gain ever made by the Welsh in their efforts to cohere as an independent nation. This bitter pill was rendered sickly-sweet with the offer of recourse to English justice – but it was a massively demoralising era for those in Wales who still clung to the ancient dream.

In the ensuing reign of Edward II, the Welsh remained constrained, and the only significant ember of resistance was the uprising of one Llywelyn Bren of Senghennydd, in early 1316. However, despite a partially successful attack upon nearby Caerphilly Castle, Bren surrendered within months to the overwhelming forces of Humphrey de Bohun (Earl of Hereford), John de Hastings (Lord of Abergavenny) and Henry de Lancaster (Lord of Monmouth and the Three Castles) – whereafter he was horribly executed by Edward II's friends the Despensers and his mutilated remains were interred in the House of the Grey Friars at Cardiff.

The Welsh were utterly despondent in the wake of Bren's defeat, for their disillusionment had never been greater, and not until the 1370s would another leader even aspire to throw off the Anglo-Norman yoke – Owain Lawgoch – a descendant of Llywelyn the Great, who had lived all his life in France. Recognised as the rightful Prince of Wales, and financed by the French who esteemed him as a soldier of fortune, Lawgoch made a series of abortive attempts to stage an invasion of south Wales with the assistance of a French fleet – his efforts being monitored with interest by the English, who in 1370 prudently strengthened Carreg Cennen Castle in the south-west, so as to secure the borders of what had once been Deheubarth.

In 1373 John of Gaunt, the incorrigible son of Edward III, marched fruitlessly across France, his forces harried by Lawgoch's Gallic-Welsh mercenaries, and five years later in 1378, as Lawgoch prepared once again to arrange an invasion of south Wales, he was treacherously assassinated by an English agent, almost certainly in Gaunt's pay – and all Wales's hope seemed extinguished.

The 1300s had been a miserable century of death, oppression, penury and plague, which had weighed all too heavily upon Wales. Under Edward II and Edward III, Edward I's regime had degenerated into a grip described by Burke as 'something between hostility and government'. Meanwhile the imposition of English law across the Principality had long since supplanted the legal legacy of Hywel Dda and the Lord Rhys, and had also replaced the Welsh family system of land-inheritance known as Gavelkind – thus allowing the Marcher lords to extend their lands into Welsh territories by 'free enterprise' and simple purchase. Welsh recourse to English justice was forgotten, and in many lordships Welsh customs and traditions lay crushed beneath the Marcher heel.

In 1348 the appalling carnage of the Black Death had not only brought untold misery, but had been widely interpreted as the catastrophic failure of the medieval Church to assuage the wrath of God, either on its own behalf or anyone else's. Vast numbers of clergy had been felled by the disease, and the renewed outbreaks which had ensued had served only to confirm the impotency of clerical prayers, rituals and incantations – while for those Welsh peasants who quietly adhered to a very much older system of beliefs, it was simply the failure of the new magic to control the spirits.

Plagues had rampaged across south Wales, striking at Striguil (Chepstow) and Caldicot in 1361. Archenfield was contaminated by the outbreak of 1369 which slew Henry de Lancaster's son Henry of Grosmont, and which laid low the neighbouring township of Trellech near Monmouth. South-east Wales had fallen victim once again in 1381, and widespread outbreaks had blighted the years 1375, 1379, 1390 and 1391. The emaciated Welsh always suffered more than most, and afterwards they suffered again when there were shortages to be endured and the Marcher lords required villeins to restore the status quo – and yet, even as the 1300s crawled dismally to a close, those oppressed Welsh who were still able to care remembered that they were the Cymry – outsiders in their own land; weakening, as they were undermined politically, economically and territorially, and so they were not slow to absorb the more revolutionary ideas of the time.

In the second half of the century the credibility of the medieval Church was already at an all-time low, even before the papal divide of the Great Schism plunged it into chaos. Meanwhile, with the population drastically reduced, for the first time the peasantry could bargain for their services. Suddenly both the spiritual and the material bonds had come loose, and at this moment men such as William Langland and John Wycliffe famously opposed the corrupt and corpulent Anglo-Norman Church – and the hedgerow-preacher John Ball (Mad Priest) of

Kent peremptorily castigated all wealth and privilege, and proceeded with Wat Tyler to lead the Peasants' Revolt which so nearly destroyed the English Crown in 1381.

In the Welsh borders of south-west Herefordshire and Archenfield, the words of Langland, Wycliffe and Ball were exceptionally well received, and they were accompanied at the wayside crosses by a very much older tune – for also performing at the waysides were the minstrels. In England they made comic verse, but the road behind the Welsh minstrels was long, and it led far into the dominion of the bards. Here the territory was mountainous and dangerous, and as the century waned it thrilled once again to the Dark Age 'Song of Prophecy', which told of those who would return. Once a tribal cry, then a Druidic chant, and more recently a Dark Age song, it had found a new resonance in medieval times. Soon it would lend its ancient strains to a new Son of Prophecy – a shining warrior reborn to liberate Wales and to repulse the Saxon invader – and his name was Owain Glyndŵr . . .

LEGEND 9 : CROWS

One cold and blustery day, when Jack of Kent was a young farm hand at Caerphilly, his master left instructions for him to spend the day scaring the crows from the fields. When the master returned, he was furious to find Jack warming his feet by the farmhouse fire. 'Why aren't you guarding the crops from the crows?' he cried, to which Jack replied, 'No problem master, they are all confined to the castle keep.' 'Nonsense!' retorted his master and stormed out across the fields, where, strangely, there was not a crow in sight. Puzzled, he went to the castle keep and opened it, whereupon a black cloud of crows poured forth and pecked his eyes out.'

Other versions

Also in Glamorgan, it was sometimes said that Jack of Kent (Siôn Cent) had confined crows by closing the park gates at Eglwys Ilan near Abertridwr, where a road was shown as the route he later took to Kentchurch in south Herefordshire. However, the story of crows recurs at Kentchurch when Jack of Kent confines the crows not in a castle keep but in a barn, as occurs in all the oldest versions of this story, and this is said to have been an ancient building once known as Jacky Kent's Barn, which stood until modern times beside the Pontrilas to Garway Road (see photographs). In another Herefordshire version, Jack was told to protect the wheat while his master was away at Hereford Fayre (another version says Grosmont Fayre), and later that day the master was furious to meet Jack at the event. 'Ay, ay, master,' said Jack, 'the crows be alright, they be all in the barn,' according to Leather (The Folk-Lore of Herefordshire), as in all the earliest versions, it was a roofless barn, and the master of the crows, 'The Old 'Un' (the Devil), was sitting on a cross-beam keeping the crows in place until Jack's return.

'He was like a big old crow was their master and every now and then he said – Crawk! Crawk!'

According to Levett (The Story of Skenfrith, Grosmont and St Maughan's) after the fayre Jack led the farmer to the barn with the assurance that the crows would be asleep, but would leave upon his (Jack's) order. The farmer noticed a particularly large crow (the Devil), apparently sitting sentinel upon the barn wall, and not realising its true identity, raised his bow, but found that the arrow would not leave the string.

Finally, as 'an old woman' confirmed to Archdeacon Coxe in 1801, 'sure enough the crows were there, for they made a terrible clatter and would not fly away until Jack himself came and released them.'

[See also Appendix 1, p. 277.]

FIVE

OWAIN GLYNDŴR
(1380–1400)

O wain Glyndŵr was born at Glyndyfrdwy near Carrog in
north Wales in *c.* 1354 – and behind him was the
heritage we have discussed. He began his career
conventionally enough, holding his estates of Glyndyfrdwy
and Sycharth directly from Richard II and acting as a minor
Marcher lord, a Welsh diminutive of the powerful Anglo-
Norman nobility who dominated the Borders. Having spent
seven years in London studying law, he subsequently, like any
other Marcher lord, performed as a soldier when summoned
by the English king – and thus served Richard II in the
Scottish campaign of 1385.

Aided by those who have hailed Glyndŵr as the ultimate
hero of Welsh nationalism, these details have inevitably created
a market for the opposite point of view – namely that his
uprising was little more than the spontaneous tantrum of an
overblown 'English' lawyer in middle age, who failed in an
attempt to manipulate the Welsh cause in his own self-interest.
While the truth, as always, lies neither in one camp nor in the
other, these two positions regarding Glyndŵr are far from new,
for as we shall see they are precisely the same two positions
that were popularly adopted at the time. Our own thesis,
however, will reveal a man who lies in the ancient tradition of
Welsh leaders.

Owain Glyndŵr would have been in his early twenties when
Owain Lawgoch was killed in 1378, and we need have no doubt
that in common with many of his countrymen Glyndŵr was

bitterly disappointed. Perhaps it was at this very moment that the idea of his own uprising was first suggested to a youthful Owain – albeit tempered with the wisdom that it must be many years in the planning, and that the moment must be carefully chosen.

Just as a modern terrorist or freedom-fighter takes advantage of the facilities of an enemy state, so Glyndŵr proceeded to use his service in the English army to perfect his military skills to such a standard that he was celebrated by his colleagues. Simultaneously he deflected any suspicion regarding his loyalty to the Crown while gaining an intimate knowledge of the workings and weaknesses of the English military machine.

Between campaigns, Glyndŵr would return to the area of Llansilin upon the borders of north-east Wales, to his manor and lands at Sycharth – of which a certain bard once sang:

> The court of a baron, a place of courtesy
> Where many bards come, a place of the good life . . .
> Orchard, vineyard, white fortress . . .
> Ploughs and strong steeds of great frame . . .
> The deer park within that field
> Fine mill on a smooth-flowing stream . . .
> Dovecot, a bright stone tower . . .
> A fish pond, enclosed and deep . . .
> His land a board where birds dwell . . .
> Peacocks, high-stepping herons . . .
> His serfs do the proper work . . .
> Bringing Shrewsbury's fine beer . . .
> Whisky, the first-brewed bràgget . . .
> All drinks, white bread and wine . . .
> His meat, fire for his kitchen . . .
> His children come two by two . . .
> A fine nestful of princes. . . .

The author of this ode was none other than Owain's personal bard Iolo Goch ('Red Iolo'), a highly qualified and outstanding eulogist whose work earned lasting renown, and who numbered Glyndŵr upon a list of wealthy patrons. In the light of the fact that he was already 'a great teacher and minstrel' to the Welsh literary patron Rhydderch ab Ieuan Llwyd, and in consideration of matters yet to be discussed, Iolo Goch emerges as a 'Gandalfian' figure – an elderly mentor to Owain Glyndŵr.

In examining Iolo's work it is hard to avoid the conclusion that Glyndŵr was his favourite subject for eulogy. The extent to which he abandons formulaic praise in favour of radiant enthusiasm when dealing with the subject of his beloved Owain almost oversteps the mark – a fact which has provoked debate as to whether Iolo had at some point incited Glyndŵr to war. So persistent is this issue that Professor Dafydd Johnston (*Iolo Goch: Poems*) is compelled to make it the burden of his analysis, in which he gently protests that it was not the case. Nevertheless, as we are about to observe, Iolo Goch was extraordinarily forthright, as a few choice lines may illustrate. For example, in his ecstatic eulogies to Glyndŵr, Iolo describes him as the great-grandson of Madog Fychan who had 'reaped Angles' during the uprising of Llywelyn Bren, ameliorating the hair-raisingly recent nature of this reference by breaking Madog's name on to different lines; of Owain he intimates that 'if I were to raise a cub for anyone . . . for him I would do it'; he calls him 'a prince of an old family' who 'will be an heir, overpowering is his judgement'; he compares him with Cai, one of Arthur's chief warriors, observing that Glyndŵr has 'the same battle, the same eye, the same hand'; he declares that 'a day will come . . . when he will get a belief which is asserted'; and he calls him 'sole head of Wales' – but abruptly, in the midst of all this, as if aware that he has gone too far, Iolo suddenly interrupts himself by saying, 'Let us be quiet, it is best to be quiet, we will say nothing about him, good are teeth in front of the tongue'.

It seems that Iolo was even willing to jeopardise his own trade with such ardour, dangerously announcing that 'worthless is every single baron except the stock from which this one comes', before declaiming Glyndŵr's unique lineage from the royal lines of both north and south Wales – but above all, it is significant that in doing so Iolo points very specifically at Owain's descent from the line of the Lord Rhys.

'The Lord Rhys's line, summons to battle,' Iolo enthuses, as if recalling the assemblage at Corwen near Carrog which in 1165 'threw off the Norman yoke' – and he further observes that Glyndŵr was a descendant 'of Gwenllian from fair Cynan', the latter being the great-grandfather of the Lord Rhys (whose mother, wife and daughter were also called Gwenllian). Furthermore, Iolo confirms his awareness of Deheubarth and its royal line in terms which we already understand: he praises the house of Glyndŵr's chief allies the Tudors as being 'a re-creation of the hearth of Rheged'; he praises Urien's son Rhun, brother of Owein of Rheged, for reasons which will later become apparent; he invokes and praises Urien's personal bard Taliesin, co-founder with Merlin of the militant Dark Age tradition of bardic prophecy; and he refers to Glyndŵr in the context of his southern lineage as 'a bear of fine sense from Deheubarth'.

All of this itself makes sense when we recall that the Dark Age kingdom of Rheged, once led by Urien and his son Owein, has been correctly identified by Steve Blake and Scott Lloyd (*The Keys To Avalon*) as the very area adjoining Ystrad Clwyd in north-east Wales which later enfolded Glyndŵr's medieval estates of Glyndyfrdwy and Sycharth, and it is thus interesting to observe that Iolo also makes use of corvine imagery. He bemoans the current state of Mon (Druidic Anglesey) by observing that 'bright Mon's head has been struck off – it is empty'; he regularly invokes crows (i.e. ravens) in such phrases as 'you fed your army – human crows' and 'a squire's crowfeeding armburdening spear'; and he refers to Glyndŵr as 'feeding the crows' in battle.

I suggest that Iolo Goch *did* incite Owain Glyndŵr to war, having known his lineage well and having steered him upon this course since his formative years – in support of which I offer a large piece of evidence which has hitherto been overlooked.

Despite being a bard of Dyffryn Clwyd in north-east Wales, Iolo Goch knew the southern kingdom of Deheubarth and its lineage very well indeed, for it is recorded that in 1356 he journeyed there to witness the funeral of his great friend Sir Rhys ap Gruffydd of Llansadwrn in Cantref Mawr – the contemporary descendant of the Lord Rhys. However, the best guide to *precisely* how well Iolo Goch understood the south-west, and its strategic importance, comes in the form of his well-known poem entitled 'The Conversation Between the Body and the Soul', which we shall henceforth call the 'Strolling Tour', and of which Dafydd Johnston observes: 'The dialogue between the body and the soul was a common form in medieval literature . . . here used purely as a dramatic device to give an account of one of Iolo's bardic circuits around Wales, making good use of the convention that the soul is free to wander while the body lies in the grave – or rather lies in a drunken stupor', but we shall disagree.

While the traditional approach to the analysis of such poetry is to discuss its style and metre within the context of the contemporary bardic tradition, another technique is to take the road-map out of the glove-compartment of one's car, and stick map-pins in all the places which Iolo visited – at which point it becomes apparent that the 'Strolling Tour' is no mere idyll – it is a military document . . .

Iolo's Tour begins in the area of Newtown and Kerry (Ceri), a few miles from Offa's Dyke in the central Welsh borderland. This is position 'A' for the defensive control of Wales, since an English advance through this area leads straight to Machynlleth, thus providing the fastest way to cut Wales in half while offering access to the back-door of Deheubarth by getting around the back of the Cambrian mountains. The next three stops, Maelienydd, Elfael and Builth, lie in close association in the central borderlands somewhat to the south. Together they neatly seal and guard that funnel-shaped lowland region through which invaders such as Henry III had notoriously passed when intending to travel either via certain natural conduits to the far side of the Cambrian mountains (so as to gain even quicker access to the back-door of Deheubarth) or straight down the time-honoured invasion-route through Brycheiniog into south-west Wales. From here, Iolo heads immediately for Deheubarth's eastern border, the Tywi Valley, mentioning it directly and fervently, while singling out Caeo in Cantref Mawr – the birthplace of the Lord Rhys, and currently the home of Llywelyn ap Gruffydd Fychan, who would prove to be one of Glyndŵr's most committed supporters. Next he lists Kidwelly, another region of long-standing concern regarding the strategic viability of Deheubarth, and currently the home of Henry Dwn, who would become one of Glyndŵr's most prominent and powerful chieftains. At this point Iolo makes an easterly diversion which is so utterly impractical that it belies the idea that this is a genuine bardic tour. Here, north-west of Cardiff in the spiritual homeland of Llywelyn Bren, he meets the head of a Cistercian House in 'the Upper Taf Valley', who directs him to the Cistercians' headquarters at Whitland in Dyfed. The Cistercians were, of course, traditional supporters of the Welsh cause for reasons already discussed, however, not only does Whitland also mark the site of Hywel Dda's famous Welsh Assembly, but strategic control of this site specifically severs Carmarthen from the Anglo-Norman stronghold in south-west Wales, thus neutralising the strategy put in place by Henry I. Finally, pausing only to rejoice in Ceredigion, Iolo completes his circuit of Deheubarth's strategic defences with a visit to the Cistercian abbey of Strata Florida – the sentry-point to Deheubarth's back-door.

This is not coincidence. Other details within the poem also confirm that it is no whimsical jaunt. Iolo refers to Powys and Deheubarth as 'the two Gwynedds yonder', which seems to imply a greater agenda. As he lists the various places he visits, he praises the bravery of their people, and lists the resident Welsh nobility, landowners and clergymen, along with the wealth or material support which they can offer, and it is clear that above all he views with exuberance the level of support available in the Tywi Valley – of which, speaking as the wandering 'soul', he declares to the slumbering 'body':

> Thick were your tracks in Ystrad Tywi . . .
> The rich land was the prosperity of the country . . .
> a country which has always been most renowned. . . .
> The three cantrefs are stronger than six, . . .
> Caeo is better than nine [cantrefs] of heaven. . . .

Eventually it transpires that the 'body' is indeed not dead but drunk, doubtless with Shrewsbury beer, for it lies asleep at Sycharth – Owain Glyndŵr's home. This brings us to the final revelation that this is not Iolo's wandering soul in conversation with his own body, but rather Iolo assessing the level of support in key areas of the south and reporting back to Owain Glyndŵr. It is a conversation between Iolo the moving-spirit, and the body of a sleeping warrior, patron, protégé, friend and drinking partner.

If this were a real bardic tour, it would be amusing to imagine Iolo settling himself upon some tavern stool and announcing to the populace, 'Listen very carefully – for I shall sing this only once'. Instead it is more likely to have been copied and circulated by the monks of the Cistercian Order in the Upper Taf Valley, Whitland and Strata Florida, not to mention their close associates the Premonstratensians of Talley Abbey, who were already well-known for supporting Welsh causes.

Estimates of when the 'Strolling Tour' was written vary between 1375 and 1387 but, in agreement with the *Dictionary of Welsh Biography*, we shall tend towards the later date, noticing that this is also when Owain Glyndŵr, upon some unknown pretext, seems to have 'retired' from the English army. Like so many before them, Owain and Iolo were well aware that in order to raise Wales and to evict the English, it was essential to restore the integrity of Deheubarth and thus to remove the alien grip upon south Wales. Later we shall further substantiate the assertion that the 'Strolling Tour' is a military document, but for the time being we shall conclude that it essentially says: 'Let everyone in the following areas remember their history, for these are the key places which must be held.'

Meanwhile, the ecclesiastical network of Welsh-supporting Cistercian and Premonstratensian monks and scribes were to prove invaluable in disseminating such information to key landowners and the populace, as would certain other aspects of the legacy of the Lord Rhys . . .

Owain Glyndŵr knew that this time the Welsh nation would be hard to raise, for their spirits had sunk so low. In 1318 Llywelyn Bren had been let down by the many who had refused to rise, and in 1378 Owain Lawgoch had been cut down before he could even hoist a sail. Knowing this, and recognising that in strategic terms everything hinged upon raising the south, Glyndŵr must have spent many a long afternoon considering the legacy of the last man to do so – the Lord Rhys.

Not only had Rhys demonstrated that Deheubarth could be rekindled from its ashes, but the history of Deheubarth also contained a principle which Glyndŵr could employ in raising an embittered and demoralised Wales. Except for the Cambrian range, Deheubarth lacked the mountainous terrain that protected the kingdoms of mid and north Wales; the territory of the south-east was notoriously weak and indefensible, and the River Tywi was more an article of an ancient tribal faith than it was a physical barrier. Nevertheless Deheubarth had survived, even when compressed into the woods of Cantref Mawr, by a policy of 'all hands to the pumps' – for its leaders had traditionally engaged with, and rallied the full support of, the indigenous Welsh population. This they had achieved by remaining as close as possible to the thoughts and beliefs of their people, which may be characterised by the following passage from Lecky (*History of the Rise and Influence of the Spirit of Rationalism in Europe*)

The country people continued . . . to practise the rites of their forefathers . . . innumerable superstitious rites which occupied an equivocal position, sometimes countenanced and sometimes condemned – hovering upon the verge of [Christian] faith, associated and entwined with authorised religious practices.

Thus in Deheubarth, such rites had traditionally been countenanced, and this is why the Lord Rhys had not hesitated to invoke the power of the pagan Raven, even in the late 1100s: it was popular with the peasantry; it successfully roused the spirits and memories of an agricultural folk who still knew the goddess in all her aspects, especially the Morrigan, just as well as they knew the land itself; and in harking back to Urien, who had surely made the same appeal, it also recalled the old songs and the vengeful dream of a Celtic Britain.

This was an example which Glyndŵr must have viewed with great interest – for the peasantry of Wales had changed very little since the days of the Lord Rhys, and Glyndŵr knew that he too must generate a similar groundswell among the population, both of Deheubarth and beyond, for as R.R. Davies (*The Revolt of Owain Glyndŵr*) observes: 'Such a challenge could only be undertaken with the support, be it willingly given or an automatic response, of the populace of Wales, or a goodly proportion of it.'

So it was that in the late 1300s Owain Glyndŵr and Iolo Goch faced a dilemma regarding their propaganda campaign. During his uprising Glyndŵr would draw upon the legacies of both Llywelyn Bren and Owain Lawgoch, but in the strategically crucial area of Deheubarth it was paramount that he be identified with the Lord Rhys, thus highlighting his own connection with the House of Rheged. This was hardly a problem, since Glyndŵr was descended from the Lord Rhys on his mother's side, and as Welsh nobility he currently exercised a tiny islet of Welsh rule within the territory that had once been Rheged. Considering the Welsh penchant for names in Arthurian genealogy, it was therefore inevitable that Owain would soon be hailed in song as the new Owein of Rheged. However, corvine complications were certain to result.

To summon the spirit of the Lord Rhys was to flirt with an agenda which Iolo and Owain could not openly embrace – for although invoking the Raven would surely raise the grass-roots of Deheubarth and Wales, it would also invite allegations of paganism from clerical and baronial enemies, as the connection to the House of Rheged was swiftly made and Urien's marriage to the Morrigan was recalled. Not only would this bring accusations that Glyndŵr was a heathen and a sorcerer, who, according to the medieval Church, must therefore derive his powers from the Devil – but it would thus jeopardise potential alliances; nor did it sit very comfortably with the fact that both Iolo and Owain considered themselves Christians, or at least Marians with a Romano-Celtic heritage. Nevertheless, in the south there was no substitute for the spirit of the Lord Rhys, and no option but to fly with the Raven, and so a religious strategy was required to refute the inevitable allegation that Glyndŵr was pursuing a pre-Christian agenda.

It is possible that we can glean something of Glyndŵr's religious position by examining that of Iolo Goch, whose poetry demonstrates that he was at ease with superstition in its positive forms – seeing no problem in mentioning such entities as Nudd, a Dark Age Celtic saint linked to the Romano-Celtic healing-deity Nodens, nor in declaiming a spell-like blessing which would effectively render the Bishop of St Asaph invisible during his dangerous journey to Scotland, nor in linking the Holy Spirit with the Druidic symbol of the oak tree. However, Iolo apparently refers with repeated disapproval to the dark or black 'Irishness', which may be construed as a veiled reference to the Morrigan,[13] and he effectively applauds the story of how St Patrick ended the worshipping of stones and the evil spirits they contained. Furthermore, Iolo appears to have been a prominent fan of the Virgin Mary in the official Christian sense, and no doubt Glyndŵr's position was similar.

In such equanimity also lay the compromise which Glyndŵr could adopt when addressing the Welsh peasantry. While adhering strictly to Mary, he would also urge the restoration of the see of St David's and the rehabilitation of the old Celtic saints, and thus invoke the memory of Romano-Celtic Christianity – a senior form of Christianity that was distinct from the Anglo-Norman medieval Church and which had an identifiable Welsh heritage and a tradition of tolerance towards peasant beliefs.

The problem, however, lay in the legends (then widely accepted as actual history) which surrounded the House of Rheged – specifically its embroilment with the pagan Raven and the core allegation that Owein's father Urien had shared a bed with the Morrigan.[14] In response to this, folklore indicates that efforts were made by the Welsh to cast Urien as an early

Christian,[15] although it was also possible to absolve Urien's offspring by reciting the well-known story that Urien's son Rhun (Owein's brother) had become a Christian missionary in Northumbria during the brief era of distinctively Celtic Christianity once propagated from Iona – and this is why Iolo is careful to say, 'good was Rhun himself, who was born of love' in his writings.[16]

Research by Professor Gruffydd Aled Williams at the University of Wales has recently revealed that a hitherto unallocated poem was actually penned by Iolo Goch – and sure enough in it he refers to Glyndŵr as 'the last of the Three Owains', the first of whom was surely Owein of Rheged and the second almost certainly the Lord Rhys's northern ally Owain Gwynedd. Meanwhile, the same research has also demonstrated that Iolo Goch did not, as previously assumed, die in *c.* 1398. Instead it seems that he lived to see the early years of Glyndŵr's uprising, ascendant in its initial success, and therefore ended his career in the belief that victory was imminent. Thus we may remember Iolo in his final days as exultant, extolling the poetic prophecies of Merlin and Taliesin (the bards of Arthur and Urien of Rheged respectively) and proclaiming their relevance in the brave new era of Owain Glyndŵr – the warrior who was foretold.

However, the fact was that the prophetic power of the Dark Age bardic tradition was rooted in the remnants of Druidic beliefs, such as the oral preservation of British history in story and song, a belief in reincarnation, the study of astronomy and astrology, the magical divination of the future by scrying in reflective water pools, entrail-augury and oracular skulls, and the occult significance of the Raven – and as we know, the entire system was derived from a goddess-based earth-mother principle which had descended from the Neolithic. In Wales this had produced a supernatural landscape which was literally alive and immanent with ancestral spirits, and in which Druidic Anglesey was the fertile Mother of the World.

In the Middle Ages the Welsh bards had continued to preserve many such elements of their ancient heritage by a system of training involving great feats of memory. They were also expert genealogists and frequently good astronomers, and for entertainment they had even maintained the Druidic right to roam the land as 'wandering minstrels'. Furthermore, just as the Romans had once feared the supernatural powers of the Druids, so there lingered among the medieval English an uneasy belief in the cursing potency of the Welsh bards.

Since time immemorial such minstrels had succeeded in extracting extravagant gifts from noble patrons who feared that eulogies might be abandoned in favour of a bitter strain of song known as the 'glam-dicin' – an enchantment with the power to affect the health of its victim, or even to kill. Within a few years Owain Glyndŵr would be hailed by bards who were described by the fearful English as lethal – and we can imagine how their concerts progressed.

They surely began with the ever-popular 'Armes Prydein', a blistering rock-'n'-roll which urged the expulsion of the Saxon from Britain, prophesied that Cadwaladr would return to claim victory, abhorred the suppression of the Welsh saints (especially St David), and called for a Celtic alliance of the Welsh, Irish, Cornish, Picts and Celts of Strathclyde to drive the English into the sea – whereafter they would drift with nowhere to land.

Pausing only to proclaim that Glyndŵr was descended from Cadwaladr via Rhodri Mawr and the Lord Rhys, they would doubtless have launched next into a prophetic Dark Age ballad known as 'The Ohs of Merlin', which is preserved for posterity in *The Black Book of Carmarthen* and thus applied their harps, and other instruments akin to violin and flute, to the following refrain:

> A bear from Deheubarth will arise
> and his men will spread out
> over the lands of Monmouth.
> Over the Moon
> will the waiting of Gwenddydd be when a lord of Dyfed
> will be the occupier . . .
> yet I foretell
> the battle of Llwyfain woods
> and stretches all red
> before the rush of Owain . . .
> by Owain's band.

Finally, we may be certain that Iolo Goch would have led the bards in a string-laden crescendo of Taliesin's praises to the Arthurian hero Owein of Rheged, insisting that Glyndŵr was not only descended from him via the Lord Rhys, but was of the same land, and the same name.

Meanwhile, the magical powers available to the Welsh were not merely confined to peasant witches and spell-binding bards, for yet another belief had descended from the Neolithic via the Druidic to persist into the Middle Ages – namely that Celtic tribal leaders themselves possessed occult powers – and Owain Glyndŵr was no exception. Like all true tribal kings and natural princes of Wales, Glyndŵr would have inherited a primordial ability to converse with the birds – a gift also attributed to one of his late ancestors, the Lord Rhys's father Gruffydd of Caeo, who had dwelt in the woods of Cantref Mawr as the husband of heroic Gwenllian. Furthermore, we may be confident that Glyndŵr had a special ability to communicate with the ravens, with whom he had special kinship via the Lord Rhys and Owein of Rheged, and from whom he could glean prophetic information.

Glyndŵr is also said to have possessed a magic stone[17] – which we are promptly unsurprised to find described as a 'Ravens' Stone'. This afforded him the militarily useful powers of invisibility and of weather-control – and regarding the latter we may even infer how the ritual was performed, for in the *Mabinogion* tale of 'The Countess of the Fountain', it was none other than Glyndŵr's corvine ancestor Owein of Rheged who famously unleashed a furious rainstorm by the method of dashing water from a fountain upon a certain magic stone.

The Neolithic mechanics of this sympathetic ritual will not be lost upon the attentive reader[18] – nor will the fact that Glyndŵr's name is essentially derived from 'Glen of the Headwaters of the River Dee', or more specifically 'Glen of the Sacred Waters of the Battle-Goddess of the Dee'. Indeed, Shakespeare himself, writing in the 1500s, has Glyndŵr say:

> I can call spirits from the vasty deep
> and teach thee to command the Devil.

The first line here implies the creative-darkness of the Celtic 'deep', its ultimate union with the waters of the sea (Môr), and its deep relationship with the dark aspect of the Triple-Goddess often known as the Morrigan. Accordingly we find Morvran (i.e. 'mor-bran', or 'sea-raven') in the *Mabinogion*, ocean-going 'battle-ravens' upon the flags of Viking ships, and a persistent folk-belief that dark Morriganesque spirits occasionally rise from the depths of village wells.

Meanwhile the second line recalls Glyndŵr's subsequent identification with Jack of Kent, a folkloric character frequently described as 'the Devil's Master', who is the subject of a play written by Shakespeare's colleague and contemporary Anthony Munday – which also mentions 'the learned Owen Glenderwellin' (see Epilogue). Finally, in talking of commanding the Devil we should note that Shakespeare is simply adopting the policy of the conventional Church towards all supernatural powers other than those emanating from God – and is therefore ascribing those of the Morrigan to the Devil – but as we know, the deep powers at Glyndŵr's command were far older than the Christian 'Devil', and they frequently took the form of a raven.

As if this were not enough, strange portents had also surrounded Owain's birth. His father's horses were alleged to have been found standing up to their knees in blood in their stables, and it was said that the infant Glyndŵr would not cease crying until his hand was laid upon a weapon. Furthermore, effects both astrological and agricultural were cited, once again by Shakespeare in *Henry IV*, wherein Glyndŵr declares:

> . . . at my birth
> the front of heaven was full of fiery shapes . . .
> the frame and huge foundations of the earth
> shaked like a coward . . .
> the goats ran from the mountains, and the herds
> were strangely clamorous to the frightened fields.
> These signs have marked me extraordinary,
> And all the courses of my life do show,
> I am not in the roll of common men.

Once again, such rumours might have added to the prophetic hue and cry, but they also laid Glyndŵr open to the accusation that he was the spawn of Hades, the Devil's apprentice, or a direct descendant of the Morrigan, all of which in the eyes of the medieval English Church and state amounted to precisely the same thing.

Welsh leaders and their people had been demonised by the English ever since the Dark Ages, when the expediently converted Saxons had first deemed it their destiny to punish the Celts for not adhering sufficiently closely to the new decrees of Rome. In the Middle Ages, monotheistic Christianity continued to offer an exquisitely sharp instrument of state control regarding such outsiders as the Welsh, and thus in the Welsh Marches we find Bishop Charlton of Hereford (1327–43) being urged by Edward III at a moment of Scottish danger to 'secure the loyalty of the Welsh people of the borderlands, and to restrain by spiritual or other censures all disturbers of the peace' – these probably being the same Marcher Welshry whom Bishop Charlton had recently described as 'satellites of Satan'. No doubt the Welshry of the Monnow Valley who lived beneath the unrelenting glare of Grosmont Castle were similarly viewed, as they continued to cling stubbornly to their ancient beliefs. In 1358 Ewias Harold Priory was abandoned because 'religion cannot flourish there', and Kilpeck church was covered in Celtic carvings (as it is today), with its holy water in demand for purposes of witchcraft. In c. 1390 Kilpeck's rector was said to be so unfirm in faith that his flock made 'solemn processions at night with fantastic spirits', in 1424 Kilpeck's Benedictine priory was closed 'due to the natural ferocity of the people', and in 1484 the abbot of Grace Dieu at nearby Skenfrith would resign because of 'harassment'. From all of this it is clear that whatever the Anglo-Norman state decreed, at grass-roots level an older reality persisted among the local spirits of the soil, a reality with its own logic, its own agenda and its own version of history.

Meanwhile, as is reflected in a local debate regarding the origins of the name Skenfrith, we may assume that the superstitious Welsh peasantry of the Monnow Valley also had their own nomenclature and their own territorial feeling for the land. Why, for example, is the River Monnow so named? No one seems to know. In the 1200s it was the *Mone* to the Norman Marcher lords, while to others it was the *Munwi* – but did the Welsh who lived along its muddy banks remember the old name for Anglesey (*Mon*) – or did they remember *Muni(n)*, one of the two ravens ('Thought' and 'Memory') that once sat upon the shoulders of Odin? If so, then the Monnow is truly the 'River of Memories', as well as that of ergotine dreams, for wordplay and word-association were rarely wasted upon the minstrel race.

As 'Jack-daws' (*Corvus Mon-edula*) circled overhead, the medieval Welshry undoubtedly recalled the connection between the raven and the skull,[19] and feared according to a superstition which persisted even into modern times that they would therefore be decapitated. Even in the late 1300s, as they attended those churches which had been built upon pagan waterside sites, they continued in the ancient Druidic ritual of placing metal offerings into the adjacent rivers or lakes. They still knew, as Baring and Cashford (*The Myth of the Goddess*) observe, that 'birds were believed to make the weather', and when the earth shook, they dreaded, as Delaney (*The Celts*) describes, that 'the earth opened and the spirits stalked the land' – a land in which certain sacred stony sites still functioned as portals to a submerged Otherworld.

So much for the religious position of the Welsh Border peasantry in the year 1400. Politically they were the children of the Peasants' Revolt, and while some lamented the failure of John Ball and Wat Tyler, others with equal bitterness simply wished a plague upon anyone who brought more fear and terror. Meanwhile, far above their heads, Iolo Goch and Owain Glyndŵr brooded darkly in north Wales, Henry Bolingbroke was waiting in the wings – and King Richard II was clinging to the remnants of his reign.

LEGEND 10 : SPADEFULS

At Burton Hill in south Herefordshire, Jack of Kent and the Devil threw spadefuls of earth to see who could throw furthest. When the spadefuls landed they formed the 'butts' (a series of local hills). Jack won with his spadeful which landed to form Canon Pyon Butt.

Other versions
Here, a similar tale is also told of Robin Hood and Little John, while an alternative version sees a jumping competition between the pair, who proceed to make various heelmarks and divots.

[See also Appendix 1, p. 278.]

LEGEND 11 : MAGICAL THRESHING

Once, Jack of Kent had to thresh a bay of corn in the barn in a single day. He had with him a little black stick which he always carried, which contained, in a hollow at one end, a thing like a fly which was one of the Devil's imps, and once laid down beside him, this stick enabled him to do almost anything he wished. Thus, he removed his boot and put it on top of the heap of corn, wherein it miraculously threw the sheaves down to him one by one. He put his flail on the floor and it threshed the corn of its own accord. Meanwhile, he played his fiddle and chanted 'Nobble, stick, nobble. Play, fiddle, play!' and the bay was threshed by the end of the day.

[See also Appendix 1, p. 279.]

six

Interregnum
(1380–1400)

If the dates given by the experts for the 'Strolling Tour' are to be accepted, then plans had existed for Glyndŵr's uprising since at least 1387 – but Owain may have stayed his hand during the reign of Richard II because circumstances offered to deliver Wales without war. Richard had assumed the throne with so little baronial support that his credibility looked thin and his shelf-life short, but in 1382 he had done a remarkable thing in marrying his beloved and popular wife Anne of Bohemia, whose arrival in Britain was recorded at the time by the following strange tale:

> Scarcely had the Bohemian princess set her foot upon the shore, when a sudden convulsion of the sea took place, unaccompanied with wind, and unlike any winter storm; but the water was so violently shaken and troubled, and put in such furious commotion, that the ship in which the young queen's person was conveyed was very terribly rent in pieces before her very face, and the rest of the vessels that rode in company were tossed so, that it astonished all beholders.

This event was alleged by many, but we would surely be accused of the merest crystal-gazing were we to credit Anne of Bohemia with some ancient Celtic or Morriganesque influence upon the face of the deep, or even if we dared connect her with the lunar Triple-Goddess – were it not for a tide sufficient to drown all scepticism.

It is recorded that the marriage between Richard II and Anne of Bohemia was officially commemorated by a celebration of St Anne, the 'Great Mother' of the Virgin Mary, whose feast-day was subsequently observed each year. However, St Anne, popularly known as 'God's Grandmother' and thus a lady of problematical purity, inevitably became a divine earth-mother who was even more open to Gnostic interpretation than her daughter. Worse still, St Anne was a beatitude superimposed by the early Roman Catholic Church upon the last Great Mother of the pre-Christian world, namely the pagan Anna (derived from Inanna-Ishtar), a Neolithic Triple-Goddess of the Moon who was still known to the Celts as 'Ana'. This full-lunar entity was as positively famous for her child-nurturing breasts as her dark-lunar sister was negatively notorious as the child-devouring Morrigan. This may be why we find the following lines in a contemporary religious poem by Iolo Goch – who appears exceedingly wary of St Anne's potential association with the 'dark Irishness':

> then Mary, bright word
> will be on her pure knees . . .
> lifting up, supportive complaint . . .
> her hands to beseech . . .
> her son and her lord and her protector, . . .
> golden her voice for her task, . . .
> our golden sister, and requesting . . .
> heaven and mercy for us. . . .
> We will get a place through the strength of Anna's daughter,
> . . . and because of that, wise word,
> . . . it is best for me to adore Mary. . . .

Anne of Bohemia came from a land via which the ancient goddess had traditionally travelled to the west, for having emerged from the Coptic Church, the goddess, frequently clad in a Gnostic disguise, skirted the Black Sea and visited the significantly named city of 'Sophia' before reaching Bohemia in central Europe.

Anne of Bohemia, however, was purportedly much bolder. As

if to underscore her influence upon the waves, she allegedly arrived in Britain wearing an outrageous Bohemian/Syrian head-dress comprising a pair of 2ft high lunar horns. Popularly known as her 'Moony Tire', this bifurcating image recalled either the heavenly dominion of the celestial Virgin Mary, or a much older entity – namely Inanna-Ishtar, the lunar-horned Neolithic Triple-Goddess who had preceded Yahweh in Chaldea, and who had been referred to in the Old Testament as the 'Whore of Babylon'.

In the late 1300s, 'Moony Tire' was apparently considered so daring a fashion-statement that it was widely imitated by the ladies of Richard's court, while being denounced by the Anglo-Norman Church as the same type of head-dress condemned by Ezekiel. Nevertheless, it was reported that at their wedding the royal couple were pursued by carriages crammed with court ladies sporting spectacular versions of 'Moony Tire', a lunatic display said to have been enjoyed by the vast throngs lining the streets of London.

Anne of Bohemia won not only Richard's heart and mind, but also those of the people. Wed in the wake of the Peasants' Revolt, she interceded in a spirit of mercy and forgiveness and successfully persuaded her doting husband to end the retributions against the peasantry with the following remarkable speech:

> Sweet! – my king, my spouse, my light, my life! – sweet love, without whose life mine would be but death! – be pleased to govern your citizens as a gracious lord. Consider even today, how munificent their treatment. What worship, what honour, what splendid public duty, have they at great cost paid to thee, revered king! Like us they are but mortal, and liable to frailty. Far from thy memory, my king, my sweet love, be their offences; and for their pardon I supplicate – kneeling thus lowly on the ground.

Whereafter the Bohemian princess proceded to invoke the honourable spirits of the kings of Ancient Britain, Brutus and

Arthur, in this, the first of her invariably successful pleadings, which must also have pleased the Welsh.

Such talk would normally have pleased the establishment, since the Norman contingent had been claiming ownership of the Arthurian tradition ever since their own scribe, Geoffrey of Monmouth, had produced a romanticised version of it which later became the basis of chivalry.[20] However, coming from a Bohemian lady wearing 'Moony Tire', and whose husband had lately been showing a disturbing interest in the Welsh, it may be that the barons feared she was familiar with something rather older and more dangerous than Geoffrey of Monmouth's authorised version of British history.

Furthermore, since Anne's brother, King Wenceslas of Bohemia, was the heir-presumptive to the Holy Roman Empire, Anne had been hailed as 'Caesar's Sister' – and Caesar was a title which had been eulogised by the Welsh since the golden age of Romano-Celtic-Christian Britain.

In 1382, Anne of Bohemia collaborated with her mother-in-law, the legendarily beautiful Joan of Kent, Princess of Wales, to protect the life of John Wycliffe, the founder of Lollardy, a movement harmonious with the (Gnostic) Cathar Church of Provence in its urging of self-education. Constantly engaged upon good deeds, and consequently known to the people as the 'Bounteous Queen' and 'Good Queen Anne', her actions were those of a consort with a conscience on behalf of the oppressed. Prominent among these were the Welsh, and shortly thereafter we find Richard II not only restoring Welshmen to positions of military and administrative authority (despite the fact that this contravened the laws laid down by Edward I), but also bringing large areas of Wales under his personal dominion.

In 1386, Richard II was in trouble, for his wife's achievement in steering him towards popularity with the lower orders, the Welsh, and those of a libertine lunar leaning, had not endeared him either to the authoritarian barons or the Church – both of whom saw in this Bohemian drift a threat to their own status and control. In the same year the barons seized government, and left Richard shorn of power. In 1387

Richard's star declined as the old order took charge, whereupon Owain Glyndŵr promptly retired from the English army and perhaps Iolo Goch wrote the 'Strolling Tour', in preparation for war.

However, in 1389 Richard regained power, and ruled competently until the tragic death of his wife in 1394 – an event which led him to destroy their idyllic retreat at Shene and to view the remainder of his life as a wilderness. With Anne of Bohemia gone, Richard invested his faith in esoteric attempts to divine the future by geomancy, in contemplation of his personal patron-saint John the Baptist (whose prophetic oracular 'head' and association with water were of long-standing significance to both the Knights Templar and the Celts), and in the mystical lunar symbol of the White Hart, which was also of ancient significance in Wales.[21]

Thereafter, Richard continued upon his forlorn course and brought even more lands in Wales under his direct lordship, until by 1395 his collection of Welsh territories spanned the Principality from north to south, and formed the largest single power-bloc in the British Isles. In 1397, he further added to his Welsh interests and, having terminally fallen out with the nobility and the city of London, Richard even hired a force of Welshmen to intimidate certain English barons. At last it seems that he was hoping, in his madcap caprice, to rule a restructured kingdom of Britain from his new establishments in Chester and Wales.[22]

Such proceedings had so far stayed the hand of a certain squire in his service, Owain Glyndŵr, who had been looking forward to an era of vastly increased wealth, opportunity and religious tolerance in Wales, which, even should Richard fail without issue, might still be delivered without war by Richard's appointed heir Roger Mortimer, Earl of March, the king's Royal Lieutenant in Ireland. A man friendly to and esteemed by the Welsh, Mortimer was related to Llywelyn the Great, and may well have been pivotal in steering Richard and Anne towards Wales. Sadly for the Welsh, however, in July 1398 Roger Mortimer died in Ireland at the age of 24, leaving his young son Edmund suspended in wardship as the theoretical heir to the throne – and as Richard's own position deteriorated rapidly, Glyndŵr's hand must have tightened upon the handle of his sword.

In 1399, the king set out for Ireland – heedless it seems, not only of the suspicious timing of Mortimer's demise, and of the barons who were conspiring against him – but with many among his company, such as the Tudors of Anglesey and Henry Dwn of Kidwelly, who would soon be found among the key supporters of Owain Glyndŵr.

As July ended, Richard abandoned his ill-considered absence in Ireland and returned to the mainland, landing in south Wales only to find that Henry Bolingbroke, the son of John of Gaunt, had already occupied his new power-base at Chester, and had rallied the barons with the intention of de-posing the king. From the Cistercian headquarters at Whitland, Richard attempted to raise the Welsh in his support – but it was all too little and too late, for Bolingbroke had seized the initiative, and when Richard appeared at Flint he too was seized and transported to the Tower – and on 29 September the usurper Henry Bolingbroke became Henry IV of England.

These events must have been watched with resignation by Glyndŵr and his entourage, for the fragile raft which Richard had steered against the current of the English establishment had been sinking for some time; swamped by the loss of Queen Anne, it was holed below the waterline by the death of Roger Mortimer, the cargo of Welsh hopes – and only the rapids lay ahead.

In the year 1400, the situation in Archenfield and the Monnow Valley seemed normal enough, but the advent of Henry IV had brought unease for many reasons. There was a sense of loss and disbelief among the Welshry regarding Richard II, a king who had lacked the normal hostility towards them – and rumours abounded that he was still alive. There was also great bitterness concerning the illegality with which Bolingbroke had usurped the throne – and much dispute regarding the validity of his claim in comparison with that of the Mortimers. Furthermore, as the son of John of Gaunt (d. 1399), Bolingbroke had recently inherited Gaunt's

Lancastrian lordship of the Three Castles – and the last time a king of England had held dominion there was in the time of Henry III, when Llywelyn the Great had rampaged across the land and Grosmont itself had been attacked. Well might the inhabitants of the Monnow Valley feel such foreboding, for history would soon repeat itself – and somewhere in north Wales, Glyndŵr's sword was already sharpened for what would be no small feud, but the renewal of a millennial war – the result of much thought and preparation – which in Hereford had already been under way for some time . . .

In 1375, after an endless procession of Normans and Englishmen, a Welshman had managed to become Bishop of Hereford. John Gilbert, the former Bishop of Bangor in north Wales, was described as 'a civil servant . . . taking little share in the factions of the time', but his main achievement from our point of view was that in 1384 he ordained to the order of Sub-Deacon a certain Adam of Usk – a chronicler whom we shall meet again.

Gilbert, however, had set a precedent, and when Richard II regained power from the Council in 1389 he not only approved Gilbert's transfer to the see of St David's in south-west Wales but also his replacement at Hereford by another Welshman, one John Trefnant from the village of Trefnant near St Asaph, in north-east Wales.

Let us suspect that this approval of John Trefnant as Bishop of Hereford was not only an example of Richard II's positive attitude towards Welshmen in positions of authority, but also a symptom of a libertine religious agenda in which the Provençal-educated and Bordeaux-born Richard and his late lunar-horned wife shared a certain Bohemian interest with the Welsh. Furthermore, bearing in mind Richard's network of lands and supporters among the Welsh nobility in Chester and north-east Wales, we may also suspect that John Trefnant, a canon of St Asaph's Cathedral, had been presented to him by the local Welsh nobility of that area, including Owain Glyndŵr, with just such advancement in mind. Glyndŵr himself was linked to St Asaph's Cathedral through his prominence, his proximity, and his personal bard Iolo Goch who was probably educated there and whose patrons included the archdeacon and the bishop. Considering this, in the light of everything else we have learned, let us examine the career of Bishop John Trefnant at Hereford.

We have seen that sympathy with Lollardy and Ballardy came naturally to the Welsh, in so far as such causes deplored the corpulent Anglo-Norman Church and threatened to empower the common man at its expense. These movements were therefore condemned as heresy, and at Hereford it was Bishop Trefnant who famously presided over the trials of two alleged Lollards, Swynderby and Brut (Bryt), the latter being a rampantly patriotic Welshman who believed the end of the world was nigh, and that his countrymen were destined to fight the Anti-Christ. At these trials, Trefnant, although renowned for his love of legal technicalities, is described as having shown 'no significant interest' and 'no signs of persecuting zeal', and when on one occasion Swynderby failed to appear before him, the bishop's response was merely to offer him an escort. Furthermore, Trefnant was sufficiently respectful of the arguments put forward by both Swynderby and Brut that their defences relating to the Apocalypse were registered in full and at great length.

It has been suggested that the complete absence in Bishop Trefnant's library of any Lollard literature, poetry or works of the oratory of Greece demonstrated his lack of interest in such matters, but I suggest that it actually implies precisely the opposite – for Bishop Trefnant was a very careful man.

It is recorded that in his ordinations of priests to the diocese of Hereford, the Welsh Bishop Trefnant 'attracted an unprecedented number of his countrymen', including some of his relatives. In other words between 1389 and 1400 John Trefnant flooded the Hereford diocese with Welsh priests, a practice that would have raised more than eyebrows had it occurred under Edward III, but which under Richard II might merely have mirrored the acceptability of Trefnant's own appointment – were it not for the following interesting details.

Between 1391 and 1398, the influx of Welshmen from such places as St Asaph and Carmarthen also included five monks from the Premonstratensian abbey of Talley in Cantref Mawr – all of whom immediately became priests.

This already outstrips the total number of arrivals from Talley at Hereford during the entire tenure of Trefnant's Welsh predecessor John Gilbert (1375–89). Furthermore, to these five we may add four or five more, all going by the name of 'ap Madoc', who appear to have been monks of a daughter-house of Talley.

Despite the fact that before Bishop Gilbert's tenure monks from Talley were virtually unknown at Hereford, and that Trefnant appears to have doubled Gilbert's intake in half the time, we might still consider this a function of the general increase in Welshmen admitted by Trefnant during the period when the pro-Welsh Richard II was in control (1389–98). However, the acid test is to observe what happened after July 1398, when Mortimer's death left Richard suddenly isolated in his terminal conflict with the barons – for at this moment our thesis would predict that Glyndŵr's network went on to red alert, and sure enough it did. Reinforced by two grey Franciscan friars from Carmarthen and two white Cistercian monks from the diocese of St Asaph, a further six Premonstratensian monks arrived from Talley Abbey within the next ten months, the last four of whom immediately became priests, thus bringing the 'tally' at Hereford to sixteen.

I suggest that while the Franciscan and Cistercian Orders were lending their traditional support to the Welsh cause, the elite of Owain Glyndŵr's secret service in south Wales were the Welsh monks of the French Premonstratensian Order, which had been established by the Lord Rhys, the Raven of Dinefwr, in the notoriously remote and inaccessible Talley Abbey in the forest of Cantref Mawr.

To Hereford they came, in December 1398 and May 1399, Morgan ap David, John Pontham, Mathew April, Mathew ap Llywellin, David ap Jevan, and Jevan ap Joram, to conjoin with the ap Madocs and the many others who had preceded them, and to mingle as priests among the Norman Marcher lords of Archenfield – seeking out those barons who might throw in their lot with the Welsh.

I further suggest that Bishop Trefnant's appointment to Hereford in 1391 was approved by Richard II as part of a Bohemian religious agenda which he shared with his friends among the Welsh nobility of north-east Wales, and I believe it is no coincidence that within two years Richard had brought Talley Abbey under his personal protection. Nor do I consider it coincidental that when Richard stayed at Kidwelly Castle in May 1399, in preparation for his last doomed visit to Ireland, he did so in the personal company of the contemporary descendant of the Lord Rhys, Thomas ap Gruffydd, the grandson of the Sir Rhys ap Gruffydd whose funeral had been attended by Iolo Goch.

Could it be that, through his esoteric interests, and his adoration of the Bohemian Moon-Goddess who had been his wife, Richard II had become secretly possessed by the persuasive power of a pre-Christian principle?

In 1397 Bishop Trefnant lent money to Richard II, but just two years later, on 1 November 1399, he founded a chantry at Ledbury to pray for his own soul and that of the new king, Henry IV – and as 1400 dawned, Trefnant swiftly left the country to announce the change of monarch to the Pope – for he knew that it was an excellent moment to depart.

On 16 September 1400, at his manor of Glyndyfrdwy near Corwen, Owain Glyndŵr was proclaimed Prince of Wales by those long privy to his plans. It was treason, but it was only the start of Glyndŵr's great ambition to revive the fortunes of a long-downtrodden people. The big question was, could he get it off the ground?

LEGEND 12 : THE SCOTTISH ARMY

During the Civil War between Charles I and Parliament, when the Scottish army had finished besieging Hereford they came to plunder the neighbourhood of Kentchurch and Grosmont in the Monnow Valley, but the magician Jack of Kent went into a field of corn, and with one blast of his horn turned the cornstalks into such a field of soldiers that the intruders were immediately forced to retire.

[See also Appendix 1, p. 280.]

SEVEN

UPRISING
(1400–2)

Henry IV soon knew the insecurity of the usurper, for the spectre of Richard II still roamed the land, maintained by persistent rumours of his survival, by the rebellions of his supporters and by the Franciscan allegation that he was alive and well and living in Wales. Meanwhile, Henry lived in constant fear of assassination by foul means, such as a plot to oil his saddle with a poisonous substance. In the autumn of 1400, having returned with his army from a foray into Scotland, the new king was at Northampton when he heard of the insurgency in north-east Wales.

On 18 September, Owain Glyndŵr gathered a rebel force of 500 local men and staged a series of lightning attacks upon the English settlements in Dyffryn Clwyd. Taking advantage of an ongoing feud which he maintained with his powerful English neighbour Lord Grey,[23] Glyndŵr also crossed the River Dee and devastated Grey's town of Ruthin. It was an episode strongly reminiscent of the feud which had once existed between the Lord Rhys and his neighbour Walter de Clifford in the south.

Ruthin already lay in ruins as the rebels brought havoc to Denbigh, Rhuddlan, Flint, Hawarden, Holt, Oswestry and Welshpool, and north-west Wales rose under the leadership of Owain's cousins, the Tudors of Anglesey. Glyndŵr had yet to attract the level of popular support necessary to besiege a castle, let alone to prosecute a war, but he had broadcast a resounding advertisement of his intent – and offered a barbed invitation to the king.

As Henry IV and his vast army diverted from Northampton and

bore down upon north Wales, Owain promptly retreated with his fledgling force to Corwen – from where the Lord Rhys had once called all of Wales to arms. Here Glyndŵr raised the royal Welsh standard of the ancient kingdom of Gwynedd with its four lions rampant[24] – before melting into the hillsides like a morning mist.

On 26 September, a flustered Henry arrived at Shrewsbury and charged hotfoot into north Wales like a bull summoned by a red rag. By the time he returned, on 15 October, the English army had trampled right across north Wales, calling upon Caernarfon, Cricieth, Harlech, Conwy, Denbigh and Beaumaris, destroying Llywelyn the Great's Franciscan friary on Anglesey, burning numerous villages and towns including Bangor, looting and embezzling livestock, dispensing summary justice upon the innocent and guilty alike, and executing one of the Tudors – but signally failing to find Glyndŵr.

Having deposited garrisons in six castles, Henry IV nevertheless celebrated at Shrewsbury in the erroneous belief that this was a job well done, and that he would not be hearing from the Welsh again in the foreseeable future – yet even as he raised a goblet to his lips there came disturbing reports of orchestrated Welsh raids upon English towns along the length of the border. Before long it was evident that Henry had played into Glyndŵr's hands by raising north Wales to a seething state of resentment – and in October, as Anglo-Welsh tension escalated along the Marches, Henry issued a general pardon to any Welshmen who would submit, but little more was heard from the rebels in that year.

Owain Glyndŵr, the former lord of Glyndyfrdwy and Sycharth, had abandoned a comfortable lifestyle to become an itinerant guerrilla leader, for his estates had already been seized and would soon be regranted to the Earl of Somerset. With winter closing in, Owain retreated with a handful of men into the bleak, impenetrable mountains of Snowdonia, confident that the fuse which he had lit in north Wales and the borders would still be smouldering in the spring – but he knew there could be no hope of victory unless the whole of Wales, and crucially the former Deheubarth, came to arms. As Glyndŵr and his men wintered in freezing caverns amid the peaks, a rebel network of priests, bards and wandering minstrels hurried far below, urgently infiltrating key areas of Wales and the Marches, intent upon a propaganda, reconnaissance and recruitment campaign. Three constituencies of discontent were being targeted – the frustrated legacy of the Ballards, the disaffected members of the barony, and the great critical mass of the Welsh peasantry – and Owain could only hope that it would work.

Warfare was traditionally suspended during winter, so both sides were preparing for the spring. Glyndŵr's emissaries garnered support from as far afield as Oxford and Cambridge Universities, whereupon Welsh students returned home in force, and Welsh labourers also returned from England, while the English sent spies into north Wales upon a fruitless search for Glyndŵr, paying particular attention to Merionethshire, the Llŷn Peninsula and Eifionydd.

The approach of spring saw fresh apprehension growing in the English border towns and anti-Welsh sentiment running at fever pitch along the Marches, and in March 1401 the Crown once again did Glyndŵr's work for him when Parliament enacted a programme of insupportable legislation against the Welsh, who were henceforth

- communally responsible for any damage caused by rebels
- barred from holding positions of even minor authority
- not permitted to stage any gatherings or congregations without English permission and supervision
- not permitted to own defensible houses
- not permitted to serve in English castles
- not permitted to own land in the (Anglicised) Welsh towns, or in England
- not permitted to carry arms
- not permitted to support 'Wasters, rhymers, minstrels or other vagabonds in Wales'.

Thus the Welsh were officially informed of their inferior status as outsiders in their own land, but these measures, which were in fact a measure of Glyndŵr's achievement so far, created precisely the combustible atmosphere which Glyndŵr required for his spring offensive – and the spark was provided on 1 April 1401, when the Tudors made a fool out of Henry IV's regime.

This was Good Friday, the day recognised by the medieval Church as commemorating the crucifixion of Christ, i.e. the Friday before Easter Sunday. However, Celtic Christianity had disagreed about the calculation of the date of Easter, and so the rebels were unconstrained.

Early on Friday morning, while the English garrison at Conwy Castle was deep in prayer, the Tudors and their men gained access to the castle by a subterfuge, seized the armoury and proceeded to the chapel, where they captured the entire garrison and its commander at a stroke – thus relieving England of one of its most prestigious and impregnable fortresses. As well as being horribly embarrassing for Henry IV, this seriously undermined baronial confidence in both the competence and credibility of his regime – and it put great heart into the Welsh.

While the Tudors torched Conwy and repeatedly frustrated English efforts to regain the castle, the population of north Wales joined the rebels, and a jubilant Glyndŵr set off to light the fuse in west Wales with a series of incendiary raids upon the English holdings in Ceredigion and northern Dyfed (Pembrokeshire).

By May, insurgents were abroad in Ceredigion and Powys, the villeins of Abergavenny had rebelled, unrest had broken out in what had once been Deheubarth, and a garrison was required at Kidwelly. At the end of the month, Glyndŵr sent the following letter to an abrasive Welsh landowner in south-west Wales, Henry Dwn, a fellow member of the Welsh nobility who had also risen to prominence under Richard II:

We inform you that we hope to be able, by God's help and yours, to deliver the Welsh people from the captivity of our English enemies who, for a long time elapsed, have oppressed us and our ancestors. And you may know from your own perception, that now their time draws to a close and because, according to God's ordinance from the beginning, success turns towards us, no one need doubt that a good issue will result, unless it be lost through sloth or strife.

Glyndŵr was requesting Dwn's support during an imminent raiding expedition into the south-west. However, having anticipated precisely this, Henry IV was already at Worcester, where he had prepared a substantial force with the intention of cornering Glyndŵr in south-west Wales. Nevertheless, Henry was anxious lest he should fail once again to locate the notoriously elusive Welshman. Thus, when early intelligence was received of Glyndŵr's presence near Machynlleth, the decision was taken to engage in a pre-emptive strike. The king's fourteen-year-old son Prince Hal descended upon Machynlleth from the north, while Lord Charlton approached from the east, and an Anglo-Flemish army from the Crown stronghold in Dyfed arrived from the south via Ceredigion. What followed became known as the Battle of Hyddgen, an encounter that took place in the hills of Pumlumon (Plynlimon) near Machynlleth in June 1401, and which has confused historians as much it must have done the combatants – for it would seem that Glyndŵr achieved an extraordinary victory armed with only 120 men. What probably occurred, however, was as follows:

Various contingents of Glyndŵr's raiding party were converging towards a rendezvous in the area of Machynlleth, with the intention of moving southward through Ceredigion to stage a swift inflammatory raid upon south-west Wales, when the English came upon them. At the last moment the Welsh heard of Prince Hal's approach, and one of their contingents intercepted Hal's force at Cadair Idris north of Machynlleth, whereupon Hal promptly reported that he had been 'ambushed by Owain Glyndŵr'. Glyndŵr was in fact at Machynlleth, where he was simultaneously attacked from the east by Lord Charlton – whose report then served to reinforce the rumours of Glyndŵr's magical ability to be in more than one place at a time. Thus thwarted, and having only narrowly evaded capture, Glyndŵr was still roaming the hills south of Machynlleth with just 'one hundred and twenty reckless men . . . riding in warlike fashion' when the Anglo-Flemish army of 2,000 men arrived from the south.

Owain promptly fled, pursued by the Anglo-Flemish force, into the cloud-burdened summits of Pumlumon. In the shambles that followed, the Anglo-Flemish army was repeatedly harried by Glyndŵr and by other nearby Welsh contingents using the traditional Welsh tactics of ambush and archery, until their numbers were depleted and their morale worn down by constant rainfall and boggy conditions. At last they were confronted by Glyndŵr with his 120 men upon an open heath. Here, driven by dread of the proximity of Prince Hal and Lord Charlton, and fearful of a terminal failure, the Welsh fell furiously upon the enemy 'with courage whetted by despair' – and won an anomalous victory from which their enemies fled in chaos and dismay.

Hyddgen was an impromptu affair. Briefly triumphant, but nevertheless prevented from appearing in the south-west, Glyndŵr made the best of the situation by making a speech from the pair of white-quartz stones which stand not far from the sources of the Severn and the Wye, which are called Owain Glyndŵr's Covenant Stones, and which are aligned exactly north–south. From here he appealed to the men of the south-west to rally to his cause – many did, and there came an influx of influential supporters from both Ceredigion and the riverbanks of the Tywi in Carmarthenshire.

Glyndŵr immediately vanished. Henry IV dismissed his force at Worcester, and on 14 June Prince Hal dispatched spies into north Wales with instructions to seek Owain in the uplands of Nantconwy and upon the lowly shores of Traeth Mawr. Hal, based at Chester and responsible for north Wales, also confiscated numerous rebel lands, and issued even more intolerable restrictions upon the local Welsh – including barring people of even half-Welsh origin from the towns. In Chester three Welsh people together were deemed to constitute a gathering, and would therefore be arrested and imprisoned, and furthermore any Welshry found within the town walls after sunset would be executed.

However, it was all too late, for Glyndŵr had already succeeded in his actions and appeals, and Hal's brutal 'Ordinances' simply made matters worse. The chronicler Adam of Usk reported that all of north, central and western Wales as far south as Cardigan rapidly defected to the rebel cause, English towns and property came under widespread attack from the Welsh population, and the flagship castles of Harlech and Aberystwyth were besieged. Defections in central Wales spread as far south as Builth and the middle-March, and southern unrest required the garrison at Kidwelly to be doubled and a garrison to be installed at Swansea. Meanwhile financial insurrection broke out in Carmarthenshire, where tenants refused to pay debts and dues on the grounds of anticipated revolt.

As the summer of discontent reached August, Glyndŵr turned his attention to the east, devastating the town of Welshpool where the castle was stubbornly defended by the Charltons, and ruining the town and castle of Montgomery. Pausing only to destroy Bishop's Castle, Glyndŵr immediately embarked upon a campaign to ignite Radnorshire in the middle-March – the strategic importance of which we have already discussed. Upon descending from the north, Glyndŵr therefore torched Radnor town before storming its castle, which had once been held by the Lord Rhys. Sixty surviving English defenders were decapitated and their heads set on display – their heaped skulls destined to be unearthed by church workmen in 1843.

It was vital that Glyndŵr exercise as much influence upon Radnorshire as possible – an area the strategic importance of which had already bequeathed it a history of repeated devastation at the hands of both English and Welsh, and had instilled in its inhabitants a despairing border-pragmatism in their loyalties. Typical of this was the nearby Cistercian abbey of Cwm-hir, which Glyndŵr now razed to the ground in an action which, since the Cistercians were traditional supporters of the Welsh, has perplexed some commentators. However, Cistercian abbeys such as Tintern, Margam, Neath, Ewenni, Dore and Cwm-hir were Anglicised at this time, and placed in an impossible position, they had chosen to oppose Glyndŵr, who therefore pressurised or destroyed them.

If our thesis is correct, Cwm-hir's lack of support is also the reason that Iolo Goch omits the abbey from his 'Strolling Tour', even though his route takes him straight past it. However, what has puzzled others is that Abbey Cwm-hir had once supported Llywelyn the Last (d. 1282) and still provided the last resting-place for that fallen hero's remains. It has thus been claimed that in destroying Abbey Cwm-hir, Glyndŵr had desecrated a shrine sacred to the Welsh cause. However, this is to forget that Llywelyn's head was taken, not by the ravens but by the English, and put on display in London. Thus, as Glyndŵr's supporters were well aware, Cwm-hir was never the custodian of Llywelyn's soul.

Finally, having freed Llywelyn's mortal remains from English Cistercian custody, Glyndŵr did just as Llywelyn himself had done, driving south from Radnorshire to raid the areas of Hay-on-Wye, Grosmont, Abergavenny and Usk. Whereafter, having lit the fuse of eastern Wales, it is possible that Owain paused to hoist some unrecorded flag, before disappearing into the thin September air.

By October Henry IV faced a serious situation. The great Edwardian castles of Harlech and Aberystwyth were dependent upon desperate relief missions. Glyndŵr had slipped through his fingers at Machynlleth to claim a ludicrous victory before attacking the middle-March, and while Henry had dismissed his force at Worcester so as to avoid further expense, the ongoing financial insurrection and unrest in Carmarthenshire might yet prove more expensive still. For all these reasons the situation could not be allowed to continue, but even more worrying was the damage to Henry's credibility and the fact that Glyndŵr's ambition was clearly to liberate ancient Deheubarth. Henry was as aware as anyone of the vital importance of the south-west with regard to the strategic viability or otherwise of an independent Welsh nation – so it was time to act decisively, and with overwhelming force.

On 1 October, Henry set out from Worcester in the company of many thousands of troops, asserting that 'all the remaining parts of our said country [Wales] and the marches will surrender to the said rebels if we are not there in person to resist their evil'. Whereupon, ignoring the plight of other, less crucial parts of

Wales, the royal muster wasted no time in marching straight into the south-western heartland of the former Deheubarth – the Tywi Valley. Seeking rebels and news of Glyndŵr, the English came to Caeo in Cantref Mawr where the Lord Rhys was born, and interrogated its incumbent, the Welsh nobleman Llywelyn ap Gruffydd Fychan. Famously, sixty-year-old Fychan offered to betray Glyndŵr, and led Henry and his army on an intricate dance through nearby hills in search of the rebel leader, whereafter he brazenly declared himself a red herring, and admitted that two of his sons were in Owain's service. Fychan's death was abominably slow, grotesque, and public, and was performed in Llandovery town square under the personal supervision of Henry IV.

However, Deheubarth's tradition of ultimate resistance remained alive, and other rebels also chose to die rather than to betray Glyndŵr, and so an enraged Henry embarked upon an orgy of persecution and terror, heedless as ever of innocence or guilt. As an English chronicler relates, 'ravaging them with fire, hunger and sword, [he] left them a desert, not even sparing children or churches'.

Determined to be recompensed for the financial insurrection, and that the Welsh should pay for their own suppression, Henry thundered down the Tywi, impounding lands, imposing prodigious fines, seizing chattels and stealing cattle. Via Dinefwr (Llandeilo) and Carmarthen, Henry's royal river poured across south-west Wales to Cardigan, before turning north to force the back-door of Deheubarth, where the Welsh Cistercian abbey of Strata Florida stood guard upon the graves of Deheubarth's ancient kings. Here Henry chose to stay as an uninvited guest, stealing the holy silver, murdering many of his monkish hosts, burning the outbuildings, and stabling his horses in the church.

At last the English left, part of their plunder comprised of nameless Welsh children – helpless orphans who were marched in chains towards a foreign land where their unnumbered lives were spent in slavery to Anglo-Norman barons. Behind them they left a south-west in shock, ring-fenced by garrisons at numerous castles, including Hay-on-Wye, Painscastle and Builth, and by major deployments at Cardigan and Aberystwyth.

In all its punitive horror, Henry's aim was clear: to terrify the south-west into submission, to lock it, seal it and place it permanently beyond the reach of Owain Glyndŵr – and it seemed he had succeeded. Early November saw an inconclusive skirmish near Caernarfon in the north, after which an anxious Glyndŵr sought to raise the stakes with a new flag, the Golden Dragon of Uther Pendragon (Arthur's father) rampant upon a white field – thus declaring himself the king of the Britons – but even as it fluttered rather forlornly in the breeze, there came the news from the south which he must have feared. The Welshry of Cardigan and Carmarthenshire had surrendered to the Crown.

Both Henry IV and Owain Glyndŵr knew the significance of this submission, which must have plunged Glyndŵr into the deepest gloom, for with the prize removed the race seemed over. When Henry had terrorised the north, it had brought indignation and outrage from a mountainous domain in which Glyndŵr was present and well known, but in the south-west the king had gone much further in his actions, and the result was very different. What had once been Deheubarth had been scared out of its wits by Henry's campaign – it was prostrate, heavily occupied, lacked natural defences, and was surrounded by a chain of re-garrisoned castles. Accordingly, it had capitulated, and barely had Owain's brave new flag been hauled down from the stake upon which it hung than a message arrived, offering him an opportunity to do the same at Worcester.

Either through instinct or because of information received, Glyndŵr declined to attend the parley at Worcester, and this was wise – because it is known that the English did not intend him to leave there alive. Winter was pressing, and with negotiations abandoned both sides engaged once more in planning for the spring.

So far, Owain had failed to appear in the south-west and the improvised victory at Pumlumon which had halted his only attempt to do so had almost been a disaster. That nightmarish escapade had surely convinced him that for as long as Aberystwyth and Cardigan Castles and the Crown emplacement in Dyfed (Pembrokeshire) were in business, it would remain reckless to attempt a back-door descent into Deheubarth along the coast, even for raiding purposes – furthermore, any retreat from the south would be fraught with danger without simultaneous control of Radnorshire.

With the south-west secured by the Crown, and with much of the state infrastructure still functioning in Wales, any ancient prophecies or plans that Glyndŵr may have entertained regarding his leadership of the Britons in the following year were shelved. He was currently the author of a spectacular uprising, but until all Wales was on its feet it could never become a full-scale war; worse, he had been thwarted, his position was unsustainable, and he knew that he must find new ways to destabilise Henry's regime – and he spent the darkness of winter planning to do precisely that.

Inserting his shining blade into a rocky niche from which it would not easily be extracted, Glyndŵr retreated to an ill-lit corner of his mountain cavern and prepared, wearily, to wield the pen instead of the sword. To Robert III of Scotland he wrote:

> Brutus, your most noble ancestor and mine, was the first crowned king who dwelt in this realm of England which was formerly called Great Britain. Brutus begat three sons, Albanactus, Locrinus, and Kamber. You are descended in a direct line from Albanactus. The descendants of Kamber reigned as kings until Cadwaladr, who was the last crowned king of my people. I, dear cousin, am directly descended from Cadwaladr . . . the [Merlinic] prophecy says that I will be delivered from the [English] oppressions and bondages by your aid.

He wrote similarly to the Irish, although without much hope, and then addressed a letter to Charles VI of France, reminding him of the recent services of his forebear Owain Lawgoch to the French nation, and of French promises of support for Wales. At last he signed it 'Prince of Wales', prepared to write separately to the Bretons, blew out the candle, threw a log upon the small fire and made his way to the cave entrance, where one of his most faithful companions, a wild-eyed man with a mane of dark hair, stared intently at the stars.

It was a sign that things were not going well for Glyndŵr at this time that his latest letter to Scotland was intercepted. Worse still, Owain knew that while potential allies continued to ponder their responses there was every risk that his entire effort would stall. Therefore, in defiance of winter, he launched a late January raid upon Dyffryn Clwyd in which he renewed hostilities with Lord Grey and enlisted the support of the current Bishop of St Asaph – of whose 'palays and all his other three mannoirs' there was 'no styke left'.

In April, having spent most of the winter deep in thought, Glyndŵr beset Lord Grey within his castle at Ruthin – but it was a fumbling siege staged by what seemed like a spent force, and before long it was suggested to Grey that he might do well to rush the Welsh and deal with them peremptorily. Sure enough, as the Lord of Ruthin and his men sallied forth into the spring sunshine, the besieging Welsh fell rapidly into disarray and fled for the hills, with Lord Grey and his men hard upon their heels – but as the English rounded a bend they were suddenly appalled to see the glint of countless ranks of Welsh armour hidden in the trees upon a nearby slope. Horrified at the presence of what was clearly a superior force, Grey's company instantly changed direction – and fled straight into the teeth of a massive Welsh ambush.

Glyndŵr's chicanery had worked. The suggestion that Grey should leave the castle had originated among castle servants in Owain's pay, while the ranks of soldiers who had stood so imposingly amid the trees were said to have been but rows of cloaks and helmets set on poles – and the result was not only the total annihilation of Grey's men, but the capture of Lord Grey himself.

Owain Glyndŵr had embarrassed Henry IV's regime anew, and Welsh spirits soared – just as a supernatural entity pierced the night sky like a silver sword arising from the river of the Milky Way. This was the great comet of 1402, a celestial visitor like that which had once inspired Uther Pendragon to mighty victories against the Dark Age Saxons. As it passed over Europe the comet provoked apocalyptic predictions of death and disorder – but in Wales it was jubilantly hailed by the bards as heralding the final destruction of their enemies.

The elements were certainly disturbed, for the comet was followed by atrocious and abnormal weather conditions which included electrical storms of a strikingly demonic nature. In England rumours spread that Glyndŵr and his magi were now controlling the weather, allegedly with the aid of the Franciscans, and the Crown also became nervous, as if it too feared the fulfilment of some dire prophecy.

With Thomas Percy, Earl of Worcester, in charge of south Wales, and 'Hotspur' Percy in charge of the north, the Principality was urgently garrisoned from end to end. Castles such as Monmouth and Kidwelly were repaired and prepared for attack, although they were far from imminent danger. Soldiers were installed in all the castles of north Wales which were not currently under siege, and in the south, a string of isolated fortresses were reinforced, including mighty Carreg Cennen on the eastern flank of the Tywi.

In early May, 'Armes Prydein' played sordine in the hillsides, the sword of destiny sliced the sky in its brief pursuit of sunset, Lord Grey stared bleakly from a window in the fastness of a stronghold in Snowdonia, and summer smiled weakly upon the middle-March – for it knew what was to come.

What passed for summer in 1402 began with a series of vicious Welsh raids upon Radnorshire, as Glyndŵr once again set about establishing his dominion in that delicate domain, which was currently held for England by Edmund Mortimer, the uncle and namesake of the young Earl of March, son of Richard II's intended heir to the throne. In a brutal campaign Glyndŵr's forces devastated the minor fortresses of Knucklas, Bleddfa, Cwm Aran and Cefnllys, plundering and torturing, torching village churches which paid tithes to the enemy, and threatening the castle at Radnor which had only recently been reoccupied by the English. For the next few weeks

Glyndŵr haunted the middle-March, and made his personal presence known.

It was not long before the English responded. At Ludlow an army of at least 3,000 men was mustered, comprising the combined forces of Mortimer and almost the entire county levy of Herefordshire, including many of the Welshry of Archenfield in the paid service of the Crown. At Ludlow they recruited more such 'loyal' Welsh volunteers, who swelled the ranks of Welsh archers serving among the English host.

During the third week of June, Glyndŵr was at Pilleth just south of Knighton, where many of his forces, led by his chief lieutenant Rhys the Terrible, were encamped in the valley of the Lugg. It was a damp summer's evening which fell strangely still and silent in the aftermath of an electrical storm, as Glyndŵr and his shadowy companion climbed slowly up the steep slope of a nearby hill.

Halfway to the summit, they came upon an ancient religious site where there stood a small church known as the Chapel of Our Lady of Pilleth, in whose honour the slope had been lately dubbed Bryn-glas (Blue Hill).[25] This was a well-known site of pilgrimage for devotees of the Virgin Mary, but, as was so often the case, behind one lady stood another, for at the rear of the Lady Chapel was an ancient sacred well, which had recently been decorated with a statue of the 'Virgin'. For Glyndŵr and his companion there was no conflict here, and he is said to have visited both sites with equal reverence. After all, the date was 21 June – midsummer – a moment traditionally celebrated by the Celts and considered a special time for the visiting of sacred wells – and as Glyndŵr and his seer must have known, this was also the night upon which could be seen the spirits of all those who would die in the year to come.

The next morning, 22 June, Glyndŵr stemmed the flow of tithes from Our Lady of Pilleth to the English Crown by setting the tiny church ablaze – just as the English muster from Ludlow pounded down the valley of the Lugg. Seeing the smoke and the Welsh encampment upon the valley floor, the English forces crossed the river and pursued the Welsh up the steepness of Bryn-glas, labouring in their heavy armour and repeatedly failing to gain ground. Halfway up, the exhausted front-runners suddenly realised that the hill, which from below had appeared to be a continuous slope, was not – and in the hidden ground the 'fleeing' Welsh had conjoined with a substantial force of 600 men who had emerged from a gulley behind the blazing church. Worse still, as the English gasped in horror, they came under fire not only from archers who had appeared all along the summit overhead, but also from the Welsh bowmen in their own ranks.

What followed was chaotic and is little understood, but it is known that the Welsh archers in Mortimer's contingent, many of whom were probably infiltrators sent by Glyndŵr, switched sides – with catastrophic results for the English. Felled amid a whirring hail of arrows, both flanks of the English force soon lay helpless, as the central contingent, including many prestigious Marcher knights of Radnorshire and Herefordshire, reeled under the assault of a massive downhill charge of Welshmen, both on horseback and on foot. Soon almost all the English force was slain or taken prisoner, and the most prestigious captive of all was Edmund Mortimer.

Pilleth was a nightmare for Henry IV – and one which England has been trying to forget ever since, although more than 150 years later it was alluded to by Shakespeare in *King Henry IV: Part II*:

> But yesternight: when all athwart there came
> A post from Wales loaden with heavy news:
> Whose worst was, that the noble Mortimer,
> Leading the men of Herefordshire to fight
> Against the irregular and wild Glyndŵr,
> Was by the rude hands of that Welshman taken . . .

Written off, and written out of the history books, the fact remains that on 22 June 1402 the Welsh inflicted a severe military defeat, and punitive casualties, upon the English Crown. Despite its inferior numbers, Owain's army had taken on and destroyed the combined English musters of two royal counties. Nor could the nation which had invited Glyndŵr to his death at Worcester complain of treachery, for their own actions had long-since declared that all was fair in love and war. Afterwards it was claimed that local Welsh women performed obscene mutilations upon the bodies of fallen Englishmen, a charge denied amid claims that it was no less than they deserved for their own recent behaviour – and so all is swiftly chaff and propaganda.

Equally uncertain are the details of Glyndŵr's subsequent campaign into the south-east. Doubtless confident that whatever ritual had been performed upon the Blue Hill had invoked the blessing of a cosmological 'Lady', Owain may even have reached Newport and Cardiff at this time,[26] but at any rate his level of support henceforth escalated, notably in Archenfield and west Herefordshire. By July he had besieged Brecon and was pressing upon Usk in Gwent, where the population rallied to his cause and forged a platform from which he could raid the southern March. By the end of the month, Glyndŵr may well have entered Glamorgan to threaten the sprawling castle of Caerphilly (which was reputed to be in a significant state of disrepair) and to raise the spectre of Llywelyn Bren – and it has been rumoured that he then proceeded to establish another platform somewhat to the west in Glynrhondda, in the impenetrable forest surrounding Pen-rhys.

If so, I suggest that Glyndŵr was once again being guided in his actions not only by a wealth of ancestral prophecy which was intimately connected with the strategic geography of the landscape, but also by elemental forces inherent in the supernatural landscape, all of which constituted the ancient wisdom handed down by seers and bards such as Iolo Goch. Having envisaged Iolo's role as a visionary mentor to the youthful Glyndŵr, we have already observed his advice regarding Owain's military plans in the 'Strolling Tour', and noticed that his poetry makes much of his devotion to the Virgin. Meanwhile the young Glyndŵr had been named after his birthplace on the Dee, a river supreme in its ancient supernatural significance to the Celts, and which was once called *Aerfen* ('Battle-Goddess') but which by Glyndŵr's time had become *Dyfrdwy* ('The Waters of the Goddess').

While it is far from conclusive, it is nonetheless interesting that Glyndŵr's thrust down the eastern side of Wales in 1402 can be interpreted as having three main ports of call – Pilleth, Usk and Pen-rhys – and that at each of these places there was an exceptionally prominent cult of 'The Lady'. Fanciful, perhaps, but I therefore call this south-eastern campaign of 1402 the 'Three Marys Tour'[27] – and I suspect Iolo's fingerprints upon the plans.

News of Glyndŵr's success soon reached Rome, and for the first time his uprising started to attract international support. France was showing an interest in coming to Wales's aid, pending the involvement of the Scots. The Scots seemed amenable, and both Breton and Scottish pirates were already helping the Welsh to harass the English at sea. Although Ireland was a lost cause,[28] Owain knew that his letters were being taken seriously elsewhere, and he was surely cheered by the landing of a Welsh-Breton party in south-west Wales, not only equipped with a contingent of Owain Lawgoch's former soldiers, but allegedly bringing Lawgoch's heart for secret burial in Llandybïe church.

Throughout all of this one might imagine that the English despaired, but while the rebels ran rampant across the summer months the Crown ploddingly continued to take measures designed to impede Glyndŵr's long-term progress. Various castles were reinforced, including Radnor, Clifford and Swansea, new regional commanders were installed, and the Earls of Arundel and Stafford were instructed to shore up the Anglo-Welsh border in the north and south.

In August, Glyndŵr returned to the north, where he raged unchecked, but as autumn beckoned Henry IV embarked upon a final effort to bring the Welsh to heel. With the castles of Caernarfon and Beaumaris in dire straits, and the coastal castle of Harlech stranded between the 'Devil' and the deep blue sea, Prince Hal was dispatched upon a desperate mission to relieve Harlech and Caernarfon while the king prepared the hammer-blow.

Early in September, at the head of a truly colossal army consisting of tens of thousands of men mustered from all over

England, Henry IV marched majestically into north Wales. Thus arriving in the very centre of the north, he prepared to seek out, confront and crush Glyndŵr before the year was out, and having massacred its inhabitants he announced his intentions by setting fire to the rebel town of Llanrwst. However, it did not burn for long – for a supernatural hissing soon arose from the embers of Llanrwst as a deluge of bizarre proportions descended upon the monarch's head, and the bonfire which Henry had intended to make of north Wales became one of the dampest squibs in English history – for here was weather of the most outlandish variety. In the downpour which followed, as the English army struggled miserably across a swollen river, the king himself was almost swept away by the tremendous force of the torrent which tumbled from the mountains. Day after day vast storms of appalling power raged above their heads, lightning leapt from peak to peak, and the river valleys of the Dee, the Severn and others turned to seas.

Already unable to travel, and with their supply-lines severed and submerged, the English army hunkered into the quagmire underfoot as the supernatural storm redoubled its force and the temperature began to plummet. There could be no doubt that such conditions were the work of the wizard Glyndŵr, and the king himself, fearing the worst, took to sleeping in his armour.

That night, as the storm raged all around, it is recorded that Henry was awoken by an enormous crash followed by a stunning impact, whereafter he found himself pinned unceremoniously to the ground by the central pole of his collapsed royal tent. Saved by the skin of his steel pyjamas, the unhappy usurper could only struggle and watch as a flash-flood entered the tent and washed all his belongings away.

Thereafter, the rain turned to hail, and even September snow descended from the purple-laden clouds. Humiliated and numbed with shock and cold, the king was forced to abandon his royal expedition to Wales in the face of overwhelming supernatural forces – whereafter Shakespeare has Glyndŵr observe:

Three times hath Henry Bolingbroke made head
Against my power. Thrice from the banks of the Wye
And sandy bottomed Severn, have I sent
Him bootless home, and weatherbeaten back . . .

Returning from the realm of the supernatural, the possibility appears that the inclemency of Welsh weather was exaggerated on these occasions. After all, meteorological sorcery offered the perfect excuse for royal chroniclers to explain the colossal waste of time and money involved in such a monumental and unsuccessful expedition; they could always blame it on the elements, and simultaneously demonise Glyndŵr. On the other hand, it has also been suggested that the frequently bizarre weather conditions of the early 1400s marked the onset of the climatic change which culminated centuries later in the London Frost Fair which was held upon the frozen river Thames. Meanwhile, to this day there are those who believe, on an existentialist basis, in the sympathetic principles of a once Neolithic science, underpinned by its three elements of Stone, Water and the Moon. Explanations are thus available from the sceptical to the credulous, but it is nevertheless highly likely that Glyndŵr and his magi were indeed *trying* to influence the weather, and they may well have been delighted with the results.

Like his alleged partner, the medieval Devil, Owain Glyndŵr had become a 'Prince of the Air', at least in the popular mind, capable of both pluripresence (see Preface) and of influencing the weather. If ever Owain was a Jack of Kent, as we shall see that he was, then amid the gigantic shaking of the firmament and the thunderous rebounding that confounded the Crown in the autumn of 1402 we can surely hear he and the Devil at play. Henry's disastrous campaign had left the rebels running amok in Wales, as the English were reduced to the bare bones of Marcher policy, defending the border and clinging grimly to the essential south-west.

Within days of Henry's failure the Scots spuriously declared that Richard II was alive and on their side, and a Scottish army boldly invaded northern England – only to be confronted by the

Percies of Northumberland, who inflicted upon them a truly reverberating defeat at the battle of Homildon Hill on 14 September. Here the flower of Scottish nobility was culled, and many were captured, along with French nobles marching in their ranks. Although the Welsh would always hope for Scottish aid, the Scots were left reeling from a blow that had shattered both their confidence and their capacity, and with Ireland useless, Wales would henceforth have to look to France and Brittany for aid.

Glyndŵr, however, remained rampant, and as September drew to a close it was the English in Radnor Castle who pleaded for help. As the Crown infrastructure in Wales began to collapse, financial records in the Principality went missing from the end of September onwards – and in October and November Parliament was reduced to issuing anti-Welsh legislation regarding those issues which it could still control, such as forbidding inter-racial marriages between the English and Welsh.

As 1402 neared its end, the question of ransoms came to a head, and in November Glyndŵr released Lord Grey to the Crown in return for the princely sum of £666 – an amount which would surely have been welcomed by the 'Prince of Darkness' had the Devil dealt in pounds. Meanwhile Henry IV ignored the plight of another of his captured retainers, Edmund Mortimer. Whether he had been unimpressed by Mortimer's performance at Pilleth, or perhaps because he already doubted the loyalty of a man who was the uncle of a rival claimant to the throne, we can only guess, but he chose not to rescue him from Glyndŵr's clutches – and the consequences proved grave for the English Crown, for on 30 November 1402 Edmund Mortimer married Catharine Glyndŵr, Owain's eldest daughter.

The result of this romance, allegedly both passionate and political, was that the Welsh cause received the services of all those loyal to Mortimer, thus consolidating Glyndŵr's influence in Radnorshire at a stroke. Furthermore, on 13 December, Mortimer issued a letter in which he declared himself a rebel, aligned himself with 'Oweyn GlenDŵr', and proclaimed that 'if Richard be dead' then his own incarcerated nephew and namesake was the true heir to the English throne – and at last Glyndŵr must have smiled, for it was a year which had ended so much better than the last . . .

LEGEND 13 : STOLEN CATTLE

One day, the monks of a certain monastery were very upset because their cattle had been stolen, but Jack of Kent said that he would get their cattle back for them, and he did, with the aid of one of the Devil's imps. (From the Welsh tradition of Siôn Cent.)

[See also Appendix 1, p. 281.]

EIGHT

WAR
(1403)

Once again the rebel Welsh pushed on into the winter. While Glyndŵr and Mortimer kept their counsel, pressure upon the coastal castles of Harlech, Caernarfon and Beaumaris was stepped up and agitators from the Llŷn Peninsula infiltrated Flintshire where they raised a rabble force to burn the town of Hope near Chester, to lay waste the English borderlands, and to raid like a plague of locusts into Shropshire.

In March, Glyndŵr himself emerged into the sunlight to survey the chaos which was wrought, to receive new recruits from Dyffryn Clwyd and also to gaze from the summits of northeast Wales south-eastwards into Mortimer's former lands in Shropshire, where news of the latter's marriage to Catharine had been lately spread abroad. It was a fine spring morning, and the Welsh leader knew the promise of the year, for unknown to his enemies, they were already dancing to his tune.

As the battle season approached, an impecunious Henry IV viewed the situation in north Wales with great anger and concern. In the west the torment of the coastal castles worsened each day, and in the east the English border towns of Flintshire and Shropshire were still smarting from the winter raids and dreading the approach of spring. Peremptorily Henry made a scapegoat of Hotspur, whose efforts he had repeatedly failed to fund, dismissed him from his military responsibilities in Wales, impounded some of his lands, and left him furious.

On 1 April, Prince Hal, now aged sixteen, was installed as the Royal Lieutenant in Wales, equipped with a retine of barons, a substantial personal army, a promise from the Exchequer, and unitary authority over all those local officers who remained in the Principality. A month later, Hal entered north-east Wales with a cohort of 5,000 soldiers engaged upon a punitive raid, the main achievement of which was the destruction by fire of Glyndŵr's abandoned and once beautiful estates of Sycharth and Glyndyfrdwy. Afterwards, Hal wrote to his father observing that the blaze had gone well, but warning that the northern border defences remained weak, the besieged castles on the western coast of north Wales were within ten days of disaster, and predicting that if action were not taken immediately the Crown would be compelled to retreat into England, 'there to be disgraced forever'.

So it was that the English dispatched massive reinforcements by sea to the maritime castles of north Wales, including a garrison of 1,300 men sent to Harlech in early June, and sought urgently to shore up the northern border defences between Montgomery and Flint. Meanwhile Glyndŵr and his men smiled slyly – and slipped southward into mid-Wales as they had planned. Here their numbers swelled rapidly and they launched a major assault upon the strategically sensitive border zone of Radnor, already made vulnerable by the defection of Mortimer, and next they headed south, gathering ominous strength, attacking Builth and sending a rabble force eastward to destabilise the adjoining lands of Herefordshire – from which the Archdeacon of Hereford appealed in great distress:

> The Welsh rebels in great numbers have entered Archenfield, and there they have killed the inhabitants, and ravaged the country to the great dishonour of our king, and the unsupportable damage of the country. We implore you to consider this very perilous and pitiable case and pray to our sovereign Lord that he will come in his royal person . . . to rescue us from the invasion of the rebels. Otherwise we will be utterly destroyed, which God forbid . . . and for God's sake remember that honourable and valiant man, the Lord of Abergavenny, who is on the very point of destruction . . .

On 15 June, the Crown received frantic warnings of new unrest in the south, but these went unheeded by a desperately overstretched regime that was currently concentrating upon the north, and in any case it was too late – for suddenly the embattled castles of Radnor, Builth and Brecon were marooned amid a rebel sea, and mid-Wales was awash with Glyndŵr's master-plan.

Before examining this master-plan in more detail, we should consider the manner in which it was forged. As we shall later see in the language of a document called the 'Tripartite Indenture', the relationship between Dark Age history and the sacred anatomy of the Welsh landscape loomed large in Glyndŵr's mind – as did the ancient giants who slept upon its tribal boundaries. Furthermore, the strategic truths regarding Wales had never changed, for they coincided with the anatomy of the land – and thus, while a strategy might be devised by the leaders of the day, it was essential that they should consult the historians of Wales, the bards, and not proceed without the assent of their close associates, the seers. In this way, both the battle-wisdom and the blessings of the ancestors were received, via the bards and the seers respectively, and thus the Dark Age tribal kings (lately repackaged as Celtic saints) sent aid from the Otherworld.

At some stage Glyndŵr had constructed such a plan, working in close consultation with those bards and seers most highly versed in the history and prophecy of Wales, and known for time-honoured reasons as 'masters of Brut' (see Chapter 1). While Glyndŵr's long-standing talisman in battle was none other than the dark-haired, wild-eyed companion of cavern and hillside who was the seer Crach Ffinant (i.e. 'Crach of the Border Stream'), Glyndŵr's main strategic mentor remained that wizened senior bard, the enigmatic Iolo Goch, who was probably still alive.

Regarding the master-plan itself, if we accept the orthodox date for the writing of Iolo's 'Strolling Tour', then we may assume that it was devised and sanctioned sixteen years earlier in 1387; on the other hand, in view of Iolo's longevity, it might well have been written more recently – for I now suggest that the 'Strolling Tour' was not merely a message of reconnaissance – it was the battle-plan itself.

In late June 1403, Owain Glyndŵr amassed in mid-Wales the biggest Welsh army that the horrified English had ever seen (said to number in excess of 8,000 men), and, as has been noted elsewhere, 'they started with Newtown' – the first stop on Iolo Goch's 'Strolling Tour'.

After this, we can follow the course of Glyndŵr's massive and decisive 1403 campaign simply by referring to Iolo's poem – for once massed in mid-Wales the Welsh wasted no time in heading:

> . . . through Ceri, excellent land
> and the smooth-planked Newtown,
> borough on the model of Paradise

and moving southward they proceeded next to Maelienydd and Radnor, where they could count on the support of, and significantly spare,

> . . . the houses of the sons, Lleon's host,
> of fine, brave, wise Phylib Dorddu

and a little further south they raised the land of Elfael, whose native menfolk Iolo promptly describes as,

> . . . proud valiant stags,
> alive and well, there are no finer hawks.

As we know, they next targeted Builth, immediately listed as being of 'kingly appearance of a famous bright region', and then, with Radnorshire and Builth secured in bonds of verse, they made straight for the Tywi Valley, the heartland of Deheubarth and the key to all Wales.

We have already suggested, and we shall repeat it here, that Iolo's words predicted substantial support for Glyndŵr in this time-honoured region of his mother's line – but this time we shall quote Iolo in full:

> Thick were your tracks,
> God's vengeance, in Ystrad Tywi,
> like Adam's tracks they were numerous,
> when he was driven, he was summoned long ago
> for the apple, harsh punishment,
> with his tribulation from Paradise.
> The rich land was the prosperity of the country,
> a country which has always been most renowned.
> The three cantrefs are stronger than six,
> Caeo is better than nine [cantrefs] of heaven.

And how right Iolo was – for at this very moment, even as Glyndŵr prepared to march with his unprecedented army straight into the heartland of ancient Deheubarth, the cry of the Raven surely went up from among the general populace of that land, and reports came of a massive uprising in the Tywi Valley at the instigation of Henry Dwn.

Glyndŵr had summoned every power at his command, not only the physical but also the metaphysical. By geomancy he had travelled the supernatural landscape of Wales, identifying the significant points of worldly and Otherworldly power, by invisibility he had evaded capture and unwise confrontation, by unknown means he had performed the trick of pluripresence, and by his inherited gift of augury he had consulted the birds and their auspices. Acting upon his behalf, his trusty seer Crach Ffinant had lately dashed the Water upon the Stone and caused the heavens to break repeatedly upon the English in the hills – and even at this moment, in the seclusion of a nearby cave, that dark-haired wild-eyed magus sought with the aid of an oracular skull, some said Urien's own,[29] to determine the triple outcome of the Fates.

'Tall, strong, and fair' was the foretold warrior who commanded the summits of mid-Wales with his silver force arrayed – as far below a seething ocean of buckles, shields and spears glittered in the midday sun, creaked, sweated and sent up a metal murmur of deadly anticipation. On either side his bards, like archers, restrung their harps – preparing to fire their kinsmen in battle and to lacerate their foes with a lethal 'glam-dicin'.

Meanwhile, stretching far behind their glorious leader into a shadow-land which belay the noon, there massed a supernatural army of even greater proportions. Here were the colossi of bygone days, the ancient kings whose long-dead skulls sang battle-hymns of future dreams, and the subterranean spirits whom today we treat so lightly – goblins, hobgoblins, trolls, sprites, watersprites, elves, aech-elves, pixies and imps – all much feared. Even sylvan nymphs were summoned from the woods to melt beneath the long grass and to subvert the Saxon upon the battlefield. Finally, towering over all, as her chattering servants gathered eagerly upon the air, a spectral entity of prehistoric power was forming in the sky, a gigantic Morrigan, her vast primordial wings overarching Glyndŵr's forces like a storm-cloud, crying from the Neolithic dawn.

It was time. Glyndŵr gave the sign. The peasant contingents emitted a raucous din as they blew their Celtic battle-horns, designed to imitate the croaking of ravens, as the final order came, to advance upon the Tywi Valley . . .

As Glyndŵr's army bore down upon Llandovery, preparing to evict the English from their battery of strongholds along the River Tywi, there was a risk that the stupefied Crown would recover in time to enter south Wales from Hereford and confront the Welsh upon the riverbank thus cornering Glyndŵr in south-west Wales. However, as noted in our earlier analysis of Iolo Goch's excellent poem, there was one location which made no sequential sense in the case of a genuine bardic tour – namely the abrupt reference to the Upper Taf Valley, where Iolo had abstractedly met a cleric, as follows:

> The head, master of monks,
> of the White House is there, he is fair and fine;
> saviour of all, it is true,
> the good man is the best of men.

I suggest, that to prevent the English from arriving inconveniently in south-west Wales, the relatively defensible area of the Upper Taf Valley which stood in their way was to be prepared to resist and obstruct them at this critical moment. However, although this makes perfect strategic sense, and the term 'of the White House' denotes the Cistercian Order, there would appear to be a problem since there were no Cistercian houses in the Upper Taf Valley – the explanation nevertheless, is close at hand.

The nearest White Cistercian house, Llantarnam Abbey, lay somewhat to the east in the Valley of the Crows (Cwmbrân). The current head of this house (which as we know was founded by the Lord Rhys), was none other than Abbot John ap Hywel, who would shortly become famous as Glyndŵr's most indomitable warrior-monk, and whose canonical cry was apparently 'Death to the Saxons!' I suggest that this is the man whom Iolo claimed to have met in the Upper Taf Valley – and I do so because the abbey of Llantarnam was well known for its ownership of a large grange at Pen-rhys.[30]

Pen-rhys, as you may recall, lay in Glynrhondda at the terminus of Glyndŵr's campaign into Glamorgan the previous year. Here he is said to have established a headquarters in the homeland of another warrior-ally named Cadwgan of Glynrhondda. Furthermore, Pen-rhys lay just west of, and directly adjacent to, the Upper Taf Valley, where its strategic location offered a perfect base from which to hold the Upper Taf against an incoming English offensive. Thus Iolo might very well have happened upon the Cistercian Abbot of Llantarnam, John ap Hywel, in the defensive area of the Upper Taf Valley[31] at Pen-rhys.

Furthermore, in Iolo's poem the abbot of the 'White House' (reiterated) immediately proceeds to recommend a visit to Dyfed, saying:

> . . . if you go you'll get a gift
> send an authorised messenger
> to fetch a mark, and ask for more.

This can only mean Whitland, the headquarters of the Cistercians in Wales, the strategic value of which, as we previously observed, was that it severed Carmarthen from the Crown presence in Dyfed (Pembrokeshire), and Haverford West.

The conclusion is thus simple. Having delineated the course of Glyndŵr's attack as far as the Tywi Valley, Iolo is taking time out in the poem to explain how two 'White Shields' orchestrated by the Cistercians will defend the 'Tour' from interference by the English. Under the leadership of Abbot John ap Hywel, the Upper Taf Valley would obstruct any English advance from the east, while the Cistercian Abbot of Whitland would be responsible for obstructing any English response from Dyfed.

Thus, as John ap Hywel and Cadwgan of Glynrhondda prepared the Welshry of the Upper Taf, and the Abbot of Whitland prepared his defences there, Glyndŵr came upon Llandovery with a vengeance. Here was a prosperous English trading town for which Glyndŵr had no time at all – firstly because speed was of the essence, secondly because Llandovery was a heavily defended obstacle at the entrance to the Tywi Valley (fortified in 1400 at Henry IV's personal expense), and thirdly because it was here that Henry IV had made a spectacle of the barbarities he had performed upon the Welsh martyr Llywelyn ap Gruffydd Fychan.

On Monday 2 July, Owain Glyndŵr erupted into the Tywi Valley with ravening ferocity, wreaking terrible destruction upon Llandovery, with the full support of the local Welsh. Seeking revenge for the untold years of oppression and the appalling cruelty of the last royal raid, the invaders went berserk, laying waste the lordship and the lands, devastating the town, massacring the inhabitants and leaving 300 men to besiege the exposed castle, its garrison and its constable, while Glyndŵr's wrath moved on.

Eight thousand avengers careered down-river in a bloody cascade, aided by the populace in hunting down the 'Englishry' who had fled into the trees – for at last the boot was on the other foot. Welcomed in Cantref Bychan and Cantref Mawr, Glyndŵr's men came to Llandeilo to find it freshly sacked and burnt by the locals – and the Lord Rhys's sovereign stronghold of Dinefwr already beset by the allied forces of Henry Dwn – whereupon the Welsh hacked and bludgeoned their way south-west to surround the nearby fortress of Dryslwyn, which surrendered on Wednesday, and where Glyndŵr briefly set up camp.

That evening, it is known that Glyndŵr made himself comfortable at Dryslwyn – for the whole of the south-west was within his grasp – and he was expecting a visitor. Outside, amid the cheering hordes, the smouldering and the corpses, could be heard the old battle-cries of the Lord Rhys, and shouts of 'Owein!, Owein!' which would echo far into the night – for here above all Glyndŵr was of the House of Rheged, and for the peasant population of the Tywi the Raven had finally returned.

Meanwhile, in the adjoining valley of Is-cennen, the jubilant inhabitants were helping Glyndŵr's forces to besiege the towering fortress of Carreg Cennen, where the Constable was one John Scudamore of Kentchurch Court in south Herefordshire.

At a time variously suggested as before, during or after the war, John Scudamore is known to have secretly and treasonably married Glyndŵr's second-eldest daughter Alice, and the connection between the Scudamores and Owain Glyndŵr is still commemorated today. At Kentchurch Court the Scudamores possess an ancient portrait in oils which they now describe as a picture of Jack of Kent, but which in the 1800s they said was of Owain Glyndŵr. Also at Kentchurch Court is an ancient tower known as Glyndŵr's Tower, within which a secret passage leads to a room called Owain Glyndŵr's bedroom – which is also known as Jack of Kent's bedroom. Meanwhile it is also variously said that Jack of Kent was once confined in a dungeon directly beneath this bedroom (Legend 19); that his ghost is said to emanate from a wall-panel in the bedroom on dark nights; and that his flying satanic steeds were alleged to be kept in the stable-cellars beneath Kentchurch Court. He is said to have taken 'Old Scudamore' to London on the back of one such horse while flying above the great oak tree known both as Glyndŵr's and Jack of Kent's, and many of his legends cluster about the Kentchurch and Grosmont area of the Monnow Valley.

On this basis, many have suggested that the real Jack of

Kent was Owain Glyndŵr himself, and it is true that based upon the legends and upon certain other factors, it is also possible to make a very strong case for identifying Glyndŵr with Jack of Kent – much stronger than for any of the other candidates. Furthermore he is the only candidate other than the rector of the 1380s (see Preface) who can be shown to share Jack's close relationship with the Scudamores.

At Dryslwyn in July 1403, Owain Glyndŵr's nocturnal visitor was none other than John Scudamore of Kentchurch, the current Constable of Carreg Cennen Castle, who had been spirited away from the besieged fortress and brought to parley with Glyndŵr under truce. We know this because of a remarkable letter written by Scudamore to the Receiver of Brecon, which is dated the following day:

> Worshipful Sir, I recommend me to you, and forasmuch as I may not spare no man away from me, to certify neither the king, nor my lord the prince of the mischief of these countries about, nor no man may pass by no way hence, I pray you and require you that ye certify them how all Carmarthenshire, Kidwelly, Carnwaltham, and Ys Kennen, be sworn to Owen yesterday, and he lay last night in the castle of Drosselan [Dryslwyn] with Rees ap Griffith; and there I was and spake with him upon truce, and prayed of a safe conduct, under his seal, to send home my wife and her mother, and their company, and he would none grant me; and on this day he is about the town of Carmarthen, and there thinketh to abide till he may have the town and castle; and his purpose is from thence into Pembrokeshire, for he holds him sure of all the castles and towns in Kidwelly, Gowerland, and Glamorgan, for the same countries have undertaken the sieges of them until they be won. Wherefore write to Sir Hugh Waterton, and to all that ye suppose will take this matter to heart, that they excite the king hitherwards in all haste, to avenge him on some of his false traitors the which he has overmuch cherished, and rescue the town and castles in these countries, for I dread

full sure there be too few true men in them. I can no more as now; but pray God help you and us that think to be true. Written at the castle of Carren Cennen ye 5th day of July.

John Scudamore.

This is a fascinating document indeed – but of greatest interest to ourselves is the fabulous line in which Scudamore states that he had asked Owain, in vain, for safe conduct to send home his wife and her mother.

Numerous authors have suggested that John Scudamore's marriage to Alice Glyndŵr may already have occurred in the 1390s – i.e. before the uprising – but in the light of Scudamore's letter this would be utterly bizarre. Surely we cannot be expected to believe either that Henry IV had no idea who Scudamore's wife was, or that Glyndŵr himself was so inept as to refuse safe passage to his own daughter Alice and her mother Margaret Hanmer, his own wife – who would one day be captured by the English and imprisoned in the Tower of London.

Furthermore, since the legislation of 1402 that rendered English-Welsh marriages illegal backdated any such offences only to the start of the uprising in 1400, it could not easily have been used (as later it was) to prosecute Scudamore for an offence committed before this date. Scudamore must therefore certainly be referring to a previous wife and her mother, and sadly it seems that they did not leave Carreg Cennen alive.

We must pause here to consider the loyalty of John Scudamore to the Crown in 1403 – for it is intriguing that, like the houses of the sons of wise Phylib Dorddu in Iolo's poem, John Scudamore's home at Kentchurch seems to have escaped all the raids unburnt – and it has been suggested that he was already secretly in Owain's pay. At this time the political climate was rife with disaffection, dissent and disrespect for Henry IV, the usurper whom many still referred to as Bolingbroke, and whose accession in 1400 was recorded in the chronicle of Adam of Usk (the former rector of Mitchel Troy near Monmouth), who was present at the coronation: 'First, in the procession he lost one of the coronation shoes . . . secondly one of the golden spurs fell off . . . thirdly at the banquet a sudden gust of wind carried away the crown from his head . . .' – whereafter the putative king apparently dropped his offering and reacted so badly to the anointing oil that 'there ensued such a growth of lice especially on his head, that he neither grew hair, nor could he have his head uncovered for many months'. These were the months during which, as we know, Henry spent most of his time in the saddle, terrified that it too might have been anointed with poisonous oil by the many factions who were plotting against him.

Against this backdrop it is recorded that John Scudamore's impulsive younger brother Philpot of Mitchel Troy near Monmouth (the patron of Adam of Usk), had already joined Glyndŵr and had been fighting for him from the outset. It is thus evident that the Scudamore family had already been targeted by Glyndŵr for conversion to his cause – and for this I offer the following explanation.

According to Compton Reade (*Memorials of Old Herefordshire*), the Scudamores of Kentchurch had 'for many generations . . . sympathised with the Welsh' and certainly the family shared with the Welsh a history of opposition to the Crown: they had sided not only with the rebels of Simon de Montfort during the 1200s, but also – perhaps very significantly – with those of Thomas de Lancaster after 1321. One possible reason for a natural sympathy between the Welsh-speaking Norman family of Scudamore and the Welsh might well be a shared agenda of religious Gnosticism. Until their replacement by the Knights Hospitaller, the Knights Templar had been established high upon Garway Hill behind Kentchurch Court, overlooking the deerpark, and it is therefore interesting to note that the current John Scudamore of Kentchurch suspects Templaresque architecture at the Court.

Meanwhile, continuing in this religious vein, we notice that until at least 1408 John Scudamore of Kentchurch also held the important Scudamore seat of Holme Lacy near Hereford, at which point we are delighted to discover that upon these lands (known then as Hamm), there stood another abbey of those turbulent priests, the Premonstratensians. Therefore, if our suspicions regarding their infiltration of the Hereford diocese in *c.* 1400 are correct, this means that, having arrived at Hereford, the very first port of call of the Welsh Premonstratensians from Talley would undoubtedly have been Holme Lacy – where the resident Scudamores were sitting baronial targets for conversion to the cause.

However, when the rumour first reached the Scudamores, perhaps via the Premonstratensian monks at Hamm, that a massive new uprising of the Welsh was imminent, it was but one rumour among many – and it may be that the reactions of John and Philpot were very different. John was the older brother, the proud owner of widespread lands and influence, who had already risen to high office in the English establishment – whereas Philpot was younger, wilder and had much less to lose. I suggest that Philpot's reaction was essentially, 'I'll be with them if they rise – and so will many others! Bolingbroke is a usurper and a fool, and he'll be a loser too!', whereas John's reaction was much more cautious and perhaps along the lines of 'Hmmm, we'll see how it goes. It'll probably never happen.'

In 1400 the uprising began, and Philpot hurried to join Glyndŵr's cause, but for the time being at least his older brother remained 'true' to the Crown. In July 1403, John Scudamore suddenly found himself in charge and under siege at Carreg Cennen in the face of overwhelming odds, whereupon he succeeded in arranging a parley with his brother's new employer, a parley at which he unsuccessfully sought safe passage for his wife and her mother. At this stage Glyndŵr's apparent refusal thus hardly suggests a situation in which John Scudamore was already secretly in his pay, nor one in which the ladies in question were Glyndŵr's own close relatives.

Having honourably refused to surrender the castle, perhaps earning Glyndŵr's respect in the process, John Scudamore returned to Carreg Cennen, where he wrote his letter on the following day. The castle was besieged for an unknown period of time. We know that provisions ran short and the castle was badly damaged before it fell, and we shall find good reason to suspect that Scudamore's wife did not survive the assault – but it is not clear whether she died of illness, injury or privation, or perhaps was killed with her mother in a desperate attempt to cross enemy lines without safe passage.

Within days, Glyndŵr would be master of the militarily crucial south-west, and therefore of much else besides. Even as John Scudamore dispatched his letter on Thursday 5 July, Owain had already completed his triumphant march down the Tywi Valley by reaching Carmarthen, where the capital stronghold of the English Crown still squatted upon Welsh hopes and dreams. That day he burnt and sacked the town, and on the Friday he received the surrender of the castle, and the Tywi campaign was complete. It was his greatest victory.

During the next two days Glyndŵr established himself at Carmarthen, and paused for breath in glory. He had flatfooted the enemy and felled fortress after fortress along the whole length of the Tywi, he had ridden an historic wave of chaos and bloodshed which had surged the length of Wales to break upon the shore at Carmarthen, he was the Lord Rhys, Owein of Rheged, Urien, Cadwaladr, Rhodri Mawr, Hywel Dda and Cunedda all rolled into one, the fulfilment of a thousand years of prophecy. Hereafter, all of Wales and more must surely follow – and meanwhile the next fortress merely awaited its fate . . .

If Henry IV wished to know where Glyndŵr intended to strike next, then he need only have consulted Iolo Goch's 'Strolling Tour' – for immediately following the section on the Tywi Valley Iolo strolls straight into Kidwelly, of which he observes:

> Fine bright street, I saw three;
> it was enough for me, good scions,
> to see the three, princes of battle.

This destination is entirely logical for two reasons. Firstly, because Kidwelly was traditionally regarded as fundamental to the strategic viability and consolidation of Deheubarth, and secondly, because if Glyndŵr were to proceed instead from Carmarthen into Dyfed (as Scudamore had suggested in his despairing letter) and thus engage the Crown emplacement there, there would be a serious danger of his being embroiled until the king had forced his way past the defenders of the Upper Taf Valley – whereafter Glyndŵr would soon be trapped in the south-western corner of Wales.

For two days Owain warmed his aching limbs by the flickering embers of Carmarthen, overhearing the dying of many of its Anglo-Saxon citizens and having ordered his men to dismantle, tear down, destroy and render useless as much of the castle as possible. Having a healthy respect for English siege-technology, and unable to spare soldiers from the field for garrisons, the Welsh generally destroyed castles rather than attempting to hold them – and this was precisely what Glyndŵr was intending to do at Kidwelly, when a messenger suddenly arrived.

This unrecorded message may well have come from the Abbot of Whitland and it surely gave Glyndŵr a shock. Aided by the English emplacements in Dyfed a certain Lord Carew of Narberth had not merely failed to be intimidated by recent events but had reacted with exceptional speed and efficiency, raising a substantial force from among his neighbours and the local tenants. Worse still, Whitland was overrun – and Carew was already advancing upon Carmarthen to engage Glyndŵr. The 'White Shield' at Whitland had failed.

As a soldier and a military strategist, the last thing Glyndŵr wanted was to be engaged by Carew's makeshift brigade when he was about to leave for Kidwelly – but it was not merely a military inconvenience. Something else was wrong, because for the first time something had happened which was not *meant* to happen. Glyndŵr's master-plan had been weighed by the high priests of Brut, the bards and seers, against the great mass of prophecy, and they had predicted success for a given order of events, and so far it had proceeded like clockwork – but suddenly there was a problem – for although his task was to fulfil the prophecy, he could not make for Kidwelly with Carew's force clinging to him like a guard-dog to a thief.

There was no time to lose. Carew must be removed from the equation, and in extremely short order. Glyndŵr and his army immediately went out to meet Carew's men, thus breaking the rule about not pressing into Dyfed. The two forces met on 9 July at St Clears, and Glyndŵr was aghast when he saw the substantial scale and condition of Carew's army. The result was a stand-off. Glyndŵr was equipped with a superior force but could not afford to engage for reasons of time and prophecy, and Carew was leading a force that faced certain defeat. Then Owain had an idea – it was obvious.

Glyndŵr sought a parley, Carew agreed, and the next day the two men met at Laugharne. At this moment Glyndŵr was surely prepared to offer Carew his life, riches, Kidwelly, one of his daughters, anything, if he would just do what Mortimer and countless lesser men had already done – switch sides – or simply go away. Indeed, from the moment that Carew had agreed to parley, Owain must have started to feel better – for surely the prophecy dictated that Carew would cooperate? However, Carew did not cooperate – the parley was abandoned, and Glyndŵr was plagued with anxiety. If only they had not rested at Carmarthen! Had they offended the Virgin? Were the spirits displeased? How could they make amends? What should he do?

It is recorded that Glyndŵr sent 700 men back towards Carmarthen with instructions to stay in the uplands north of the town and thus secure the prophesied route of return to north Wales, which Iolo's poem confirms was via Ceredigion, and then he sent for the best seer in the south, one Hopcyn ap Thomas of Gower.

While Glyndŵr waited, things got worse. Anticipating a Welsh retreat through Ceredigion, Lord Carew proceeded to ambush and slaughter the 700 men in the hills north of Carmarthen, and then began to engage Glyndŵr's main force. With each passing day the risk was increasing that the king would enter south Wales, and even worse Glyndŵr had an urgent appointment in the north – and yet his actions continued to be dictated by considerations of prophecy.

Glyndŵr believed that when he was successful it was because the prophecy was working – but when things went wrong, it was because there was a problem with the prophecy. Had he been acting entirely rationally, he would have left the south-west immediately, dispersed his men and gone home – and ironically that is essentially what Hopcyn the Seer advised Glyndŵr to do.

Compared by a contemporary to 'Elffin', the patron of Taliesin, Hopcyn ap Thomas was already an elderly man. In his youth he had been a courageous warrior and a generous patron, and later still had come to be regarded as a man of outstanding wisdom and a 'maister of Brut'. In 1403 it is recorded that Glyndŵr had summoned Hopcyn 'so that he schuld do hym to understonde how and what maner hit schuld be falle of hym' if he were to attempt to go towards Kidwelly. Hopcyn prophesied that the outcome would be Glyndŵr's defeat and capture beneath a black banner between Carmarthen and Gower – and that was enough for Glyndŵr – Kidwelly was off.

From Newtown to Ceri (Kerry), to Maelienydd, to Elfael, to Builth and into the Tywi Valley, Owain Glyndŵr's massive summer campaign of 1403 had followed the path of Iolo Goch's 'Strolling Tour', until his intended 'stroll' to Kidwelly was prevented by Lord Carew. At this point, Glyndŵr attempted to safeguard his retreat along the route dictated by the rest of Iolo's poem, and immediately consulted a seer. I suggest this confirms that our thesis regarding the 'Strolling Tour' is correct.

Meanwhile, Glyndŵr's failure to reach Kidwelly did not alter the fact that his achievement in the south-west was already a spectacular triumph, and a massive disaster for the Crown, as is witnessed by the cessation of English administrative records in Wales after July 1403. Although Glyndŵr's movements went unrecorded in the wake of Laugharne, it is almost certain that he was heavily embroiled by Lord Carew and the English defenders of Dyfed, his planned line of retreat was obstructed, and he may well have been forced to disperse his troops in order to disengage. However, what would prove to be far more important in the long run was that he missed his vital appointment in the north.

Hotspur (Percy) had been let down frequently by Henry IV and was still fuming from his recent dismissal. He, too, knew the strategic significance of south-west Wales, and it appears very likely that he had made an arrangement with Glyndŵr along the lines of 'Contact me when you get to Carmarthen'. Glyndŵr was established at Carmarthen on 6 July, and stayed for two full days during which we may assume that he dispatched an unrecorded message to Hotspur, which was received at Chester on 9 July. In essence the message was 'All is well, I shall join you in a few days' – and in expectation of this, Hotspur raised the flag of rebellion at Chester on 10 July and declared against the king, who was then near Leicester. What Hotspur could not know was that just twenty-four hours after sending the message Glyndŵr had been embroiled by Lord Carew.

Hotspur had already rallied the men of Chester and Shropshire to his cause when he was joined by his uncle Thomas Percy, Earl of Worcester, whereafter the Percies proceeded to assemble a massive army of 15,000 men at Shrewsbury. At best, the king would not arrive at Shrewsbury with his army for another ten days, and meanwhile the Percies awaited the arrival of Glyndŵr, who was expected to return from south-west Wales via Ceredigion. His route, which Iolo's poem once again supplies, was essentially as follows. Passing north of Carmarthen and through Ceredigion via the area of New Quay, Glyndŵr was meant to travel along the coast via Aberystwyth, thus benefiting from the potential support of Welsh and Breton warships offshore. Meanwhile a third 'White Shield' (again essentially non-sequential in the poem) would be provided by the Cistercian abbot of Strata Florida, who would 'let you suffer no distress'. Thereafter, having also been protected from interception by his recent domination of Radnorshire, Glyndŵr would return 'if well' to his own homeland of Sycharth, a position neatly to the rear of Hotspur's forces which were encamped on high ground just north-west of Shrewsbury. After this, the poem ends with an invitation to make 'furtively' for the Bishop of St Asaph's, where a 'Lord's feast' would await!

However, as we know, Glyndŵr was stuck in the south and was nowhere to be seen on 20 July when the king and his colossal army of 25,000 men arrived in Shrewsbury and proceeded to attack the Percies on the following day. The ensuing battle was a contest between two huge and well-matched armies, and it produced one of the most miserable bloodbaths in British history. In addition, it resulted in the deaths of both Hotspur and his uncle, a serious facial injury to Prince Hal which disfigured him for life, and a victory for the king that was so expensive as to constitute a draw.

Meanwhile, England still neglects its hero of Narberth, for Lord Carew had not only confounded the Welsh prophets, but had changed the course of history by placing a modest but exquisitely timed spanner in Glyndŵr's plan. Had Glyndŵr been allowed to return to the area of Sycharth and thus support the Percies as planned, the Crown would surely have suffered a terminal defeat at Shrewsbury, and the result would have been a different map of Britain from the one we know today.

Nevertheless, Glyndŵr's Tywi campaign of 1403 was an historic success which still proved sufficient to see English power broken in Wales. In late July, the men of Flintshire rose under one of Glyndŵr's chieftains to burn Flint, Hawarden, Hope, Overton and Rhuddlan, before brazenly invading Shropshire where the king was still present. North Wales was firmly under Welsh control, and during the remainder of the year England was finally compelled to relinquish its grip upon the ancient south-western kingdom of Deheubarth and its heartland of the Tywi Valley.

August saw Henry Dwn partially realise Glyndŵr's plan for Kidwelly. Although he failed to take the massive castle, he annihilated the town and seized all the lowland crops for miles around in a suitably corvine manner. In the same month the English were defeated at the Battle of Stalling Down near Cowbridge west of Cardiff, in a conflict which was said to have seen 'the horses up to their fetlocks in blood', while a certain Lord Berkerolles continued to cling on grimly in the nearby castle of Coety.

Newport and Cardiff were assaulted next, and a subsequent attempt by the seafarers of Bristol to loot Llandaf Cathedral was beaten off by the men of Glamorgan. Glyndŵr, who may have secretly remained in the south after his encounter with Lord Carew, then attacked Llantrisant, and particularly Caerphilly, with such a ravenesque success that the local economy was still suffering twenty years later. Glyndŵr also attacked Crickhowell before taking and burning Abergavenny, allegedly when a citizen of that town allowed Glyndŵr's forces in through a gate in 'Traitor's Lane'. By the end of the month the surviving Lord of Abergavenny, a kinsman of Lord Grey of Ruthin, who had doggedly defended his castles at Abergavenny and Ewias Harold, reported that he was utterly ruined by the revolt. Meanwhile, Herefordshire was reduced to buying off Welsh raids with substantial sums of silver, and the remaining English castles in Wales were isolated and pleading in vain for assistance.

In mid-September came the English response – both heavy and impotent. Arriving at Hereford on 11 September, Henry IV assembled a large army and marched, as usual, into the wreckage of the Tywi Valley. Having persecuted and slaughtered many in Cantref Bychan and Cantref Mawr, the king was at Carmarthen on 24 September where he briefly rebuilt the castle walls, ran out of money, stole some cattle and left the Earl of Somerset in charge of 270 men, who ten days later wrote him a letter saying that they would not stay over a month 'for anything in the world'.

Glyndŵr's domination of the south was palpable, and within a week he was back in control. Kidwelly was attacked again, with significant aid from French and Breton land-forces. They sacked the town but were still unable to take the near-impregnable castle despite a siege which lasted for the rest of the year. In October, an English relief expedition sent by sea from Somerset to Cardiff degenerated into another abortive attempt to loot Llandaf Cathedral, while the men of Monmouth and Gwent ran amok on Glyndŵr's behalf.

By November the English garrisons at Caernarfon and

Beaumaris in the north, which were wholly dependent upon seaborne relief, were attacked by a French fleet under the command of 'John the Spaniard'. Finally, Aberystwyth and Harlech were vigorously beset with the aid of French siege-technology, as Wales heaved violently in an effort to rid herself of the coastal castles.

As this tumultuous year neared its extraordinary end, the sole surviving achievement of Henry's brief south-western campaign was the restoration of Carmarthen Castle to the Crown, where the Duke of York took over at the end of the month with a garrison of over 1,000 men – but even that would not prove permanent.

Meanwhile, those English garrisons which survived elsewhere were stranded, struggling to survive until the next relief mission arrived. Almost no revenue was raised in Wales during 1403, Henry IV was bankrupt, Owain Glyndŵr was ascendant from north to south, and before long England would find itself expelled from Wales and resigned to a long-haul policy.

LEGEND 14 : PIGS

One dark and rainy Saturday, Jack of Kent and the Devil went to the market to buy pigs. In the gloominess of the afternoon, the Devil opted to collect his share of the pigs from Jack the following morning, and asserted upon leaving that he would have those pigs which hung their tails straight and that Jack should have the ones whose tails were curly. As soon as the Devil had departed for his infernal comforts, Jack drove all the pigs home, through countless puddles, put them into his very warmest barn and pampered them with a good supper and some clean dry straw, all that is except for the most miserable specimen, which he left outside in the rain all night. The next day when the pigs were paraded one by one, all their tails were pertly curled up, 'like worms in a drought', all that is, except for the damp and miserable one, which belonged to the Devil.

Other versions

This is perhaps the best known of the agricultural tales, and it is usually set at Grosmont or Hereford market. In another version Jack persuades the pigs' tails to curl by the dubious method of feeding them with bean–haulms on the way home. It is also said that on a subsequent occasion the Devil attempted to outwit Jack by demanding ownership of the pigs with curly tails instead (whereupon Jack promptly played the same trick in reverse), and in other versions Jack drenches the pig's tails with a pail of water. There is an interesting further version in Simpson's The Folklore of the Welsh Border in which the two buy their pigs at Chepstow market having agreed that whoever's pigs still had straight tails the following morning should pay for both lots of pigs. The story goes on to tell of how the Devil then sat up all night 'with curling tongs, titivating the tails of his animals, – which by dawn were so tired that their tails hung hopelessly limp': It is also interesting that in the Norton Collection (Journal of Folklore) Jack is referred to as 'Dicky Kent'.

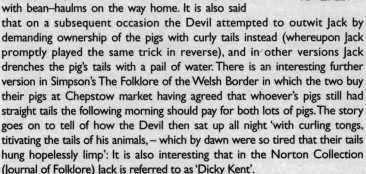

[See also Appendix 1, p. 281.]

107

NINE

MILLENNIUM
(1404–5)

Early in 1404, Henry IV made the Duke of York responsible for the south, while the Earl of Arundel replaced the injured Prince Hal in the north – whereafter Hal shuttled between Leominster and Hereford as the overseer of them both. Meanwhile, in the middle-March, Radnor Castle was restored, re-garrisoned and replaced in English hands, although it stood in a wasteland, isolated and constantly under threat – and this was the whole of the Crown's achievement during the spring.

The Welsh, however, were busy, and their hands were free. Pressure upon the English coastal castles escalated, and it was clear that they must soon fall. Meanwhile, in the south-east Welsh upland tenants in the king's own lordship of Brecon had refused to recognise Henry's sovereignty or to pay debts until the king had subdued the rebels in Glamorgan and Gwent, and in Monmouth, Grosmont, Whitecastle and Dingestow no courts would be held that year because the tenants were rebels.

In April, Owain Glyndŵr welcomed the sworn allegiances of two senior and prestigious clergymen, Bishop John Trefor of St Asaph and Bishop Lewis Byford of Bangor. Two pillars of the former establishment, they brought both their credibility and their international contacts to Glyndŵr's cause – and it is with this in mind that we return to consider John Scudamore of Kentchurch.

As discussed earlier, John Scudamore may have possessed a natural sympathy with the Welsh, and also shared the general dissatisfaction with Henry IV – meanwhile his brother Philpot was already fighting for Owain. Henry IV was a usurper who looked increasingly like a loser and a fool, and Glyndŵr was a leader of great charisma for whom the future was expanding by the day. Nevertheless, in July 1403 John Scudamore had remained true to the Crown, and had returned to make a stand at Carreg Cennen, and to write a pleading letter for help, which never came.

Carreg Cennen then fell to the Welsh, along with the south-west and consequently all of Wales – but it is evident that Scudamore himself was carefully spared – for Glyndŵr's policy had always been to target those baronial Border families who would be responsible for defending the Marches (and especially the strategically paramount south-west) – using such secret agents as the Premonstratensians of Talley to convert them to his cause. For this reason, we should not be too surprised to hear that Philpot Scudamore of Troy had joined Glyndŵr from the outset – that John Scudamore would soon secretly marry Alice Glyndŵr – that having returned from abroad during 1403 Lord Croft of Croft Castle near Leominster would soon secretly marry another of Glyndŵr's daughters (Janet), or that Ralph Monnington of Monnington-on-Wye, the Constable of devastated Llandovery, had miraculously survived one of the most vicious assaults of the conflict: nor should we be surprised to hear that one of Monnington's relatives, Roger Monnington of Monnington Straddel (directly adjacent to Dorstone and probably owned by John Scudamore of Kentchurch), quietly married yet another of Glyndŵr's daughters (Margaret), probably by the same process, and at the same time, that John Scudamore married Alice.

In 1404, Glyndŵr rose towards the summit of his power, whereupon his daughters were undoubtedly at their most attractive. The first real trappings of Owain's success had included the acquisition of the two bishops in April, and I suggest that it was almost certainly between April and the end of the year, and perhaps under the auspices of one of these two bishops,[32] that a widowed and disillusioned John Scudamore finally followed the precedent so recently set by the mighty Mortimer, and secretly married one of Glyndŵr's daughters, Alice. The marriage was covert, as was Scudamore's future role in support of Glyndŵr's cause. Reluctant to take to the battlefield as a public rebel, and thus risk all his lands and authority, I suggest that John Scudamore henceforth agreed instead to use his considerable influence on Owain's behalf, and to act as an undercover agent among the English barony. It was an arrangement which suited both parties.

Interestingly, the suggestion that one of the bishops may have played some part in overseeing the marriages of Owain's three daughters to Marcher nobles whose properties lay along the Herefordshire border is supported by the fact that Bishop Lewis Byford, whose pontificate was at Bangor in north Wales, actually derived his name and his financial support from Byford in south-west Herefordshire, right next door to the Monningtons.

In April 1404, Glyndŵr's great ally in France, the Duke of Orleans, began to write an amusing series of letters to Henry IV, repeatedly challenging him to a duel, suggesting that:

> We will not employ any incantations that are forbidden by the Holy Church – but make use of the bodily strength granted to us by God, having armour as may be the most agreeable of his person and with the usual arms; that is to say, lance, battle-axe, sword and dagger and each to employ there as he shall think most to his advantage, without aiding himself of any bodkins, hooks, bearded darts, poisoned needles or razors.

However, Henry declined.

Meanwhile the Welsh were raiding at will, striking terror into English communities along the length of the border, where the boroughs regularly bought off the Welsh with fines of silver and gold while writing desperate appeals to the king, and Abergavenny town was burnt yet again, even as it rose from its last ashes.

On 10 May, Wales felt the first glow of independence as Glyndŵr's 'in-laws' the Hanmers led an official Welsh delegation abroad to meet with the erratically insane King Charles VI of France in order to formalise the Franco-Welsh alliance. Meanwhile, a combined French, Breton and Welsh navy fought the English both in the Channel and all around the coast of Wales, where the English maritime castles were crumbling – and by the end of the month the coastal castles had begun to fall. The precise dates when the various castles came into Welsh hands have been lost, but the last recorded letter from Harlech was dated 23 April, whereafter it succumbed to John the Spaniard, and Aberystwyth and Beaumaris are said to have fallen soon afterwards. Thenceforth Glyndŵr began to develop Harlech Castle as his regal headquarters in Wales, and soon used all the fallen coastal castles as arsenals and storage facilities from which to defend his new domain (some say that the rousing anthem 'Men of Harlech' was written at this time).

In June, the war raged through the area of the Monnow Valley. Herefordshire and Archenfield were hard hit, and the Welsh were accused of attacking a nunnery at Aconbury, where a member of the de Clifford family is said to be buried under the church wall. Welsh forces then pressed into Gwent, where the long-suffering Lord of Abergavenny, William Beauchamp, was rescued only by the intervention of his young kinsman the Earl of Warwick, who defeated the Welsh in a pitched battle on Campstone Hill near the castle of Grosmont. At Campstone it was alleged that Glyndŵr was almost captured, and he may well have been present, for the Welsh forces came next to Caerphilly, where a significant tradition maintains that Glyndŵr himself took the castle. The next target was Cardiff, where Glyndŵr razed the town, ruined the castle and destroyed the Bishop of Llandaf's fortified palace. Only Llandaf Cathedral and the Grey House of Glyndŵr's Franciscan allies were spared – the latter standing guard over the remains of Llywelyn Bren. Afterwards, the Franciscans of Cardiff complained that they had put their library into the castle for safekeeping – to which Owain replied that they should have had more faith.

The Son of Prophecy was indeed in an imperious mood, for at this time his strength was further bolstered by an influx of other influential Welshmen to his cause, whereupon Glyndŵr took a momentous step towards the consolidation of his brave new Wales – he summoned a Welsh Parliament at Machynlleth.

This was the first National Assembly of Wales since Hywel Dda's Assembly at Whitland in AD 945 – upon which it was probably based. It was convened with great ceremony in late June, in the presence of ambassadors from France, Scotland, Spain and Brittany, and it was presided over by Glyndŵr himself, resplendent with the Crown Jewels of Wales, an orb, a sceptre, and a crown, which have never been found. Thus enthroned, he was styled *Owynnus Dei Gratia Princeps Wallie* and his Great Seal was duly struck. Thereafter, Glyndŵr's Parliament ratified the formal treaty of alliance to be agreed with France – and the English were left to fulminate as an array of Welsh glitterati met with preposterous impunity to purport a new world order.

It could be argued that this was the event which finally brought the mesmerised English to their senses. Glyndŵr had demonstrated that it was possible, with sufficient planning and effort, and under the right circumstances, to render the English presence in Wales unsustainable. However, in the process Wales had become an utter wilderness, in many areas scorched and starved beyond foreseeable repair – whereupon it occurred to England that such a Wales was itself unsustainable. While Glyndŵr's Parliament met, the English began to re-garrison a string of castles along the border. It was a containment policy, the aim of which was to develop an effective economic embargo.

July saw substantial reinforcements at numerous castles, including Welshpool, Oswestry, Bishop's Castle, Radnor, Hay, Brecon, Abergavenny and Carmarthen, and Prince Hal wrote to the king bemoaning a Welsh raid upon Herefordshire and pointing out that he could not keep his men together without pay or provisions. Whether he received anything is unknown, but no relief came to Herefordshire for many months.

On 14 July, the formal Treaty of Alliance between Wales and France was signed in France by the Hanmers and by three French bishops, stipulating that Wales was officially entitled to French military aid, and that neither country would make peace with England independently. Furthermore, the negotiators returned to Wales bearing gifts for Owain from the French king – including a suit of French armour.

In August, after a French fleet under Jacques de Bourbon had floated ineffectually around the Channel, the Welsh chose 20 August on which to launch three simultaneous attacks in different parts of Wales, two of them in the south-west. In Dyfed the Welsh finally overran Haverfordwest, while Henry Dwn launched another assault upon Kidwelly, yet again burning the town but yet again being confounded by the impenetrable castle. Meanwhile at Craig-y-dorth near Trellech a swingeing offensive by the Welsh routed the opposition and chased the surviving Saxons all the way to the gates of Monmouth in a spectacular confirmation of 'The Ohs of Merlin' (see Chapter 5). At this time the Anglo-Norman tenants of nearby Skenfrith were corralled in the castle while their pillaged lands decayed, and at Pennallt south of Monmouth it was said that 'all the tenants left the patria, and certain of them are killed, and their lands lie in the lord's hands for lack of tenants'. Not only the crops but many local mills were also burnt, including those at nearby Dixton, Mitchel Troy and Rockfield (although the fate of a certain mill at 'Kaueros' near Kentchurch, which may have belonged to the Scudamores, went unrecorded).

For a while the English observed the curious sight of a Wales with a mind of its own, and a body devastated, driven and fuelled only by an ancient dream, and then they began to interfere once again in the south. In November and December, two formidable English forces entered Glamorgan to relieve the long-standing siege of Coety Castle, where the indefatigable Lord Berkerolles was *still* holding out – and in December the English retook and re-garrisoned Cardiff Castle. These incursions had little immediate impact on Glyndŵr's dominance of Wales, for the English were merely testing Welsh resolve while continuing to slowly strangle cross-border trade and the flow of illegal support from such places as Hereford. Meanwhile Glyndŵr rejoiced at Harlech as the sovereign of his people, defended by artillery for the first time, and hailed in verse, some say by Iolo Goch, as he 'whose symbol was a conquering sword'.

By the year's end, two of the characters who had brought this tapestry to life had passed away, the first being Iolo Goch. We have suggested that Iolo, doubtless in cahoots with a clique of other magi and masters of Brut, had nurtured and moulded Glyndŵr for his unique destiny since his youth, truly believing that Owain was 'not in the roll of common men' but was the deliverer of Wales prophesied in the Dark Ages. Having masterminded and incited an extraordinary millennial war, during which he wrote the 'Strolling Tour' and many other interesting things, Iolo lived to a ripe old age but is likely to have died by the end of 1404, having witnessed Glyndŵr's triumph in the Tywi Valley, his first Welsh Parliament, his enthronement at Harlech, the Saxons expelled, Wales resurrected, and the ancient prophecy confirmed. So it was that Iolo died, self-contained and victorious, and was allegedly buried at the Cistercian abbey of Valle Crucis near Glyndyfrdwy.

The second Welsh rebel to leave the stage that year was Bishop John Trefnant of Hereford, who is recorded as having died in office in the spring. At Glyndŵr's request he had flooded the Hereford diocese with Welsh priests before the uprising, and had given priority to certain priests from Talley Abbey, before promptly leaving the country in his capacity as an Auditor of Rome. When he returned is unknown, but his death in 1404 might well be construed as suspicious. Henry IV was undoubtedly engaged in a witch-hunt for Welsh agents by the time Trefnant returned, and the fact that for some time a recently absent Welshman had been Bishop of Hereford was guaranteed to look bad. Such suspicions are strengthened when we discover that Trefnant was replaced at Hereford on 2 July 1404 by one Robert Mascall, a Carmelite Friar who at a very young age had gone straight from Oxford to become Henry IV's personal confessor. Was Henry vengefully determined that the next Bishop of Hereford should be a safer pair of hands? It was usually preferable not to be seen murdering the clergy in England, particularly an Auditor of Rome, so it was far better if they met with an accident, such as a nasty attack of food poisoning. In 1404, John Trefnant was laid to rest in the cross-aisle of Hereford Cathedral, under the church wall.

As 1405 began, the rebel forces in north Wales were reported to be 'in haughty spirits', as they surely were, and Shropshire and Herefordshire were still being raided. Meanwhile Henry IV's credibility was at an all-time low – as were his finances – and a number of plots were brewing against him in England. Early in February, the widowed Lady Despenser, a recent resident of Glamorgan, arranged the escape from royal custody of the young Mortimer heir to the throne (Edmund's namesake and nephew), who as the son of Richard II's appointed successor had long since been incarcerated by Henry Bolingbroke in Windsor Castle. In the company of young Mortimer and his younger brother, Lady Despenser left London for Harlech, intending to reunite the two boys with their uncle and thus to bring applause from rebels across the land. Lady Despenser was at Cheltenham when she was intercepted and arrested on 5 February, and so what was nearly a masterstroke by the Glyndŵr/Mortimer alliance at the start of 1405 was thwarted.

Nevertheless, the next stage of the rebel plan went ahead on 28 February when an historic agreement was signed between Owain Glyndŵr, Edmund Mortimer and Henry Percy, the Earl of Northumberland. The latter was both Hotspur's father and the father-in-law of Mortimer's sister[33] and while protesting his innocence to the Crown, he had orchestrated the insurgency of the Percies all along.

The document the three men signed was the famous Tripartite Indenture a treaty that apportioned Britain between the three signatories in anticipation of the Crown's capitulation, and had Lord Carew not prevented Glyndŵr from attending the Battle of Shrewsbury it might even have become the map of Britain which we know today. Signed for Glyndŵr by his two bishops, Byford and Trefor, the northern counties of England as far south as the Midlands and East Anglia were apportioned to Northumberland. Mortimer would rule in southern England, while Glyndŵr presided over a greatly expanded Wales bounded not by Offa's Dyke, but by the River Severn – the dominion remembered from the Dark Ages as the Old Wales of Urien's day. Many have claimed with hindsight that added to the innate optimism of the Tripartite Indenture itself, Glyndŵr's intention to control the whole of 'Old Wales' was wildly overambitious – but why? It was the territory of his ancestors, and he would have it back, and furthermore, as R.R. Davies (*The Revolt of Owain Glyndŵr*) remarks: 'The remarkable claim to a much enlarged Wales . . . may suggest that Owain was losing touch with reality; but it may also suggest that he realised that the vulnerability of his allies was his opportunity to drive a very hard bargain.'

One of the most interesting aspects of the Tripartite Indenture for our purposes is its language, which serves to confirm Glyndŵr's interest in an ancient agenda. While Northumberland and Mortimer list their territorial ambitions as a series of counties, Glyndŵr delineates his intended domain using landmarks from Dark Age history. Thus, having proceeded northward from the Severn estuary along the river boundary of Old Wales unto Worcester, Glyndŵr describes the next boundary point as follows 'and from thence directly to the ash trees known as "Onnenau Meigion" which grow on the high road leading from Bridgnorth to Kinver', which for Glyndŵr and the medieval Welsh was the legendary site where Cadwallon (father of Cadwaladr), 'the last hero of the British race', had defeated the Northumbrians in AD 633.

In March, Glyndŵr's cause suffered a seminal reverse. A great rabble army had been raised, possibly under the direction of Glyndŵr's lieutenant Rhys Gethin of Builth, from among the Welsh peasantry of Glamorgan and Gwent. This marauding mass is said to have plundered its way through Cardiff and Newport before attacking the castles of Caerleon and Usk and then heading north. Described as 'a tumultuous crowd who had thrown down the fences and taken the land in common', in a manner which would have been heartily applauded by John Ball (see Preface), they had skirted Abergavenny before coming to the time-honoured royal Lancastrian border-town of Grosmont, which faced Kentchurch across the River Monnow.

On Wednesday 11 March the Welsh attacked the town of Grosmont, while many of its English citizens either fled into the woods or took sanctuary in the cathedralesque church.

However, while engaged in the usual process of burning and looting, the rabble army was violently interrupted by a 'small body' of royal forces dispatched by Prince Hal from Hereford and led by his royal cousin Lord Gilbert Talbot. The Welsh were routed with heavy casualties, and the Welsh chieftain in charge was captured.

This event raises several issues, not least concerning the numbers involved. Prince Hal's estimate that the rabble army had comprised '8,000 men by their own account' is almost certainly an exaggeration designed to enhance the scale of Lord Talbot's achievement at a moment when the English desperately needed to hear good news. Similarly, his claim to have inflicted almost a thousand casualties upon the Welsh has also been questioned. Although there is no known mass-burial site at Grosmont, it has recently been suggested that such a site may exist beneath the 'King's Field' – an area historically in the possession of the Scudamores. Meanwhile, it may also be significant that a local tradition cites the final rout as having occurred in the region of the nearby Graig hill, while perhaps symbolically siting the mass-grave beneath the preaching-cross within the precincts of Grosmont church.[34] While fanciful, this latter claim is interesting, since in the immediate wake of the Tripartite Indenture, which had marked the high point of Glyndŵr's aspiration, the battle of Grosmont can claim to mark the turning point in Owain's fortunes. Is this why 'Jack of Kent' is also said to have been buried at Grosmont church, occasionally beneath the preaching-cross but much more famously 'under the church wall'?

On 2 April, with his home at Kentchurch yet again miraculously unscathed by recent events, John Scudamore was promoted and appointed as 'Constable of Carmarthen for life'. Interestingly, while evidently not realising what Scudamore, Monnington and Croft were up to with Glyndŵr's daughters, it may well be significant that in the same month Henry IV declared Bishop Byford's income from Byford forfeit, because he was 'in the company of Glyndŵr'.

Also in April, perhaps suspecting that both the rout at

Grosmont and the economic embargo were beginning to have the desired effect upon the level of Glyndŵr's support, the Crown stiffened its resolve. Prince Hal, having recovered from his injury, returned to the field as the King's Lieutenant in north Wales with a retinue of 3,500 men, and a further 2,000 men were sent to reinforce the garrisons of seven key castles. Meanwhile, preparations were made in the south to press upon Gwent, where many Welsh had returned shocked, starving and demoralised from the slaughter at Grosmont, and where Glyndŵr's new sovereignty at Harlech seemed most remote.

In early May, Sir John Greyndour and Lord Codnor, Talbot's colleagues at Grosmont, joined forces with Sir John Oldcastle and Sir David Gam (Dafydd Gam) and moved swiftly into Gwent, where they secured Usk in order to pave the way for a planned invasion by the king. In response, a rapidly raised rebel force arrived under the leadership of a number of prominent Welsh chieftains and proceeded to attack Usk town and castle on 5 May, apparently unaware of the exceptional strength of the English forces packed within. The English returned bowshot for a while so as to lure more rebels in, before breaking out in full strength and pursuing the Welsh across country in a rout which culminated on the hill of Pwll Melyn ('The Yellow Pool'). This location has never been identified, but it is interesting that at nearby Raglan the moated castle was once known as 'The Yellow Tower'.[35] Meanwhile, at Usk three hundred Welsh are said to have been captured and beheaded, in addition to an unknown number of casualties, but the worst news for Glyndŵr in the wake of Pwll Melyn was that several of his most celebrated chieftains lay dead. These included not only John ap Hywel, the warrior-monk of Llantarnam, but also Glyndŵr's look-alike brother Tudur, whose corpse was initially hailed by the English as Glyndŵr's – until the absence of a wart above one eyebrow served to distinguish the two. Nevertheless, this episode may have served to spread nervous rumours across Wales that Glyndŵr was slain, causing widespread fear and trepidation that were only partially ameliorated by the truth that his brother was dead. Furthermore, the additional news that

Owain's son Gruffydd was captured at Pwll Melyn and subsequently incarcerated in the Tower of London must also have contributed to a growing realisation that the hitherto untouchable Glyndŵr was mortal. However, in south-east Wales, I suggest that the impact of the Welsh failures at Grosmont and Pwll Melyn was much more serious than that.

When it came to maintaining popular support, Glyndŵr needed credibility in south-east Wales almost more than anywhere else. This was the indefensible zone which had once formed the weak south-eastern kingdoms of Morgannwg and Gwent, traditionally used by the English and other invaders as a doormat upon which to wipe their feet before attacking Deheubarth. Therefore, to ask the peasant population of *this* area to rise against the overpowering might of England was asking a great deal – for geography placed no obstacles between them and the terrible repercussions which invariably came. Already they had suffered such consequences repeatedly, their lives and their economy had been destroyed, and by 1405 they were wretched and starving for lack of crops. In March, representatives of Glyndŵr from other parts of Wales had arrived and urged them to rise again. Reassured by talk of prophecy and surprise attacks, they had done so – and the result had been a thousand of them slaughtered at Grosmont. In May, more representatives of Glyndŵr had arrived and asked them to rise again – and again they had done so, and this time the result was Pwll Melyn. Always the English seemed ready for them, and Harlech offered no protection, and so the sceptics in the area finally began to win the day. Soon, except for a few fanatics, those who had followed Owain and the prophecy were either fools, dead fools, or living liabilities who threatened to bring yet more terrible repercussions upon everyone.

Here, in Glamorgan and Gwent, where doomed forces had been raised to attack Grosmont and Usk, the final victor was thus a dark and bitter scepticism which descended upon both areas – meanwhile, in adjacent Archenfield, repeatedly raided but rarely daring to rise, the opinion was similar. They had had enough.

The *Annals of Owain Glyn Dŵr* state that in the wake of Pwll Melyn 'Glamorgan made its submission to the English, except for a few who went to Gwynydd, to their master', and while this may be premature, we shall conclude that it was following the battles of Grosmont and Pwll Melyn that Owain finally began to lose his credibility with, and his grip upon, the people of the traditionally vulnerable south-east – Glamorgan, Gwent and Archenfield.

Indeed, as if in confirmation, folklore offers an amusing tale regarding the Battle of Pwll Melyn, which seems to contain an element of ridicule aimed at those who had urged support for Glyndŵr, for it is said that a Welsh priest who survived the carnage had spent the morning promising the Welsh soldiers that he would join them 'that very evening, to supper at Christ's table . . . where the toast will be to you men' – but when things went badly, it is said that he quit the battlefield with the excuse that this was one of his fast-days!

On 14 May, Henry IV was at Hereford amassing a royal army with the intention of campaigning into south Wales via Usk, but at this moment Northumberland raised a new rebellion in the north of England with the aid of Lord Bardolf and Richard Scrope, Archbishop of York. Henry immediately abandoned the planned campaign in south Wales, summoned Hal and went north, where he crushed the rebellion in force. As Northumberland and Bardolf scurried sheepishly into Scotland, Henry abandoned the rule about not murdering the clergy and executed Scrope – whereafter the Church accused him of sacrilege, and pointed triumphantly to a subsequent downturn in his health as an example of divine retribution.

In June, Glyndŵr suffered another reverse, this time in North Wales, when the King's Deputy Lieutenant in Ireland crossed the Celtic sea to take Anglesey and to regain the maritime castle of Beaumaris. Also in the same month, Glyndŵr's close personal friend and confidant John Hanmer was captured and imprisoned with glee by English troops, who received a substantial award testifying to the pleasure of the Crown.

In July, despite such troubles, Glyndŵr besieged Rhuddlan Castle and attempted to keep up appearances in the south-east by arranging a rally of support, which I suggest took the form of a marauding mass of imported supporters from elsewhere – thus lowering his credibility even further with the locals. Indeed, so unimpressed were the local English commissioners that by the end of the month they were in Usk and Caerleon agreeing the terms by which the region would surrender, and in north-east Wales an assortment of Glyndŵr's leading supporters also abandoned the cause and surrendered voluntarily to the Crown.

Meanwhile, in the north-west Glyndŵr was holding his second Welsh Parliament – this time not at Machynlleth but in the greater security of Harlech, where ambassadors from France, Scotland, Brittany and Spain enjoyed an international tourney of jousting. In the face of recent setbacks, it is probable that Glyndŵr was comforting himself with the fact that his international friends were present, that military aid was available from France, that Northumberland had promised at some future point to raise 10,000 troops in northern England, and that there was even a possibility of Scottish involvement. Meanwhile, having raised the necessary cash, he and Mortimer were about to hire a French force of 2,000 men to take part in an epoch-making attempt to realise the Tripartite Indenture.

From a Welsh point of view the raid upon Usk seems to have been an ill-prepared knee-jerk response which led to the disaster of Pwll Melyn, but the rabble assault upon Grosmont may have been a premeditated endeavour to prepare the way for what would now be Glyndŵr's ultimate attempt to restore Old Wales – and for Owain it could not come soon enough. He knew that he must maintain the support of the populace at all costs, and he knew that no amount of weather-control could restore the crop-shortages which were already causing that support to haemorrhage by the day, especially in the south-east. It was now, or never.

On 22 July, the French contingent of 2,000 soldiers left Brest for Milford Haven, keen to restore French honour and to make amends for the embarrassing failure of the ineffectual Bourbon mission the previous year – which had attracted as much derision in France as in Wales. This time the French force was of excellent quality, comprising 800 heavy cavalry, 600 crossbowmen under Jean de Hengest, Grandmaster of the Crossbows of France, and 1,200 French and Breton footsoldiers – but the voyage did not go smoothly – and for two weeks an anxious Glyndŵr was forced to wait, pacing the clifftops as the downward trend continued among his grass-roots support.

The French fleet was becalmed in mid-Channel while all their warhorses died of thirst. Nevertheless, they drifted slowly on, finally arriving at Milford Haven on 4 August, where they were met by Glyndŵr with a Welsh army at least as great as that with which he had invaded the Tywi Valley two years earlier. This was an unhappy landing for the French, who were already bemoaning the loss of 800 of the finest French warhorses that their nation could supply. Furthermore, while the Welsh scrambled to re-equip the French cavalry with unfamiliar and inferior steeds, the French crossbowmen were apprehensive about their inability to match the firing-rate of any longbowmen they might encounter, and the French footsoldiers were not looking forward to the undulating unpredictability of both the Welsh weather and terrain.

Nevertheless the French went rapidly into action, pounding the re-garrisoned castle of Haverfordwest with their sophisticated siege artillery, while the Welsh looked on in admiration. Once they had breached the walls they left the locals to finish the job while the Franco-Welsh army moved on to destroy Picton Castle before coming next to Tenby, where they were reportedly joined by a contingent of 'two thousand Welsh knights'.

Despite having constructed a battery of siege engines in preparation for the assault, it is said that the French departed 'à la Jacques-Robinson' when a rumour reached them that an English fleet was approaching offshore, and so they decided to attack St Clears instead. Meanwhile, having ignored the phantom fleet and finished the job at Tenby, the Welsh caught up with the French at St Clears – only to find them engaged in chivalrous negotiations with the English garrison there – who had fabulously agreed to surrender if Carmarthen did so first.

This, however, proved not to be a problem – as the alert reader may well have guessed. Despite its status as the most heavily defended and important English castle in the south-west, the Welsh siege of Carmarthen went with unprecedented smoothness and an extraordinary lack of bloodshed. The French ceremoniously undermined the castle walls, and the Constable of the castle surrendered on condition that the defenders went free, leaving all their equipment behind. Some may have been surprised at this, but we are not – for the new Constable was none other than Glyndŵr's son-in-law, the recently appointed John Scudamore of Kentchurch.

Leaving the castle freshly ruined, the Welsh and French then marched eastward into Glamorgan, Glyndŵr, in appreciation of his guests perhaps wearing the suit of armour sent to him by the King of France. However, if our thesis is correct it is likely that Glyndŵr was both disappointed and embarrassed in front of his visitors when the hordes he had so fondly hoped would rally to his cause upon this epoch-making march sourly declined to show their support.

Having failed to take Coety Castle, and with their ranks unswelled, the Welsh and French moved next into Gwent, where they followed the route taken by those who had come to grief at Grosmont earlier in the year. Through Caerleon and Usk they marched, desperately trying to incite the inhabitants to rise and march with them, but again they met with the same dour, embittered and unenthusiastic response – and the French grew increasingly nervous. Past Grosmont and into Archenfield they marched, still gaining no significant support.

For Glyndŵr this was a tragedy. This campaign, for which he had worked so long, had been intended to combine the peasant masses who had lately formed the rabble armies of Glamorgan and Gwent with his Franco-Welsh force, and thus create an unstoppable Welsh surge into England. He had hoped that this would be the march of the millennium, a gargantuan thrust back along the invasion-route so regularly used by the English to invade south Wales. Its ultimate destination was Worcester on the boundary of Old Wales, where the river Teme meets the Severn, and with French aid it was intended to deal the English such a blow that they would capitulate and allow the implementation of the Tripartite Indenture – but it never happened.

When Glyndŵr reached Worcester his troops were tired, demoralised and saddened, and the French were deeply uneasy. They had been led to expect that things would be very different, and that disaffected factions in England would also rise in support – but Henry's comprehensive crushing of Scrope's rebellion had caused many potential rebels to abandon their plans.

Henry IV had heard about the French landing at Milford Haven while he was at Pontefract on 7 August. Summoning 8,000 soldiers to arms, he headed south, arriving at Worcester on the 19th, where Glyndŵr's men may have begun to burn and sack the town. Glyndŵr had dreamed of leading an army of historic proportions which nothing could withstand – but instead he was confronted by the English king with an army the equal of his own. At this point, in a manoeuvre that has baffled historians ever since, Glyndŵr retreated with his forces to a place called Woodbury Hill, ten miles north-west of Worcester. The result was a stand-off, and a parley, whereafter it is said that these two vast and evenly matched armies fought eight days of chivalric jousting which produced 200 casualties on each side. The fact was that neither side could afford to risk everything in such an evenly matched contest. The French were particularly reluctant – and the nearest thing to a battle which occurred was when Henry decided to leave the armies on the battlefield and retire to the safety of Worcester, whereupon the Welsh are said to have ambushed his baggage train. The details of what happened at Worcester are obscure – but with his supply-lines stretched and his provisions running out, Glyndŵr is subsequently said to have led his forces northward along the Severn before turning west, plundering and rampaging as he went, frustratedly, back into Wales.

As August ended, John Scudamore was simultaneously and independently accused by two common criminals in England of having raised money and support there for Glyndŵr. We might tend to believe them – but fortunately for Scudamore Henry IV didn't, and so the pair were executed and their accusations were swiftly forgotten.

In September, Henry IV led a major campaign into south Wales, finally relieving the siege of Coety Castle, but choosing to ignore Glyndŵr's Franco-Welsh force which was encamped dejectedly near Cardigan on the south-west coast. Henry was learning not to risk wasting his resources – and Glyndŵr's were running out.

In October, Owain was losing support in Brecon, and on 1 November all the French commanders except a man nicknamed 'One-Eyed Bellay' set sail for France, leaving their troops behind. Once in France the officers engaged in an orgy of feasting and self-congratulation, despite being lambasted by the French peasantry for their outrageous behaviour.

By December, Gwent and Glamorgan had capitulated to the Crown – and Glyndŵr was left with many guests but precious little food for the table. Meanwhile the rain fell in a downpour which was not of Owain's making, and his military activities, while not over, seemed to stall.

LEGEND 15 : SIÔN CENT'S HOUSE

At the beginning of the twentieth century in the areas of Merthyr Tydfil and Caerphilly, the schoolchildren told stories of Jack of Kent, and they sang the following song

> It's raining and the wind is blowing
> And Siôn Cent's House is shaking
> And little Sioni bach is running out
> In case the house falls down.

[See also Appendix 1, p. 282.]

LEGEND 16 : HIDDEN TREASURE

Once, it is said that Jack of Kent (Siôn Cent) conveyed a monk who was called 'truan bach' ('a poor little thing') to a cave piled high with hidden treasure.

[See also Appendix 1, p. 283.]

TEN

TURN OF THE TIDE
(1406–9)

At the start of 1406, Owain's Wales resembled a marathon runner collapsing from exhaustion as the prize slipped from his grasp. The disillusioned Welshry of Glamorgan, Gwent and Archenfield, so recently subdued by the English, had watched with scepticism as Glyndŵr had trampled across their lands en route to Worcester, accompanied by the Grandmaster of the Crossbows of France, and when they heard that it had come to nothing, they and many others knew that Glyndŵr had shot his bolt.

In England the royal cash crisis which had seen Henry IV pawning his own jewellery would be resolved by the end of the year, and meanwhile it was painfully clear that Glyndŵr's Wales was starving, disillusioned and vulnerable to renewed pressure. With this in mind, and with the south-east having already submitted to the Crown, the decision was taken to make the island of Anglesey the target of a major English offensive.

During January and February 1406, Anglesey was attacked by English ships assisted by a quadrupled garrison at Caernarfon. If Anglesey could be wrested from Glyndŵr's control it would serve English interests as a permanent offshore troop-carrier, and its capture would have a triply demoralising effect upon Glyndŵr's regime – firstly by demonstrating his inability to maintain his grip upon a territory so close to Harlech, secondly by cutting off the important food supply from fertile Anglesey to Wales (especially to Harlech), and thirdly by crushing underfoot the time-honoured significance of Anglesey in the Welsh (bardic) tradition.

On 1 February, with his father's health deteriorating, Prince Hal was requested by Parliament to serve once more as the King's Lieutenant in Wales with an extended retinue of 5,000 men – but Hal was reluctant. Campaigning was far more glamorous upon the continent and Hal knew that victory in Wales was only a matter of time – he also knew that within a few years he would be king, and he did not wish to incur the hatred of the Welsh as their conqueror. Furthermore, it is said that he had come to respect Glyndŵr as a military adversary even to the point of affection. In the event, Hal agreed to act as the King's Lieutenant in Wales – but resolved to put commanders such as Gilbert Talbot at the forefront of the campaign.

The siege of Anglesey continued for most of the year as the rebel Welsh fought furiously to maintain their grip upon the island – but in March, Glyndŵr's cause suffered another blow with the loss of the important northern Welsh stronghold of Halkyn Mountain in a major battle which resulted in the death of yet another of Owain's leading chieftains.

In the same month, a French fleet set sail for Wales with every appearance of offering support for Glyndŵr in his hour of need, but actually with the intention of collecting the French troops abandoned at Cardigan the previous year. Thereafter, with countless Gallic shrugs, the French sweetened their piecemeal retreat with murmurs of future support, while steadily abandoning Wales. However, even as the ebb-tide carried Glyndŵr's fairweather friends away in the south, a capricious current cast two old allies upon the shoreline in the north. Forced from hiding in Scotland by a plot to exchange them for Scottish prisoners captured at Homildon Hill, Northumberland and Bardolf had followed in the footsteps of numerous outlaws of northern England – they had fled to Wales.

To what extent Glyndŵr was cheered by the arrival of Northumberland and Bardolf is unknown, but they are described by R.R. Davies (*The Revolt of Owain Glyndŵr*) as 'broken reeds . . . more of a liability than an asset'. It is unlikely that they had significant numbers of followers to boost Glyndŵr's cause – and their arrival coincided with more bad news. On 23 March, eleven rebels publicly submitted before the new Justiciar of north

Wales, Hal's prominent commander Gilbert Talbot, and by the end of the month all hopes of future aid from Scotland were ended when the heir to the Scottish throne was captured by the English. Glyndŵr was in trouble, he was on his own and he had to think of something.

Since 1378 the international Church had been divided by the Great Schism, after the notorious corruption of Rome had led to the establishment of two alternative Popes, one in France at Avignon and the other at Pisa in Italy. Thereafter each of the three Popes (all claiming to be the 'Supreme Lord of the Universe') had excommunicated the others as Anti-Christs and had hired mercenary armies with which they intended to destroy the lands and followers of their rivals – but by 1406 the main contest was between the Popes at Rome and Avignon.

On 31 March 1406, Glyndŵr made a desperate attempt to obtain further help from France. In a remarkable document known as the 'Pennal Letter', he followed Scotland's lead and transferred Wales's allegiance from Rome to the French Pope at Avignon. Considering the unique religious background and the ancient Welsh longing for an independent Church, it would be simplistic to make the cynical assertion that this document represented nothing more than the shameless triumph of temporal necessity over spiritual fidelity – furthermore, the Pennal Letter is interesting.

Having duly condemned 'the madness of the Saxon barbarian', and called for the usurper Henry IV to be branded as a heretic and to be 'tortured in the usual manner', Glyndŵr requested ecclesiastical help in establishing two Welsh universities (north and south) and asserted that future papal appointments to the Church of Wales should consider only those individuals who knew the Welsh language. He also demanded the restoration of the bishopric of St David's as a metropolitan see at the heart of an independent Welsh Church, and the freedom of his own private chapel from diocesan control, a privilege enjoyed by monarchs of England such as Richard II, and also by the Lord Rhys of Deheubarth.

As Owain waited to see whether his alignment with Avignon would bring the French cavalry to his rescue, the French opened two new fronts against English interests in France, both of which would see the French defeated by the autumn. Meanwhile, in an emaciated Wales things went rapidly from bad to worse for the Mab Darogan.

On 23 April, the area of Carnwyllion near Kidwelly submitted to the English, probably in response to a substantial English victory which brought the death of one of Owain's sons. Thereafter, Glyndŵr's efforts increasingly bore the hallmarks of a regime which was not only running out of steam but also out of ideas. The big idea had been the march upon Worcester, but its failure had put all plans and prophecies in limbo. Mass support was ebbing away, the margins of Wales were submitting and slipping irrevocably beyond Glyndŵr's control, and all that Owain could do was to stage ever more vitriolic raids in a desperate effort to stamp his influence upon local populations and to raise much-needed cash by looting. It was pragmatic resistance, but without the luxury of strategy.

In May, as the weight of England continued to press inexorably upon key areas of Wales, Glyndŵr responded with endless raids upon the Borders, where the townships and denizens of Powys, Shropshire and Herefordshire met the cost, and where Owain's supporters were increasingly alienated from his cause. In June, a force commanded by Northumberland and Bardolf was comprehensively defeated by Lord Edward Charlton in north-west Powys, whereafter the hapless duo fled to France and sought assistance in vain. Meanwhile the English noose tightened around Anglesey, and support for Glyndŵr began to crumble in Flintshire. In August, Henry Dwn staged yet another raid upon Kidwelly before plundering the resources of the south-west, and Glyndŵr himself led a major looting expedition into Clwyd – while seven of his leading supporters in Flintshire publicly submitted to the Crown.

In September, the consequence of Dwn's efforts in the south-west was a substantial desertion of supporters from Glyndŵr's cause in the regions of Gower, Ystrad Tywi and Ceredigion, while in the north many of the leading Welshmen of Denbighshire surrendered. All across Wales local populations, starved and battered beyond endurance, were finally turning against Owain, who had promised them dreams at the price of destruction and grief, but who had delivered neither food nor security in return. Indeed, their current experience of Glyndŵr's representatives was that they would arrive and forcibly take away what little food they had.

For many, Owain Glyndŵr had become a liability, as the English were well aware, and so it is probably to this period that the curious tale of an attempt upon Owain's life belongs. Owain is long said to have been at odds with his cousin Hywel Sele of Merionethshire, but they had agreed to meet to resolve their differences. No sooner had they met than Sele lunged at Glyndŵr with a dagger, only to find his blade turned aside by armour beneath Glyndŵr's robe. Glyndŵr's revenge was to burn Sele's home to the ground and to immure his would-be assassin alive in the concavity of a great oak tree which subsequently became known as *Ceubren yr Ellyll* ('The Hollow Tree of the Devils'). Four hundred years later, in 1813, a portion of the tree collapsed, whereafter it was alleged that a party of English travellers measured its girth at 27 feet and described a skeleton holding a rusted sword which was visible in the tree's interior. The original story may have been embellished by the bards, but it is echoed by numerous 'Glyndŵr Oaks' which dot the landscape, including the legendary 'Fairy Oak' at Newcastle on the Monnow and the mighty 'Glyndŵr's Oak' in the deerpark of Kentchurch Court (sometimes called 'Jack of Kent's Oak'), which is said to have been old in Glyndŵr's day. Meanwhile the idea of an attempt upon Owain's life is also reinforced by the tale of another assassination attempt made upon him by one of his arch-opponents, a squinting, red-haired soldier-dwarf known as Dafydd Gam, whose residence Glyndŵr also burnt down.

By October, the fall of Halkyn Mountain had allowed English officials to re-establish administrative control of Holywell, Caerwys, Rhuddlan and St Asaph along the eastern coast of north Wales, and, on 9 November, Anglesey effectively submitted when 2,000 local Welshmen there paid fines, received pardons and capitulated to the Crown. Thirty-four of these men were clerics. A further ten clerics were refused pardons and became outlaws.

The loss of Anglesey was a bitter blow indeed for Glyndŵr, and four days later on 13 November he vented his spleen by devastating much of north-east Wales in a blood-curdling attack which was probably intended to teach the area a lesson for harbouring certain English spies. However, its main achievement was simply to alienate many former supporters who were shocked at the indiscriminate nature and scale of the violence. As Glyndŵr returned to Harlech with insufficient manpower or support to consolidate control of the north-east, the English moved in and re-garrisoned the castles there, and the sands of time subsided in the hourglass of Owain's Wales.

The year 1406 had begun with many false hopes for Glyndŵr, none of which had been realised, and as it came to an end some fifty-two churches in a ten-mile-wide region of the Shropshire border lay in ruins, looted and razed to the ground. Throughout the winter Glyndŵr's rebels continued to raid the borders and north-east Wales for food and resources, but it profited them little and further reduced their support, and we can only guess what desperate thoughts were racing through Owain's mind as the unsustainability of his achievement became apparent. Whereas in previous winters he had eagerly anticipated the fraying days of spring, this time he must have dreaded what was to come.

In January 1407, the English finally consolidated their grip upon Anglesey, and in February, Glyndŵr lost the public blessing of Bishop Byford, who had been unhappy with the transfer of ecclesiastical allegiance from Rome to Avignon and had resigned as Bishop of Bangor. In March, over 1,000 men from Flintshire submitted before the dreaded Justiciar, Gilbert Talbot, and agreed to pay a communal fine in return for pardons for their support for Glyndŵr. Flintshire was returned to English administrative control, and was rapidly followed by Denbigh and Dyffryn Clwyd while similar submissions occurred in other parts of Wales. By April only Caernarfonshire,

Merioneth and northern Cardiganshire adhered to Glyndŵr, whose main hope now lay in seaborne aid coming to his coastal castles of Aberystwyth and Harlech.

In May, the detached part of Flintshire held by the Hanmers and known as Maelor Saesneg submitted. Prince Hal agreed to serve a further six months in Wales equipped with 600 men-at-arms and 1,800 archers, and the Justiciar Gilbert Talbot toured the north with impunity and an escort of 400 men – levying massive fines and terrorising the fearful and humiliated communities with his pronouncements regarding pardon or execution. As Glyndŵr's remaining western territories came under attack, his rebels resisted as best they could, even harassing English ships in the Menai Straits, but by the end of the month the English were confidently preparing for the kill.

Finally, under the auspices of Prince Hal, and with a colossal budget of £7,000, a glittering array of English nobility marched at the head of a formidable army, equipped with siege engines and artillery, straight into the midriff of Glyndŵr's remaining territory. At this stage there was nothing the rebels could do to stop their advance, and the invading English travelled directly to Aberystwyth, where they surrounded the castle and prepared with great pomp and ceremony to give its Welsh defenders a firework display they would never forget. Among the besieging assembly were such luminaries as Lord Carew, Lord Audley, Sir John Greyndour, the young Earl of Warwick and Sir John Oldcastle. Featuring cannons and a vast amount of gunpowder shipped from Bristol, this was meant to be not merely a siege but a celebration, a feast of public conquest and a brazen demonstration of English power.

In June, as the siege of Aberystwyth began, Gilbert Talbot engaged upon a sixty-day tour of Caernarfonshire and Merionethshire, during which he held courts, issued fines, pardons and executions, dispensed justice and injustice alike, and generally established himself as the hated public face of restored English authority in the very heartland of Glyndŵr's support. Meanwhile, mopping-up operations were concluded in the north-eastern borders around Chirk, Yale, Bromfield, Oswestry and Welshpool by Lord Charlton.

In August, the English consolidated their control of Denbighshire, patrolled the Menai Straits in the unlikely case of any seaborne aid arriving from France, and accepted the formal submission of Glyndŵr's broken ally, the Earl of Northumberland. Meanwhile the siege of Aberystwyth continued, as its defenders put up unexpectedly stubborn resistance under the leadership of one of Glyndŵr's most feared and respected surviving chieftains – Rhys Ddu ('Rhys the Black').

It has been said that Rhys Ddu was so-named 'because of his dark deeds' and his fearsome reputation, but we may note with interest that he hailed from the tiny hamlet of Morfa Bychan on the coastal neck of the Llŷn Peninsula near Harlech. *Mor-fa* means 'sea-marsh', and Morfa Bychan is directly adjacent to Black Rock Sands, therefore Rhys the Black was actually 'Rhys of the Black Rock beside the Sea' – and bearing in mind the connection of the Morrigan with the waters of the Celtic 'deep', perhaps we can discern here the spectral shape of 'Rhys the Raven' – Glyndŵr's companion upon the wing, and therefore one of his own 'bodyguard of fierce ravens'.

By September, the siege of Aberystwyth was not going as well as the English had expected. Not only were Rhys and his men putting up much fiercer resistance than had been anticipated, including a deadly and apparently infinite hail of arrows, but the castle itself was extremely robust, and one of the English cannons had exploded, bringing bloodshed and embarrassment for its owners and hearty cheers from the Welsh within the castle. Meanwhile, Rhys and his men were anxious about the inevitability of their fate, and also worried about running out of food, and at this point Rhys Ddu succeeded in negotiating a truce that was due to last until 24 October, under the terms of which the Welsh would have free entry of provisions so long as they ceased firing arrows at the English. A deadline of 1 November was also agreed regarding Welsh surrender, and in the meantime Rhys set out to meet with Glyndŵr in the north to tell him of the arrangements.

According to the *Welsh Annals*, Glyndŵr was incandescent with rage at any talk of defeat and frogmarched 'Rhys the Raven' straight back to Aberystwyth under threat of decapitation – along with anyone else who might be thinking of surrender. Once at Aberystwyth, Glyndŵr allegedly relieved Rhys of his command and took over the defence of Aberystwyth in person, free of any obligation to the truce. This story has frequently been cited as an outstanding testimony to the unswerving loyalty which Glyndŵr inspired among his supporters, as it demonstrates that he remained firmly in command until the very end – which may well have been the very purpose of the tale.

Nevertheless, it is true that Glyndŵr was not destined, nor was it in his nature, to surrender to the 'barbarous Saxon'. Instead, it is said that he sent the English a message attached to an arrow, declaring that they could keep the money by which the truce was secured in place of hostages – after which he is reputed to have ordered the immediate execution of the English hostages held within the castle, and catapulted their severed heads into the besieging mass below.

In November, events in France eclipsed any realistic possibility of French aid for the Welsh, and in December the French signed a treaty with England in blatant contravention of their agreement with Wales – a curious land where, as the Lord Rhys and his kin had long since demonstrated, hope springs eternal and surrender is impossible to arrange.

Even as France turned its back on Wales, it appears that Glyndŵr embarked upon a final effort to involve the Scots. Envoys were received in Scotland by the regent acting in the Scottish heir's absence. Meanwhile, Northumberland, doubtless fearing for his future and still harbouring his hatred of Henry IV, also headed into the freezing north, in the company of Lord Bardolf and Glyndŵr's former bishop, Lewis Byford.

At Aberystwyth, as no doubt in the north of England, heavy snow soon blanketed the ground, as it would for the next four months, and during this exceptionally hard winter the siege-spectacular of Aberystwyth found itself on ice. Both besiegers and besieged froze miserably at their arctic stations – all across the land countless animals died of cold and starvation became the main enemy, as once again Owain seized control of the weather.

Nor was Northumberland idle. On 19 February 1408, he and Bardolf raised the standard of rebellion among their remaining adherents in northern England and came southward with a contingent of Scots, only to be confronted by the forces of the Sheriff of Yorkshire upon a frozen wasteland near Tadcaster. Here, at the battle of Bramham Moor, Northumberland and Bardolf both died, their cause was crushed, and among those taken prisoner at the battle was the unarmed Lewis Byford, who was subsequently released.

In March, Harlech Castle also came under siege, and once again the English faced vigorous defiance from the Welsh resulting in heavy casualties on both sides. It was clear that Glyndŵr's flagship castle would not go down easily. May saw two Welsh envoys adrift in Paris, as Owain desperately hoped that help might yet be dispatched by sea while Aberystwyth and Harlech still held, but it was a vain hope indeed. Meanwhile in north Wales, a gang of weatherbeaten rebels who expected no pardons took to outlawry in the upper Conwy Valley, seeking along with other scattered groups of Welshry to ambush English convoys travelling overland.

In June, the Crown redoubled its attack upon Aberystwyth, and still the Welsh held on, despite having endured a perishing winter and sixteen months of assault and battery by English siege engines and artillery. July and August passed, but, in September, Rhys Ddu, who had apparently been restored to command, made a despairing attempt to negotiate with the attackers. His efforts were rebuffed, and the defence of Aberystwyth collapsed. As the old and the wounded surrendered at the end of the month, legend has it that Rhys Ddu and some of the more able defenders escaped by sea before, according to legend, making their way northward along the coast to assist in the defence of tormented Harlech.

As 1408 ended and a new winter began to bite, Harlech clung grimly on, as another English cannon exploded and every rebel sinew strained to the bitter end to deny the English what they sought – dominion over Wales and the head of Owain Glyndŵr. Within the shattered walls, exhausted and weakened along with the rest through cold, lack of sustainance and sleep, is alleged to have been Glyndŵr himself, and perhaps an unknown number of his sons. Certainly, known to be present were Owain's wife Margaret Hanmer, two of their daughters including Catharine, Owain's great ally and son-in-law Edmund Mortimer, who had wed Catharine in happier days, and Mortimer's four children by Catharine – three daughters and a son who were Owain's grandchildren.

By February 1409, Harlech was set to fall and Mortimer was already dead, variously by starvation, a cannonball or while repulsing an attack upon the walls – and the victorious besieger in charge was none other than the gloating Justiciar, Gilbert Talbot, who was accompanied by his brother John Talbot, Lord Furnival.

Before the month was over Harlech had surrendered, and Margaret Hanmer, her two daughters, and Catharine's four young children by Edmund Mortimer had been rudely seized by John Talbot and taken in great distress to the Tower of London to share in the misery of Glyndŵr's son Gruffydd, who had been captured four years earlier at the battle of Pwll Melyn. After four long years of incarceration, Catharine and two of her daughters died, and were buried in the vanished church of St Swithin's in London, soon to be followed into oblivion by the rest of Glyndŵr's captured family. Where, oh where – they must have wondered – was Owain?

It is far from established that Owain was present at the sieges of either Aberystwyth or Harlech, and the idea that he was has been reinforced by the natural identification of a leader with his last strongholds. At Aberystwyth, we are asked to believe not only that Glyndŵr gained access to a besieged castle, but that, having briefly taken over command, he also succeeded in leaving again. Therefore, notwithstanding Owain's alleged powers of invisibility, I suggest that the tale in which he relieved Rhys Ddu of command and then reinstated him is merely a device intended to demonstrate that Glyndŵr's authority remained unquestioned to the very end. Instead, we shall accept that the message from Glyndŵr to Rhys Ddu regarding surrender was simply an uncompromising order to behead anyone who suggested it, accompanied by a message to the English that the truce was off and that they could keep the money. At Harlech, we are again asked to believe that Glyndŵr was present and in command, and that he somehow succeeded in leaving the besieged castle. The story here is that when the castle surrendered he escaped disguised as a peasant among the elderly men, women and children who were freed by the English upon payment of a fine – but it would be strange if Glyndŵr alone succeeded in escaping thus, while his family of women and children all failed to do likewise.

It has also been suggested, both at Aberystwyth and at Harlech, that Glyndŵr escaped along the beach at night, perhaps implying that he left the area by sea – but we may be certain that if the English either believed, or were led to believe, that Glyndŵr *was* present at Harlech then they would have spared no effort to ensure that no such escape was possible. The claim that Owain Glyndŵr deserted his wife and family at Harlech is one which is still used by those who are keen to discredit him – but it is almost certainly a piece of English propaganda, disseminated when Glyndŵr's absence became infuriatingly apparent. Furthermore, while the tales of Glyndŵr's apparent entries and escapes from Aberystwyth and Harlech are of equal improbability, there are other reasons which reduce the likelihood of his presence even further.

Firstly, the moral obligation that Owain should remain with his family was somewhat reduced by the presence at Harlech of Edmund Mortimer – it could, for example, be argued that Catharine did not necessarily require the presence of both her father *and* her husband. Meanwhile it may have been accepted by all that Owain had a moral responsibility to his supporters to keep the Welsh cause alive and to fulfil his Dark Age obligation as the eternal Son of Prophecy by evading capture and by permanently depriving the enemy of the opportunity to put his head upon a pole. Secondly, only one commander is required to defend a castle, in this case evidently Mortimer, and it would have made no military sense for the rebel Welsh to have put all their eggs into the one basket of Harlech. Thirdly, all England's military might was focused upon Harlech, which was consequently a siege too great to be deterred by any offensive action from within. However, from outside the castle Owain could offer hope – he could communicate with his remaining forces, intend to conspire with Northumberland, appeal to the French and Scots, hope to raise a force capable of relieving the siege, and try to strangle the siege by orchestrating the harassment of English supply-lines with ambushes such as those staged around the upper Conwy Valley. Finally, in an effort to buy time and to further constrict the English supply-lines, we may be certain that Owain was also desperately urging his magi to do everything in their power to invoke a winter like that which the previous year had frozen the siege of Aberystwyth – but it was all to no avail.

As Edmund Mortimer lay dying in Catharine's arms, and Margaret Hanmer told her grandchildren a fairytale in which their grandfather rode a white charger to the rescue, their eyes surely widened, not with wonder but with terror. The white horses of the sea raged against the castle's western walls while the English thundered from the east – and meanwhile, somewhere in the mountains of north Wales, Owain Glyndŵr was aghast, as his brief dominion collapsed, one by one the straws at which he grasped all failed – and Harlech fell.

In May, a small company of French and Scottish soldiers, motivated either by great loyalty to Glyndŵr or by great hatred of the English, or both, landed upon the coast of north Wales – and provoked hysterical warnings from a jittery English Crown to the effect that Glyndŵr had engineered a Franco-Scottish invasion. It wasn't true – but he *was* summoning a last-ditch brigade.

Three months later, at the end of August, Owain led a small army of his most dedicated supporters in the direction of Shrewsbury. Marching defiantly at his side were a handful of his surviving chieftains, including Rhys ap Tudur, Philpot Scudamore, and apparently Rhys Ddu. Little or nothing is known of their intentions, or of what they achieved. Some say that, having won a bloody victory near Welshpool, they proceeded to take and burn Shrewsbury before pressing ever deeper into Shropshire. Perhaps it was nothing but a final gesture of defiance, or even a death-or-glory adventure in which they imagined that the peasantry of Shropshire and the Midlands would arise and march with them all the way to the Tower of London in an echo of the Peasants' Revolt of 1381. Owain's family would be rescued, the usurper-king would be deposed, and all would be well in the Island of Britain. In reality, however, they were stopped, apprehended by Crown forces, and heavily defeated. Rhys ap Tudur, Philpot Scudamore and Rhys Ddu were captured, and all three were hung drawn and quartered by the end of the year.

Owain, however, avoided capture as always, returning to the mountains of north Wales, where he spent the autumn orchestrating ambushes and raids. After ten years he was finally back where he had started – a guerrilla leader desperately trying to kindle the flames of rebellion.

LEGEND 17 : HORSES

Jack of Kent did not win all of his dealings with the Devil. He once challenged the Devil that he could keep his stables with a hundred horses perfectly clean, but try as he might, by the time Jack had finished cleaning the last stable, the horse in the first stable had performed once again!

Other horses

There are numerous references to the 'flying horses' kept by Jack of Kent. It is said that they could not only 'outstrip the wind' but could 'traverse the air with a speed only equalled by Lapland Witches', and it is said that he kept them in stables beneath Kentchurch Court and would ride them up the slope and onward into the sky, with their shoes on backwards to deceive pursuers. On Sundays he would compel local farmers to hunt with him, and the flying horses would bear them far away into unknown lands. On one occasion, one of Jack's horses refused to leave a certain local barn for three weeks, but it burst out to join the flying throng as the hunt flew by. Once, Jack drove a whole team of horses over the heads of the terrified villagers, and sometimes he was seen flying over the rooftops on a stolen mount.

[See also Appendix 1, p. 283.]

LEGEND 18 : SPREADING DUNG

Once, when Jack of Kent was spreading dung in the fields, the Devil appeared and offered to do it for him, adding, 'But make sure you are out of the field before I finish!' Jack agreed, but, knowing what a fast worker the Devil was, he began to run straightaway, whereupon the Devil whipped around the field and finished the task in no time at all. He then pursued Jack at tremendous speed before catching him by the coat-tails in the corner of the field! But it was an old coat, and the coat-tails broke, allowing Jack to jump over the stile and escape into the trees.'

Other versions
Another version has the Devil faced with the task of 'filling the dung-cart before Jack is out of the sheepfold', whereupon Jack immediately drops his pitchfork and flees to gain the same escape.

[See also Appendix 1, p. 288.]

ELEVEN

OUTLAW
(1410–24)

I n 1410, ill-health saw Henry IV resisting calls for his abdication, but nevertheless handing over the reins of government to his prodigious son Prince Hal. Intent upon restoring its preferred version of normality, the Crown had dispatched letters the previous year to the Marcher lords, instructing them to concentrate upon suppressing discontent in their native lordships, and to deter their officials from buying local truces with Owain Glyndŵr – thus reducing one of the last sources of revenue for the rebel cause. Meanwhile, income flowing from much of Wales to the Crown was still running at only a third of pre-rebellion levels, and in northern Cardiganshire and Merionethshire it remained impossible to collect taxes in an area that continued to be a hotbed of rebel support long after other regions had been subdued.

In March, renewed unrest on Anglesey sparked a major English naval alert and the deployment of 900 men into north Wales – and nor was north-east Wales entirely quiescent, for despite its official submission in 1407, outlawed rebels still found support and sustenance here, English supplies were stolen and sent to rebel hideouts in Snowdonia, and local officials were regularly ambushed and murdered, or kidnapped and ransomed.

In 1411, Hal imposed heavy fines upon Wales for its non-payment of rents as he embarked upon a relentless policy of fund-raising (which he also pursued in England), whereupon Glyndŵr's heartland of support in Cardiganshire and Merionethshire reignited in a fresh burst of rebel violence which would last until the end of the following year. However, when attempts to negotiate with Glyndŵr were rebuffed, the Crown under Prince Hal adopted a subtler policy and negotiated separately with local leaders, some of whom accepted pardons, official positions and even military postings overseas. Meanwhile, the rebel Bishop of St Asaph, John Trefor, was replaced by a safe pair of Crown hands in Robert de Lancaster (Bishop of St Asaph and Valle Crucis, 1411–33), as castles across Wales were steadily restored and rebuilt, and the system of taxation was slowly reconstructed.

The year 1412 found Carmarthenshire suffering exceptionally heavy fines under the current Constable of both Carmarthen and Kidwelly, Sir John Scudamore, who had held a lifetime grant of the latter post since 1401. Having secretly married Alice Glyndŵr in 1404, surrendered Carmarthen Castle to Glyndŵr with remarkable ease in 1405, and having been accused of raising funds for the rebels in the same year, Scudamore's career had nevertheless gone from strength to strength. He was knighted for his services in 1408, made Sheriff of Herefordshire in 1409 and appointed Steward of Archenfield in 1411. However, his stewardship of Kidwelly, which had lately seen his acquisition of a lucrative string of forfeited rebel estates, had set him at odds with Glyndŵr's turbulent, formidable and independent-minded ally Henry Dwn, whose lifelong ambition had been to raze Kidwelly Castle to the ground. The result was a feud that would culminate by 1413 in a stack of local charges being laid against Scudamore, including oppression, personal aggrandisement, the sale of offices, extortion, demanding forced gifts of cattle and goods, compelling tenants to cultivate his lands, and plotting the murder of Henry Dwn.

Significantly absent from these charges, most of which were doubtless instigated by the irrepressible Dwn (who was currently the subject of similar charges himself, and who wanted his own lands returned by the Crown) was any mention of Scudamore's secret marriage to Alice Glyndŵr. Dwn may well have been aware of the marriage, but as Glyndŵr's ally he may have chosen not to exploit it. Furthermore, Scudamore's marriage to Alice Glyndŵr was scarcely a matter which Henry Dwn was in any position to couch in terms of an 'accusation' – and if men like Dwn declined to mention such a thing, it would have been a powerful signal to all local Welshmen who valued their necks that it was not a matter for open discussion. Nevertheless, Scudamore's embroilment in this substantial acrimony in south Wales may have led to a limited whispering regarding his marriage among knowledgeable denizens of the south-west.

Meanwhile, in north Wales life was becoming ever tougher for Owain Glyndŵr. The year 1411 had brought the news that his son Gruffydd had died piteously in the Tower of London, officially of pestilence. This doubtless added to Owain's gloom, and may have played a part in the renewed violence in Ceredigion and Merionethshire.

1412 saw the start of a steady influx of English troops into Wales in a policy which rapidly consolidated the Crown's grip upon the lowlands, and increasingly confined the Welsh rebels to the cropless hills and forests. Meanwhile English agents were everywhere, seeking Glyndŵr, who in his late fifties was forced to stay constantly on the move between mountain cavern and forest lair, while still managing to organise rebel activity.

In the spring of 1412, the squinting, red-haired dwarf Dafydd Gam, Henry IV's personal retainer who had been appointed Master Sergeant of Brecon two years earlier, was abducted by Owain's men in Gwent and transported to the fastness of Snowdonia, whereafter he was ransomed and released to the Crown by August. It was a relatively minor embarrassment and expense to the Crown in comparison to those it had suffered during the height of the war, but it brought a degree of cheer to the remaining rebel camp – and its conclusion marked the last significant military achievement of Owain Glyndŵr.

Had the rebel cause been less impoverished, Owain might well have preferred to settle his score with the squinting dwarf who had earlier attempted his assassination. However, he had other things on his mind – and perhaps he already knew that this would be his last action as the leader of the Welsh cause against the Saxon barbarian. In the seven years since the failed march upon Worcester, Glyndŵr had seen his great dream of a resurgent Wales disintegrate, and the widespread support he had once enjoyed ebb away – until to many he was simply the man whose ambitions had laid Wales waste, for nothing, and whose loss of Harlech had seen him fall both publicly and irrevocably from a very great height.

Owain nevertheless still inspired a certain loyalty and solidarity in Wales, doubtless reinforced by the ubiquitous presence of potentially violent former rebels, but his actual credibility survived only among his diehard supporters, and it was clear that he would never lead a Welsh army into battle again. In the capture and ransom of Dafydd Gam a final gesture of defiance had been made, and funds had been raised which would sustain the cause for a short while, but he was tired and hard-pressed, and soon he would confer the leadership of the Welsh rebels upon his faithful son, Maredudd.

In 1413, news arrived that Owain's eldest daughter Catharine and her two young daughters by Mortimer had died of neglect in the Tower of London, and perhaps it was then that Owain finally stood down, overwhelmed by grief, guilt and dismay. He had been responsible for an enormous failure, for which many of his best friends and supporters had given their lives and suffered terrible fates at his behest. He had lost a loyal wife, several sons, a daughter and much else besides, and many have suggested that he was now a broken man. What, he must have wondered, would Iolo Goch – who lay in victory – have thought if he could have seen him now?

In March 1413, Henry IV died, and his son Prince Hal ascended the throne. At his father's coronation Prince Hal had famously borne the ceremonial sword 'Curtana', representing 'justice without vindictiveness', and this would be reflected in his policy. Within forty-eight hours the new Henry V had authorised the admission of all rebels in Wales into the king's peace, issuing instructions that their lives should be spared, but their lands impounded and sold – and many complied. Henry's ambitions lay in France. He needed money, and he wanted no more trouble from Wales.

In July, Henry displayed even-handedness when he prosecuted an investigation into misconduct by Crown officers in Wales during the war, and in September the lordship of Kidwelly was investigated by a commission of fines and pardons, thus bringing another occasion upon which the marriage of John Scudmore may have come to light.

In November, Henry issued a specific pardon to the counties of north Wales, depersonalising local grievances by writing off all debts and arrears outstanding since November 1411, and replacing them with a general fine in the form of an annual levy to be paid over the next seven years. The result of this intelligent device was that specific vengeances were defused, and the sins of the rebels were spread across the whole population, as well as across time, thus steadily deflating any local esteem in which the rebels were still held.

In the south, the end of the year saw Henry Dwn cheerfully repossessed of his lands and successfully evading payment of the attendant fines, his quarrel with John Scudamore resolved. Meanwhile in the north, northern Cardiganshire and Merionethshire adhered stubbornly to the rebel cause and refused to pay rents, while elsewhere the King's Chamberlain helped tenants to restock their lands with cattle at royal expense.

Among those diehards in the north who remained committed to the rebel cause, Maredudd Glyndŵr was doubtless seen as a popular and capable leader who had stayed at his father's side through thick and thin. However, at this moment he scarcely held a winning hand. To what extent he remained in contact with his father we cannot be sure, but certainly neither Owain nor Maredudd had accepted any pardons. Meanwhile, the rebel cause continued, a few Welsh envoys persisted in the haunts of Paris to appeal hopelessly to the French, while their shattered homeland smouldered across the Channel – and Maredudd watched with interest from a forest lair, as an event unfolded upon the Welsh Borders which might conceivably offer hope.

Sir John Oldcastle (see Table II) was a Herefordshire Marcher lord whose lands at Almeley adjoined those held by his Crown colleague Sir John Scudamore of Kentchurch at Monnington Straddel. Oldcastle was a friend of Henry V's, and during the war he had remained a loyal officer, fighting alongside Sir Hugh Waterton against the rebels of Gower in 1403, and subsequently taking part in the siege of Aberystwyth. As Sheriff of Herefordshire in 1406, Oldcastle had been responsible for attempting to prevent support flowing from the city of Hereford to Owain Glyndŵr, but he had been replaced in that capacity by Sir John Scudamore in 1409.

Oldcastle thus had more time to spend in cultivating his well-known sympathy for the religious doctrine of Lollardy, which had been inspired in the early 1380s by John Wycliffe, who had subsequently become the intellectual voice of John of Gaunt's Anti-Clerical Party in Parliament. Wycliffe's ideas included stripping the clergy not only of their wealth and corruption but also of their authority to interpret the Latin Bible, which he demanded should be translated into English. Once this was done, everyone could read the word of God for themselves, and thus be rid of these corpulent priests. Having instigated just such an English translation of the Bible, Wycliffe then went even further by denying the miraculous ability of the priests to turn bread and wine into the flesh and blood of Christ during the Mass. Many of his adherents were alienated and shocked by this attack upon such a hallowed ritual, and so the Church promptly seized the opportunity to condemn all Lollard beliefs as heresy, punishable under Henry IV's Statute of 1401 by burning.

Nevertheless, in January 1414 Sir John Oldcastle defiantly declared himself a Lollard, in outright opposition to the orthodox religious position held by his old friend the king, and was therefore hailed as the noble leader of the Lollard cause, for which he was immediately arrested, excommunicated and tried as a heretic, while Lollards across the country rose in his support.

This was the last thing Henry V needed, just when he had virtually subdued the Welsh and was busy making plans for an invasion of France. Worse still, even as Henry tightened his grip in south and west Wales for fear of a Lollard-Welsh alliance, Sir John Oldcastle escaped from captivity, cheered by the Lollards of London who may have assisted him, and fled to the Welsh borders of Herefordshire where he declared himself a rebel and is said to have met with Maredudd Glyndŵr.

There is, however, no mention of Oldcastle having met with Maredudd's elderly father Owain Glyndŵr, who had faded from all historical records during the previous year. Therefore, although he may well have been in the area, we must assume that as a sixty-year-old outlaw he was too tired, too infirm, or perhaps too ill, to act as anything more than an adviser or as an intermediary in such proceedings. However, since we may assume that he *was* alive, his warrior's eyes must have flickered anew at this potential lifeline for the Welsh cause.

The Crown, at least, seemed to think that Owain lived, for in February 1414 a woman in north-east Wales was forced to swear that she would not support him – but on 10 March, 600 former diehard rebels knelt in the mud and rain outside the town of Bala to swear loyalty to the Crown in the name of Henry V. Was Owain still alive? All we can say is that during the following year, 1415, the Crown continued to exercise either the belief or the assumption that Owain lived.

Throughout 1415, Merionethshire remained rebel despite the Crown's efforts at negotiation, and Crown officers in the county dared not leave their castles in order to collect taxes. The summer saw Henry V still nervous about the possibility of an Oldcastle-Welsh revolt, but nevertheless continuing with his preparations to invade France, where Welsh envoys originally appointed by Owain remained active. Furthermore, there were worrying rumours of a renewed plot to proclaim the young Earl of March, Edmund Mortimer, as king.

On 5 July, Henry V offered a formal and specific pardon addressed to both Owain and Maredudd Glyndŵr – but there was no reply. In the brief silence which ensued, Henry crushed the plot to proclaim Mortimer king and departed for France in August – and among those knights who accompanied him was Sir John Scudamore.

It is possible that whisperings of Scudamore's marriage to Alice reached the ears of the king at about this time, and it may well be significant that in July 1415 Scudamore was removed from his post as Steward of Kidwelly, despite having been granted it 'for life' in 1401. Furthermore, in view of the fact that no other action would be taken against Scudamore regarding his marriage for another eighteen years (see Epilogue), it makes good sense for the marriage to have become known to the king at this moment. Henry was currently far too busy, and had far too much at stake, to risk making waves among either the senior barony or the Welsh just when he was about to leave for France. Since the beginning of his reign Henry had pursued a calming policy of 'justice without vindictiveness', and his strong desire to close the door upon his father's problems with Wales had recently culminated in his public offering of a pardon to the House of Glyndŵr. Therefore, we may assume, Henry gave Scudamore the nod – and they left for France.

'On September 21st, 1415,' wrote the Welsh chroniclers in 1422, 'Owain disappeared so that neither sight nor tidings could be obtained of him in the country. It was rumoured that he escaped in the guise of a reaper bearing a sickle, according to the tidings of the last who saw and knew him, after which little or no information transpired respecting him, nor of the place or name of his concealment. Many say that he died, the seers say he did not.'

This is an interesting assertion regarding the fate of Owain Glyndŵr – which proceeds to offer either his death in a wood in Glamorgan, or his supernatural survival with soldiers in a cave in Gwent, awaiting a time when England would be 'self-debased' – but it is utterly unreliable. As we know, Owain had been hailed by the bards and seers as the eternal Mab Darogan (or Son of Prophecy), whose duty in the ancient tradition of Celtic leaders was never to be taken by the enemy, nor to manifestly die. Indeed, Glyndŵr is distinguished as the only Welsh leader known to have been hailed as the Mab Darogan during his own lifetime. Accordingly, we are merely told that

Glyndŵr went into hiding, whereafter he deliberately disappeared from the pages of history so as to live forever in countless Welsh folk traditions, wherein he is depicted sleeping with his soldiers beneath myriad mountains and in countless caverns – waiting like his forebears Owein of Rheged and King Arthur himself for a legendary bell to sound, signifying the call of the Cymry to awake and liberate Wales.

It was thus the task of the Welsh chroniclers to obscure the time and place of Glyndŵr's death as much as possible, assuming that they were even privy to it, and one method was to supply vague and misleading information – for example, we remain uncertain as to whether the chronicler intends to imply that 'many said that he died' on or soon after 21 September – or whether he 'died' or 'did not' subsequently.

We can, however, ponder the interesting fact that 21 September happens to be the last day upon which the hours of daylight are longer than those of the night. It is also St Matthew's Day, a saint traditionally depicted as an old man, and 21 September was 'St Matthew's Day in Harvest', which tallies very conveniently with the image of Glyndŵr escaping bearing a reaper's sickle. Furthermore it is interesting that in his capacity as a 'Raven', Glyndŵr was a raider and a reaper of crops (i.e. corn), and that corn in its capacity as bread is capable of becoming flesh – not only as the body of Christ in the Christian Mass but as part of the natural cycle by which man consumes the fruits of the land and returns to it before springing forth once more. 'Corn as flesh' therefore signifies resurrection in both Christian and pre-Christian symbology – representing either Christ's body, or the body of an ancient fertility goddess of the earth. Moreover, in the tradition of the Celtic saints, 21 September is the feast-day of St Mabon, a hunter blessed with eternal youth. Therefore, we may conclude that the significance of 'September 21st, 1415' as offered by the Welsh chroniclers regarding Glyndŵr's departure is not only heavily laden with symbolism, but is also very likely to be deliberately misleading, may in any case be inaccurate, and so cannot be considered trustworthy regarding either his disappearance or his demise.

Finally, there is also another reason why September 1415 would have been an attractive moment for the Welsh chroniclers to declare Glyndŵr's voluntary disappearance. Henry V's campaign in France culminated a month later in the celebrated Battle of Agincourt, at which the young king brilliantly defeated the superior forces of the French. In Henry's army were numerous Welshmen and prominent former Welsh rebels who had opted to accept pardons and take up paid careers in the English army – albeit against Wales's former allies – and indeed it was Henry's Welsh archers who famously won the day. The actions of these men, including such as Henry Dwn's grandson Gruffydd, must have caused bitter controversy in Wales, particularly among those closest to the core of Owain's cause, and his Welsh envoys in Paris would have been embarrassed.

I therefore suggest that, by allocating Glyndŵr's disappearance to September 1415 (and thus implying his disdain for the pardon offered in July), the Welsh chroniclers had extended Owain's life as far as possible without requiring him to preside over this apparent desertion of so many of his prominent supporters. In other words, they are saying that 'by the time of Agincourt, Owain had disappeared'. We have already seen a desire among the Welsh chroniclers to preserve the image of a Glyndŵr who commanded loyalty to the very end, and ornamented by its symbolism, this may well be a similar propaganda regarding an Owain who never lost control.

25 October 1415 saw Henry's victory at Agincourt, following which the chronicler Adam of Usk described the death and burial of Glyndŵr as follows:

> Died Owen Glendower after that [Agincourt], during four years he had lain hidden from the face of the king and the realm, and in the night-season he was buried by his followers. But his burial having been discovered by his adversaries, he was laid in the grave a second time, and where his body was bestowed, may no man know.

Adam of Usk was a Welsh cleric brought up within the auspices of the English establishment, on a Mortimer estate, during the 1370s. Educated under the patronage of the Mortimers, in 1382 Adam became rector of Mitchel Troy near Monmouth, where he is likely to have become acquainted with the young Philpot Scudamore. His appointment seems to support the likelihood that the Scudamores were long-since politically and ecclesiastically aligned with the Mortimer/ Richard II camp – and thus also tends to confirm that John Scudamore's marriage to a daughter of Owain Glyndŵr was influenced by Mortimer's marriage to Catharine. Meanwhile, Adam of Usk was rapidly promoted up the ecclesiastical ladder when in 1384 the Bishop of Hereford ordained him as an Acolyte and as a Sub-Deacon on the same day, and two years later Adam served as rector to the senior branch of the Scudamore family at Upton Scudamore in Wiltshire – whereafter his clerical career took off, and he began to develop an increasingly independent frame of mind.

Despite having been educated by the Mortimers and patronised by the Scudamores, Adam of Usk was allegedly involved in the downfall of Richard II in 1399, and was thus richly rewarded by Henry IV. Nevertheless, this did not deter Adam 'the kingmaker' from criticising Henry IV's government, for which he was exiled in February 1402, and spent some years in Rome as a result. Returning in secret as Glyndŵr's war waned and Henry IV's health declined, Adam took refuge with Owain and his rebels before receiving a pardon from Prince Hal in 1411, whereafter he claimed to have joined Glyndŵr only under duress, having left 'as quickly as he could'. In his chronicle written between 1415 and 1421, Adam mentions Philpot Scudamore's severed head being on display at Shrewsbury, and describes Owain and Maredudd as having lain 'miserably in hiding in the open country, and in caves, and in the thickets of the mountains'. Meanwhile, he also makes a show of disapproval towards Glyndŵr which, as R.R. Davies (*The Revolt of Owain Glyndŵr*) observes, renders him among 'the least convincing' of all apparently reluctant rebels. In the light of all of this, what should we make of Adam's account of Owain's death and burial?

Adam is certainly an independent-minded witness who had personal knowledge of the Welsh cause – but he makes mistakes and he seems to have relied upon hearsay. Furthermore, despite his links with the Scudamores, Adam is strangely alone among other sources in listing Sir John Scudamore as having fallen at Agincourt – and there is no doubt that this is incorrect because there are subsequent records of the careers of both Sir John Scudamore, 'Knight', and his son by his first marriage, another John Scudamore, who is referred to as 'Esquire'.

It is true, however, that Sir John Scudamore had not returned from France. Possibly as a reprimand for his marriage to Alice, and doubtless to avoid baronial disputes, Henry V had appointed Scudamore to serve as Captain of Harfleur in 1416, whereafter successive appointments in France kept Sir John effectively exiled and away from Kentchurch until late 1422. Therefore, we must conclude either that Adam was sufficiently poorly informed in these fractured times as to be misled simply by the fact that Sir John had not returned, or that he was deliberately helping to spread the rumour of Sir John's demise, so that those barons who suspected him of treachery during Glyndŵr's war would forget him for a while.

Adam's implied date for Owain's burial was the winter of 1415/16, in the 'night-season', in contrast to the 'day season' of St Matthew when the Welsh chroniclers claim that Owain disappeared. However, if, as Adam suggests, Owain had already lain 'hidden from the realm' for four years, then this would imply that Owain had vanished as early as 1411 – which is certainly not the case – and so Adam is wrong again. I suggest that Adam of Usk is every bit as unreliable as the Welsh chroniclers, whose obscuring agenda he may well have shared. He was also careless, and like many others he relied upon the hearsay which drifted across the tortured wasteland of Wales regarding the fate of Owain Glyndŵr.

As 1415 drew to a close, Wales was largely subdued, except for Merionethshire, where insurgency continued and from where the Gwylliaid Cochion Mawddwy ('The Red Rebels of Mawddwy') staged raids across mid-Wales.

The year 1416 saw Henry V offer another pardon to Maredudd Glyndŵr on 24 February, but it is unclear whether Owain was included. The explanation for this is unlikely to be, as some have suggested, that Henry did not know where to find Owain, since that would certainly have been the case regarding the previous pardon – and neither Maredudd nor Owain were in the habit of providing their addresses – but it may indicate that by 1416 the Crown had begun to suspect that Owain was dead. Again there was no reply to the pardon from either Maredudd or Owain, whereafter Henry V nevertheless pursued his calming policy towards the Welsh, and also restored the estates of Mortimer and Percy. Meanwhile the incorrigible Henry Dwn had contrived to die, without paying any of the fines which had secured his entry into the king's peace.

On 23 January 1417, Henry V issued a warrant for the arrest of his old friend Sir John Oldcastle, and on 30 April he offered a third pardon to Maredudd Glyndŵr in which Owain was not mentioned. In Wales rebel activity continued under Maredudd's leadership, with Crown officials continuing to be abducted and ransomed in the north-west, despite armed escorts, and with Merionethshire being seen as the source of the problem. Meanwhile, Henry continued to press south and west Wales for contributions towards his war-effort in France.

At the end of the year, Maredudd's hopes were dashed when Sir John Oldcastle was captured by Lord Charlton in Powys, possibly en route to Merionethshire – and to the alleged delight of Henry V (who had opposed Lollardy since 1406) the Lollard rebel was dragged with a broken leg to the Tower of London. On 14 December, Oldcastle was simultaneously hanged and burnt as a heretic at the age of thirty-nine, being hailed as a popular hero and martyr among the peasantry who may well have regarded him as another Jack of Kent (see Table II).

The year 1418 also saw the death of the Lollard cause, except for a haunt of heretics who continued to meet in secret along the borders of south-west Herefordshire and Wales in the area between Almeley and Kentchurch. Meanwhile Owain Glyndŵr's long-serving ambassador in Paris, Gruffudd Young, finally gave

Jack of Kent's Stones (also known as Harold's Stones) at Trellech (Tri-lech) near Monmouth were said to have been hurled by the Devil and Jack of Kent (see Legends 2 and 6). (Photograph: *Tania Milne*)

The Standing Stone at Stroat near Chepstow, thrown by the devil during a competition with Jack of Kent (see Legend 4) (Photograph: *Lynn Harrison*)

Jack of Kent's Stone at Huntsham (also known as the Quin Stone or Queen Stone) stands near Goodrich south of Ross-on-Wye and was shown on the 1840 Tithe Map. The vertical grooves are due to rainfall erosion of what were originally horizontal rock strata. (Photograph: *Lynn Harrison*)

Jacky Kent's Bake Oven on the Graig Mountain near Grosmont, possibly a hidey-hole used by outlaws such as Owain Glyndŵr.
(Photograph: *Lynn Harrison*)

Siôn Cent's Quoits at Gaerllwyd between Usk and Chepstow are the remains of an ancient cromlech. (Photograph: *Alex Gibbon*)

Jacky Kent's Barn, an ancient building which stood at Bagwllydiart near Kentchurch until the 1960s, and which contained a beam inscribed 'I. O'Kent 1596'. This was said to have been the barn in which Jack confined crows (see Legend 9). (© *James family*)

The Devil's Heelmark on the flanks of the Skirrid Mountain near Abergavenny is the result of a landslip possibly caused by an earthquake (see Legend 2). (Photograph: *Alex Gibbon*)

Jacky Kent's Bridge over the River Monnow links the villages of Kentchurch and Grosmont (see Legend 1). (Photograph: *Alex Gibbon*)

Jack of Kent and the Devil in embrace, an engraved tombstone formerly in Grosmont churchyard, sketched by Richard Symonds, a soldier in the Royalist army in 1645. (© *British Library*)

Jack of Kent's Oak (also known as Owain Glyndŵr's Oak) in the deerpark at Kentchurch Court. (Photograph: *Richard Jordan*)

The sign of the Bridge Inn at Kentchurch shows Jack of Kent and the Devil on Jacky Kent's Bridge (see Legend 1). (Photograph: *Alex Gibbon*)

Grosmont church. The folkloric Jack of Kent is said to be buried under the church wall at the lower left of the picture.
(Photograph: *Lynn Harrison*)

The early oil-painting known as 'Jack of Kent' (also said to be a portrait of Owain Glyndŵr) is owned by the Scudamores of Kentchurch Court. (Photograph: *Richard Jordan: reproduced courtesy of John Scudamore*)

The Premonstratensian Abbey of Talley (Talyllychau) in Cantref Mawr was founded by the Lord Rhys. Another such abbey adjoined the Scudamore lands at Holme Lacy near Hereford. (Photograph: *Lynn Harrison*)

Llanwrda Church, a possession of nearby Talley Abbey on the River Tywi between Llandovery and Llandeilo (Dinefwr) in south-west Wales. (Photograph: *Lynn Harrison*)

up and returned to Britain to become the Bishop of Ross in Scotland – where the Scots had recently reverted from Avignon to accept the papacy of Rome.

In 1419 Henry V continued his efforts in France, and in 1420 the rebels in Merionethshire and Caernarfonshire still refused to accept pardons. However, on 8 April 1421, Maredudd Glyndŵr finally accepted a pardon from the King – and became a courtier to the English Crown.

Maredudd may well have been finally demoralised by the failure of Oldcastle's cause, and also by the failure of the Welsh to ally with it to any noticeable extent. In addition to the general exhaustion and disillusionment of Wales, there may also have been a religious problem. While the Welsh ecclesiastical and political position largely tallied with the Lollard manifesto, the Welsh (like many others) could not swallow Wycliffe's rejection of the transformation of bread and wine in the Mass, a concept which was confirmed by some of their own ancient beliefs regarding the natural cycle – which returns us to the important question, 'was Owain still alive?'

It is possible to construct an argument for Owain's death having occurred in early 1421, on the basis that Maredudd would have refused to accept a pardon while his father still lived. On the other hand, it is also possible that Owain's long-standing and well-founded distrust of the English Crown had simply rubbed off on Maredudd, despite Henry V's apparent leniency. However, there was another reason why Maredudd may have chosen to accept a pardon from Henry V in 1421 – for by this time it may already have been evident that the king was unwell. Henry V was suddenly preoccupied with his health – and with three pardons already offered, 1421 was the optimum moment for Maredudd to acquiesce to the Crown. The king's illness was rumoured to be dysentery, and might therefore prove fatal, and if he were to die while his son remained in infancy the country would soon be run by a 'scrum' of barons intent upon settling old scores – whereafter pardons would become both rare and dangerous. At any rate, we must conclude that Maredudd's late surrender does not constitute evidence of his sixty-seven-year-old father still being alive in 1421.

In August 1422 the 35-year-old Henry V died of dysentery near Paris. He had been a popular and successful king, and his loss brought great grief to England. From September onwards government was performed in the name of his infant son, the nine-month-old Henry VI, by a Council of unruly barons. Presiding over their ignoble machinations was the acting Regent, Henry V's ineffectual brother the Duke of Gloucester, whose position was later undermined when his wife was accused of witchcraft by the Earl of Suffolk – such was the baronial scrum that Maredudd had avoided by accepting a royal pardon the previous year.

Also in 1422, as the disparate and embittered remnants of the Lollard and Welsh causes mingled among the populace of the Welsh Borders in south-west Herefordshire, the Benedictine Priory at Kilpeck was suppressed because of the general hostility and the superstitious paganism of the local Welsh peasantry (see Chapter 5). Meanwhile, at nearby Kentchurch we find Sir John Scudamore swiftly returning from abroad at the onset of winter, anxious to set out his stall among the mêlée of competing barons and to attend to affairs regarding his family.

At this point it becomes necessary to consider the career of Sir John Scudamore's son by his first wife, John Scudamore 'Esquire', who had been living at Kentchurch during his father's long absence and had doubtless functioned as head of the family there. In this capacity he was thus the protector of his stepmother Alice and also of his younger half-sister 'Jo-anne', Owain Glyndŵr's granddaughter who had been born in *c.* 1405 as a result of Sir John Scudamore's marriage to Alice the previous year. Now aged sixteen, Joanne had married Gruffydd Dwn in 1421 in a ceremony which had doubtless formally healed the rift between the Scudamores and the Dwns, while also commemorating their mutual alliance with Owain Glyndŵr.

Confusion abounds regarding the configuration of the Scudamore family at this point, but I have no doubt that the situation was as I have just described. John Scudamore 'Esquire' was consequently *not*, as some have suggested, 'a grandson of

Owain Glyndŵr'. The recorded details of his life imply that he was born in the late 1390s (see Table IV), and that he was therefore the son of Sir John Scudamore by his *first* wife – the unknown lady who perished at the siege of Carreg Cennen in 1403.

In 1417, while his father was away in France it was therefore young John Scudamore 'Esquire' who was old enough but foolish enough to witness a deed on behalf of a certain John Abrahall, relating to the grant of the manor of Gillow just downriver from Kentchurch. John Abrahall was a very undesirable character, and when Sir John Scudamore finally returned from abroad in late 1422 he must have been appalled to find his son committed to Abrahall's side in a bitter dispute with none other than the even more undesirable Lord of Goodrich in Archenfield, Sir John Talbot (brother of the late Gilbert), who had recently returned from hammering the prostrate Irish in an exceptionally brutal display.

John Talbot, also Earl of Shrewsbury, was a powerful and unpleasant figure within the hierarchy of the Crown, and was therefore an influential player in the baronial scrum which was running the country. When Talbot returned from Ireland to find his interests in Archenfield effectively embezzled by Abrahall with the support of the young John Scudamore 'Esquire', we can imagine his displeasure. One consequence of this may have been that Talbot immediately obstructed the careers of both John Scudamore 'Esquire' and his father – for it is recorded that in 1423 Sir John Scudamore senior encountered difficulties in obtaining his son's inheritance from the family of the Lollard Walter Brut (Bryt), which also makes us wonder if Scudamore's first wife had connections with the Bryt family (see Epilogue). At any rate, the upshot of the Talbot versus Abrahall/Scudamore conflict was that in the same year (1422), we suddenly find John Talbot hauling the Abrahall/Scudamore faction into court upon a spectacular charge, namely that on 26 March:

> John Abrahall senior of Gillow, Richard Abrahall [his father], John Abrahall junior of Ivorstone (Sellack) . . . John Skidmore [Scudamore] of Kentchurch *Esquire*, Maurice Skidmore of

Wormbridge Esquire, George Skidmore of Holm Lacy [and others from Kilpeck, Kaueros, Ewias Harold and other parts of the Marches of Wales] . . . gathered together 1,000 men armed with arrows and other arms in warlike fashion . . . they came to Michaelchurch and Gillow in Irchenfeld [Archenfield] for the purpose of committing treason and treachery, and lay in wait to murder and kill Lord John Talbot, and William Talbot [his younger brother].

On 18 July, Talbot issued further indictments, alleging that the same faction, including 'John Abrahall, Maurice Skidmore, and Thomas Skidmore of Rolleston, with 80 men arrayed for war', broke into the house of Maurice Dawe (a Talbot supporter) and 'murdered him with four lances valued at two shillings'. Meanwhile on the same day it was alleged that 'William Skidmore of Euiasland [Ewias Harold]' was involved in another murder and three abductions at Aconbury, whereafter the victims were carried off to Ewias and imprisoned until they each agreed to pay a ransom of £20 for their release.

Regarding the culmination of this substantial feud, which had already brought misery to the non-partisan inhabitants of Archenfield, it has been observed by Elizabeth Taylor (*Kings Caple in Archenfield*) that: 'It was John Scudamore of Kentchurch who had married Owain Glyndŵr's daughter, and if legend is true, Glyndŵr was in hiding at Kentchurch at that time. There is a strong suggestion that there was more to this outbreak of violence than mere thuggery and a personal vendetta between the two leaders.' This is an interesting idea, the subtext being based upon the fact that '1,000 men in warlike fashion' is a very substantial muster, certainly tantamount to a small army, and that the charge levelled by Talbot was one of treason. Again, we ask, 'Was Owain still alive – aged almost seventy and in hiding at Kentchurch as late as 1423?'

Detailed investigation of this dispute, and of the parties concerned, confirms that it was essentially the result of a power-struggle between the Talbots and the Abrahalls, in which the Scudamores had become embroiled. By 1423, Abrahall was already notorious for maintaining a substantial private army at his fortified headquarters at Gillow, and while it is highly likely that their ranks were swelled on this occasion by the disaffected remnants of the Lollard and Welsh causes who haunted this part of the border, there is no evidence of the direct involvement of either Maredudd or Owain Glyndŵr.

It would certainly be fabulous to imagine that an aged Owain was still alive at Kentchurch in 1423, planning perhaps to take advantage of Sir John Scudamore's influence in Herefordshire, his anger at the beheading of his brother Philpot, and his marriage to Alice, in order to create a new 'Mortimer scenario' with Sir John Scudamore in the leading role and raising a small army against the Talbots, who were so hated by the Welsh. One might even imagine that, had Talbot been killed or abducted, the attack was intended to be coordinated with other actions elsewhere. However, the fact is that it may well have *required* 1,000 men to even attempt to overwhelm Talbot's considerable personal guard, and there is nothing here which cannot be explained within the basic framework of the Talbot versus Abrahall/Scudamore dispute – once again, there is no evidence of Owain's survival, and so, finally the time has come to ask, 'What really *did* become of Owain Glyndŵr?'

LEGEND 19 : THE DUNGEON

Once, Jack of Kent was a highwayman (outlaw) who was imprisoned in the dungeon under the tower at Kentchurch Court, but he escaped by sawing through the iron bars that confined him, and fled to Grosmont via a tunnel which ran from Kentchurch Court under the River Monnow.

[See also Appendix 1, p. 288.]

TWELVE

END-GAME
(1413–14)

As he faded from history during 1413, Owain was in no mood for celebrating his 59th birthday, nor was he in any condition to continue dwelling 'miserably in the open country'. At his last known battle, in enemy territory in late 1409, all the remaining chieftains who had accompanied him were captured or killed; Owain may have been lucky to have escaped, he may well have been injured and he was surely utterly demoralised. Since then he had lived a wretched life as an outlaw in north Wales, and I suggest that by 1413 he was in very poor condition, and perhaps did not expect to live for very long. Thus, while Maredudd and the rebels remained on the run, Owain, no longer able to keep up with them, finally 'retired'.

What could he do? For some time he had been an outlaw of the mountain thickets, perhaps clad like Robin Hood in Kentsdale Green (see Preface), but that was a lifestyle which had finally become impossible for an old man who had suffered much, and whose health may well have been in decline. Worse still, English agents were swarming across Wales, looking for newcomers among local communities and hiring Welsh informers to discover where Owain was in hiding. This was particularly so in Glyndŵr's native north Wales, where cattle now grazed upon the charred remains of his old home, and his face, voice, habits, supporters and general demeanour were dangerously well known.

It is thus likely that, as the winter of 1413 approached, Owain shaved off his trademark forked beard (which appeared upon his Great Seal at Harlech), tonsured whatever remained of his long hair, dispensed with his forest garb and donned another of the disguises so favoured by outlaws – either a shepherd's garb or a grey monk's habit. Having thus obeyed the general principle of Green-to-Grey (see Preface), he confirmed his reputation as the classic 'Jack of Kent' and perhaps made his way slowly southward towards the margins of Wales and south-west Herefordshire, where a strong and logical tradition claims that he ended his days, and where his remaining daughters, Janet, Margaret and Alice, were married to the lords of Croft, Monnington Straddel and Kentchurch respectively. It was 1413, the marriage between John Scudamore of Kentchurch and Alice was still unknown, and John Scudamore, as the current Steward of Archenfield, might offer a degree of protection . . .

Here endeth the recorded history of Owain Glyndŵr. Nevertheless, we shall press on and attempt a reconstruction of Owain's journey into obscurity with the aid of three informants – extrapolation, tradition and folklore. In a general absence of historical records, we shall employ our intelligence and our understanding of Owain Glyndŵr, of the Scudamores and of Jack of Kent to calculate the probable course of events – and for the faint-hearted and sceptical who follow such a path reluctantly, we shall observe that even recorded history rarely offers the kind of proof that might be obtained by access to a time-machine – and within two chapters we will perhaps reach an historic conclusion.

There is a tradition that Glyndŵr arranged a fake burial for himself at Llanrhaeadr-ym-Mochnant church just south of the Berwyn Mountains in north Wales, immediately before he went into hiding – and this would indeed be plausible if he was known to be infirm. Having been hard-pressed in the north, it is also understandable that Owain would have come to the southern foothills of the mountains, and so we have no particular reason to reject either this story or Llanrhaeadr-ym-Mochnant as Owain's general starting point.

Having heard that his 'funeral' had gone well, and would be deployed as a decoy in due course, Owain Glyndŵr donned his disguise as a Grey Friar and left the mountains, making his way slowly southward, passing near the hallowed source of the River Severn. Then, moving shadowlike amid the fringes of the Forest of Radnor, he crossed Elfael before coming upon the border in the form of Offa's Dyke. A little further south he would have slipped from Radnorshire into Herefordshire, perhaps at night or by offering in a priestly manner to pardon the sins of any who questioned him. This would have brought him rapidly to Croft Castle, where his daughter Janet was married to Lord Croft.

If such a thing *did* occur, then it is wonderful to imagine the scene whereupon one October evening in 1413, an old priest weary with pain and experience would have approached the guard-house of Croft Castle and requested hospitality for the night. Even more so, when in offering prayers for the Lord and Lady, the itinerant Grey Friar slowly raised his hood to reveal that he was Owain Glyndŵr . . .

Sure enough there is a considerable tradition, originally oral but later written down, which suggests that Owain did indeed come to haunt the region of Croft from time to time, which is as follows: 'A Welshman could always get a night's lodging with a palliasse of straw in the attic floor, a large one at Croft Castle, and it may well be that this comes down from the time of Glendower.' Thus Owen Croft discussed in 1949 the family tradition that an aged Glyndŵr occasionally stayed at Croft Castle, possibly in the Welshman's Attic, which is thought to have been used by drovers of sheep travelling to and from mid-Wales.

Tito Livio, an Italian scholar writing in *c.* 1436, claimed: 'This Owen, for feare and in dispaire to obtain the king's pardon, fledd into desart places without companie; where in caves he continued and finished his misserable life . . . he died vppon the toppe of Lawton's Hope Hill [near Croft] in Herefordshire, as is there stated and affirmed.'

Lawton's Hope Hill is given as the site of Owain's death in a translation of Tito's work which appeared in 1513. It is nonetheless a confident assertion, stating that the truth of this was confirmed by the locals at the time. Regarding Glyndŵr's fate, Tito was duly anti-Owain, since he had been invited to England by the Duke of Gloucester (the head of the baronial scrum) to write a history of his late brother Henry V.

In 1671, a Herefordshire landowner named Aubrey, wrote: 'Owen Glendour . . . was of Lincoln's inne and dyed obscurely I know not where in this county, keeping of sheepe . . . Skydemore [Scudamore] of Kenchurch married his sister, and Vaughan of Hengest [Hergest] was his kinsman, and these two mayntayned him secretly in the ebbe of his fortune.'

Aubrey is wrong about Scudamore marrying Glyndŵr's sister, for Alice was Glyndŵr's daughter. The reference to Lincoln's Inn alludes to Glyndŵr's early career as a lawyer, while the absence of a 't' in Kentchurch reminds us of the fact that it was inserted by Colonel Scudamore in 1840, to avoid his mail going to Kenchester. Hergest Ridge, where Glyndŵr's kinsman lived, is close to Croft Castle in precisely the area we are discussing, and it adjoins Offa's Dyke on the Herefordshire side. Therefore, it may well have been via Hergest Ridge that Glyndŵr was able to slip across the border and perhaps spend some time keeping sheep – always prepared to slip back across Offa's Dyke if necessary. It is also reasonable that at this time Owain is said to have been disguised as a shepherd, for this was sheep-country, and to change regularly from a priest's habit to a shepherd's habit would have been an excellent idea.

In H. Thornhill Timmins's *Nooks and Corners of Herefordshire* is recorded the following:

> Hope under Dinmore, and if Dinmore should fall,
> The Devil would have Hope, and Dinmore and all.

This charming verse regarding Jack of Kent's colleague, adversary and *alter ego* at nearby Hope and Dinmore Hill perhaps indicates the locals' sharpened awareness of a time when the prayers of the monks at Dinmore Abbey were their sole protection from the 'Devil' Glyndŵr.

Between Croft Castle and Hergest there was also a potential safe-house called Chapel Cottage in Deerfield Forest near Lingen, where John Oldcastle is suspected of taking refuge following his escape from Crown custody in early 1414. The talks he is said to have held with Maredudd Glyndŵr could have been held here in the presence of Owain.

Finally, Carte and Williams (*Monmouthshire*), also confirm that Glyndŵr spent some time wearing a shepherd's habit in the region, and observe that, from Croft, Owain was also within easy reach of Monnington.

There has been much confusion in this arena between Monnington-on-Wye, which lies upon a bend in the Wye, and nearby Monnington Straddel, which lies just to the south-west upon the River Dore and directly faces Dorstone on the opposite bank. The distinction is as follows (see Map 2).

Ralph Monnington was Constable of Llandovery during Glyndŵr's spectacular invasion of the Tywi Valley in 1403 (see Chapter 8), and it was also from the Audley Lordship of Llandovery that the Monningtons held Monnington-on-Wye in south Herefordshire, where (at nearby Monnington Straddel) Roger Monnington was currently married to Owain's daughter Margaret. It is thus suggested that Glyndŵr would have come southward from Croft to visit Margaret at Monnington(-on-Wye). This was also within easy reach of neighbouring Monnington Straddel on the Dore, which was held by the Scudamores of Kentchurch, along with a small piece of land directly across the river at Dorstone.

Having established this, we might wonder what sort of welcome Owain received from the Crofts and the Monningtons. Were Janet and Margaret willing to forgive him for the ruin and destruction of their family? Were their husbands unimpressed with the legacy of Owain's failed war, and the dangerous liability of his outlaw status?

At Croft, one gets the feeling that while Glyndŵr might have enjoyed the occasional night in the attic, he probably spent most of his time keeping sheep for his kinsman at Hergest. Meanwhile at Monnington (on Wye), we might suspect that the owners were relieved when Owain moved on to nearby Monnington Straddel, where we shall find reason to believe that he was invited by the Scudamores to camp across the river at Dorstone. If so, then it was the Scudamores who were ultimately prepared to take responsibility for Owain's presence on their land, and this would imply that Owain found the warmest welcome at Kentchurch, with his daughter Alice and her husband Sir John Scudamore – and it would also explain why Jack of Kent ultimately came to be associated with Kentchurch Court.

As Glyndŵr approached the gatehouse of Kentchurch, cowled in grey, he was surely a classic outlaw who may well have already earned the popular title of a 'Jack of Kent' by the process described in the Outlaw theory (see Preface). Added to the fact that from the name Owain can be derived Yvain, Ifan, Iuean, Sion (John) and thus Jack (Sioni), and noting that (like the English) the Welsh also have an Everyman tradition of simply calling people Sioni (Jack), we thus have a very viable mechanism by which Glyndŵr could have acquired the popular title *Sioni Cent* ('Jack of Kent').

With this in mind it is interesting to recall that following his victory in the Tywi Valley (whereafter he was embroiled by Lord Carew), Glyndŵr is said to have hidden for a while in the south – I suggest in the forestland east of the Tywi, where today we promptly find 'Llwyn Jack Farm' (Jack's Grove Farm) south of Llandovery, and 'Coed Shon Farm' (Jack's Wood Farm) south-east of Llangadog. Then, just a month later after his victory at Stalling Down near Cowbridge, it is recorded by local folk-tradition there that Owain concealed himself for a while in a wood on the hill of Bryn Owen, where he was remembered by the locals as 'Sion Gwdffelow'. This reference to Owain as 'Jack Goodfellow' (Professor G.J. Williams 'Iolo Morganwg' 1953) concerns the well-known hobgoblin 'Robin Goodfellow' who was associated with Robin Hood[36], and so it is also interesting that after the battle Glyndŵr and his men are said to have 'taken away from the rich and distributed the plunder among the weak and poor' in a very Robin Hoodly manner. Therefore, not only do we have an example of 'Robin' and 'Jack' being used as popular alternatives, but of an outlawed Owain hiding in the woods and being known in the Welsh tradition as 'Jack'. Furthermore, Owain Glyndŵr and Jack of Kent have a great many other things in common.

Firstly, both Owain Glyndŵr and Jack of Kent are said to have made themselves at home with the Scudamores at Kentchurch Court in south Herefordshire, where an oak tree, a tower, a bedroom, a ghost and even an early portrait in oils are still said by the Scudamores to be both Jack of Kent's and Owain Glyndŵr's. Meanwhile there are resident legends of Jack of Kent at Kentchurch Court which sit very well within the context of an outlawed Glyndŵr (Legends 17 and 19), and which describe 'Old Scudamore' as having been Jack's patron.

Secondly, both Owain Glyndŵr and Jack of Kent are described as wizards who were 'in league with the Devil', and they also share an association with the Franciscan Order – burial in the grey habit of which formed the standard medieval means of evading the posthumous attentions of Satan (see Legend 23).

Owain Glyndŵr stands head and shoulders above all of his suggested rivals or predecessors when envisaged in the role of Jack of Kent, 40 per cent of the Legends either being interpretable within his context or referring to him directly (see Appendix I). Meanwhile the three key areas in which Glyndŵr's support first succumbed to the scepticism of the locals, Glamorgan, Gwent (Monmouthshire) and Archenfield, are the same three areas where the significant traditions of Jack of Kent remain – perhaps reflecting the fact that the sceptical view of Glyndŵr as a 'Kent-educated' lawyer of 'Lincoln's Inn', who devastated Wales during a mid-life crisis, is not an invention of his modern discrediters – especially since lawyers in the Middle Ages enjoyed much the same reputation that they do today.

On the basis of the above, there is surely a substantial possibility that at Kentchurch Court, Owain Glyndŵr and Jack of Kent were indeed essentially one and the same, as tradition in the Monnow Valley has long maintained (See Appendix I; Legends 1 & 25). If so, we may assume that in the years following the public exposure in c. 1430 of John Scudamore's earlier illegal marriage to Alice Glyndŵr (see Epilogue), rumours promptly ran rife among the Border peasantry as they and others realised who the Scudamores' priestly lodger must have been. Aided by the Devil, the outlaw Glyndŵr had evaded capture to the very end, and thus he had become the latest and greatest of all Jack o' Kents – and this explains why Kentchurch has become the iconic and geographical epicentre of the Jack of Kent legends, as it remains today.

With this in mind, let us therefore finally accept the tradition which suggests that there is a real connection between Owain Glyndŵr and Jack of Kent – and with the aid of folklore, attempt a reconstruction of Jack's last days in the Borders of Wales and south-west Herefordshire . . .

The welcome from Janet and Lord Croft had been perfunctory, and while shepherding at nearby Hergest, Owain remained as desolate as the wretched lands which he had created and crossed. He had become an embarrassment, Lord Croft had much to lose and Janet had never forgiven him for the fate of her mother at Harlech. So it was that Owain preferred to reside alone in the safe-house at Dorstone, which the Scudamores had said he could call his own, and which was also nearer Hergest. At Dorstone, Owain had become known as a strange and bitter old man who cut a sorry figure and kept very much to himself – as well he might – for the terrible spectre of the condition which now enveloped him had stalked him ever since 1407 when Wales first began to slip from his grasp. Only the Day of Judgement stalked Owain now, meanwhile his sole refuge was anonymity, his only friends the flock he herded near Hergest and a scattered few who still, in desperation, dreamed.

Owain had recently returned from an extraordinary meeting at Chapel Cottage near Croft, where he had briefly been reunited with his son Maredudd, and had participated as best he could in the early negotiations with the Lollard outlaw John Oldcastle. Still Owain dreamt bitterly of revenge upon the English Crown, but upon this particular morning, in the spring of 1414, he strove to set aside such thoughts – and dreamt instead of seeing Alice.

The sun shone and the birds sang in a language which only he could understand, as he made his way slowly southward from Dorstone along the River Dore towards Kentchurch. He travelled downriver along the eastern bank, avoiding the English Cistercian Abbey of Dore on the western side. As he traversed the Golden Valley, the flanks of Mynydd Myrddin ('Merlin's Mount') rose to his right before he came to Pontrilas ('The Bridge of Three Streams'), which was then known as Heliston ('Witches' Stone'). Here he could either carry on or cross to the Grosmont side, crossing the river Monnow by the span still known today as Jacky Kent's Bridge. In either case this left him but a short journey from the gatehouse of Kentchurch, the home of Alice and Sir John Scudamore.

Assuming that he had not hitched a ride upon a passing cart, it would have taken the weary Owain a full day to reach Kentchurch on foot, and somewhere along the way he changed his humble shepherd's garb for the grey habit of a Franciscan friar – for a priest was a far more plausible guest of nobility than a shepherd, and the Scudamores were already associated with the Franciscans.[38] At Kentchurch, unlike at Monnington and Croft, Owain received a warm welcome from his devoted daughter Alice, and was allowed by Sir John Scudamore to stay awhile.

Sir John was frequently away on Crown affairs, but Alice remained at home, delighted to see her father and anxious at his frail condition. To the general household Owain was but a visiting Grey Friar, perhaps a learned acquaintance of Sir John's, and so the servants soon grew accustomed to the sight of this elderly cleric sitting in the deerpark of Kentchurch Court beneath the shade of the great tree, which is still known today as Glyndŵr's or Jacky Kent's Oak.

The weather was fine and as Alice gazed across the deerpark at the lowly distant figure, deep in thought and occasionally making notes in a book of personal prayers, perhaps it occurred to her that it would be both pleasant and fitting that an artist should make a drawing, or even an oil-painting, of her fragile father . . .

The oil-painting of 'Jack of Kent' at Kentchurch (see front cover) is in the style of early Flemish oil-painters, such as Jan van Eyck who pioneered oil techniques during the early 1400s and his apprentice Petrus Christus, who was in the area in

1428. While the building in the middle-distance is said to be medieval Kentchurch Court, the hill in the background bears no resemblance to Saddlebow Hill, which would actually be visible from this angle, and nor does the peak upon its summit depict, as some have said, 'Grosmont Castle in a state of ruin', for upon closer inspection it is simply a mass of distant trees, and in any case Grosmont would lie far to the right of the picture. Nevertheless the landscape, with its winding road, is said to be among the finest surviving examples of the Flemish technique.

In the foreground is an elderly and enigmatic cleric, wearing the red robe normally associated with a cardinal, who stares sharply into infinity while preparing to write in a book – the edging of which bears a gophering pattern similar to that found upon a medieval breviary of 1494 (Glasgow University Library, L. Hunterian MS 25) but which, rather than being gilt, appears to have been burnt on.

Art historians differ regarding the date of the painting alleged to be of Jack of Kent, but in common with a majority, Nicholas Rogers (*Bulletin of the Board of Celtic Studies*, 31, 1984) notes the book's similarity to the Glasgow breviary and ascribes the painting to the later 1400s, after 1480. If true, this would certainly have been too late for Glyndŵr to have sat for the portrait – but as we shall see, it does not *necessarily* mean that it is not a picture of him.

It has been noted by many that the format of the painting is generally consistent with the traditional depiction of St Jerome in the Garden, many examples of which still exist, and in which St Jerome is traditionally shown as an old man wearing red cardinal's robes and either reading a breviary or writing in a personal prayer-book. However, Jack of Kent differs from such pictures because, as Rogers also notes, St Jerome is always figurative whereas Jack of Kent is clearly a portrait of a real individual. Combined with his piercing stare, this difference amounts to the fact that while St Jerome is generally a bland and passive figure, Jack of Kent is most certainly neither.

Several of the candidates regularly offered as Jack of Kent have inevitably been suggested as the subject of the portrait – particularly one of Glyndŵr's contemporary rivals in the role, a

Welsh bard who styled himself Siôn Cent. However, as we shall see in the Epilogue to this book, while Siôn Cent wielded a pen to great effect, he has, despite what so many have said, no demonstrable link whatsoever to Kentchurch. Furthermore, his hostility to baronial wealth, worldly vanity and its 'ill-coloured illusions' would probably have precluded such portraiture, and he would have been an unlikely subject for such an expensive work of art.

Various cardinals have also been suggested, including Cardinal John Kempe (d. 1454), the traditional confusion between Kempe and Jack of Kent perhaps relating to Kempsford (a village adjoining the Scudamores' senior family seat in Wiltshire, where until lately mumming plays featured a character known as 'Jack of Kemp') but doubtless deriving from 'Kentsdale' (Kendal) in Yorkshire, where the green-dyed cloth so favoured by outlaws (see Preface) was indeed woven in a factory founded by the famous Flemish weaver John Kempe during the 1330s under the auspices of Edward III. So, who is the man in the painting – and could it still be Owain Glyndŵr?

A physical analysis of the portrait of Jack of Kent was undertaken immediately prior to publication of this book by the National Museum of Wales (See Appendix 2) which confirms the general opinion of experts that the painting is too late for Glyndŵr to have met the artist. If so, the only way in which this painting might yet represent Owain Glyndŵr sitting in the deerpark of Kentchurch Court in the spring of 1414 would be if (though painted many years later) it was based upon a sketch or line-drawing which had been made at the time.

If so, it would be the only picture of Owain Glyndŵr in existence. Furthermore, what would be more fitting than for the elderly Owain to be portrayed as St Jerome – an early tutelary of pagan birth, who underwent a true conversion during the time of the Roman occupation of Britain when Celtic Christianity flourished, and who later became a hermit? In any case, it can do no harm to let this fascinating painting illustrate a page of history which has hitherto been lost – as we continue with our attempt to reconstruct events at Kentchurch in the spring of 1414.

LEGEND 20 : THE CHRISTMAS BLOCK

Once, Jack of Kent wanted to put a Christmas Block (a Yule Log) on the fire, but it was so big that everyone said he would never get it into the house. Telling them to wait, he proceded to get four goslings, and tied them to the log, and upon his order they pulled the log indoors just as easily as if they were horses.

[See also Appendix 1, p.289.]

LEGEND 21 : THE MINCE-PIE

One day, at Christmas, Jack of Kent went from Kentchurch to London to take a mince-pie to the King. He set off at dawn on one of his legendary horses and was in London in time for breakfast. As for the pie, that was still quite hot! On the way Jack lost one of his garters which was later found at the top of a spire. It had been caught in the weathercock of a church as he went flying by.

Other versions
In a similar tale, Jack's patron (Old Scudamore) is told that he must be in London the following morning, an impossible request in those days, but the problem was solved when Jack took him there on the back of a flying black horse.

[See also Appendix 1, p. 290.]

THIRTEEN

HALCYON DAYS
(1414–15)

If we are correct, Owain Glyndŵr spent the best of his last days in the deerpark at Kentchurch Court during the spring and summer of 1414, treasuring every moment, but perhaps fearing that this was the nearest thing to Heaven that he would ever know. Lately he had made a slow and painful pilgrimage across the fields to visit the nearby chapel at Kilpeck, where he was greatly preoccupied with prayer, eternity and repentance. Nothing brought more solace than to pay his respects at such a place, for Kilpeck was not only dedicated to St David, but was also uniquely emblazoned (as it remains today) with stone carvings and imagery which spoke of Celtic Christianity.

When he visited Kilpeck, Owain would stay at a nearby safe-house, still known today as 'Raven's Seat', and the next morning he would make his way determinedly westward to visit the chapel at Kenderchurch (see Appendix 1: White Rocks), once a major centre of Celtic Christianity. Here the dedication was to St Keneder (Cynidr) – often identified with Cunedda – and doubtless Owain paid his respects to his great ancestor before returning quietly 'home' to Kentchurch, and to an anxious reception from Alice at the fireside.

The next day, as he sat beneath the oak tree with his pen and book, the grey-cowled Glyndŵr sketched the dappled outline of a stag amid the apple-trees which lined the banks of the River Monnow towards Kaueros (Corras). The white hart had been the emblem of Richard II, and the stag also represented the soul of the Welsh hero Llew Llaw, who could only die under certain conditions – but the apple-trees in which the young stag stood spoke to Owain of many other things . . .

Sweet apple-tree that grows upon the riverbank
Because of the current,
No steward can reach its glistening fruit.
When I was in my right mind
I would be found at its foot
With a fair, playful maid, a slender lemmun.
Ten years and two score have I been moving on
Through twenty bouts of madness
With wild ones in the wild, after not so dusty things,
And entertaining minstrels,
Only lack does now keep me company
With wild ones in the wild.
I don't sleep now, I tremble,
My dragon, my lord Gwenddolau
And my nearest and dearest.
After suffering illness and longing
Around the forest of Celyddon[39]
Let me be a blissful hireling
With the Lord of Hosts . . .

Sweet apple-tree, with flowers foxglove pink
That grows in secret in the forest of Celyddon,
And even though you look for it, it is all in vain
For it is strange
Until Cadwaladr comes from his meeting of warriors
To the lowland of the Tywi, and the River Teifi,
With the terrible horde of pale faces
To tame the wild with the long hair . . .
The Welsh will win, glorious shall their dragon be.
Everyone shall have their rights
The Brython's morale will be high
The horns of celebration will be blown
The song of peace, of prosperity.

'Merlin's Apple Trees',
The Black Book of Carmarthen

As witnessed by the Arthurian apples of Avalon, the apple-tree was of ancient significance to the Druidic Celts, and also to other deep-rooted cultures across Europe and the eastern world – and in Wales it had become the bardic symbol of poetic immortality.

The apple-trees of south Herefordshire, which once lined the Monnow at Kentchurch, were also traditionally associated with the Scudamores, who by the 1500s would demonstrate a significant affection for them (see Epilogue). Meanwhile, Owain was soon distracted by the numerous doves which fluttered constantly among the leaves of the oak tree beneath which he sat, and which flew to and fro above the deerpark between Kentchurch Court and Garway Hill.

High above the River Monnow and the deerpark, the suppressed stronghold of the Knights Templar on Garway Hill had been replaced during the 1300s by the Order of the Knights Hospitaller, although as Kissack observes (*The Lordship, Parish and Borough of Monmouth*), the Monnow Valley retained the tradition of sanctuary, established here by the Templars. The dove had been adopted by the Templars as their symbol, and in Owain's day a large dovecote on Garway Hill which featured 666 nest-holes bore the inscription: 'This Columbarium was made by Brother Richard de Biri: 1325' as can still be seen today. However, even as the Templars' doves fluttered down into the deerpark from the summit of Garway Hill, they would have encountered the doves who dwelt at the other end of the deerpark, in a dovecote maintained by the Scudamores at Sancta Keyna, their private chapel at Kentchurch. Indeed, such was the Scudamores' penchant for doves that Sir John Scudamore's local ancestor Ysenda, Lady of Kaueros (fl. 1240), had once used cumin (the food of doves) as her medium of exchange, and so we may be certain that Owain would have been surrounded by doves as he sat beneath the oak tree – and it was surely well-known to him that in Christianity they represented the Holy Spirit, having previously represented the messengers of the creative 'Sophia', and earlier still the full-lunar birds of the positive aspect of the ubiquitous Neolithic Triple-Goddess.

Furthermore, while the medieval Church was consequently keen to depict the Virgin Mary receiving the attentions of a dove sent by God, for those such as Owain Glyndŵr, Iolo Goch and others with a keen interest in the House of Rheged, the dove was also the symbol of the famous St Columba, founder of the celebrated Celtic-Christian monastery on Iona which, in the days of Urien the Raven, had formed the main opposition to the agenda of St Augustine.

Finally, the dove may also have held a more ironic significance for Glyndŵr, since the story of Celtic Britain seems to echo the story of the Flood in Genesis, a tale which first appears in the *Epic of Gilgamesh* wherein the same words are used to describe how the lunar-horned Neolithic Triple-Goddess Ishtar had initiated the Flood before releasing her birds across the waters. In the Bible, however, it was Noah who released two birds from the refuge of his Ark as the waters began to subside. First, he released a *Raven*, which as the Bible observes 'flew hither and thither from mountain top to mountain top' (whereafter we hear no more of its fate), and secondly, a *Dove*, which subsequently returned with a sprig of foliage in its beak, thus demonstrating that the fertile lowlands had reappeared, and were available for the taking.

This is also the story of the Celts in Britain, where the Anglo-Saxons repeatedly occupied the lowlands and confined the Celtic 'ravens' to the mountain tops. It happened to Urien and Owein of Rheged in Cumbria and the Pennines; it was both the history and the geography of north Wales; it was repeated when the Normans seized the lowlands of south Wales; it was reflected when Llywelyn Bren was driven into the highlands of Glamorgan in 1316; and more recently it had been the bitter experience of Owain Glyndŵr himself.

Suddenly there was a pause in the gentle 'hu-ing' of the doves and then, deep in the late afternoon from somewhere high upon Garway Hill, in the vicinity of an area known as White Rocks, the silence was punctuated by the 'crow' of a cockerel – and a dark thought entered Owain's mind, for this was said to herald the imminence of a death.

As a descendant of the ancient princes of Wales, Owain Glyndŵr possessed the ability to understand the language of birds, a talent he had inherited through his mother's line via the family of the Lord Rhys (see Chapter 5). Robert Graves (*The White Goddess*) suggests that the cry of the dove, 'Hu-hu', essentially meant 'Where? Where?', and this was a question which surely preyed upon Owain's mind at this time. Where, he must have wondered, was his soul destined to fly?

As evening fell, Glyndŵr closed his book and made his way wearily back to Kentchurch Court. He cut a shadowy figure as he moved silently across the deerpark in his clerical attire. It was dusk, and a low silver mist had arisen from the river and spilt eerily across the fields. According to the old beliefs, this meant that the spirits were rising via the water-cycle, and that one should therefore be upon one's guard. Owain thus pulled the Franciscan cowl more tightly around him, seeking the protection that it offered against the Devil, at least in death, and remembering that its hue, so loosely referred to as 'grey', can also be interpreted as 'dove-pink'.[40]

Before returning to Kentchurch Court, Owain made sure to check the cellar-stables which then existed beneath the great house, and where he tended to Sir John Scudamore's horses while the latter was away on Crown affairs in London. Few knew more about horses than Owain Glyndŵr, save perhaps Sir John himself, who was not merely a knight but a chevalier.

Horses would have been an interest passionately shared by Sir John Scudamore and Owain Glyndŵr, who were both exceptional experts in the field, and this would explain why so many stories emanate from Kentchurch Court concerning the 'flying horses' which Jack of Kent kept in stables beneath the house, and which were therefore the 'Horses of Annwn', the Celtic Underworld or the subterranean 'deep'. Referred to in the Welsh tradition of 'Sioni Cent' as his 'fiery coursers' or 'satanic steeds', these horses were generally black (as is traditional regarding horses associated with the Devil) and Jack is frequently said to have ridden them through the air to strange lands (as in tales of witchcraft). In the context of Glyndŵr as an outlawed Jack of Kent, such horses might well have been useful in the event of sudden discovery, and in another story, Jack is said to have deceived his pursuers by putting his horse's shoes on backwards. This is a tale which is also told in north Wales regarding the alleged military tactics of Owain Glyndŵr – and it is not the only Jack of Kent legend concerning horses and military tactics which can be related directly to the former Welsh leader (see Legends 12 and 17).

Later that evening Owain abandoned his usual caution. Although weak, he was nonetheless elated to be no longer living in damp caves and in freezing forests, but staying instead at a manor, and in a manner to which he had once been accustomed – and he had not lost his appetite for the 'beer and braggart' which he had once shared with his old friend Iolo Goch.

Despite Alice's protests, Owain made his way alone by moonlight, his shadow preceding him, through the apple-trees and along the riverbank until at last he came to a peasant tavern somewhere beyond Kaueros. For too long he had been isolated from the everyday Welsh peasantry and from ordinary situations; he no longer commanded a private army of spies and agents who brought him information, and he wished to hear at first hand the tavern-talk regarding the failure of the war.

It was not unusual for a Grey Friar to be seen in a dark hovel such as this, and indeed Owain's main concern was that there might be others of the local Franciscan Order there who would question his presence. Sadly for St Francis of Assisi – a truly remarkable man – his grey-cowled representatives had long since acquired an unparalleled reputation for debauchery and corruption, the linings of their habits were frequently sewn with forbidden riches, and they were consequently popular with other men's wives. Fortunately, however, it turned out that Owain was the only representative of St Francis in attendance.

At first the evening was as convivial as could be expected. The ill-lit room was dense with smoke from a dangerous fire. The landlord was a wounded former soldier, rolling drunk and refusing to indicate which side he had taken during the war. Meanwhile Glyndŵr's hollow-cheeked glance at the serving wench who poured weak Skenfrith ale into a leather pint-Jack proved sufficient to cool her ardour for the clergy – especially when she saw his bleak demeanour and evident frailty. After a few snatched conversations with the farm labourers who jostled him upon a creaking bench, his attention soon turned to three hussies who sang a bawdy song, and then Owain retreated to a dark corner where he sipped the sickly brew and listened to the many conversations which continued all around.

For a long time there was no talk of the war at all, and Owain felt increasingly adrift and alone, as he steadily consumed more and more of the brew, which was ladled from a cauldron loaned from Skenfrith Castle into the cracked jug which the buxom serving wench brought round, staggering and spilling it upon the evil-smelling floor as she progressed. The hour grew late, then later still, and it was just as Owain was preparing to leave that he was suddenly assailed by a raucous outburst to his left: 'Jack a Kent! – what *that* Jack? Some Jack a Kent was he who left all his womenfolk in the Tower, as they still do say – and who left us all with even less! Let the ravens take him and be done forever. No outlaw-hero he – more *"Jack a Kentigern"* as I do say!'

Peals of laughter exploded around Owain on all sides. It was all he could do to make unsteadily for the door, while striving to contain the boiling rage which coloured his thin white cheeks. The speaker had come from Herefordshire, but it had been Welsh laughter that he heard – the sceptical mocking cackle of the Welsh Border peasantry of Archenfield – and the popular joke regarding St Kentigern had been all too plain.

It was well-known that Glyndŵr had been hailed as the corvine descendant of Owein of Rheged, and that he had descended from the area of St Asaph in the north to raise the 'raven' of the south against the oppression of the English Crown. After all, this had been the entire thrust of his unwritten message to the illiterate peasantry of Wales, as expressed by minstrels in just such taverns as this, in terms which the locals would understand. Unfortunately, those Dark Age Saxons who had wished to discredit the Celts had long since reinterpreted the tale of Owein of Rheged so as to highlight his illegitimate fathering of St Kentigern – the founder of

St Asaph's Cathedral – whereupon it was said that Owein of Rheged had callously abandoned his unwanted family. Thus Glyndŵr's alleged abandonment of his own family at Harlech offered this popular jest at his expense, while also evoking memories of St Kentigern's alleged meeting (possibly near the River Kent in Cumbria) with a man named Lailoken, a forest-dwelling wizard-outlaw who had gone insane as the result of a battle in which he had been blamed for a terrible slaughter.

Still nursing an impotent wrath, Owain stumbled miserably back to Kentchurch, horribly reminded of all that had gone wrong in his tumultuous life – but resolving to say nothing to Alice, whose identity remained unknown behind the fortress walls of Kentchurch Court. The next morning he felt unwell and sick at heart, and so undertook only a short journey to the Scudamores' private chantry, Sancta Keyna.

The name of the original chapel at Kentchurch was already somewhat Anglicised by the time of Owain's visit in 1414, insofar as a 'k' had been substituted for the Welsh 'c', and the chapel had become known as Kencherge or Keynchirche (see Table I). Nevertheless, as Owain, the local Welsh and the Scudamores must surely have been aware, the chapel had been recorded in the *Book of Llandaf* as 'Lann Cein' in 1130, and therefore may have been dedicated to the Celtic saint whose feast-day was 8 October and who was variously known as Ceinwen, Cain, Cenau or Ceneu – allegedly a daughter of Brychan, the first king of ancient Brycheiniog (Breconshire) after the departure of the Romans. However, while it is true that the cult of this beautiful virgin saint ('Cein/Mor-wen') was popular in south Herefordshire, there was also an earlier Celtic saint available. Also called Ceneu, his feast-day was 15 June, and he too was associated with Brecon, being the son of Urien's forebear King Coel of Rheged, and the father of Môr.

As Owain knelt in solitude and silence before the altar, images from the previous night repeatedly interrupted his prayers: if only he had had a sword; if only he still had the strength; if only he were not the Son of Prophecy, he could have made his presence known . . . Meanwhile it began to rain, the raindrops falling hard upon the little chapel of St Ceneu and scurrying in vast sheets as if driven by an Otherworldly wind far across the open deerpark, to drench the summit of Garway Hill – for once again, the spirits were on the move.

Owain knew well what modern archaeologists suspect – that at a site called White Rocks on the Templar lands of Garway Hill high above Kentchurch, certain ancient Celtic chieftains lay in a burial site surrounded by the sacred stones that had once formed their tombs. As rainfall moistened their remains, their vital essence still flowed down the flanks of Garway Hill into the Monnow, thence into the tribal boundary river of the Wye, thence into the Severn estuary, and finally into the mysterious Môr, the creative 'deep' of the virgin ('Mor-wyn') sea.

At White Rocks was once a legend concerning ancestral Giants heaving stones, which would later be adapted to feature Jack of Kent and the Devil (see Legend 5) – and scattered across the deerpark from Garway Hill to Kentchurch Court lie other boulders known as 'Kent's Stones' – but even they do not mark the end of Jack's territory. As far away as Huntsham near Goodrich is a monolith which stands directly beneath another Celtic burial site on high ground above a loop in the River Wye, which is sometimes called the Quin Stone but which on the 1840 Tithe Map is marked as Jack o' Kent's Stone. Meanwhile between Usk and Chepstow, high above another tribal border-stream is a crumbled tomb or cromlech known as Siôn Cent's Quoits, while on the banks of the Severn at Thornbury, and at Stroat under Tidenham near Chepstow, are more stones said to have been hurled by Jack o' Kent and the Devil (see Legend 4).

It was at places such as these – invariably on high ground above tribal river-boundaries or border-streams – that great Celtic leaders traditionally chose to lie and 'flow away' (see Chapter 1). Owain had long-since consulted the seers regarding his own appropriate place of burial, and his two main advisers had been Iolo Goch and Crach Ffinant ('Crach of the Border Stream').

At this moment the chapel door of St Ceneu's suddenly burst open, and there entered the unexpected figure of Sir John Scudamore himself, a tall powerful man with a shock of white hair who had evidently returned to Kentchurch upon a matter of great urgency – but even as Owain turned to greet his old friend, Sir John had already begun to deliver the bad news. Henry V was planning the invasion of France which would soon lead to Agincourt, and many Welshmen including some of Owain's former soldiers and chieftains were sworn to march among his forces – but even worse was to follow. A rumour was abroad that knowledge of Sir John's marriage to Alice Glyndŵr had been brought to the ears of the king, possibly by the Talbots. At this moment Sir John Scudamore must have feared Henry V's reaction – although as we know, the king would exercise his usual policy of 'justice without vindictiveness' and take Scudamore with him to France, before posting him there for the next seven years. In the meantime, however, there was no doubt what must be done – Owain must leave immediately.

The return to Dorstone was hard, for the rain still fell and Owain struggled to reach his humble abode in the cold and darkness. Once there, he lit first a candle, then many candles, and finally a meagre fire, before remembering the single apple which he had brought from Kentchurch, and which he now cut in half. At last, after much prayer and while deep in thought, perhaps he wrote a poem which lay scrawled across the open pages in the darkness, long after he had extinguished the flickering lights and gone sadly to his bed. It read:

> The torment of subduing vengeance
> Alas is afflicting me.
> Woe to the one, woe to the many
> Who shall endure a portion of my torture
> Hear my groaning and sorely complaining,
> Like a wolf on a chain.
> Do not, heavenly Lord, I beseech thee
> Take me from the world in a state of burning

> God of heaven forgive me the sins
> I have committed so long;
> Before dying – before the fierce summons of death
> My day it is approaching . . .

This poem is part of an amalgam of material known as 'The Deathbed Stanzas', and it has generally been attributed to the elusive but important contemporary Welsh bard who used the name Siôn Cent – and who as a putative Jack of Kent is also supposed to have sat beneath the great oak tree in the deerpark of Kentchurch Court while writing poetry. However, despite repeated conjecture on the part of earlier investigators (see Epilogue), there is in fact no *substantive* reason whatsoever to suppose that the Welsh bard Siôn Cent was ever at Kentchurch – or had anything at all to do with the Scudamores.

M. Paul Bryant-Quinn of The Centre for Advanced Welsh & Celtic Studies at the University of Wales is a leading expert in the study of the bardic tradition, and a specialist in the works attributed to Siôn Cent. He too has reached the conclusion that there is no evidence linking the bard with Kentchurch, and in his opinion many of the works produced by the authentic Siôn Cent were written in about 1430, or even as late as 1445 – thus demonstrating that he was certainly not, as some have suggested, identical with Owain Glyndŵr. However, both the life and the work of the authentic Siôn Cent, who wrote in the wake of Glyndŵr's war, offer reasons to suspect that he may have been an outlaw too (see Epilogue). If so, both Owain Glyndŵr and Siôn Cent may have benefited from the useful anonymity supplied by the popular label Jack of Kent – but is it possible that they *both* wrote poetry?

M. Paul Bryant-Quinn has found 'The Deathbed Stanzas' impossible to allocate in terms of their authenticity, not least because they are fragmented, and they reappear in numerous documents. However, of all the material which cannot be ascribed with certainty to the authentic Siôn Cent, he considers 'The Deathbed Stanzas' to be the most credible and enigmatic. Whether or not any of the 'Stanzas' might have been written by Owain Glyndŵr is thus impossible to say – although, since

Glyndŵr was not merely a patron but an active student of the bardic tradition, it is quite possible that he might finally have felt impelled to wield the pen instead of the sword – and it is interesting that Ian Skidmore (*Owain Glyndŵr: Prince of Wales*) has observed that 'The Deathbed Stanzas' are reminiscent of Henry IV's final request for the *Miserere* to be sung, with its prayer for the forgiveness of blood-guilt.

The next morning Owain Glyndŵr left Dorstone in fear and haste, dreading that rumours might rapidly spread and lead to a search of all the Scudamore lands by officers of the Crown. He arose feeling most unwell, the hard journey of the previous evening and the cold and damp having taken their toll. Packing just a few small comforts and his writings, and the half-apple which remained upon his desk, he headed north once more into the area of Hergest and Croft, where his daughter Janet's marriage remained obscure.

It was September. Winter had come early, and for a short while Owain survived once again as a shepherd, until his health finally deteriorated beyond repair and left him nothing but a lowly hermit, weathering the night-season and the elements in a makeshift hut near Lawton's Hope just south of Croft. Here he was sustained only by the charity of a scattered few who were Maredudd's agents in west Herefordshire, and it was one day in the mid-winter of 1414/15, in the company of two such men, that Glyndŵr was taken suddenly ill and collapsed upon the slopes of Lawton's Hope Hill.

As one of his companions ran for help, Owain slumped into semi-consciousness, knowing that his day had come at last, and that he would never see Alice again – and so perhaps his last thoughts were of the sunlight pouring down the Golden Valley, of doves that cried 'Where? Where?', and of the sweet apple-trees that once grew upon the riverbank at distant Kentchurch.

This is the scenario dictated by Tito Livio's 'affirmed' assertion that Glyndŵr died upon Lawton's Hope Hill near Croft. Glyndŵr's companions surely knew that he was dying, and they also understood from Maredudd that certain arrangements existed for his burial in a great and time-honoured tradition, and that, as in his later life, his location in death must at all costs remain secret. It was therefore most certainly not an option to attempt to blunder past the guard at Croft Castle, inexplicably carrying the body of a dying shepherd for the immediate attention of the Lord and Lady – especially not at a time when Glyndŵr's whereabouts might already be under scrutiny, for this would jeopardise everything, including the welfare of Janet Glyndŵr and the career of her husband Lord Croft.

On the contrary, everything that happened next had to be characterised by the utmost pragmatism and secrecy – and Owain could not be left on top of Lawton's Hope Hill. The procedure from here on therefore follows a logical course (see Map 2). Faced with the impossibility of going to Croft Castle, there was only one alternative destination in the Croft area where Owain, if he still lived, could safely receive help in private, and that was at Hergest, the home of his kinsmen the Vaughans. However, the route there lay across country and was obstructed by Kington, and furthermore, as his companions were well aware, it was the Scudamores who knew the secret of where Owain was to be buried. Therefore, the procedure was as obvious as it was decisive and bold. In broad daylight, Owain's companions carried him straight down the hillside and directly on to the old Roman road which led south towards Hereford and the River Wye. A horse and cart of some kind was procured, and Owain's body was laid within beneath a rough covering and a layer of farm detritus, and then the party made their way straight down this medieval version of the A4110 which brought them swiftly to Canon Pyon (where Jack of Kent shares a legend with Robin Hood).

Coming next to the region of Tillington, they turned right upon another Roman road which took them across the River Wye at Kenchester. Passing close to Eaton Bishop, another right turn took them through Shenmore,[41] and with no intention of causing a sensation at either Monnington-on-Wye or Monnington Straddel, they crossed the River Dore at Peterchurch before travelling the short distance up the Golden

Valley to Owain's former accommodation on the Scudamore lands at Dorstone.

By this time it was late afternoon, and almost dark, and Owain's companions forced the door and got him inside. We cannot say at this stage whether or not he still lived, or even was conscious, nor whether word was sent immediately across the river to Monnington Straddel – but we might imagine that candles were lit and prayers were said – and before long Owain Glyndŵr was dead.

The month was perhaps February, 1415. Contrary to various other theories and indications – and for an excellent reason which will be revealed in due course – I therefore suggest that Owain Glyndŵr almost certainly did not survive the winter of 1414/15. Indeed, the popular idea that he lived beyond this date is simply consistent with his own intention that he should seem to linger on and on forever, remaining alive in a shadow-realm of rumour and deliberate misinformation which would eventually blur into legend and thus preserve his image as the Mab Darogan who would one day return to fulfil the prophecy of Wales.

Why am I so confident that Glyndŵr died at Dorstone? Firstly, because it has a certain logic, as we have just seen, and because Sir John Scudamore of Kentchurch did indeed hold this small and obscure piece of land at Dorstone, just across the river from his lesser seat at Monnington Straddel (it had been bestowed upon him by Richard II in November 1396). Secondly, because it is confirmed, not only by the numerous and persuasive traditions of Glyndŵr's presence in the general area which we have already discussed, and by his identification with Jack of Kent, but also by another legend which is unique to Dorstone, and which is very interesting indeed.

This story, set and told at Dorstone (see Legend 24), concerns the death of a character called Jack of France, whom I have suspected of being identical with Jack of Kent ever since I began my researches – partly because Dorstone is situated deep within Jack of Kent territory, partly because the story also involves the Devil and has much the same feel to it as the legends regarding Jack of Kent's demise (Legends 22 and 23), and partly because, like Jack of France, Siôn Cent is also described (in the Welsh tradition) as 'a terror to everyone in South Wales,' (Davies, *Folklore and Place-Names of Caerphilly District*). Furthermore, while we have built a coherent argument explaining why Owain Glyndŵr should have been called Jack of Kent, it is even easier to understand why he might also have been known as Jack of France.

At the beginning of his war, Glyndŵr made great play of the fact that he was the natural successor to his late relative Owain Lawgoch ('Owain of the Red Hand'), the previously proclaimed Prince of Wales who had lived all his life in France and who had repeatedly threatened to invade his homeland with the assistance of a French fleet during the late 1300s.[42]

The legacy of Owain Lawgoch was thus deliberately targeted by Owain Glyndŵr, and it was duly rumoured that some of Lawgoch's former supporters had crossed the Channel and landed in south-west Wales, bringing Lawgoch's heart for burial at Llandybïe before lending their support to Glyndŵr. Furthermore, during the pivotal year of 1405, Glyndŵr's father-in-law Sir David Hanmer publicly mourned Lawgoch as part of his activities as Glyndŵr's envoy in Paris, while Glyndŵr took full advantage of the fact that within the great Welsh (bardic) tradition of reincarnating leaders, it is those named Owain who have made the greatest show of identifying themselves with one another across the ages.

Owain Glyndŵr thus did everything within his power to be hailed not only as the new Owein of Rheged (via the Lord Rhys) but also as the new Owain Lawgoch – a man who was actually known as Yvain de Galles – and since we know that Yvain is a variant of Owain which is easily converted to Jack (via Ifan and Ieuan), there is no doubt that Owain Lawgoch (Yvain de Galles) was most certainly a Jack of France. However, having proclaimed himself the new Yvain de Galles, Owain Glyndŵr immediately proceeded to demonstrate the fact by allying himself with the French, transferring the allegiance of the Welsh Church to the French Pope and marching with French soldiers all over south Wales and the Borders, very possibly in the suit of armour given to him by the French king. His final act in this respect was to march from south-west Wales to Worcester, via Herefordshire, at the head of a Franco-Welsh army.

Lawgoch and Glyndŵr were thus both undeniably Jacks of France, but whereas Lawgoch had ultimately failed to cross the Channel, had never raised his rebellion and had made no impact upon south Herefordshire, Glyndŵr most certainly had – and he is therefore very possibly the Jack of France about whom the following story is told, as related by E.M. Leather in *The Folk-Lore of Herefordshire*:

> There once lived in Dorstone a man called Jack of France, an evil-doer and a terror to all peaceable folk. One night, the Eve of All Souls, he was passing through the churchyard, and saw a light shining in all the windows of the church. He looked in and saw a large congregation assembled, apparently listening to the preaching of a man in a monk's habit, who was declaiming from the pulpit the names of all those who were to die during the following year. The preacher lifted his head and Jack saw under the cowl the features of the Prince of Darkness himself, and to his horror heard his own name given out among the list of those death would claim. He went home and, repenting too late of his evil deeds, took to his bed and died.

This story is approximately reproduced in the Dorstone church booklet. I suggest, in view of all that we have learned, that it is very likely that Owain Glyndŵr ended his days at Dorstone, where he is remembered in the oral tradition by the story of Jack of France.

Finally, there is a third reason why I confidently believe that Glyndŵr died at Dorstone. This reason is connected with the details of the story of Jack of France, specifically with the candle-light in all the windows of the church, and also with Glyndŵr's actual place of burial, and it will be revealed in the penultimate chapter of this book.

In this chapter, however, there remains but one thing to discuss, and that is the existence of a persistent and relentless assertion that Owain Glyndŵr was laid to rest either at Monnington-on-Wye or on the Scudamore lands at Monnington Straddel, directly adjacent to Dorstone. For example, John Webb, writing in 1833, reports: 'It is said that [Owain] retired to his most esteemed daughter Mary [Margaret] Monnington in Herefordshire . . . Browne-Willis Esquire in his history of the Bishop of Bangor says Owen Glyndŵr died and was buried at Monnington, the 20th September 1415.'

Naively accepting the date offered by the Welsh chroniclers for Owain's death, this tradition has meant that Monnington-on-Wye and Monnington Straddel have been endlessly and romantically discussed as Glyndŵr's burial site, in the absence of any other reasonable theory. However, while superficially attractive, there is an enormous problem with this idea. The whole point of Owain's incarnation as the Mab Darogan was that he should disappear *forever*, so that following the deaths of those few trusted individuals who inevitably knew the secret of his burial, the knowledge of his whereabouts would be lost forever – or at least until the Fates decided otherwise.

Monnington-on-Wye belonged to the Monningtons whose scion Roger and his wife Margaret (Glyndŵr) lived at nearby Monnington Straddel which currently belonged to Sir John Scudamore and his wife Alice [Glyndŵr] – and therefore I suggest that it is most unlikely that the Mab Darogan would wish to be buried at either place, let alone to be displayed in a prominent burial mound such as that offered at Monnington Straddel. Maredudd Glyndŵr's rebels, still known as Owain's Folk, took Glyndŵr's commemoration as the Son of Prophecy very seriously. They were certainly not fools, and they knew perfectly well that the 'secret' marriages of Janet, Margaret and Alice were guaranteed to become known sooner or later – as of course they did. The Croft and Monnington marriages were common currency within a century of Owain's death, while Scudamore's marriage to Alice was well known as early as 1430 (see Epilogue) and may even have been rumoured by 1415. It was thus inevitable that there would come a day when people would look for Owain's grave upon the Croft,

Monnington and Scudamore lands. This is precisely what *has* happened – and it is also precisely why Owain is not there.

I suggest that the idea of Owain's burial at Monnington simply originated as a result of the inevitable search of the Scudamore, Monnington and Croft lands following the public discovery of the marriages of Glyndŵr's daughters – and it was doubtless a popular canard by the 1500s. In 1680 a burial mound on the former Scudamore lands at Monnington Straddel was duly excavated and found to contain a skeleton 'whole and entire and of goodly stature', which was duly declared to be that of Owain Glyndŵr, but which conveniently crumbled into dust before anyone could examine it – whereafter the story was reiterated by Browne-Willis in 1720 and subsequently by others such as Harper and John Webb. It is nonetheless ludicrous, if one accepts that Glyndŵr's burial site was intended to remain secret for any significant length of time.

For the same reasons we can safely assume that Owain is not buried either at Croft or at Kentchurch. However, what happened to Owain's body in the *immediate* wake of his death at Dorstone is harder to say. If Sir John Scudamore feared that the king was already aware of his marriage to Alice, this might have caused him either to hurry or to delay making the necessary arrangements for Owain's secret burial. As we shall discover, Glyndŵr was almost certainly laid to rest at a long-planned burial site within eight weeks of his demise in early 1415 – but there remains a possibility that he first received a temporary burial in the vicinity of Dorstone before being moved to his pre-ordained resting place as dictated by the seers and the great (bardic) traditions of Wales.

If, as we have suggested, Sir John Scudamore's marriage was already being rumoured at this time, then it would certainly not have been a good idea to keep Owain's remains either at Kentchurch or at Monnington Straddel – unless his body had been cremated. The possibility of this (see Appendix I: Legend 22) is slight since in the Middle Ages (as per the burning of witches) such a process was usually believed to prevent resurrection (reincarnation) on the Day of Judgement, and therefore we can assume the likelihood that he remained intact. This being the case, there were two main options for a temporary burial. Depending upon the degree of anxiety over the imminent discovery of Sir John Scudamore's marriage to Alice, it might have been decided to keep Owain precisely where he was, since Dorstone was a relatively obscure piece of Scudamore territory on the far side of the River Dore from Monnington Straddel. The alternative was to risk taking Owain out of Dorstone for temporary burial elsewhere, but we shall never know which option was preferred.

Since the cessation of official history in 1413, both extrapolation and tradition have supported Glyndŵr's subsequent presence in south-west Herefordshire, where Jack of Kent bestrides the supernatural landscape. These two informants have brought us as far as February 1415 – at which point we have assumed, for a reason which will later become apparent, that Owain died. However, with both history and tradition now exhausted, only one source of information now remains which might enable us to follow Owain upon his final journey – folklore.

According to Evans, writing in 1810 in *a Topographical & Historical Tour of the county of Monmouthshire*:

> A prevailing tradition is that an old wizard, disguised in a shepherd's habit, once frequented Kentchurch House, and roamed about the neighbourhood of Grosmont. His remains are said to be buried under the stone called John of Kent's tomb. This person was probably Owen Glyndŵr, who is reported to have taken shelter at the house of his son-in-law (John Scudamore of Kentchurch), but who at that period is stated to have resided at (owned) Mornington [Monnington Straddel]. After his defeat, he is known to have escaped, habited as a shepherd, and he might have retired to this sequestered spot, and been privately interred here, though his body might have been afterwards removed, or a cenotaph erected to his memory in another place.

Thus we are not the first to observe that both Owain Glyndŵr and Jack of Kent were wizards with an interest in the Monnow

Valley (see also Appendix I: Legend 1) and whose shared identity might imply a shared place of burial. While the folkloric Jack of Kent is occasionally said to have been interred beneath the preaching-cross in Grosmont churchyard (which may be a comment regarding the fate of Glyndŵr's cause following the battle of Grosmont), by far the dominant tradition is that Jack was buried *'under the church wall'*, sometimes at the Scudamores' chapel at Kentchurch but usually across the river at Grosmont church, where the tombstone mentioned by Evans protrudes from beneath the wall of the south transept.

This tombstone is part of the pathway adjoining the church – and when the sunlight falls at a shallow angle it can be seen that whoever once repaired the path took the trouble to write 'Jack of Kent' in the wet concrete with a stick! This well-known site was pointed out to me by the late vicar of Grosmont, Bill McAdam, when I first began my researches, and while we will soon discover that neither the folkloric Jack of Kent nor Owain Glyndŵr was actually interred at Grosmont, it is nevertheless significant that this alleged burial site is indeed 'under the church wall'. Furthermore, by being buried 'Half-in and Half-out' of the church, Jack is said to have swindled the Devil to the very end (see Legend 23).

Owain Glyndŵr faded from history during 1413, having disappeared entirely by the autumn. We have already concluded that he did not survive the winter of 1414/15 and have therefore assumed his death in February 1415 – and upon revealing his intended place of burial, we will find confirmation that he was almost certainly laid to rest before 18 May of that year. This is the eighteen-month gap in which official history fails, and which we have been attempting to bridge by other means. If the faint-hearted and the sceptical will therefore accompany us across this spectral bridge into the next chapter, it may be that they will be reassured by our discovery of the location of Owain Glyndŵr's intended grave at a place which has never previously been considered.

LEGEND 22 : THE DOVE AND THE RAVEN

On his deathbed, Jack of Kent requested that his liver and lights (lungs) should be impaled upon Grosmont, or some say Kentchurch, steeple. He prophesied that a dove and a raven would come to fight over them, and said that his soul would be saved only if the dove won.

Other versions
This tale is traditionally told in conjunction with Legend 23, and while no one knows how the battle ended, it is often added that a dove was seen flying from Jack's tomb, and it was said by W.H. Greene in the late 1880s that a white dove had appeared on Jack of Kent's tombstone before flying upwards pursued by a jet black raven (after a fierce conflict, the raven returned beaten to the earth, as the dove spiralled upwards out of sight). While three spikes projecting from the tower of Grosmont church are said to have served for the impaling, another version suggests the spiked railings around the same church, and there is also a little-known version in which the outcome would simply be a good harvest if the dove won. Another account asserts that consumption of the remains by birds would constitute proof of Jack's wizardry, while it has also been said that Jack's destiny revolved purely around whether or not the remains were devoured by carrion birds.

There is also a strange variation of 'The Dove and the Raven' preserved in the Welsh tradition (Peniarth MS. 114,110), which is as follows: 'When Sioni Cent heard that the Devil was preparing a place for him in Hell, he made his friend heat up an oven, and he went inside to burn himself. He said that afterwards he should be taken out, and his heart removed and put to one side, while keeping it away from any crows (ravens) which might attempt to make off with it. He also told his friend that when doves were seen flying overhead, they should be allowed to carry the heart away, and that if they did his soul would be saved, and it was said that this happened.'

[See also Appendix 1, p. 290.]

LEGEND 23 : HALF-IN and HALF-OUT

Jack of Kent was a wizard in league with the Devil. While still a boy he had sold his body and soul to 'The Old 'Un' in return for supernatural powers, and the contract was to stand whether he were buried inside or outside the church. But Jack arranged to be buried Half-in and Half-out, directly under the church wall, thus swindling the Devil to the last. A stone protruding from under the south wall of Grosmont church is said to mark Jack's grave.

[See also Appendix 1, p. 292.]

FOURTEEN

THE DOVE AND THE RAVEN
(563–1415)

While evidence exists that Sir John Scudamore's illegal marriage to Alice became known considerably earlier, its official exposure occurred in 1433 as the culmination of a dispute with the Earl of Somerset (see Epilogue), whereupon it brought an ignominious end to Scudamore's glittering baronial career. Scudamore's lands and activities would certainly have been investigated at that point, and it would also have been suspected, especially by those in the Monnow Valley who remembered the visitations to Kentchurch of a certain Grey Friar from Dorstone, that Scudamore had at some stage given shelter to his outlawed in-law.

We certainly share such suspicions, not only because after Scudamore's marriage to Alice in *c.* 1404 it appears that he became a secret agent working *against* the Crown, but also because we have accepted the basic premise offered at Kentchurch Court – namely that in the Monnow Valley and south Herefordshire of 1433, Jack of Kent had become synonymous with Owain Glyndŵr. This being the case, let us take a final leap of faith – and consider the logical implication that the fabulous folklore describing the death and burial of Jack of Kent (see Legends 22 and 23) might actually refer directly to the death and burial of Owain Glyndŵr.

Until today, the modern inhabitants of south Herefordshire and Monmouthshire have long since forgotten whether the folkloric Jack of Kent should be identified with a rector of Kentchurch in the 1380s who happened to rejoice in the common medieval name John of Kent, a Welsh bard who styled himself

Siôn Cent, Owain Glyndŵr, or perhaps one of the various earlier candidates with whom the name has also been associated (see Preface). However, while ignoring Jack's ultimate identity, the locals have remained fascinated by the purported story of his death – and the two birds which attended it.

Upon his death Jack is said to have requested that his liver and lungs should be impaled on Grosmont church steeple, for he prophesied that a dove and a raven would come to fight over them, and declared that the outcome would indicate the destiny of his soul. This has hitherto been seen simply as a spiritual metaphor regarding whether Jack would go to Heaven or Hell – as may well have been the intention of whoever first appropriated this story to the demise of Jack of Kent (Owain Glyndŵr). However, as we shall see, the origins of this tale lie in a very different era, and it has many layers which belie its apparent simplicity.

The first thing to remember regarding the flights of the Dove and the Raven through time and space, is that both birds were originally pre-Christian pagan symbols, long-recognised by the Celts as representing the opposite aspects of a virgin who was originally the Neolithic Moon-Goddess – i.e. she of both the full-lunar whiteness (Dove) and the creative darkness (Raven) of the Celtic 'deep'. However, in Britain it was the Raven and not the Dove which achieved major cult status, since the positive (white) aspect of the goddess was more popularly symbolised by creatures more directly associated with fertility – such as the cult of the White Sow (Pig).

In those days no disharmony existed between the forces of light and darkness, for the Celtic Otherworld accepted and embraced both forces as opposite aspects of the same creative and destructive deity, the virginal goddess, whose capricious whim controlled the mysteries of time and tides, and regarding whose 'fowl of the air' we will start by considering the flight of the Raven.

As we have seen, from the days of Neolithic sky-burial to the entrail-inspections of the Druids (see Chapter 1), the Raven-cult was traditionally at home in northern Europe, especially in Viking Scandinavia and also in Celtic Britain where great tribal leaders and warrior-kings were 'Ravens', corn was the recycled flesh of the earth, and corvine raids upon it were a regular feature of everyday life. Then came the Roman occupation of Britain and the adoption of Christianity as the official religion of the Roman Empire. As we know (see Chapter 2), instead of provoking a religious conflict in Britain between the Celts and their Roman masters, this had produced a Romano-Celtic-Christian compromise wherein the Celts were allowed to interpret the new religion in terms of the old. As a result the Celts remained partially pagan, and the flight of the Raven continued alongside Christianity, both during the Roman occupation and after the Roman departure in AD 410 – whereupon the Celts were harassed by the Anglo-Saxons who were raiding and invading the eastern coast of Britain.

The initial Anglo-Saxon invasion was at best a piecemeal affair, but in the late 500s matters came to a head when it became evident that Celts could no longer pass east of the Pennines because all the lands there were controlled by Anglo-Saxons who considered themselves a superior race. Britain was split along its length by the central Pennine divide across which the heathen Angles of Northumbria faced the nominally Christian Romano-Celtic 'ravens' of the north-west, led by Urien and his son Owein – the legendary Ravens of Rheged.

At this stage, the modernisation of Christianity, which had been proceeding apace in an embattled Rome, had had little or no impact upon mainland Britain where the Anglo-Saxon barbarians had overrun half the country, paganism still frequently ruled the roost and the corvine cosmology of the Morrigan was more likely than Yarweh to have inspired King Urien when he prepared himself for battle.

Ireland, meanwhile, was a relatively tranquil island which had recently become one of the most erudite cultural centres in western Europe. Here, early Christianity had not only taken root but had blossomed into an independent Celtic-Christian tradition – and so it was that in 563 there set sail from Ulster a legendary 'Dove' – St Columba of Donegal – whose historic ambition was to convert the pagan Ravens of north-west Britain to a truer Celtic Christianity.

The Dove and the Raven

Doves, of course, belong to the family Columbidae (and are thus the inhabitants of 'columbariums'), and so Christianity having appropriated the symbol of this bird (not least as a useful antidote to the Raven-cult of the pagans of northern Europe), St Columba swiftly founded his own ecclesiastical 'dovecote' just off the west coast of Scotland, on the island of Iona. With his monastery thus established, there rapidly ensued a supernatural contest between the Dove and the Raven as they met for the first time since leaving the Ark – their conflict being a spiritual clash between the Christian concept of Heaven and Hell (schizophrenically opposed and each absolute) and the old Celtic Otherworld (embracing both light and darkness as aspects of a greater whole).

It is only possible here to relate a few details of St Columba's mission to northern Britain, but it constituted what was initially a purely metaphysical struggle for Christian supremacy over the old Celtic Otherworld. At Loch Ness, Columba is said to have mastered a terrible water-monster which arose from the dark waters of the Celtic 'deep' (Môr), and to have serenely defied an occult wind impeding the progress of his boat along the loch, whereafter he is said to have expelled evil spirits from the waters of a well. These are pro-Christian tales, in which Columba defies with impunity the ancient goddess of the elements in her capacity as the mistress of the 'deep'. However, St Columba did not get it all his own way in the folkloric account, as is illustrated by the following tradition which recalls a disagreement between St Columba and his 'brother', St Oran (who may either have been one of his monks or a purely figurative character). This is a dispute which not only illustrates the difference between the Celtic and Christian Otherworlds, but which also shows the Raven in conflict with the Dove.

Upon Iona it is said that the walls of St Columba's monastery collapsed just as fast as they were built (very much in the manner of Jacky Kent's Bridge, and doubtless due to a similar presence of 'evil' pre-Christian spirits within the stones: see Legend 1). The only solution was to consecrate the ground with a Christian burial, and therefore, having recently argued with Columba regarding the nature of Heaven and Hell, St Oran boldly volunteered to be buried alive, and descended accordingly into the earth. Twenty days later his burial site was excavated – whereupon Oran's head made the following inconvenient announcement . . .

> Heaven is not what it is said to be
> Hell is not what it is said to be
> The saved are not forever happy
> The damned are not forever lost.

An embarrassed Columba at once declared that an evil spirit must be speaking through Oran's mouth, and ordered that the pit be filled once and for all, after which he is said to have observed Oran's soul ascending to Heaven in the midst of an airborne battle between Angels and Demons.

St Oran (or 'Dobhran') is, of course, a Raven opposed to St Columba's Dove – and a bold and disconcerting one at that. As a typical Romano-Celtic Christian, he lay stubbornly in the middle-ground upon which paganism and Christianity had originally made their compromise under the Romans – and thus, while prepared to nod in the direction of the Lord, and to accept Jesus Christ as an example of a great king, he still believed the forces of creation and destruction to be interdependent parts of a greater recycling whole – Mother Nature.

Until about AD 300, the female principle of creation had been accommodated in Christianity by 'Sophia', but she had since been suppressed and demonised. In Columba's time, St Oran was thus a Devil's Advocate in the form of a singing skull – for in Gaelic *oran* means to 'sing', as per the singing of oracular skulls. Furthermore, Oran's performance on Iona was indeed that of a classic pagan Celtic tribal leader, undergoing a voluntary death before returning from the Otherworld to sing prophecies, observing that the new Christianity was fundamentally wrong about the afterlife, while proving that Christ was not the only great king who could return from the dead for the benefit of all.

In the end, the upshot of this dispute was an airborne conflict between the forces of light and darkness over St Oran's ascending soul – thus testifying that St Columba had set himself a substantial task in attempting to convert the pagan Ravens of the north-west – for as Delaney remarks (*The Celts*) – 'the Morrigan appears as the goddess of war, and when the Christians arrived . . . clearly offered a challenge to any new belief'.

At this early stage in the battle between the Dove and the Raven it is interesting to notice the delicacy with which the dove-like St Columba approached the problem of impressing Christianity upon the pagans of the north-west at a time when the most prominent of its leaders was that mighty Raven, Urien of Rheged. As an Irishman who had recently supported the aspirations of the bards in Ireland, Columba was himself a Celt, and thus when seeking to interest the pagans of northern Britain in Christianity it is said that he finally decided to put it to them thus: 'Christ is the new Druid' – after which the Celts cheerfully persisted even into the Middle Ages in referring to all reincarnated leaders and great kings, including Jesus Christ and Owain Glyndŵr, as Mab Darogans or Sons of Prophecy.

Was Urien of Rheged converted at some stage from a Raven to a Dove – or was he that third bird, piebald and so controversial to the Celts, a magpie? We cannot be sure, but it is certainly interesting that Urien's personal bards were Llywarch Hen, who rescued his skull after his assassination in *c*. 590, and the legendary Taliesin, co-founder with Merlin of the Dark Age bardic 'Song of Prophecy' which predicted the return by reincarnation of great ancestral Celtic leaders. Indeed, Taliesin once famously declared: 'I am old. I am new. I have been dead. I have been alive.' – thus showing that he sang exquisitely from the songsheet of St Oran.

Whether or not Urien's son Owein remained pagan is much harder to say, although his brother Rhun apparently became a Christian missionary (see Chapter 5). On the other hand, Owein of Rheged is remembered for his 'bodyguard of fierce ravens', and in the opinion of Rutherford (*Celtic Mythology*) he was 'probably a pagan'. In fact of course it is impossible to know precisely where, or upon what compromises, such individuals pitched their spiritual tents, or to what extent they may have later adjusted their positions. This was a moment when paganism and Christianity were fused and in a state of flux, and Ravens such as Urien and Owein, whose familiarity with Christianity derived from the Roman era, were receiving the fresh attentions of the Dove of St Columba. However, it is this very ambiguity regarding the religious credentials of the House of Rheged in *c.* 600 that would one day lay Owain Glyndŵr open to questioning as to whether his claim of descent from Owein of Rheged made him a Dove – or a Raven.

It is a remarkable characteristic of the Neolithic goddess that throughout history she has proved impossible to suppress, not least because her principle is so deep-rooted and widespread, and her imagery is so endlessly reiterated in nature and in agriculture. The Romans in Britain had merely drawn a veil of Christianity over the goddess and the Otherworld, and so in 563 we find St Columba's attempt to bury St Oran in consecrated soil still thwarted by the fact that for many the subterranean realm remained the Celtic 'deep'. Thus, for all the progress which Columba subsequently made, and which caused him to be remembered as one of the greatest Christian missionaries of his day, the goddess and the Otherworld persisted, the Morrigan flew on into the Dark Ages, and the Raven survived its first encounter with the Dove.

In 597 St Columba died, and in the same year St Augustine arrived in Kent (see Preface). Having established himself as the first Archbishop of Canterbury, he proceeded to disseminate the modernised version of Christianity which had been developed in Rome. This was much more confrontational than the gentle 'hu-ing' adopted by Columba, and it made no compromise in polarising the afterlife and demanding a stark and immediate choice between light and darkness, Heaven or Hell. Whereas the Celtic Christianity of Columba had sought to engage ravens in gentle discussion, St Augustine simply regarded all non-Christians and deviants from the orthodoxy of Rome as manifestations of the Christian Devil, and his message was a stark 'Whose side are you on?' Nevertheless, despite the hellfire of St Augustine's preaching, which he doubtless believed was inspired by the columbine Holy Spirit, the Dove and the Raven remained in flux, as the kingdoms of Kent, East Anglia and Northumbria were first converted to Christianity and then reverted to paganism.

Meanwhile in the north, the spiritual battle between the Dove and the Raven would soon become a military conflict. The year 590 had seen the death of Urien of Rheged just as he was besieging the Angles of Northumbria. This had brought the rapid collapse of a demoralised Rheged as the network of northern alliances upon which it had depended fell apart, and the door was thus opened to Northumbrian retaliation against a Rheged that was now led by Urien's son Owein. Unfortunately for Owein, the momentum was suddenly with the Northumbrians, and the consequence was their invasion and conquest of Rheged, as they embarked upon a massive advance into Cumbria and Cheshire – a tidal wave before which Owein of Rheged and his 'bodyguard of fierce ravens' may well have fled like outlaws into Wales.

In 634, the new ruler of Northumbria, King Oswald, was converted to the Celtic Christian tradition of St Columba and thus became a Dove duly known as 'Oswald of the White Sword'. Soon afterwards, his newly Christian forces confronted a Welsh-Mercian alliance led by King Penda at the battle of 'Catscaul', which Steve Blake and Scott Lloyd (*The Keys to Avalon*) correctly site at Oswestry, and at which Oswald himself was killed.

Notwithstanding Penda's victory at Oswestry, the truth was that Old Wales was under attack and was finding it increasingly difficult to defend its eastern border along the River Severn. With the collapse of Rheged, all influence in Cumbria and Cheshire had been lost, while Celtic control of the Severn Estuary had been relinquished, and as a result the Severn boundary of Old Wales was now vulnerable to substantially increased pressure from both north and south. As a result, the Welsh were becoming ever more powerfully aware of the overwhelming strategic importance of the geographical truth which had already been highlighted by Cawrdaf – i.e. the terrible vulnerability of Deheubarth in the south-west to invasion via Radnorshire and Brycheiniog (Breconshire), and the terminal outcome for the Celtic cause if the south-west were ever to be lost.

For this reason, when Owein of Rheged fled southward from his homeland in the early 600s with his 'bodyguard of fierce ravens', it is entirely reasonable to suggest that his destination was Deheubarth, where his father is said to have held Carreg Cennen Castle adjacent to the Tywi Valley and Cantref Mawr. If this is indeed where Owein the Raven finally came to roost, then we may be certain that his last energies were spent in securing the haft of Cawrdaf's Spear in the valley of the Tywi, while urging those in Brycheiniog and Radnorshire to hold it at all costs against the Saxons. However, despite their efforts, in the course of the next century the Welsh would be driven back from the convex Severn boundary towards the flat border of the reduced (modern) Wales which would one day be marked by Offa's Dyke.

In the 800s, Wales was consolidated under Rhodri Mawr, just as the Northumbrians were suddenly overwhelmed by Vikings who arrived in ships festooned with flags depicting the Morvran (sea-raven) of the Scandinavian version of the 'deep'. Leaving Wales relatively undisturbed, the Vikings then proceeded to raze the entire network of Anglo-Saxon kingdoms until King Alfred and his family finally managed to restore the status quo during the 900s, establishing England in the process.

Next came the Norman invasion, resisted in Wales by the (Raven) family of Dinefwr (Cantref Mawr), who finally succumbed when Rhys ap Tewdwr was slain while attempting to bolster Brycheiniog (see Chapter 3) – and following which the Lord Rhys and his family proclaimed their corvine descent from Owein and Urien of Rheged as they repeatedly sought to restore Deheubarth's influence in Brycheiniog and Radnorshire.

During the Middle Ages, Rome and the Anglo-Norman medieval Church promoted the Dove as the symbol of the Holy Spirit, and tried to pave over all pre-Christian concepts such as goddesses who would not lie down, spirits of the 'deep' who evaporated from wells and waterways, and Orans who refused to sleep and made corvine remarks about the afterlife – and at last came Owain Glyndŵr's death in early 1415 – and the clash of the Dove and the Raven over the liver and lungs of Jack of Kent, folklorically impaled upon Grosmont church steeple.

As the Dove and the Raven converged in mid-air over Jack's mortal remains they were aware that they had performed this aerial ballet a thousand times before – for their struggle was not unique to Jack of Kent. In Scotland, similar tales are found commemorating Columba's efforts to convert the ravens of the north and west. At Ardmore, for example, facing Whiteface and Clashmore across the waters of Dornoch Firth, there is a tale concerning a fisherman, the liver of a fish, a boy whose soul belongs to the Devil but who tries to evade the contract, cremation, and a battle between three doves and three ravens. At Skye, the next major island north of Iona off the west coast, we find the popular tale of a dying girl who prophesies that upon her death either a dove or a raven would enter the room to determine the destiny of her soul. At Vatersay, but set upon the next island north at Uig near 'Crowlister' on Lewis (a waterlogged expanse permeated by lochs and inlets such as 'Ora[n]say' and 'Ardmore Mangersta'), there is a tale involving a corpse-candle, a stone of prophecy, the daughter of a Viking king, and a contest between a dove and a raven, wherein the dove descends to demonstrate the innocence of a dead boy.

Meanwhile, the exodus of traumatised Celts to the continent after the departure of the Romans in AD 410 had laid the basis of the traditional Welsh link to Brittany – where the following story is told: a sinful woman accused of incest, and whose soul therefore surely belonged to the Devil, once attempted to get into Heaven by being buried in a chest. When it was opened it contained only a little piece of her heart. This was placed on top of a wall by a priest, whereafter a dove and a raven came to fight over it.

The crucial conflict in such tales frequently focuses on a piece of the heart, as in the 'oven' variant of the Jack of Kent story involving cremation. In the standard version, however, the Dove and the Raven were interested in Jack's liver and lungs, which were of course standard post-battle carrion fare for ravens. Upon inspecting and ingesting such entrails, especially the liver, the Raven became a bird of prophecy and could predict the occasion and outcome of future conflicts (from which process derives the term 'lily-livered', to describe someone whose liver is pale through lack of blood). Before any battle, therefore, the liver of a sacrificial victim would be consulted by Druids and seers, and its colour considered as an omen of the outcome, a technique also once favoured by the King of Babylon (Ezekiel 21: 21). Finally, it is of course noticeable that liver and lungs would have appealed to a raven, which is a carrion bird, but not to a dove, which is not. However, following the harvest, doves and ravens scavenge the fields in close company, but in separate gangs, for fallen ears of wheat – and thus we are reminded that 'all flesh is corn' (see Chapter 1).

In conclusion, our analysis of the battle between the Dove and the Raven over Jack's remains indicates that the story is Dark Age in origin, that it concerns the conversion to Christianity of the Celts, and that it was therefore both available and appropriate during the Middle Ages for application to Owain Glyndŵr, of whom it would have posed a traditional and relevant question regarding his religious position. Furthermore, the theme of the Dove and the Raven was evidently widespread, and was popular in medieval Scotland, Wales and Brittany – and it is consequently most unlikely that anyone would have been more than mildly amused to hear it adapted to Owain Glyndŵr in the early 1400s. Indeed, even an English agent who happened to overhear this familiar religious controversy being applied to that recently deceased Jack of Kent in the area of the Monnow Valley would surely have assumed it to be an irrelevance – which, as we shall see by the end of this chapter, it is not.

Having fully considered his death, let us now examine the folkloric details of Jack's burial. In his youth we hear that Jack of Kent had sold himself to the Devil in exchange for supernatural powers, whereafter the Devil would have his soul whether he were buried inside or outside the church. Jack then swindled the Devil to the end by being buried 'Half-in and Half-out' of the church – i.e. directly under the church wall (see Legend 23).

Uncertain as to whether this refers to the Scudamore's chapel at Kentchurch or to Grosmont church on the opposite bank of the Monnow, this story has created the local tradition that Jack was buried under the church wall (see Legend 23) in one of these two places, and has led to a particular tombstone under the south wall of Grosmont church becoming known as Jack of Kent's Grave. This is a fabulous piece of folklore but, just like the Dove and the Raven, 'Half-in and Half-out' is also a Celtic tale, and its origins are probably even older.

We are first reminded of 'Half-in and Half-out' when we recall the burial sites of ancient Celtic kings, which lay upon high ground above tribal boundary rivers. As the mighty ancestral leader 'flowed away' and thus charged the defensive waters with his protective spirit, he therefore lay 'Half-in and Half-out' of the territory of the tribe.

Later, the delicate spiritual position of such venerated local ancestors was confirmed by incoming Christianity in another sense, insofar as the official policy of Rome regarding such awkward cases as dead but unbaptised infants, and those who had lived in pre-Christian times, was that they lay neither in Heaven nor in Hell, but in Limbo, which by the time of Dante's *Divine Comedy* (c. 1320) had been moved for political reasons from a neutral position to a zone on the outskirts of Hell.

It is thus reasonable to assume that the idea of 'Half-in and Half-out' was a poignant one for the Celts, especially since under the Romans they had once been allowed to remain happily 'Half-in and Half-out' of Christianity, while the Celtic Otherworld continued to offer an all-embracing and recycling Limbo, rather than a stark choice between Heaven and Hell. Thus, in metaphysical terms we can see that 'Half-in and Half-out' is where the Celtic spirit naturally lay, perhaps having its origins in the physical location of buried tribal kings upon the river-boundaries where they slept 'Half-in and Half-out' of life.

However, the arrival of Christianity in Britain also reinforced the idea of 'Half-in and Half-out' in a more physical way.

It is well known that the first churches in Britain were superimposed upon ancient burial sites of pagan significance to the Celts, and that these sites were frequently near tribal river-boundaries. Such places were often marked by revered assemblies of sacred (White) stones known as cromlechs, and so the builders of these early churches frequently faced a trilemma as to what to do with the ancient cromlech – should they destroy it, and completely alienate the people they were attempting to convert? Leave it standing, intact, next to the church? Or absorb into their new church the hallowed ancestor (who officially dwelt in Limbo) by incorporating the useful stones into the church walls? Having ceremonially blessed the stones in order to drive out any evil, and to ensure that the walls did not fall down as fast as they were built (see Legend 1), the third was obviously the preferred option. Thus the Limbo of pre-Christian leaders and ideas became physically embodied in the stones of the church wall, 'Half-in and Half-out' of Christian ground.

Such practices had begun when the first Christian saints had used the ancestral standing stones of Neolithic Britain as the basis of the circular enclosures which still surround some of the oldest churches in Wales (such as those at Yspyty Cynfyn just north of Strata Florida and at Llansadwrn in Cantref Mawr). In the days of Owein of Rheged, the need for speed in establishing new churches saw the Pope instructing the Bishop of London to appropriate heathen temples at every opportunity, whereafter a more recent example of the same principle can be found at Llanfor church near Bala Lake in north Wales, where a Dark Age stone bearing the inscription 'CAVOSENIARGII' has been incorporated into the church wall (it has been suggested that this was originally the burial site of Urien's former bard Llywarch Hen, or of Arthur's warrior Cai, although it is more probably that of Caw).

By the Middle Ages the idea of 'Half-in and Half-out' was thus a long-established theme, and it can be illustrated with examples from all over Britain. At Tolleshunt in Essex, 'Barn

Hall' is said to have repeatedly fallen down each night while it was being built, because the Devil objected to its location. A local knight therefore undertook to guard the site during the hours of darkness, whereafter he is said to have triumphed in a struggle with the Devil. However, the Devil defiantly hurled a rafter from the building into the night, declaring that 'Wheresoe'er this beam shall fall, there shall stand Barn Hall' – and predicting that he would have the knight's soul whether he were buried inside or outside the church. After this the knight eluded the Devil by being buried 'Half-in and Half-out', although in another version his heart was torn out by his adversary and was subsequently buried 'under the church wall' by his friends.

This story is reminiscent of countless tales in which the Devil objects to the location of local churches, expressing his resentment either by hurling boulders at them, dismantling them during the night, attacking them with lightning, or picking them up with the aid of a mighty wind and relocating them to the place where they are found the following day. Such stories surely record the opposition of local pagans to the building of churches upon sites of ancient significance and therefore, like the principle of the Dove and the Raven, the principle of 'Half-in and Half-out' was also concerned with the struggle between paganism and Christianity – and it was an even more widespread and ubiquitous theme. It is particularly interesting in this case that in 1131 the Lord of Tolleshunt in Essex was a certain William de Tregoyl of Ewias Harold near Kentchurch in Herefordshire, whose family and lands were closely and constantly associated with the Scudamores, not only at Kentchurch but also at the Scudamores' ancient family seat at Upton Scudamore in Wiltshire, where Tregoyl's grandson was Sheriff in 1192. Thus the Tolleshunt tale may have originated in the Dark Ages before becoming a popular tradition in the Middle Ages, and it thus offers a specific route by which the theme could have become familiar to the Scudamores of the early 1400s. However, by then it was already such a popular theme that it was in any case common currency.

Another example is found at Aldworth in Berkshire, where

the same travelling diarist of the 1600s who recorded a long-vanished relic of Jack of Kent in the graveyard of Grosmont church (see Epilogue) also noted the vanished effigy of a giant at Aldworth, of which he wrote: 'The common people call this "John-Ever-Afraid", and say that he gave his soul to the Devil if ever he was buried either in church or churchyard – so he was buried under the church wall under an arch.'

Meanwhile at Aconbury, near Callow just south of Hereford, a member of the baronial family of De Clifford was also once said to have been buried under the church wall for reasons currently forgotten by the locals, but at which we can certainly guess!

At this point we find a natural development of 'Half-in and Half-out' which was dictated by the need to conserve space within churches while also providing an opportunity for elaborate stonework to decorate prestigious ecclesiastical burials. In order to achieve both objectives simultaneously, the medieval Church soon developed a habit of interring its local luminaries in hollows under arches built into interior church walls, the tombs of such learned clerics being usually inset into the chancel where they could be celebrated on a regular basis by their surviving colleagues. However, by virtue of being 'in' the church wall and 'under' an arch, they were inevitably laid open to dark suggestions by sceptical locals (with whom they were unlikely to have been popular) that they were now 'Half-in and Half-out' themselves and were therefore not proper Christians either. For example, Friar Roger Bacon (1214–91), the Franciscan who famously invented spectacles and brought the recipe for gunpowder to Europe, was accused of witchcraft and was said to have received his knowledge at the expense of having sold his soul to the Devil. Bacon is also said to have fashioned a 'Brazen Head', the oracular function of which would have been familiar to the Celts and the Knights Templar, and which appears to have been singing from the songsheet of Oran and Taliesin when it apparently announced 'Time is. Time was. Time is passed.', before exploding into flames. Bacon is subsequently said to have eluded his contract with the Devil by constructing a cell underneath the friary wall, in which he both lived and died.

Similarly, at Brent Pelham church in Hertfordshire a hollow in the wall houses the tomb of one Piers Shonks, a 'giant' who slew a dragon representing the Devil, before being confronted by the Devil himself – whereupon the latter promptly swore that he would have Shonks's soul whether he were buried inside or outside the church. However, as Shonks lay upon his deathbed he drew his bow and loosed an arrow which struck the north wall of the church, thus indicating his equivocal burial site and outwitting the Devil to the last. A tradition dating from c. 1600 offers Shonks's date of death as 1086. However, evidence shows that, whoever he may originally have been, at least some of Shonks's current identity is derived from one Peter Shank, the local beneficiary of a grant from the Earl of Arundel (d. 1397), who interestingly was overlord to the young Owain Glyndŵr in north Wales (which reminds us that 'sionc' is Welsh for 'sprightly'). Finally we observe that a moated building called Shonks' Barn stood at Brent Pelham in c. 1700, and that the habit of firing an arrow from one's deathbed in order to determine one's place of burial was traditionally practised by a certain Robin Hood.

Meanwhile, at Tidenham near Chepstow, on the north bank of the Severn estuary there is a small stone in the churchyard wall which is said to mark the 'Half-in and Half-out' burial of the 'Tidenham Witch', and which illustrates that as time passed the use of any supernatural forces not derived from God and wielded by his priests increasingly became a matter for persecution on a 'Whose side are you on?' basis. It is also no coincidence that jackdaws and ravens became the favourite familiars of witches, who, like the Druids, practised augury, and that this was also the corvine lifestyle of a witch at neighbouring Berkeley in Gloucestershire who, having sold her soul to the Devil, dismally failed to evade the contract. A later tradition of burying witches under church walls thus arose for reasons which were originally much older, as the state continued to demonise its opponents under the auspices of Rome, on the basis of a paganism that it had once identified with the Celts.

Finally, some other salient examples spring to mind of medieval burials 'in' the church wall: the Welsh Bishop John Trefnant at Hereford Cathedral (d. 1404); the now-debunked site of Glyndŵr's alleged burial in Bangor Cathedral, which probably belongs to the Lord Rhys's northern colleague Owain Gwynedd (d. 1170); and the sinister-looking priest of unknown identity whose effigy lies surrounded by deliberately defaced stonework in Kempsford church, which faces Upton Scudamore across the Thames in Wiltshire.

Our overall conclusion is that both the 'Dove and the Raven' and the 'Half-in and Half-out' themes had emerged from the Dark Ages and were thus *available* for medieval application to Owain Glyndŵr. Furthermore, since both themes concerned the conflict between the Celtic Otherworld and incoming Christianity, they were also *appropriate* for medieval application to Owain Glyndŵr. It is true that either of these themes would have been equally applicable to *any* Celtic leader from the Dark Ages onwards, and in any case by the 1400s both these themes were surely so ubiquitous that even an English agent overhearing *both* stories being applied to the late Jack of Kent (Owain Glyndŵr) in a single breath (as they significantly still are) would have taken no notice – and yet how very wrong he would have been!

When I first began my researches into Jack o' Kent, I was intrigued by a character in folklore. Owain Glyndŵr was but one of many suggested contenders for the role. I did not expect him to prove an especially strong candidate, and I was not remotely concerned with discovering his place of burial. The task which I had set myself was in fact 'to fully account for the origin and evolution of the Jack of Kent legends as they exist today'.

It was only after I had investigated many of the other candidates and various aspects of the legends in great detail that I was almost reluctantly driven to the conclusion that in the area of south Herefordshire and Monmouthshire in the early 1400s Jack of Kent probably meant Owain Glyndŵr – and it was even more reluctantly that I would eventually take seriously the extraordinary possibility that the death and burial of Jack of Kent might therefore relate to the fate of Owain Glyndŵr – let alone be a deliberate clue as to where he was buried.

As a result, having studied the life of the Mab Darogan in his apparent capacity as a folkloric figure of Kentchurch and the Monnow Valley, I had initially dismissed as silly a certain cadence which I occasionally noticed between the high-point of Owain Glyndŵr's military career, and the death of Jack of Kent. The high-point of Glyndŵr's military career was undoubtedly his successful invasion of the Tywi Valley in 1403, an historic campaign that saw the liberation of the ancient Welsh kingdom of Deheubarth and its spiritual heartland of Cantref Mawr, with the immediate result that the English were temporarily hurled out of the Principality, and Glyndŵr's coronation at Harlech was made possible the following year. This well-planned seizure of the strategically crucial south-western key to an independent Wales was, as I have pointed out, both forecast and concealed in a poem written by Glyndŵr's personal bard Iolo Goch (the 'Strolling Tour'), in which the 1403 campaign was outlined by a cumulative sequential code, in which the elements seemed innocent enough on their own, but when added together delineated the geography of the 'Tour'.

So it was that Owain Glyndŵr's liberation of Cantref Mawr in 1403 began amid much violence when he entered the area at the north-eastern end, marked by the royal English stronghold of Llandovery, before progressing down the Tywi Valley to the south-western end, marked by the ancient royal stronghold of the Welsh rulers of Deheubarth at Dinefwr (Llandeilo). As a student of the legends of Jack of Kent, it was therefore inevitable that whenever I took the road-map from the glove-compartment of my car in order to trace the details of Glyndŵr's 1403 campaign, I could not help but notice the fact that at one end of the Tywi Valley in Cantref Mawr stood Llan-DOVE-ry, and at the other stood Dinefwr (Llandeilo), the RAVEN headquarters of the Lord Rhys and ancient Deheubarth. However, I immediately assumed that such an apparently frivolous resonance with the Dove and Raven demise of Jack of Kent was so banal as to be nothing but a coincidence, and for a year or so I forgot all about it – until one day when I was revisiting the 1403 campaign I noticed something else.

Equidistant from Llandovery and Llandeilo, and less than 3 miles from the western bank of the Twyi, is the village of Halfway. Noticing this, I think I muttered 'Good heavens! A Dove and a Raven and a Halfway!' – but it was not until the following morning, when I was embroiled in coffee, toast and marmalade, that I peered once again at the map and noticed the existence of *another* village also called Halfway, which lies on the eastern bank of the Tywi, just four miles from Llandovery. Halfway through the next piece of toast, it occurred to me that in Glyndŵr's day, as viewed from Cantref Mawr, the eastern Halfway lay on the side of the river that was directly administered by the Duchy of Lancaster and thus the English Crown, and would therefore undeniably have been 'Halfway-in', while the western Halfway lay on the side of the river which did *not* belong to the English Crown – and would therefore most certainly have been 'Halfway-out'.

Taking a pencil and a ruler I slowly drew two lines, one running straight down the River Tywi between the Dove (Llandovery) and the Raven (Dinefwr/Llandeilo), and the other joining 'Halfway-in' and 'Halfway-out'. Sure enough, the two lines bisected, forming a cross (or a sword), lying in the road on the A40 and directly obstructing the time-honoured invasion-route into south-west Wales, as if to say 'over my dead body!'. Furthermore, the two lines did not bisect in the middle of nowhere, as they might easily have done, but crossed very precisely at a little village called Llanwrda, about which I knew nothing.

For some days I stared at the 'X' on my road-map, wondering if I was still being silly and if it was simply an odd coincidence, and then I began to subject 'the four stations of the cross' to a closer scrutiny. If the 'X' in south-west Wales was indeed what I was hardly daring to suspect, then it was effectively the product of a cumulative sequential code exactly like that used by Iolo Goch in the 'Strolling Tour'. Told separately, the stories of the 'Dove and the Raven', and 'Half-in and Half-out' seemed innocent enough, but add them together, as in the case of Jack of Kent, and they suddenly meant something else – geography.

It soon occurred to me that if Jack of Kent was indeed Owain Glyndŵr, and he was actually buried at the centre of the 'X', then a burial site in Cantref Mawr could scarcely be more appropriate – for all the reasons so well understood by such military strategists as Cawrdaf, Urien and Owein of Rheged, Henry I, Henry II, the Lord Rhys, and by now the attentive reader of this book. Furthermore, with his distant northern home destroyed and under English scrutiny, a southern burial in Cantref Mawr would see Owain Glyndŵr returned to his other home, where his mother's family had facilitated his claim to the royal line of the south. It would thus simultaneously reiterate his desire to unite north and south Wales, illustrate the bottom line of Welsh military strategy in a graphic statement of defiance, commemorate the high-point of his own military career, and propagate a spiritual barrier to all foreign invaders of the south-west as his spirit 'flowed' forever into the nearby Tywi, charging the defensive boundary river of the strategically crucial Deheubarth.

However, despite this enchanting logic, I was not going to buy the validity of the 'X' so easily, and so I proceeded to question the viability of each of the four stations of the cross . . .

LEGEND 24 : JACK OF FRANCE

There once lived in Dorstone a man called Jack of France, an evil-doer, and a terror to all peaceable folk. One night, on the Eve of All Souls, he was passing through the churchyard and saw a light shining in all the windows of the church. He looked in and saw a large congregation assembled, listening apparently to the preaching of a man in a monk's habit who was declaiming from the pulpit the names of all those who were to die the coming year. The preacher lifted his head, and Jack saw under the cowl the features of the Prince of Darkness himself, and to his horror heard his own name given out amongst the list of those whom death should claim. He went home then, and repenting too late of his evil deeds, took to his bed and died. (E.M.Leather, *The Folk-Lore of Herefordshire*)

Other versions
While there are no other versions of this story as such, or any other stories of Jack of France, there are excellent reasons to presume that Jack of France is in fact identical with Jack of Kent.

[See also Appendix 1, p. 293.]

LEGEND 25 : THE WIZARD OF GROSMONT

A prevailing tradition is that an old wizard disguised in a shepherd's habit once frequented Kentchurch House and roamed about the neighbourhood of Grosmont. His remains are said to be buried under the stone called John of Kent's tomb. (Evans and Britton, *Topographical and Historical Tour of the County of Monmouthshire*)

[See also Appendix 1, p. 294.]

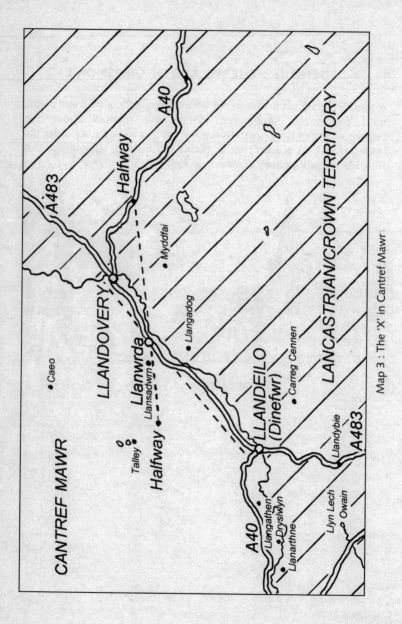

Map 3 : The 'X' in Cantref Mawr

FIFTEEN

JACK-IN-THE-BOX
(1415)

Regarding the long axis of the 'X' which, if we are correct, is defined by the DOVE of Llandovery and the RAVEN of Dinefwr (Llandeilo), our confidence increases when we hear that the holy cross was indeed sometimes depicted with a dove at the head end, in accordance with the dove's Christian role as the Holy Spirit or Messenger of God, which descends from on high – as in the baptism story. One example of this is *La Vierge Ouvrante*, which was painted in the 1300s and is now kept at the Museum of Cluny in France, while a more ancient precursor might be the cruciform goddess with a crown of lunar doves found at Knossos in Crete which dates from *c.* 1300 BC.

Meanwhile our confidence increases further when we find the holy cross effectively depicted with the Morrigan at its foot. An example of this is to be found at St Mary's church in Brent Pelham in Berkshire, where Piers Shonks (see Chapter 14) is allegedly buried 'Half-in and Half-out' in a tomb recessed into the church wall and covered by a black marble slab. The carving upon this slab not only features the symbols of the Four Evangelists (also featured in Upton Scudamore church in Wiltshire) but its central image is a cross with its foot firmly planted in the mouth of a dragon. Dragons are well known in imagery and folklore to represent the Devil (having been demonised by the Church as serpents, to the detriment of such dragon-fanciers as the Welsh), and, as we know, the Devil was used by the Christian Church to imply *all* supernatural powers which were 'not of God' – especially the Morrigan.

221

Thus the holy cross was indeed used to reflect Heaven above and Hell below, and the idea of a Dove at its head and a Raven at its foot makes perfect sense. However, such an image would have been seen very differently by those with a Romano-Celtic-Christian perspective, for they saw the forces of light and darkness as dual aspects of a single nature, and doubtless pointed out that Yahweh was also responsible for the forces of darkness. Therefore, from their point of view the bright summit of the cross was not merely incomplete, but actually impractical, without the darkness at its foot.

Among such Gnostic thinkers were of course the Knights Templar, whose temple on Garway Hill had always overshadowed Kentchurch Court. Their sympathies traditionally lay with the Cistercians and the Welsh, while their errant ways allegedly included the (Celtic) head cult. They were therefore keenly aware of Ravens, while their public symbol was the Dove, and their known penchant for laying out large-scale symbology upon the landscape might well have inspired recognition of the 'X' in south-west Wales.

Regarding the short axis of the 'X', we have already explained that it is marked by two villages on opposite sides of the river, which, if they existed at the time, would have been 'Halfway-in' and 'Halfway-out' of Crown territory. So the important question is, 'Were all four stations of the cross in south-west Wales recognisable, and available, six hundred years ago in the early 1400s?'

STATION I: LLANDOVERY

The Anglicised appearance of a dove in such diverse place-names as Llandovery ('Llanymd-dyf-ri') in south Wales and Aberdovey ('Aber-dyf-i') in north Wales testifies to a long-standing awareness that the Welsh '*dyf*', meaning water or waterway, and the English '*dove*' share the same pronunciation. However, while the unrecorded origin of the 'dyf-dove' pun has hitherto been seen as so trivial an affair that neither Welsh nor English historians have paid it much attention, we may assume that, if the 'dyf-dove' pun is still exploited today, then it would doubtless have been exploited long ago by medieval Welsh bards, who nurtured an entire tradition based upon just such macaronic themes. Furthermore, regarding the religious significance of both water and doves, the 'dyf-dove' pun would also have offered a very potent play on words regarding such important medieval matters as the Holy Spirit, the Flood, and the baptism of Christ, as we find in the New Testament (Matthew 4:16), where: 'Jesus . . . went up straightway from the water: and lo, the heavens were opened unto him, and he saw the Spirit of God descending as a dove and coming upon him.'

There is thus no doubt that the potential of the 'dyf-dove' pun increases enormously with the reversal of time, and therefore I suggest that it once circulated around medieval Llandovery ('The Church amidst the Waters') as an oral and colloquial tradition which was popular with the Marcher Welsh, primarily because it offered them a propriety in biblical terms which the contemporary English would have preferred to suppress. Finally our confidence is confirmed when we hear that Llan-dove-ry in its Anglicised form was indeed first recorded in 1116 – sixteen years before the birth of the Lord Rhys and almost three hundred years before the death of Owain Glyndŵr.

STATION II: LLANDEILO (DINEFWR)

We have seen how the Ravens of the Celtic west who succeeded Cawrdaf (c. AD 500) were once hard-pressed to defend the Severn boundary of Old Wales, and how they were thus increasingly forced to attend to the weakness of the potential invasion-route which terminated in the region of Deheubarth and Dinefwr in Cantref Mawr – a mutual concern that forged a lasting relationship between Deheubarth and Brycheiniog. We have also seen how Urien of Rheged – king of the north, husband of the Morrigan and last holder of the Celtic west in c. AD 600 – was said to have held lands in south-west Wales at nearby Carreg Cennen, and how his son Owein might later have flown southward with his 'bodyguard of fierce ravens' to inhabit those lands – where a tradition persists that he still sleeps in the Raven's Cave under Carreg Cennen Castle.

However, at this moment we suddenly find it suggested by Ralph Griffiths (*Sir Rhys ap Thomas and his Family*) that the whole idea of the descent of the House of Deheubarth and Dinefwr from Urien of Rheged was simply invented in the early 1300s by one of the Lord Rhys's descendants – namely a certain Elidir Ddu, who had adopted the name fitz-Urien – thus creating a family tradition which only later caused them to become known as 'The Blood of the Raven'. At this stage in our thesis, this might seem to come as a bombshell – but in fact it causes no problems at all, for the following reasons. Firstly, because it is an allegation that is every bit as unprovable as the Raven-claim itself. Secondly, because Elidir's alleged invention still occurred long before Glyndŵr's war, and in the Middle Ages such inventions were invariably believed (which is why they have survived) in exactly the same way that the medieval Welsh really believed that Urien had married the dark goddess, and that their ancestors had truly been giants – and just as many medieval Normans seriously believed that they could claim ownership of the Arthurian tradition. Thirdly, because at the time of Glyndŵr's death in 1415, and thereafter, the irrepressible descendants of the House of Dinefwr were rising yet again to prominence and dominance in south-west Wales, in the form of a certain Gruffydd ap Nicholas – and so no one was about to dispute the family's continuing claim of descent from Urien of Rheged. Fourthly, because a question which we have yet to address is precisely how long after Glyndŵr's death the cipher of the 'X' was actually distributed, and by whom – and while we have so far assumed that it was rumoured straightaway, it is also perfectly possible that it was written down, put in an envelope and kept in a box for another hundred years – by which time no one in the Monnow Valley remembered what it meant or was certain to whom it applied.

Therefore, for the purposes of the 'X' in Cantref Mawr, we need have no doubt whatsoever that by the 1400s Llandeilo (Dinefwr) was accepted and recognised in the tradition of ancient Deheubarth as the headquarters of the Raven.

STATIONS III AND IV: 'HALFWAY-IN' AND 'HALFWAY-OUT'

Having confirmed the long axis of the cross, we now come to the cross-bar formed by the two villages on either side of the Tywi which both rejoice in the name of Halfway. In terms of their availability during the 1400s we are immediately delighted, because this has always been sheep-droving territory. 'Halfway' is well known to be a sheep-droving name, for excellent sheep-droving reasons – and sheep-droving names and practices are among the most ancient and least changing traditions in the British Isles, to the extent that it would actually be very surprising if these villages had *not* existed in the Middle Ages. With this in mind, let us therefore deal briskly with Halfway-in – the village on the eastern side of the River Tywi, near Llandovery, in territory which in the 1400s belonged to the Duchy of Lancaster and thus to the English Crown.

The year 1977 saw the closure of the Halfway Inn, since when this little village, which once supported three pubs and a post office, has been dying with an aplomb for which it was rewarded in the local publication *Saga* (January 1999) with an amusing article which covered as many pages as there remain viable houses (four), and which observed that Halfway had lately become known as 'the falling-down village'. However, some 220 years ago, in 1780, the volume of traffic through Halfway inspired the building of a new road upon which the London–Milford mail-coach subsequently recorded the second-fastest average speed in Britain. In those days the Royal Oak, the Three Horseshoes and the Halfway Inn were doubtless thriving, and the two long-since ruined Non-Conformist chapels known as Bethesda and Horeb, whose denominations suggest an origin in the 1600s or perhaps even the 1500s, were attracting enthusiastic congregations. On the basis of this, combined with the presence of an ancient droving path parallel to the road, it seems reasonable to assume that there was a significant settlement here in *c.* 1600. I would also suggest that since Halfway lies in a defensible position adjacent to a route last used by the Romans, it may well be a very ancient settlement indeed.

In the Middle Ages, Edward III invited the Flemish weaver John Kempe (see Preface) and others to bring their weaving expertise to Britain in 1331, and this, combined with the drastic fall in population following the Black Death in 1348, led to an upturn in the sheep economy which saw Carmarthen become a major venue for the wool trade in the 1390s, and Llandovery become such a substantial centre that it continues to host a major Sheep-Drovers' Festival to this day. We may therefore be very confident that in the days of Owain Glyndŵr, Halfway-in was a bustling overnight watering-hole for countless drovers of sheep, pigs, chickens and numerous other creatures en route from Llandovery to Pontsenni (Sennybridge), and it was undoubtedly therefore available as a station of the cross in the early 1400s.

This major upturn in the sheep economy immediately before Glyndŵr's war also, of course, bodes well for the fourth station of the cross, namely the other village of Halfway which lies on the western side of the Tywi river, equidistant from Llandovery and Llandeilo, in territory which was not directly administered by the Duchy of Lancaster and the Crown in the 1400s, and which was therefore Halfway-out.

Far less information is available regarding Halfway-out. Like its sister-village it lies at a confluence of streams and is undoubtedly a former sheep-droving settlement and overnight watering-hole lying on the westward route from Llandovery to Carmarthen. The evidence for this, and also for its existence in Glyndŵr's time, comes from the fact that the Cistercian Order was famous for its substantial involvement in sheep-farming – to the extent that wherever a Cistercian abbey is found, one can be confident that its monks were effectively in charge of the local sheep economy. Having said this, it is also the case that the Premonstratensians were so closely identified with the Cistercians (see Chapter 4) that they were essentially variations upon a theme, and thus the Premonstratensians were equally enthusiastic sheep-farmers – and it so happens that Halfway-out is a mere mile from the Premonstratensian abbey of Talley in Cantref Mawr.

In a list of the possessions of Talley Abbey made in 1324 no mention is made of a place called Halfway (for which the Welsh would be 'Hannerford', i.e. 'half-road'), but just eight years later in 1332 (a year after John Kempe had come to Britain) another inventory made during the reign of Edward III promptly lists among the possessions of Talley Abbey a place called simply 'Hanner' – i.e. 'Half' – which, as Jack of Kent might say, was definitely 'Half-out'. This, then, was surely the local sheep-trading and transport-link for the Premonstratensian monks of Talley Abbey, and the overnight watering-station for drovers passing between Carmarthen and Llandovery. Fifteen years later, in 1348, the Black Death arrived, and in its wake the lack of supply and demand for crops saw the great rise of the sheep economy, and the burgeoning of the wool-weaving industry encouraged by Edward III – and thus we may be confident that both Halfways henceforth went from strength to strength, and that they undoubtedly existed in the 1400s.

Therefore, having established that all four stations of the cross were available at the time, and having also established the likelihood that Sir John Scudamore's father-in-law (Owain Glyndŵr) became known as Jack of Kent, I hereby suggest that the story of Jack's demise has nothing whatsoever to do with birds flying around church steeples in pursuit of entrails, or with his grave being beneath a wall at either Grosmont or Kentchurch. Instead, I believe it is a deliberate clue regarding the fate of Owain Glyndŵr, which has been staring everyone in the face for at least half a millennium, and it identifies his burial site, with precision, in the heart of Cantref Mawr.

If this is correct, one cannot help but wonder who would have thought of such a clue, and perhaps the man who can best help us with such an enquiry is our old friend Iolo Goch.

Iolo, as you will recall, was undoubtedly Glyndŵr's friend, perhaps even the bardic inspiration of his war, and as in the 'Strolling Tour' he was evidently a practitioner of the cumulative sequential code. He was also a senior bard, a student of the Dark Age tradition, a self-proclaimed admirer of Urien's bard Taliesin and of Rheged in general, and something of a seer, and in 'knowing Glyndŵr's descent' he would have recognised him as the Mab Darogan and thus prophesied the tradition in which he lay. In other words Iolo Goch held 'deep' opinions concerning Glyndŵr's birth and death from the outset, and thus might easily have been his adviser not only regarding his life, but also his afterlife. Furthermore, other considerations support this general train of thought – for when Iolo arrived at Glyndŵr's opulent home at Sycharth (Llansilin) on the borders of north-east Wales, he entered a building which was shaped like a crucifix, the architecture of which he proceeded to describe with his well-known penchant for precise poetic metre in a way which displays his interest in, and his appreciation of, geometry. He also delights in 'the strength of the cross' and praises the sons of Tudur Fychan as being 'as solid as squares'.

All of this, combined with his authorship of the 'Strolling Tour', portrays a man who is steeped in the cross, and whose interests include prophecy, poetry, geography, geometry and cumulative sequential codes. Furthermore, we know that this north-Walien bard not only wrote a poem outlining a certain 'stroll' around the ancient south-western kingdom of Deheubarth, but also that he had visited Cantref Mawr in person in 1356 to attend the funeral of his old friend Sir Rhys ap Gruffydd of Llansadwrn, who was none other than the contemporary descendant of the Lord Rhys of Dinefwr. Therefore, in consideration of his psychology, and the various details of his life, is it unreasonable to suggest that while visiting Llansadwrn, Iolo might also have visited his friends at the nearby Premonstratensian abbey of Talley?

If so, Iolo would have walked a mere four miles from Llansadwrn, which was actually a possession of Talley Abbey, along the sheep-droving route via Halfway-out, and thence to the abbey itself. In doing so he would have mingled with the mêlée of minstrels, monks, messengers and miscreants who meandered among the drovers of the day, and would thus have been in his element among the people who were ever the experts in travelling across country in medieval Wales.

Like Glyndŵr's house, the towering edifice of Talley Abbey was also built in the shape of a cross, and we have already discussed its probable religious agenda, its role in the subsequent war, and the fact that there was another Premonstratensian House on the Scudamore lands at 'Hamm' (Holme Lacy) just south of Hereford. Therefore we shall leave Iolo in the reception room at Talley, in earnest conversation with some Welsh monks, and perhaps offering to perform a song or two, and we shall never know for sure who first mentioned the well-known local quip about the Dove and the Raven.

The lines upon my road-map had bisected very neatly at a village named Llanwrda, where the church was also a possession of Talley Abbey. At this stage, in consideration of the welcome extended by the Scudamores of Kentchurch Court to both Owain Glyndŵr and his legendary alter-ego Jack of Kent, I had already decided that if Jack were indeed buried at Llanwrda in Cantref Mawr then it was surely the Scudamores of Kentchurch who were most likely to have buried him. This reminded me of a passage in an excellent book by G. Hodges (*Owain Glyndŵr and the War of Independence in the Welsh Borders*). Having done much better than most in attempting to unravel the mystery of Owain's fate, he discusses Glyndŵr's last haunts and talks of 'the perils of the journey to Croft, through country whose inhabitants had many scores to settle with the Welsh, and says, 'In fact the Scudamore manors, which were in Welsh-speaking country, were Owain's only safe haven' and such dangers might also have precluded the transportation of Owain's body from Dorstone, were it not for two things.

First, in early 1415 Sir John Scudamore was a high-flying Marcher lord, who was at that time both the Constable of Carmarthen and the Steward of Kidwelly on behalf of the king, and nobody was going to check *his* luggage. Secondly, as I was subsequently stunned to discover, it is an obscure detail of his career that from 1407 to 1415 *Sir John Scudamore of Kentchurch in south Herefordshire was also the Steward of Cantref Mawr*. In other words, having secretly married Alice Glyndŵr in *c*. 1404 and having surrendered Carmarthen Castle with suspicious ease in August 1405 (being accused in the same month of receiving funds for Glyndŵr himself), John Scudamore acquired the stewardship of Cantref Mawr in 1407. This was the year when the Welsh cause collapsed, the grim siege of Aberystwyth began, and it became evident that, barring a miracle, Glyndŵr had had his day.

Scudamore's tenure as the Steward of Cantref Mawr was originally prescribed to last only until 1413, but in fact it was not until 18 May 1415 that he was finally replaced by a certain Rhys ap Thomas ap Dafydd, who swore loyalty to the English Crown. This, then, provides the date by which Owain Glyndŵr was almost certainly dead and buried – whereafter Sir John Scudamore quietly stood down as Steward of Cantref Mawr. It is also the information which first led me to believe that I was correct. Surely the story of Jack of Kent's curious death and burial in the Monnow Valley was a cumulative sequential code, and one which had been well understood by the Scudamores of medieval Kentchurch – but it did not refer to the Monnow Valley – it referred to the Tywi Valley, and the lands in Cantref Mawr which had been in Sir John Scudamore's charge in 1415.

At this point I was fortunate enough to receive the enthusiastic help and encouragement of Lynn Harrison, whose delight in Celtic history and religion, and natural ability with a camera, have made a wonderful contribution to this book. Therefore, on a lovely sunny day in the spring of 2002, we finally embarked upon a journey to south-west Wales, travelling via Brecon and Llandovery to Llanwrda.

Our main interest was, of course, the village church, where we had arranged to meet the vicar. On our arrival, we were a little disconcerted to find that the structure initially appeared Victorian. However, the vicar had very kindly brought with him some interesting information about the church, including a copy of a report by Cambria Archaeology on behalf of CADW for the Welsh Historic Churches Project in 1998, which, having observed that the church is essentially medieval, and still retains some original features, proceeds to date the chancel to the 1200s – and says: 'An underfloor void is present. A crypt or vault may lie beneath the chancel.'

This is an interesting piece of information. The medieval chancel with its 'underfloor void' would therefore have been available in 1415, when it would have been accessible by stairs and a wooden door. However, having been filled with the remains of those considered prestigious enough for burial in this most sought-after part of the church, this vault has long-since been sealed and paved over, and we have no information to suggest that it has ever been opened in modern times.

Reflecting upon this, and also upon the fact that crypt burial is a Romano-Celtic custom which originally derived from the catacombs, Lynn and I meandered outside to view the battered buttress of the chancel from there. If my theory was correct, then Owain Glyndŵr lay beneath our feet in the chancel vault. Having been led to Llanwrda by the sign of the cross, it was also curious to observe leaning against that very wall, propped at a rakish angle strongly reminiscent of the 'X' on my road-map, a large wooden cross.

Until that day I knew nothing about Llanwrda, other than that it lay precisely at the centre of the 'X' in a part of Wales which could scarcely be more appropriate as a burial site for Owain Glyndŵr – the site of his greatest victory and the spiritual heartland of Deheubarth. For all I knew, Llanwrda might have been a modern village which had never possessed a medieval church, let alone one with a suitably dated 'underfloor void', and it might easily have had no other features to confirm its suitability – but it had.

The dedication of the church of Llanwrda could have been to St David or St Peter or Mary the Virgin, or to any one of the innumerable saints to whom village churches are dedicated. Instead, however, in a consecration that confirms all our earlier calculations, the church of Llanwrda just happens to be dedicated to none other than our old friend St Cawrdaf, the Dark Age Celtic warrior-king who once held Old Wales firm against the Saxons – and whose defence of the Severn south of the Teme had once defined the bottom line of Welsh military strategy. I therefore suggest that Owain Glyndŵr was buried at Llanwrda, and that his interment there was a statement of defiance to the very end.

Despite the 'wrda' in its name, and local confirmation in 1917 that the village church 'is dedicated to St Cawrdav', the dedication of Llan-wrda to 'Ca-wrda-f' has been questioned by some, such as Baring-Gould (*The Lives of the British Saints*, 2) on the basis of comparison with another church of St Cawrdaf in north-west Wales which commemorates a stronghold held by Cawrdaf's father on the Llŷn Peninsula. Here, at Llangawrda (Aber-e-rch), the replacement of the letter 'c' by a 'g' is common practice, but the 'awrda' element has been hailed as a significant improvement upon 'wrda', which is then offered by Baring-Gould as indicating 'a St Gwrda', similar to the St Cwrda who curiously appears at Jordanstone in Dyfed (Pembrokeshire).

However, nobody knows who this St Gwrda or Cwrda was, and his non-identity is confirmed at Jordanstone where it merely derives from the English name of the parish, which happens to translate as 'Tre Iwrdan'. Finally, while it has also been suggested that Llanwrda might possibly derive from 'gwr da' ('a good man'), one must agree with A.T. Arber-Cooke (*Llandovery and its Environs*) who observes: 'The name Llanwrda, often translated as "The Church of the Good Man", is really an adulteration. The Celtic saint credited with the founding of the church was probably Cawrdaf, but who is to say other than that he was a good man?' Precisely, and considering the increasing pressure put upon the (pagan) reputations of the early Celtic saints by the English, it could also be argued that there might have come a day when it was thus politic to contract 'awrda' to 'wrda'. In any case, St Cawrdaf survives with ease such spurious objections to his presence at Llanwrda.

Having dispensed with this, the other objection raised by Baring-Gould is that while St Cawrdaf's feast-day is well established as 5 December (or occasionally 21 February), the feast-day celebrated at Llanwrda was All Saints' Day (i.e. All Hallows, 1 November). However, this objection simply evaporates when one considers that All Saints' Day was a day on which *all* saints were to be celebrated regardless of their actual feast-days. Therefore at Llanwrda it is not as if the inhabitants were celebrating the feast-day of some other saint, it is simply that for impeccable reasons (which will be more fully understood by readers of the sequel to this book) they had transferred their celebrations to All Saints' Day – and so, at Llanwrda, St Cawrdaf remains unchallenged.

The reason why a powerful king of Brycheiniog is celebrated at Llanwrda is explained by the ancient and inevitable strategic liaison between Brycheiniog and Deheubarth, for as we have said Cantref Mawr is the haft of Cawrdaf's Spear. In 1282, we find Llanwrda duly recorded as 'Lanwrdaf', and I therefore maintain that since this time at least, this church has commemorated St Cawrdaf.

Finally, let us return to north Wales to consider St Cawrdaf's other church at Aber-erch (Llangawrda), where a curious custom was observed until the early 1800s, as described by *Archaeologia Cambrensis* in 1856 . . .

> On the eve of St Cawrdaf's festival [5 December] all the children brought into the church a number of candles, which they had been making themselves, or had bought – one candle for each member of their family in whom they were particularly interested, and which they had called after their names. They knelt down, lighted them, and muttered any prayer they recollected as long as the candles continued burning; but, according as the candles became extinguished one after the other, they supposed that the person whose name was attached to the candle that burnt out first would certainly die first; and so on in the order of successive extinctions.

The similarity of this ritual to the tale of Jack of France (see Legend 24) is the reason I promised earlier concerning candle-light, which reinforces the likelihood that Owain Glyndŵr died at Dorstone. The death by candle-light of Jack of France/ Owain Glyndŵr allegedly occurred as the result of a ceremony remarkably akin to that traditionally performed upon the feast-day of St Cawrdaf, except that it was said to have occurred upon the eve of All Souls Day (2 November) – and thus took place on the preferred feast-day of Cawrdaf's parishioners at Llanwrda (1 November). Thus, like the Dove and the Raven story at Kentchurch, the folktale of Jack of France told on the Scudamore lands at Dorstone also appears to be a clue regarding the fate of Owain Glyndŵr – and it too points precisely at Llanwrda.

Early one morning in 1415, as February was drawing to a close, it seems that a grey dawn saw Sir John Scudamore and his party setting out from Monnington Straddel with the body of Owain Glyndŵr concealed in their baggage-train. Owain's body had temporarily been left at Dorstone, from where the route to south-west Wales was unobstructed by the Black Mountains, and thus he lay conveniently within a day's ride of his final resting-place.

No one but Sir John, and a tearful Alice who rode nearby, knew the contents of the cart which also contained Sir John's personal effects, and no one questioned the purpose of their journey, for as Constable and Steward Sir John always had important matters to attend to in Carmarthen and Cantref Mawr. Via Hay-on-Wye and Brecon they travelled, and thence along the upper Usk Valley to Pontsenni before moving on towards Llandovery along the route once taken by the Romans. Some 4 miles from Llandovery they passed through Halfway-in, where drovers and travellers scurried hastily aside, and having reached Llandovery by late afternoon they prepared to turn south-west along the Tywi, now proceeding along the old Roman road. At last they neared Llanwrda, where, upon what pretext we shall never know, there came a moment after nightfall when two men in the pay of Maredudd Glyndŵr removed the simple wooden chest containing Owain's body from the baggage cart, and bore it swiftly across the fields to Llanwrda church. By the thin light of a crescent moon the cowled figure of a Premonstratensian monk silently awaited the appointed hour in the shadow of a doorway, while nearby stood a slender woman whose fair hair shimmered as she detected their approach – it was Alice.

To make the necessary arrangements for Owain's burial Sir John Scudamore thus had no need to engage in any suspicious activity outside his usual agenda, for while his contribution was to ensure safe passage to south-west Wales he could doubtless rely upon Maredudd's network to attend to any practicalities at the Llanwrda end. Furthermore we have already observed that both the Scudamores and Glyndŵr's entourage were well acquainted with the Premonstratensians, and so – in contrast to the desperate use of shovels by moonlight which has been envisaged by some – all the conditions were perfectly in place for an interment enacted with great secrecy and speed.

Llanwrda was both a daughter-church of Talley Abbey and a possession of the Premonstratensians, and so ease of access was guaranteed – and Owain's body would simply have been taken downstairs into the crypt which forms the 'underfloor void' detected by the 1998 survey. Here, an unmarked tomb, long-since installed and assumed to be occupied, was in fact empty. Owain Glyndŵr was laid to rest inside, as prayers were said and Alice wept a last farewell – and it was over.

Thus the interment at Llanwrda solved elegantly all the practical difficulties attendant upon such a secret burial. Not only was it appropriate in every respect, but it was also well away from Kentchurch, Monnington and Croft, and it could be facilitated with great ease in a manner which caused no suspicion. It was swift, dignified and consecrated, and it left no physical traces whatsoever.

Furthermore, within a couple of months Sir John Scudamore quietly stood down as the Steward of Cantref Mawr, and handed over at the earliest opportunity to Rhys ap Thomas ap Dafydd, a Welshman distinguished by having taken no part in Glyndŵr's war, who had remained conspicuously loyal to the English Crown – and who from 18 May 1415 onwards had no idea that he was guarding the burial site of Owain Glyndŵr.

LEGEND 26 : TO SIP AN APPLE

One night, the Devil tried to carry Jack of Kent away, but he obtained permission to sip an apple before they left, whereupon he clung so tightly to the upper branches of the apple-tree that he could not be dislodged. Since then, too sinful for Heaven, but safe from Hell, he has haunted the world like a will o' the wisp.

[See also Appendix 1, p. 295.]

SIXTEEN

EPIPHANY
(2004)

The Scudamores are a very old Norman family – so old that their origins are lost in the mists of time – but it is known that they were in Britain a thousand years ago, before the Norman invasion, during which they are said to have fought for King Harold. However, several times they are later found effectively siding with the Welsh against the Anglo-Norman Crown, and several times we have wondered whether, in view of the proximity of their manor at Kentchurch to the Templars' establishment on Garway Hill, the Scudamores might have indulged (like the Knights Templars) in a certain Gnostic religious sympathy with the Welsh Romano-Celtic-Christian agenda.

A closer look at a certain site adjacent to Kentchurch may seem whimsical but I think it is worth pursuing. During the 1200s and 1300s this site changed hands between the Knights Templar and the Scudamores, and was known as the manor, chapel and mill of Kaueros. However, while other vague explanations have been offered regarding its name, the fact is that from the 1100s onwards and into the 1400s the spelling was consistently either as above or with the English 'k' substituted by the Welsh 'c', so as to produce 'Caueros' or 'Cauros'. I therefore suggest that in their long-standing ownership of 'Cauros' (see Table V) and of its chapel (which was demolished in the wake of the Black Death) the Scudamores of Kentchurch had long-since celebrated an esoteric interest in the Dark Age Celtic cult of none other than St Cawrdaf of Brycheiniog, the earliest versions of whose name were spelt 'Caur-tam'.

This apparent flight of fancy on my part suddenly becomes a

little more reasonable when one remembers that the Scudamores' other chapel at Kentchurch (Sancta Keyna) was dedicated to St Ceneu, of Brycheiniog – and that as Norman Marcher lords, the Scudamores had an interest in both military strategy and the Arthurian tradition. Furthermore, the Scudamores may also have been significantly better informed than the average medieval Norman Marcher lords, for they had been in Britain long enough to remember the true (Welsh) origins of the Arthurian tradition and to understand the military significance of what we have called Cawrdaf's Spear.

From the outset the Scudamores had recognised, just as Owain Glyndŵr had done, that if Cawrdaf's Spear could be seized and made to point eastwards once again, then Old Wales and the true Arthurian tradition might be restored – but Wales had not the strength, the ancient plan had failed, and so, as the tide ebbed against Glyndŵr in the fall of 1405, he had made a desperate lunge for Worcester – a Dark Age warrior with a broken spear.

At Worcester, Glyndŵr had found himself armed with French allies who were reluctant to fight, and faced with an English army which was the equal of his own. At this moment, which should have been the zenith of his hopes and dreams, Owain knew that his great millenial march into English territory along the line of Cawrdaf's Spear had not gone according to the prophecy, and so I suggest that once again, he sought help from the seers.

This is the reason that Glyndŵr immediately retreated with his forces, 10 miles north-west of Worcester to Woodbury Hill in a strange manoevre that David Walker (*Mediaeval Wales*, Cambridge University Press, 1990) and many others have described as 'inexplicable' – for Woodbury Hill is defensible high ground on the river Teme, waters Cawrdaf had once known well, where his influence still lingered, and which as a sacred tribal river-boundary has long been hallowed by the Celts almost as greatly as the Severn and the Dee. Here Owain remained, and as the stand-off between the two armies continued, and the French refused to fight, perhaps Owain summoned his magi once more, and under cover of darkness made his way to the banks of the Teme. What strange prayers were offered we will never know, but Cawrdaf sent no aid from the Otherworld, the French refused to fight, and the Dark Age dream dissolved.

Owain had been born in the shadow of St Collen's Church (Llangollen), where an inscribed stone (since lost) had proclaimed St Cawrdaf as St Collen's ancestor, and I suggest that like the Scudamores, Glyndŵr had chosen Cawrdaf as his personal saint (see Appendix 2).

Now Owain was gone, and only a desolate land remained. In the years to come the marriages of his daughters would be revealed, and there would be much speculation and misinformation regarding his fate. One day, it was promised that he would return, in a future age when England was self-debased, to expel the Saxon at last. Some said he would yet fulfil the prophecy, others that he had already failed – and so had never been the Mab Darogan. Later, a curious piece of folklore would cause people to look beneath church walls in Herefordshire for a certain Jack o' Kent, and much later still a twenty-first-century scribe who was doing nothing much else at the time would inadvertently stumble upon a secret which had once been known to some – and would thus be led to Llanwrda.

Llanwrda, a little village church dreaming upon the Afon Dulais brook where it babbles and flows forever into the Tywi, and thence into Môr, the 'deep' beyond Carmarthen Bay. This is a classic burial site for any Celtic king – not on the bank of the main boundary river, which would jeopardise the site in times of flood, but a little higher up on the edge of a tributary, on a border-stream (which is why the Celtic names of so many rivers survive as the names of their tributaries).

Is this where Glyndŵr still lies? Only the birds which chatter sweetly in the trees reply, in a language we do not understand. Look, I have brought an old document, which says: 'died Owen Glendower after that . . . and in the night-season he was buried by his followers. But his burial having been discovered by his adversaries, he was laid in the grave a second time, and where his body was bestowed, may no man know.'

So said Adam of Usk, but we know that he was either

hopelessly ill-informed or shared with the Welsh chroniclers an intention to disguise the truth. Furthermore, in life Owain had many 'doubles' acting as decoys and thus possessed the supernatural ability to be in two places at once, and in death he staged fake burials like the one at Llanrhaeadr-ym-Mochnant, and it might easily be to one of these that Adam refers.

Here is another document, recorded by Owain Rhoscomyl, an historian: 'The location of his grave is known – is well known. It lies not close to any church nor in the shadow of an old yew tree. It is in a more secret and more sacred place than that. Time cannot touch it; putrefaction cannot dishonour it, because this grave is in the heart of every true Welshman. There persistently, from generation to generation, Owain's heart dreams on, dreams on for evermore.'

As we sit upon the grass in the sunshine, in the churchyard at Llanwrda, we have no proof, except for the knowledge of the long road which we have travelled, a certain subtle tension in the air, and a large wooden cross propped at an angle against the chancel wall. As we turn to look back along the dark centuries of our great journey, a breeze suddenly stirs and the shadows of the ancient yew trees close to the church run wildly across our faces. The oldest was a seedling that grew out of the very Dark Ages themselves, and so at last, chased by the shadows of a thousand years and more, let us leave Llanwrda, undisturbed.

Fern Hill

Now as I was young and easy under the apple boughs
About the lilting house and happy as the grass was green
The night above the dingle starry,
Time let me hail and climb
Golden in the heyday of his eyes,
And honoured among wagons I was prince of the apple towns
And once below a time I lordly had the trees and leaves
Trail with daisies and barley
Down the rivers of the windfall light.

And as I was green and carefree, famous among the barns
About the happy yard and singing as the farm was home
In the sun that is young once only,
Time let me play and be
Golden in the mercy of his means,
And green and golden I was huntsman and herdsman, the calves
Sang to my horn, the foxes on the hill barked clear and cold,
And the sabbath rang slowly
In the pebbles of the holy streams

Nothing I cared, in the lamb white days, that time would take me
Up to the swallow thronged loft by the shadow of my hand,
In a moon that is always rising,
Nor that riding to sleep
I should hear him fly with the high fields
And wake to the farm forever fled from the childless land.
Oh as I was young and easy in the mercy of his means,
Time held me green and dying
Though I sang in my chains like the sea.

Dylan Thomas

Epilogue
(1415–2004)

If our theory is correct, Owain Glyndŵr was a charismatic Welsh leader whose unique lineage was recognised by the bards and seers at birth, and whose moment came 1,000 years after the collapse of Romano-Celtic Britain. Following the example of his prodigious ancestor The Lord Rhys, and well aware of the paramount strategic importance of the ancient south-western kingdom of Deheubarth, Glyndŵr raised the peasantry of Wales by proclaiming his corvine descent from Owain of Rheged, and attempted to resurrect Old Wales by restoring the original eastward-pointing direction of what we have called Cawrdaf's Spear.

He failed, his credibility as the Mab Darogan was questioned, and he ended his days as an outlaw in the Welsh Borders where he was popularly known as Jack of Kent. Nevertheless, supported by the Welsh rebel network which continued under the auspices of his son Maredudd, and by such families as the Vaughans, Crofts, Monningtons, Scudamores, and perhaps also the Bryts (see Appendix 2), Owain Glyndŵr remained defiant to the very end and was laid to rest by the Scudamores in the vault beneath the chancel of Cawrdaf's church at Llanwrda in Cantref Mawr, a daughter-church of the nearby Premonstratensian abbey of Talley, which had been founded by the Lord Rhys in the spiritual heartland of Deheubarth. Glyndŵr's burial here in early 1415 was appropriate not only because the Tywi Valley had been the scene of his greatest victory, or because as the haft of Cawrdaf's Spear, Llanwrda church also commemorated the military principle by which the Old Wales of Cawrdaf's day might yet be resurrected, but also because it was a dramatic statement which was understood by the bards and seers, the Premonstratensians, the

Scudamores, and even ourselves, and it still rings forth today, being essentially as follows: 'Over my dead body, does the Saxon come down the Tywi Valley into the south-west, let the north and south unite against them, I will never go home to the north while this issue is unresolved, I am still out here – fighting.' However, all such conclusions are inevitably prefixed by the phrase, 'if we are correct', for after 600 years we could very easily be wrong! – and this causes us to wonder, whether or not Owain Glyndŵr really *is* at Llanwrda.

If we are wrong, and Owain Glyndŵr does not lie within an externally unmarked tomb in the vault of Llanwrda church, then one explanation would be that while making some interesting suggestions along the way, giving a colourful account of Welsh history, and one hopes, retaining the dignity of having made a good guess, our entire thesis is spurious. On the other hand, there might be other explanations. The 'Oven' variant of the Dove and the Raven (see Legend 22) seems to invoke the possibility of Jack of Kent's cremation, a process traditionally seen as purification by fire, but which was demonised in the Middle Ages as a process which prevented proper Christian burial and which thus precluded resurrection on the Day of Judgement. Therefore, while a cremated Glyndŵr would have been easy to transport across country, and would have needed no tomb, cremation seems unlikely; furthermore in the scenario which we have described, it would also have been unnecessary. Another possible reason for Glyndŵr's absence might concern Adam of Usk's completely unreliable assertion that Glyndŵr was buried more than once, and had to be moved in great haste when his enemies discovered where he lay. In which case, Owain might have been moved *from* his intended burial site at Llanwrda, perhaps because an English agent had already heard and understood the information regarding the 'X' in Cantref Mawr. However, since we have no substantive reason to suspect that Owain actually *was* moved from his intended burial site, and every reason to believe that such rumours were either ill-informed and/or were part of a smokescreen of misinformation deliberately designed to make his grave appear not worth looking for – we can therefore only return to the more tangible question of the 'X'.

It is stated both in folklore (see Legend 17) and tradition that Scudamore of Kentchurch was Jack of Kent's patron, and if, as is long asserted in south Herefordshire, we accept that this Jack of Kent was in fact Owain Glyndŵr, then it might well be significant that Sir John Scudamore happened at that very moment to be in charge of a site in south-west Wales which can be so accurately described by the four coordinates 'Half-in, Half-out, a Dove, and a Raven'. Furthermore, the significance of this apparently increases, when the site in question turns out to be a church dedicated to St Cawrdaf, one of the last holders of the Celtic West, whose tradition at Llanwrda commemmorates not only the bottom line of Welsh military stratgy, but also Glyndŵr's greatest victory and the homeland of his mother's line. If this, and all the many other circumstantial factors which we have identified, are considered sufficient to be convincing, then our next task must be to attempt a reconstruction of the years which followed Owain Glyndŵr's death at Dorstone, and his burial by the Scudamores in south-west Wales. Glyndŵr may well have died and been buried at Llanwrda in early 1415, but life went on: the Scudamore dynasty continued at Kentchurch until the present day, some very interesting things had yet to occur, and the folkloric Jack o' Kent has always refused to lie down.

In the years which followed Glyndŵr's death, his burial site remained a secret known only to his descendants, and to the descendants of those who had buried him. Meanwhile, in time, the cipher regarding the death and burial of Jack of Kent and the 'X' in Cantref Mawr, which had presumably originated as a joke belonging to the Premonstratensians of Talley Abbey, would eventually become the sole property of the Scudamores at Kentchurch, and in this analysis, we shall assume that they made no mention of it for a long time.

In 1419, John Kemp (see Table II) became bishop of Rochester and thus embraced a vocation which lasted for thirty-five years and ended in his death as archbishop of

Canterbury – a role which doubtless caused him to be confused with Sioni Cents in general via the Everyman theory, and with John Kempe the Flemish weaver via the Outlaw theory (see Preface). As a result, this John Kemp has occasionally been suggested as Jack of Kent, or even as the subject of the oil-painting kept at Kentchurch Court.

In 1425, Gruffydd ap Nicholas, the great grandson of Elidir Ddu and consequently the latest colourful descendant of the Lord Rhys, became the King's Approver for the royal demesnes at Dinefwr Castle, whereupon he embarked upon a spectacular career in which he would not only adopt his ancestors' heraldry of three black ravens, but also the family motto of 'God Feeds the Ravens' – which presumably refers to the survival of the raven first released by Noah from the Ark. Described as 'verie wise . . . infinitlie subtile and craftie, ambitiouse beyond measure, of a busie stirring braine', Gruffydd would subsequently receive a lifetime's lease of Dinefwr Castle, and by allying himself with the generally absent Justiciar for south Wales (Lord Powicke), would not only become the 'right trusty and well-beloved friend' of Henry VI, but ultimately the effective custodian of the castles of Carmarthen, Cardigan, Aberystwyth, Kidwelly, and Carreg Cennen. Finally, having erected a prestigious manor house at Dinefwr to which he summoned a great meeting of the bards, he died a year later.

One important poet, however, who probably did not live long enough to attend Gruffydd ap Nicholas's Eisteddfod, and who would doubtless not have attended it even if he had been invited, was the enigmatic Siôn Cent, a bard whose work has recently been scrutinised by M. Paul Bryant-Quinn of The Centre for Advanced Welsh & Celtic Studies at the University of Wales. While we fully concur with Paul Quinn that there is absolutely no evidence linking him either with the Scudamores, or with Kentchurch Court in south Herefordshire, Siôn Cent was nonetheless a radical Welsh poet who was writing in the wake of Glyndŵr's war, and who may have been called a Jack of Kent for precisely the same reason as Glyndŵr – for there are reasons to suspect that he was an outlaw too.

Born, probably, in the 1360s, it is possible that Siôn Cent had once been a youthful adherent of John Ball, the 'Mad Priest' of Kent who had accompanied Wat Tyler in leading the Peasants' Revolt of 1381. Most of his poetry however, appears to have been written following Glyndŵr's war, during the period 1430–1440, and our suspicion that Siôn Cent was also an outlaw seems to be confirmed when we hear him not only lamenting the loss of the luxuries which he had enjoyed in his youth, but lamenting the loss of all his possessions, the loss of his status, and applauding the fact that the local outlaws were going from strength to strength. Furthermore, it appears that Siôn Cent may have read Langland's *Piers Ploughman* (the earliest known copy of which was found in the Welsh Borders), and that his political and religious position is that of a 'Ballard', i.e. one who lambasts all wealth and privilege, including that of the barons.

It has been suggested by some writers in the past that Siôn Cent was a supporter of Owain Glyndŵr, and some have even suggested him as Glyndŵr's alleged last follower, travelling companion, or personal chaplain. It is also interesting therefore (regarding Lawton's Hope Hill) that a popular Welsh folk song not only attributed to Siôn Cent but also said to refer to Glyndŵr should state – 'I was told that the lark has died on the mountain, if I knew these words were true, I would go with a band of armed men to bring the body home' (Dr. Robin Gwyndaf: 'The Heroic Process' p. 436. Glendale Press, 1987). However, while outlawry and disapproval of the established order might possibly have led him like many other former Ballards to throw in his lot with Glyndŵr, Siôn Cent's position does not sit comfortably with any cause other than that of John Ball, and he makes it crystal-clear that the *only* authority he is prepared to accept is that of Christ. Furthermore, it is also questionable to what extent Siôn Cent's religious views would have permitted him to fully support Glyndŵr, for he delights in the use of a poetic technique known as *ubi sunt* in which all worldly wealth, power, priviledge, pleasure, and other such distractions are shown as shallow folly in the disapproving face of the grave. Thus, while other bards eulogised the rich and powerful in return for lucrative pay, Siôn Cent acridly condemned their muse to the crematorium, accusing it of emanating from 'an oven of hellish nature', and describing the fate of a typical rich patron as follows:

> All too low will lie his bed,
> The roof-tree pressed against his head
> For coat the clogging shroud he'll take
> His cradle clay and gravel make . . .
> His body the oaken chest within
> His nose all shrunken grey and thin . . .
> His journey sure to earth addressed
> His strong arms crossed upon his breast
> Empty courts where wine flowed free
> And in his kitchen no cook will be . . .
> His wife will sure his hall forsake
> And soon a second husband take.

Siôn Cent also called the world '. . . a sermon, a cold thing', and elsewhere compared it to a bird's nest imperilled by the wind amidst the high twigs of a tree, he listed all the greatest men and the most beautiful women of the past and repeatedly asked 'Where are they now?', to which the answer was essentially 'in a box' and returning to his previous theme he pointed out 'A hideous toad, dark the house, If he looks, will be his bedfellow . . . And three hundred, they tell me, Worms are tasting him.' This is very different from Iolo Goch's account of opulent Sycharth and its lord (see Chapter 5), and among the mighty of whom Siôn Cent asks 'where are they now?' he even lists king Arthur, and thus makes no exception for the Welsh tradition, permits no reincarnations other than that of Christ, and even asks, 'Where is King Richard?' and 'Where is Owain?', which might refer to Owain Lawgoch (d. 1378) or to Owain Glyndŵr (d. 1415). For Siôn Cent, who as 'they tell me' was not without a dark sense of humour, and who shone brightly whenever he sang of Heaven, Owain Glyndŵr was therefore most certainly not the Mab Darogan. Instead, Siôn Cent believed that God would save the Welsh people only if they lived according to his Law, and he is consequently cited in the *Glamorgan County History* (vol. 3, p. 151) as an example of those Welsh who in the wake of Glyndŵr's war had blamed their own inadequacies for its failure.

It has also been claimed that Siôn Cent was a supporter of Sir John Oldcastle, on the basis that he mentions the Lollard leader in his poetry. However, M. Paul Bryant-Quinn has pointed out that the verse in question is actually 'anti-Lollard', for Siôn Cent is simply citing Oldcastle's horrific fate as an example of what happens to those who set themselves against God. Thus, like many others, it may be that Siôn Cent had been appalled by Wycliffe's rejection of the mystery of the Mass (see Chapter 11).

So, who was this elusive bard? While nobody knows, many have cited a story from a notoriously tangled web of invention and information compiled by a certain Iolo Morganwg (otherwise known as 'Edward Williams', 1747–1826). In this account, Siôn Cent is said to have started life as a poor orphan who worked on a farm at Abertridwr in Glamorgan, and who lost his job as a result of having magically confined crows in the keep of nearby Caerphilly castle (see Legend 9). Notwithstanding the rest of this story which appears in the *Myffyrian Archeology* and which spuriously connects him with both Kenchester (Hereford) and Kentchurch (and thus Jack of Kent), Iolo Morganwg also states that Siôn Cent had served for a while as a priest at Newcastle Emlyn in west Wales, and notes elsewhere that he had received a free education from his uncle at a house called 'Glyn Tridwr' near Abertridwr.

This would be of more interest were it not for the fact that Iolo Morganwg, who apparently had access to many documents since lost, and whose considerable intelligence saw him at at the forefront of Welsh scholarship, has also been described as follows: 'Unfortunately . . . his great erudition and his frequently penetrating insight were largely vitiated by the queer twists of an unusually peverse mind. Only rarely did his abnormally overactive imagination have any firm contact with historical reality. Impelled by deep-rooted psychological urges which probably had their origin in a pathological influence . . . and partly by a passionate desire to enhance the prestige and glory of his native Morgannwg . . . he was driven over and over again to distort what he actually knew' (*Glamorgan County History*, 3, p. 450). Furthermore, Iolo's history of Siôn Cent becomes even more suspect when we notice that the poet Daffyd Gwilym, a near contemporary of Siôn Cent, is recorded as having received a free education from an uncle, who happened to be the Constable of Newcastle Emlyn in west Wales; and finally, since Iolo was also distracted by recollections of previous lives, both as a sheep and as a Druid, and probably indulged in 'substance-abuse', it seems that we are probably none the wiser. In conclusion therefore, regarding the identity of this bardic Jack of Kent, who may well have been a priest at some point as well as an outlaw, and whose poetry became popular in Glamorgan, our only hope lies in what is to come when M. Paul Bryant-Quinn's forthcoming investigation, *Gwaith Siôn Cent*, is completed and published. In the meantime however, we can at least assert with confidence that the bard 'Siôn Cent' was *not* the rector of Kentchurch in the 1380s, and nor was he Owain Glyndŵr.

In 1430, the baronial scrum which was running the country instructed none other than Gruffydd Dwn to conduct an investigation into Talley Abbey. As the son of Glyndŵr's great ally, Henry Dwn, a youthful Gruffydd had once fought for Glyndŵr but had subsequently been pardoned by Henry V and had served at Agincourt in 1415. Six years after Agincourt however, in about 1421 (the year that Maredudd finally accepted a pardon from the Crown), Gruffydd Dwn had healed the rift between the Dwns and the Scudamores by marrying the daughter of Sir John Scudamore and Alice Glyndŵr, Joanne, the granddaughter of Owain Glyndŵr (see Chapter 11). It is thus very likely that Gruffydd Dwn would have been among the few who knew the secret location of Owain Glyndŵr's grave, and if our theory is correct, we might imagine that he is most unlikely to have investigated Talley Abbey or its daughter-churches too deeply, or to have tried too hard to penetrate the extent of the 'misrule' by which Talley was said to have been wasted just three years later. Also in 1430, Sir John Scudamore was opposed by the Earl of Somerset in an attempt to reverse Glyndŵr's outlawry and claim Owain's lands in right of his wife. Three years later in 1433, the baronial scrum finally exacted its revenge upon Sir John Scudamore, as his marriage to Alice was used as an excuse to strip him of all his titles and to impose upon him a fine so heavy that it could only have been paid with the aid of an extensive network of friends and supporters, and within two years, Sir John was dead.

In 1437, pamphlets circulated in England warning 'Beware of Wales!', whereupon Henry VI declared his minority at an end, abolished the baronial scrum, and wrote in 1438 to the Pope describing the Welshry of Herefordshire and Radnorshire as 'wild and untameable by nature', before targeting them for harsh punishments in 1442.

The year 1443 saw the death of the turbulent John Abrahall, whose career during the past twenty years had seen him reconciled with the Talbots, outlawed for swindling a draper in London, pardoned, and immediately appointed as a Justice of the Peace. Upon his deathbed he left a fortune, no will, and a conflict over his riches which plunged the entire family into a violent feud which brought yet more misery to the denizens of south Herefordshire in an acrimony which lasted for the next fifty years.

In 1450, a bard named Ieuan Ddu of Brecheiniog began to write in a style remarkably similar to that of Siôn Cent, just as a brief but substantial rebellion was raised amongst the men of Kent by an outlaw named Jack Cade, and two years later John Kemp became Archbishop of Canterbury, just as Henry VI began to display the first signs of insanity.

The year 1455 saw the battle of St Albans, the first clash between the aspirant House of York and the established House of Lancaster which marked the beginning of the Wars of the Roses. The history of York is suddenly interesting when we observe that Edward Duke of York, who had been Sir John Scudamore's predecessor in charge of Carmarthen Castle, had, like Scudamore, also been accused of supporting Glyndŵr at that time, and had even been briefly imprisoned on suspicion of having aided Lady Despenser in her attempt to abduct young Mortimer from Crown custody and carry him to Harlech in early 1404. Furthermore, in 1425 when the same Mortimer suddenly died, it was his uncle Richard Duke of

York, who was made to wait seven years by the Lancastrian Crown before finally receiving Mortimer's inheritance in 1432 – and therefore it is also interesting that when the victorious Yorkists arrived in south-west Wales in 1461, it was yet another John Scudamore who surrendered the castle of Pembroke to them with remarkable ease, whereupon a bard of Glamorgan named Llywelyn ap Hywel, who was familiar with the outlaw territory of Pen-rhys, sang clearly in the vein of Siôn Cent. In the same year, Edward IV became the first Yorkist king, and was succeeded in 1483 by Edward V whose reign lasted only a single year before he was deposed and usurped by the third and final Yorkist ruler, Richard III.

Although Lancaster had usurped the throne and held it for sixty years under three kings, armed with the same number of kings, the Yorkists had maintained their grip for little more than two decades when Richard III was killed at the battle of Bosworth in 1485, at which point it was alleged by the Welsh bard Lewis Glyn Cothi that his slayer had been none other than one Rhys ap Thomas, the grandson of Gruffydd ap Nicholas, and thus the latest corvine descendant of the Lord Rhys. As you will recall, Gruffydd ap Nicholas had made a great deal of his descent from the Lord Rhys and the ancient House of Rheged through his heraldry of the three black ravens, and also by his adoption of 'God Feeds The Ravens' as the family motto; and thus by the time Rhys ap Thomas led a private army in support of Henry Tudor against Richard III at Bosworth, the entire family was known as 'the Blood of the Raven'. However, from our point of view, the career of Rhys ap Thomas is interesting indeed, not only because he was the owner of a house said to have been frequented by Owain Glyndŵr at Llanarthne, or because he held the manor of Llansadwrn in Cantref Mawr where the church was a daughter-house of Talley and the senior sister of adjacent Llanwrda, or because his mentor was the contemporary Abbot of Talley, but also for another reason. Prior to the Battle of Bosworth, Richard III had correctly doubted Rhys ap Thomas's loyalty. However, he is said to have been reassured when Rhys famously announced that Henry Tudor would enter south-west Wales only *'over my bellie'*, or *'over my dead body'*, after which he was subsequently said to have lain down under Mullock Bridge while Henry's army passed overhead.

However, could it be that *'over my bellie'* was actually a private joke which the Abbot of Talley Abbey, the Tudors, and 'The Blood of the Raven' all knew referred to the statement made by the secret burial of the late Glyndŵr at Llanwrda? – and if so, is it a coincidence that the result of Rhys ap Thomas's deception, was indeed to place one of Glyndŵr's former allies, a Tudor, upon the throne of England?

Henry Tudor, henceforth Henry VII, was indeed promptly and inevitably hailed in Wales as the Welshman whose destiny was to fulfil Glyndŵr's ambitions, but despite such exhortations, as king of England he knew better than to attempt to restore the Celtic West. He was, however, careful to reward those prominent Welshmen who had supported him at Bosworth, and his subsequent elevation of 'Sir' Rhys ap Thomas to the Order of the Garter some years later was celebrated in the form of a grand tournament held at Rhys's castle of Carew near Pembroke. At this, while far away the Welsh bard 'Guto'r Glyn' sang plaintively of how the ravens had prepared the victory at Bosworth, Sir Rhys famously hoisted a banner above the entrance which showed the two patron saints of England and Wales, St George and St David, facing each other in an attitude of embrace. It was a political poster, an image so simple and so direct that it would not be easily forgotten in Wales, and while some saw in it a reconciliatory embrace, others saw Wales held in a vice-like grip which spelt the final end of the Dark Age dream – and so it was at this moment that another bard, Hywel Rheinallt, who lived near Aber-erch on the Llŷn Peninsula in north-west Wales, glumly observed 'The best of all fortresses, for a long time, is the glass castle [spiritual fortress] of Cawrdaf.'

Finally, before we leave the 1400s, we should not neglect another Jack of Kent, a suspect who has been hailed by many, and who achieved eminence just prior to the downfall of York at the hands of Henry Tudor and Rhys ap Thomas, namely a certain 'Dr John Kent of Caerleon' (see Table II) who appears in *De Illustribus Angliae Scriptoribus* (pp. 669–70) and whose works were published upon his death in 1482. Originally known, as Leland (*c.* 1540) observes, simply as 'John of Caerleon', he is interestingly called John 'Kent' by the *Scriptoribus* which calls him 'Ionnus Kentus alijs Cailegus (Caerleon)', from which, combined with the information supplied by Leland, an account of his career may be compiled as follows . . .

Born in Caerleon, perhaps in the 1420s, 'Doctor John' was a Welshman who grew up in south Wales and later received an ecclesiastical education at Cambridge, where he became a Master of Mathematics, Science and Philosophy, before turning his attention to medicine. At this he was so successful that he positively 'shone in learning' and became known as the 'Chief Doctor', and after graduating, devoted himself to studying herbalism and to discovering the means of healing illness. For the sake of future ages he recorded what he had discovered, and in Leland's day a number of manuscripts in his hand were preserved at Cambridge, their contents, in Welsh, concerning the subjects of medicine, herbalism, animals, astronomy (astrology), sacred matters and symbols, and the invocation of divine spirits for the purposes of healing. From this we gather that Doctor John was clearly something of a wizard-priest, and so it is perhaps unsurprising to find Bale (1557), while wrongly ascribing to him a doctorate in theology, referring to him as 'Joannes Kent', and pointing out that he was also known as a 'necromancer', a man who was ascribed the power to summon and consult the spirits of the dead, and thus to 'sing' or utter prophesies concerning the future. Indeed, in view of the fact that necromancy was achieved by 'enchantment', and that Doctor John wrote partly in poetry described as 'the most elegant verse', we can also assume that he was something of a bard. In conclusion therefore, 'Doctor John ('Kent') of Caerleon' seems to have been a bardic wizard-priest who arrived rather late in the field of Jack of Kent. While he was never an outlaw, it is nonetheless by confusion with him, and also with a doctor of theology called John de Went (d. 1348: see

Preface), that both the Welsh bard Siôn Cent, and the folkloric Jack of Kent, are frequently found referred to as 'Doctor John Kent of Kentchurch'.

In 1483, the year after Doctor John 'Kent' of Caerleon died, his lack of 'outlaw' credentials was momentarily compensated by the appearance another occasional suspect who was hauled into court on 18 March (Court Rolls) under the name 'John Kent', to answer charges of 'treasons, felonies, trespasses etc committed . . . in the county of Hereford and the Marches of Wales adjacent'. However, as our Outlaw theory (see Preface) would suggest, John Kent was unlikely to have been this marauder's real name, it simply meant that he was an outlaw.

In c. 1506 an interesting coincidence occurred in the Monnow Valley when a former chapel of the Knights Hospitallers called Little Garway Farm, which still stands amidst the tumble of moss-laden boulders known as White Rocks (see Legend 5) on Garway Hill, was acquired by a man called John Kent, who might conceivably have been a descendant of the family who once supplied a rector to the Scudamores of Kentchurch in the 1380s (see Preface). Meanwhile, at this very moment, Sir Rhys ap Thomas was holding his grand tournament at Carew Castle, and hoisting, in a spirit of reconciliation and forgiveness, the 'Embrace of the Two Saints', St George and St David.

In 1531, Henry VIII was upon the throne, and allegedly indulging in an afternoon of falconry when his bird was suddenly deprived of its prey by a raven, whereupon his aide is said to have suggested that the raven had best be pulled down from its perch in order to 'secure your majesty'. This story, as R.A. Griffiths (Sir Rhys ap Thomas and his Family) observes, seems to have illustrated 'the king's dynastic anxieties' regarding the 'Ravens' of Dinefwr, and so in the same year an ageing Sir Rhys ap Thomas was peremptorily hauled before the Crown and charged with use of the name fitz-Urien, and thus with intending to make treasonable claims upon Wales based upon his descent from the ancient House of Rheged. Furthermore, his grandson, Rhys ap Gruffydd (accused of prophesising England's conquest by an alliance between the Ravens of Dinefwr and the Red Hand of Scotland), was beheaded.

In 1536, the Cistercian abbot of Grace Dieu near Skenfrith was a certain Doctor John Vaughan (see Table II), a man who, while later associated with 'Jack of Kent' by a writer who mistakenly listed John de Went as the abbot, might originally have attracted the connection because the locals remembered that the Vaughans of Hergest were Glyndŵr's kinsmen (see Chapter 12).

Two years later in 1538, Henry VIII instigated the Dissolution of the Monasteries as the time-honoured clerical order was finally discredited, its assets were reaped (many said raped) by the state, and its icons were promptly demonised, including the ambivalent effigy of the Virgin at Pen-rhys, of which Bishop Latimer effectively declared, 'She hath been the Devyll's instrument to brynge many (I feere) to eternal fyre', before suggesting that she be burnt, and finally, in 1545, the abbey of Grace Dieu was closed for ever.

In the same year, the chronicler John Leland toured the region of the Monnow Valley and recorded that 'Jenkin Scudamore was a stoute fellow and had al the nile of countery thereaboute', which doubtless included some lands acquired by the Scudamores on the Grosmont side of the river, and in c. 1560, as if in response to a controversy, a writer testily declared, 'John Kent died at Llangain (Kentchurch), Herefordshire, and is buried there, Mr Scudamore was his master'. (Cardiff, MSS.50, p. 379).

In 1567, the bard Siôn Cent was confused with 'Doctor John de Went' (d. 1348) in a document noted by Ifor Williams (Summary of Pitts) and which called him Dr Sion Guent, and in 1570 *The Mirror for Magistrates* was keen to confirm that Owain Glyndŵr had been 'seduced by false prophecies', and had died miserably in the mountains for lack of food. However, while Owain was certainly in a subterranean condition, in the latter 1500s his alter-ego, Jack of Kent, was still alive and kicking, and keen to 'sip an apple' (see Legend 26), and so it seems that the period 1570–1680 was about to become Jack's heyday as a character of myth and legend.

The Dissolution of the Monasteries had seen the closure of the Premonstratensian abbey of Talley in Cantref Mawr, and also the end of the Premonstratensian abbey on the Scudamore lands at Holme Lacy ('Hamm') near Hereford. So it was that with the final passing of the monks, the old religious joke once made at Talley regarding 'Half-in and Half-out' was soon forgotten, the sheep industry which had boosted the importance of the two 'Halfways' was no longer booming, and the River Tywi no longer marked the old Lancastrian boundary of Crown territory – so the 'in' and 'out' joke had become meaningless, and disused. As for the Dove and the Raven, with the accession of the Tudors, even that had lost its poignancy, and in any case, it was a very old story.

Thus, by 1570 only the Scudamores of Kentchurch in south Herefordshire, and perhaps a handful of other families with similar connections to Owain Glyndŵr, still knew and understood the cipher of the 'X'. Meanwhile, the activities of the Scudamores during this period do not lack interest, and I suggest that for some reason possibly connected with the Dissolution of the Monasteries, they had recently come under renewed pressure to admit their knowledge of the fate of Owain Glyndŵr, a grey-cowled wizard they had once sheltered, and whom the locals still called Jack of Kent. Despite such enquiries, however, the response of the Scudamores remained consistent with their support for Owain and for the Welsh cause. As you will recall, following Glyndŵr's death, Welsh chroniclers and supporters such as Adam of Usk had been keen to offer as much misinformation as possible regarding both the timing and the location of Glyndŵr's death and burial – because distracting, frustrating, and wasting the resources of an investigation is a better policy than remaining silent. Therefore, I suggest that when pressured upon the subject during the 1500s, the Scudamores simply continued to offer 'decoys' regarding the location of Jack of Kent's grave, and the easiest way to do this, while admitting nothing, was to draw attention to the possibility that he had been buried somewhere in the region of south Herefordshire, such as Kentchurch, Grosmont, or Monnington Straddel. In 1560, or perhaps a little earlier, had come the abrupt claim that 'John Kent died at

Llangain (Kentchurch), Herefordshire, and is buried there, Mr Scudamore was his master.' From this one might imagine that the Scudamores, while confirming that Sir John Scudamore had indeed married Alice Glyndŵr, may recently have been suggesting that the strange priest remembered as Jack of Kent had actually been their rector of the 1380s, John of Kent. However, few may have been convinced by this, because the local tradition was so strong that it had been Owain Glyndŵr, the outlaw, who had been popularly remembered as Jack of Kent, not the rector of the 1380s. Nevertheless, the debate served to concentrate attention upon Kentchurch and the Monnow Valley, which was the object of the exercise.

1570, according to local tradition, saw the contemporary Lady Scudamore distributing pax cakes signifying 'reconciliation and the forgiveness of old grudges', perhaps in the spirit symbolised by the erstwhile 'Embrace of the Two Saints' which had been sponsored by the Tudors at Carew some decades earlier. At this stage the Scudamores of the Monnow Valley would, like the rest of the area, have been Welsh-speaking, and so perhaps it was from this era that there came the following poem, also reconciliatory in nature, and originally in Welsh, which is kept on a scrap of paper at Kentchurch Court:

These Were The Delights Of Siôn Cent

A musing in a sequestered thicket/A pleasant aspect/A cheerful countenance/Contentment with the circumstances that prevail/The remembrance of a friend and a beloved one/Delight in a splendid feat/Enjoyment of the fare served/Decent behaviour/Prudent self-confidence/Restraint of over-confidence/An equal struggle/ Sunshine on a mountain top/A complete shade/Countercharging a rush/A competent servant/The praise of conscience/To love and be loved/To forgive an enemy/And God forgiving everybody.

In c. 1590, according to Aubrey, 'Sir James Skydmore of Herefordshire changed his name to Scudamore, and took his motto "Scutum Amoris" when Spencer's Faery Queen came out.' So, let us pause for a moment, and indulge in a pax cake, while I speculate that this Sir James Scudamore might have taken an interest in the Scudamore family history regarding Owain Glyndŵr, and that his interest might even have been stirred by the *Faerie Queene*. Spenser's *Faerie Queene* was a celebration of the reigning Queen Elizabeth as the culmination of the (Welsh) Tudor dynasty and of its claim to represent the true lineage of King Arthur, and for Sir James Scudamore, this would therefore have brought to mind not only the 'Queen of the Fates' in her old Gnostic and Templaresque sense, but the victory which Henry Tudor had first achieved with the help of, and 'over the bellie' of, Sir Rhys ap Thomas of Carew. This in turn, might have set Sir James thinking about a hypothetical wooden box, which we shall imagine that he now removed from a high shelf where it was hidden at Kentchurch Court. Inside was a line-drawing of a gaunt old man with a sharply piercing stare, a scrap of poetry in Welsh, a piece of paper with a cross drawn upon it at a rakish angle, and some writing which stated that Jack of Kent had been buried 'Half-in and Half-out' of a church, and that a dove and a raven had competed for his remains. Also perched upon the shelf nearby, was a wall-panel painted with an unfinished portrait of 'St. Jerome in the Garden' (see Appendix II), at which Sir James now stared thoughtfully, before returning his gaze to the sketch of the enigmatic old man. It would be nice to be able to display the rapidly decaying drawing in such a way that it need no longer be hidden away, and perhaps it was then that he conceived the idea of asking an artist to paint the old man's head upon the shoulders of St Jerome. Perhaps Sir James went even further, for while as Aubrey suggests, it may be that the original form of 'Skydmore' had been derived from 'great shoe' or 'stirrup' (as per their equestrian heraldry), we are told that Sir James decided at this moment to change the family name from Skydmore to Scudamore, so as to reflect a new family motto. The full version of this was in fact 'Scutum Amoris Divini' or 'Shield of Divine Love', and so it is also curious to observe that this seems to echo a line of Iolo Goch's made in reference to Owain Glyndŵr, namely 'May God's breastplate defend him'. If copied directly, the line would not have worked as a family motto, but if altered to 'Shield of Divine Love', then the sense is preserved, and Sir John and Alice Scudamore certainly appear to have shielded Owain to the end, just as Iolo would have hoped. Finally of course, it may have been in the late 1500s that someone, perhaps Sir James Scudamore, first volunteered the information that Jack of Kent, whoever he might have been, was said to have been buried 'Half-in and Half-out' of a church, and had prophesied that a Dove and a Raven would come to fight over his entrails. It would have seemed safe enough to say this now, almost two centuries later, especially since the result was to generate local speculation that 'Jack' might lie under the wall of either Grosmont church, or the Scudamores' private chapel at Kentchurch, for while such old stories remained vaguely familiar to many, their geographical significance in the Tywi Valley in south-west Wales was long forgotten, and in the Monnow Valley, it had never been known.

Popular drama and romantic literature were flourishing in this prosperous Elizabethan era, as witnessed by Spenser's *Faerie Queene* and by the contemporary works of William Shakespeare, and just four years later in 1594, in north Wales, a play was produced and performed entitled *The Wise Man of West Chester*, which in the following year reappeared under the title *Jack a Kent, Jack a Cumber*, by Anthony Munday.

Munday was attended by historical advisors, and also did his own research, and as we have already noticed his understanding of the 'anciaunt' nature of Jack of Kent seems to coincide with our own theories regarding 'Jack's' origins. We have also noticed (see Preface) that there appears to have been an early connection between Jack of Kent and King Harold, and so with regard to the original title of the play, it is therefore interesting that the legends regarding King Harold in the 'Vita Haroldi' claim that he survived the battle of Hastings, became a hermit who roamed the Welsh Marches in disguise, and ended his days at Chester.

As a specialist in outlaw stories, Anthony Munday was doubtless also acquainted with a popular tale concerning the 1100s and 1200s called *The Romance of Fulk Fitz Warine*, which featured a prominent historical outlaw from Whittington close to Glyndŵr's home at Llansilin (Sycharth), and while familiar with the more 'anciaunt' origins of 'Jack of Kent', Munday may also have been aware that there was currently a popular murmuring in the southern Marches around the Monnow Valley, which associated 'Jack of Kent' with the outlaw Owain Glyndŵr. So it was that while writing broadly across both time and space, and mixing both at will, Munday nevertheless decided to permit 'the learned Owen Glenderwellin' to make a cameo appearance in *Jack a Kent, Jack a Cumber*, while incorporating into Jack's personality some characteristics also ascribed by Shakespeare to Owain Glyndŵr. As contemporary playwrights, Munday and Shakespeare are well-known to have borrowed material from each other, and thus while Shakespeare describes 'that great magician, damned Glyndŵr' as 'exceedingly well read, and profited in strange concealments', Munday's wizard 'Jack of Kent' promptly declares 'in youth I studied hidden artes, and profited in chiromancy much' – and while Shakespeare notes the 'several devils that were his (Glyndŵr's) lackeys', Munday observes of the wizard 'Jack' that 'he never goes abroad without a bushel of devils about him' – and whereas Shakespeare's Glyndŵr calls up 'spirits from the vasty deep', Munday's 'Jack of Kent' calls up 'ghostes' from 'foorth the vaultes beneath'. It is also interesting that Munday offers a character in his play who is called Jack's 'Master' (a recognised synonym for 'patron') and who is named as 'Sir Gosselen Denvylle', a man who Munday asserts elswhere was one of the rebels outlawed for his part in the Lancastrian Revolt of 1321. The existence of Sir Gosselen Denvylle is confirmed in Captain C. Johnson's *Lives of the Highwaymen* (copied from the work of Captain A. Smith, 1714), and of course chimes well with the Outlaw theory (see Preface). However, it is also interesting that the word 'Denvylle' is very similar to the word 'Devil', and also to the important baronial family of 'De Neville'; furthermore, that the Scudamores were also rebels (pardoned) on the side of Lancaster during the Lancastrian Revolt, and that in 1321 the main seat of the Scudamores remained at Upton Scudamore in Wiltshire, where they appear to have been associated with a string of 'Goscelyns' including a Walter de Goscelyn (fl. 1331/2), an Adam de Goscelyn (fl. 1348), and a John Goscelyn (fl. 1358), not to mention a Goscelyn de Tanner (listed in 'Upton Scudamore' by Warren Skidmore) who lived just prior to the Lancastrian Revolt in 1317.

Anthony Munday was also an early authority upon the subject of another participant in the Lancastrian Revolt, namely 'Robin Hood' (see Preface) regarding whom he wrote three plays, and who, like Jack of Kent was also a considerable 'rock-hurler' in the field of folklore. Like Jack of Kent, Robin Hood may also have had precursors, since in 1296 we find a Gilbert Robinhood who lived prior to the Robyn Hode of Wakefield who finally 'cornered the market' for the name in 1321. Furthermore, it was Robyn Hode of Wakefield who had an outlaw friend named John the Little, who appears in the early stories as Robin's equal partner, and in legend it was none other than this Little John who initiated discord between Robin Hood and the Sheriff of Nottingham. In this respect, Munday's wizard Jack of Kent may have something in common with Little John, insofar as Jack is portrayed by Munday as a fickle 'side-switcher', a sprite-like character who sows both harmony and misery, and who makes and breaks alliances upon a whim. In doing so, Jack of Kent makes great use of 'the ladies', and so we find 'Upon these loovers practise thou thy wit. Help, hinder, give, take back, turne, overturne, deceive, bestowe, breed pleasure, discontent, yet comickly conclude, like John a Kent.' Meanwhile, the Jack of Kent we have identified thoughout history is also very much a 'side-switcher'. If the Everyman theory is correct, Sioni Cent began as a theological wizard-outlaw pitched against the dictates of Canterbury and the Anglo-Saxon Crown, but after 1066, even King Harold and his supporters seem to have become outlaws who were pitched in the popular mind against the Norman regime. In 1321, the Cumbrian outlaw Jack of (the) Kent was on the side of Lancaster against the Crown, but when in 1400 Henry IV usurped the throne, Lancaster *became* the Crown, and was promptly plagued by Jack of Kent in the form of Owain Glyndŵr. Furthermore, Glyndŵr, like any baron with a view to an uprising, also employed 'the ladies' in a destabilising game of marital alliances, and had formerly fought in the English army.

Jack of Kent was thus an elemental force, a double-edged and untameable side-switcher, a capricious entity who disappeared and reappeared, incarnated and reincarnated, and who seemed to live forever. Meanwhile, Munday's inclusion of Glyndŵr in his popular play (which had been preceded by an even more popular 'novel' version, since lost) had no doubt generated publicity well beyond Chester, and had further stirred the debate regarding Jack of Kent in the southern Marches and the Monnow Valley – and so it may be no coincidence at all that in the year following the play's release in 1595, someone carved an inscription upon one of the beams of an ancient building near Kentchurch, known as Jacky Kent's Barn, which proclaimed 'I. O' Kent 1596.' This was the barn in which the locals said that Jack had famously confined his crows (see Legend 9), which were of course the same as 'ravens', but alas, the beam is lost, for the barn was demolished during the 1960s. In *c.* 1600, the terms 'Cent' and 'Kent' were confused with 'Kemp', for all the reasons previously discussed, thus producing references to 'Sion Kemp (Kempt) or Cemp', and in *c.* 1645, a book entitled *The Life of Sir Rhys ap Thomas* (written by one of his descendants) recalled Sir Rhys ap Thomas's declaration of '*over my bellie*' and added the probably apocryphal tale of his lying under Mullock Bridge.

The year 1645 was certainly an interesting year for Jack of Kent, for the Civil War was under way, and summer in the Monnow Valley suddenly found itself host to a confrontation between a Scottish army allied with Oliver Cromwell and the forces of the Crown. With Hereford already surrounded and beseiged, we hear that a division of surplus Scots then poured down the Monnow Valley, whereupon it is recorded that they stole the bread out of people's ovens. At this moment, however, as if by magic, the folkloric Jack of Kent seems to have suddenly appeared upon the scene, perhaps in three different ways. Firstly, it appears that Jack's involvement may be commemorated by a small arrangement of stones forming an enclosure on the upper flanks of the nearby Graig Mountain as it looks down into the valley. Lost amid the trees, and nearly lost forever (since this is the first time its existence has ever been written down), this is a site long known to the locals as 'Jacky Kent's Bake-Oven'.

Epilogue

Nowadays known simply as 'Jacky Kent's Oven' this enclosure is in fact just the right size and shape for an outlaw to hide in, and there are still elder residents amongst the locals who can recall being told as children either that Jack of Kent spent the night in there once, or, that 'If you go in Jacky Kent's Bake-Oven, the Devil will have you!'

Secondly, we are told that when the Scottish Army came down the Monnow Valley in August, it was none other than Jack of Kent who routed them and sent them packing, with the aid of his magical powers (see Legend 12).

Thirdly, it is recorded that on 30 July a contingent of the opposing royal army of the Crown was actually encamped in the graveyard of Grosmont church, where, sitting amidst the monuments, a soldier named Richard Symonds was busily engaged in sketching what appears to have been a large tombstone, on which was a curious engraving. This sketch has been preserved in *The Diary of Richard Symonds* (B.L. Harley, 911) and next to it he wrote: '. . . Grosmont . . . in the east end of the churchyard lies a flat stone whereon is rutt the picture of a priest callid John of Kent and a picture of the Divell', whereupon Symonds proceeded to confirm that John of Kent's local patron had been 'Scudamore', before briefly citing the tale of Horses (see Legend 17) in which Jack of Kent conveyed his patron to London upon a black horse at supernatural speed. Regarding the context of Symonds's Diary, it is interesting that the Civil War had already been under way for three years, and that only the previous year Symonds had made a sketch in a churchyard in Berkshire of the effigy of a local folkloric character in that area, of whom he wrote, 'The Common people call this John Ever Afraid, and say farther that he gave his soul to the Diuel if euer he was buried either in church or churchyard, so he was buried under the church wall, under an arch', from which we might conclude that Symonds's interest in such otherworldly affairs may well have mirrored a widespread contemporary belief that the Civil War was reflecting a cosmological conflict between the forces of Good and Evil.

Furthermore, it might also be significant that in Symonds's drawing of the tombstone, Jack of Kent and the Devil are depicted in an attitude of mutual embrace – i.e. with a hand upon each other's shoulder, and that this is the same position adopted by modern schoolchildren in Carew when asked to re-enact the 'Embrace of the Two Saints' once hoisted above the entrance to Carew castle by Sir Rhys ap Thomas in 1506. If so, I suggest that since only Jack of Kent's patrons, the Scudamores, would have possessed the money, the influence, and the inclination to procure the manufacture and installation of such an artifact in Grosmont churchyard, that it may have served two purposes. Firstly, it officially focused attention regarding the legendary Jack of Kent upon Grosmont and the Monnow Valley, and thus acted as another 'decoy' which reinforced the idea that he was buried under the church wall there. Secondly, having possibly been installed in the 1500s, very possibly by Sir James Scudamore, the embrace between Jack of Kent and the Devil might also have been a satirical remark regarding the Anglo-Welsh politics of the famous 'Embrace of the Two Saints' at Carew, and of course, in view of where Glyndŵr was *really* buried, it subtly re-echoed Sir Rhys ap Thomas's joke. Finally, if the tombstone (now lost) was indeed installed during the late 1500s by Sir James Scudamore, perhaps in *c.* 1590, then this would have allowed Anthony Munday to inspect the result while doing research for his forthcoming play *Jack a Kent, Jack a Cumber*, for as was apparently written upon Munday's own monument (also lost). 'He that many an ancient Tombstone read, ith labour seeming, more among the dead to live, than with the living, he survaid Abstruse Antiquities, and ore them laid, such beauteous colours with his pen.'

In 1651 the Civil War ended, but Jack of Kent certainly seems to have remained a live issue in the Monnow Valley at this time. If we are correct, the Scudamore's attempts to blur the identity of Jack of Kent by pointing at a conveniently named rector of the 1380s, and their intention to concentrate upon the Monnow Valley a debate inflamed by the release of Munday's play in 1595, had culminated in the calculated installation of a monument to Jack in the graveyard of Grosmont church. However, at the end of the day, the best decoy of all had proved to be the legendary story of Jack's death and burial itself, which, once identified with Grosmont church, offered such a powerful religous image concerning the destiny of Jack's soul that it effectively *prevented* anyone from imagining in their wildest dreams that it might concern geography. It is unlikely however that the Scudamores had yet forgotten its meaning, for their tradition of keeping doves can be traced all the way from 1242 when Ysenda Scudamore 'Lady of Kaueros' had used cumin seed as a medium of exchange, via a dovecote recorded at Kentchurch in *c.* 1300, to a fine dovecote which was still maintained at Kentchurch during the 1600s. Meanwhile, regarding 'ravens', Sir John Scudamore 'Esquire' may well have married into the line of Dinefwr in the wake of Glyndŵr's war (see Table IV), and in any case, as today's John Scudamore observes 'there have always been ravens in the deerpark'. In the 1600s, the Scudamores had succeeded in focusing debate regarding Jack of Kent upon the Monnow Valley. However, the powerful local folk-memory identifying 'Jack' with Owain Glyndŵr had proved impossible to erase – and it was evidently intriguing the historians and archeologists of the day. In 1680, a burial-mound at Monnington became yet another 'decoy' offered by the Scudamores when it was excavated, claimed to have contained a skeleton 'intact and of goodly stature' and announced to be Owain Glyndŵr, whereupon it conveniently crumbled into dust before anyone could disagree. In the early 1700s, the Monnow Valley was well-known as a popular hiding place for recusants and outlaws (which did the memory of Jack of Kent no harm), and in 1721 according to the Browne-Willis correspondence, a site was excavated in Glamorgan which was allegedly the grave of John of Kent, and which apparently contained his leather shroud and his pewter chalice. As we have already observed, Glamorgan was also a popular hiding place for outlaws, especially the forested valley area around Pen-rhys, and it was also the main area of popularity for the poetry of a certain Welsh bard who may well have been an outlaw too, and who was notorious for his poverty. Therefore, since a leather shroud implies a pauper's grave, it is not impossible that this was indeed the grave of the bard Siôn Cent.

So it was that in Glamorgan the tradition of Sioni Cent remained strong, not just because of Owain Glyndŵr, but also because of the popularity of an outlaw-bard who had once rejoiced in the use of the same name. Thus, even into the early 1900s, the schoolchildren of Merthyr Tydfil were still singing songs of Sioni Cent. Finally, in 1996, it was left to two popular bards from the valleys east of Merthyr Tydfil, to write and perform just one more song entitled 'Jack of Kent'. This was a ballad which recorded three of Jack's dealings with the Devil, including the 'moonlight' variant of 'The Bridge' (see Legend 1), an encounter which as Huw and Tony Williams duly sang, left Jack to walk the land forever, as 'a shadowless man'.

* * *

'All men end by lying down.'

Siôn Cent

APPENDIX 1:
THE LEGENDS' ANALYSIS

LEGEND I : THE BRIDGE

Originally a stone-working escapade of the second generation of Scandinavian trolls, this ubiquitous tale has become an interesting example of the well-known principle of 'Cheating the Devil', in which good work is done with Satanic aid. The same story appears all over Britain and Europe, with other local characters inserted into the leading role, and is consequently found at such diverse places as the bridge across the Schollen Gorge in Switzerland, a bridge between Pontypool and Trefethin in south Wales, and at 'Devil's Bridge' near the Cistercian abbey of Strata Florida in west Wales.

In the Middle Ages, bridge-building was considered a pious work, and was conducted under the direction of the learned clergy, frequently the Franciscans, as part of their well-known expertise in the fields of road-building and water-working. By providing a new river crossing, the resulting span would alter the logistics of local travel and trade, and for this reason, as well as the fact that its maintainance was likely to be paid for by local taxation, it inevitably became a political issue among the nearby peasantry, only some of whom would actually reap any benefit from the bridge. Meanwhile, the new bridge was also a spiritual issue, as the ability of the clergy to build a bridge sufficiently hallowed as not to fall down (despite being in such close proximity to the water spirits of the ancient 'deep') was put on trial. In cases where a new bridge *did* happen to fall down, whether due to poor design or to nocturnal sabotage by unruly locals (such as those who once dwelt upon the banks of the Monnow) the constructing clergy were far more likely to blame evil spirits than their own incompetence, while any local saboteurs among the peasantry nodded vigorously in agreement.

In the case of Jack of Kent and the bridge over the Monnow at Kentchurch, we thus find Jack recruiting the Devil in the pious work of bridge-building, in a manner which falls into the category of 'theological banana-skins' (see Preface) such as those placed in the path of the Anglo-Norman medieval Church and its clergy by those who remembered an older cosmology. Such stories were designed to highlight the impracticality of the polarised Heaven and Hell vaunted by the Church since the days of St Augustine, and since the ultimate example of this impracticality was the question of 'Half-in and Half-out' (see Legend 23) it is interesting that the story of the bridge at Kentchurch has sometimes been linked directly with the fate of Jack's soul.

In the Welsh tradition (James Davies, *Folklore and Place-Names of the Caerphilly District*, Caerphilly, 1920) Siôn Cent is said to have built the bridge in a single night with the aid of the Devil, in return for which the Devil would have Jack's soul whether he were buried in or out of the church (thus linking 'The Bridge' directly with 'Half-in and Half-out'). Meanwhile, in the 'Moonlight' variant, Jack's lunar shadow precedes him across the bridge as the representative of his soul, spirit, or shade, just as Shakespeare refers to Banquo's ghost as his 'shadow', and Anthony Munday makes use of pluripresence and 'shadow-play' in his *Jack A Kent, Jack A Cumber*. Meanwhile, as the modern minstrels Huw and Tony Williams in their song 'Jack of Kent' correctly observe, Jack subsequently walked the land forever as a 'shadowless man', for it is dictated by an old tradition that when students of the black arts reach a certain standard, they are required to run through a subterranean vault with the Devil on their heels. If they prove fast enough, the Devil will only catch their shadow, or a part of it, and thus they will have qualified as accomplished magicians, but they will have lost some or all of their shadow, and for this reason there exists an old saying, 'May your shadow never be less'.

Such talk of the magician Jack of Kent losing his shadow to

Appendix 1

the Devil on the bridge at Kentchurch finally brings us to consider the suitability of this legend for application to the wizardly Owain Glyndŵr, who as Evans ('Monmouthshire') observed in c.1800 was doubtless also the 'Wizard of Grosmont' (see Legend 25). It is certainly interesting to speculate that Glyndŵr's war might have seen certain bridges sabotaged by the locals at moments inconvenient to the English, and to point out that if we are correct, a grey-cowled Glyndŵr subsequently haunted the Kentchurch and Grosmont area as an outlaw-wizard-priest. Meanwhile, the local historian M.N.J. of Blackbrooke (*Bygone Days in the March Wall Of Wales*) even went so far as to cite the local tradition that Glyndŵr was Jack of Kent, and to recount the story of 'The Bridge' with the Welsh 'wizard' in the leading role.

Finally, in Celtic terms, Glyndŵr, the 'Raven' whose army had descended upon crops all over Wales and the Borders, and who was described by the Welsh chroniclers as having left the world in the guise of a Reaper bearing a sickle, sits comfortably within the context of 'The Bridge'. At nearby Kentchurch Court he is said to have tied his 'dogs' to Glyndŵr's or (Jack of Kent's) Oak, and perhaps some muttered that these were in fact the 'Hounds of Annwn', the dogs of the Celtic Underworld. Thus, as the Devil finished his work upon the bridge at Kentchurch, it may well be that he looked up just in time to see the Welsh wizard, Glyndŵr, a grey-cowled figure who had done a great deal of good and evil in his life (depending upon which view you took), hurling a loaf of bread ('all flesh is corn') across the bridge, pursued by a dog which was in fact a lost soul from the subterranean 'deep', a realm long since identified by the medieval Church with the Devil's own domain.

LEGEND 2 : THROWING STONES

The significance of a giant Celtic ancestor (later supplanted by the Devil) hurling boulders with remarkable accuracy in the direction of Canterbury, has already been discussed in the Preface. Nevertheless, there remain some interesting details to record regarding the feature known as 'The Devil's Heelmark', an indentation in the side of the Skirrid Mountain which is said to have been made by the Devil during the stone-throwing episode with Jack of Kent.

The 'Heelmark' is also sometimes said to have been made by the keel of Noah's Ark during the Flood, or by a bolt of lightning which struck the Skirrid during the Crucifixion, and these are claims which seem to support the suggestion made in the Preface that the area was subject to some vigorous Christianisation between AD 600 and 1066. The 'Heelmark', however, is in fact a substantial landslip on the side of a mountain noted for its fragile geological construction (due to inclined strata separated by layers of clay), and which stands directly adjacent to one of the most geologically active earthquake zones in Britain. It is possible therefore, that an earth tremor similar to the many recorded in the area in both modern and ancient times may at some point have dislodged a portion of the mountain and thus changed its appearance literally overnight.

The panic engendered by some of the earthquakes that have struck the area throughout history have been recorded (and will be detailed in another volume of my research). However, it is a well-known fact that any such disturbance of the earth leading to fissures in the ground (let alone a phenomenon seeming to shake the very foundations of the world) was traditionally interpreted by the pagan peasantry (especially the Celts) as being due to disquiet among the spirits of the Underworld (the subterranean 'deep'), and was thus interpreted by the orthodox Church as being the work of the Devil. The name Skirrid, meanwhile, may be derived from the Welsh for 'shivered' or 'shaken', and it may also be significant that the Devil was often said in Wales to take the form of 'a large boulder rolling downhill'. However, what seems certain is that faith in the mountain itself had been shaken at some point, and so it was perhaps in the wake of just such a quake that an attempt was made to conquer it on Christ's behalf.

Perched high upon the flank of the mountain overlooking the landslip ravine known as 'the Heelmark' is an extraordinary stone which has been called 'the Devil's Table', but which when one clambers high enough to inspect it properly, is revealed as being nothing of the sort. This stone is in fact unmistakably a gigantic 'lectern' (I hereby rename it 'the Devil's Lectern'), and it appears to have been deliberately worked, being rough-hewn from the boulders nearby. From here, if one had the voice, a truly almighty sermon could be delivered to those who might be gathered in the landslip ravine below, before soaring out into the great eternity beyond.

In view of this, it was interesting to note while walking through the landslip ravine one afternoon (after a previous excursion made in dense fog and snow) that there is indeed a remarkable 'blessedness' in the area which takes the form of a deep silence, and a peaceful stillness in the air which may be produced by the guarding walls of the landslip and the mountainside itself. Furthermore, this sensation appears to have been noticed a long time ago, perhaps not least by the medieval monks of the chapel of St Michael which once stood upon the summit (and which may have been demolished by a 'demonic' earthquake in 1222) for local farmers used to regard the soil of this place as sacred, and often took it to scatter upon their fields, or upon the coffins of the dead. Thus the Skirrid has always been known locally as 'The Holy Mountain', for as E.M. Leather once observed (*Folk-Lore of Herefordshire*, Jakeman & Carver, Hereford, 1912), 'There has been no snail upon it ever since, or worm either; that is because it is sacred; they cannot go there . . .' and as has also been said, 'Tis a haunted place, and spell-beset.'

LEGEND 3 : THE DEVIL'S QUOIT

This story, ostensibly of a stone-throwing competition between Our Lord and the Devil shows every sign of being a 'damaged' legend, not only because of the blatant Christianisation which has installed Our Lord in the leading role, but also because it is a stone-throwing competition that offers only one stone. There are however, at least two reasons to suspect that this was once a tale of Jack of Kent and the Devil, which are as follows:

Firstly, the site (at Rogiet) seems to form part of the curious Chepstow outcrop of Jack of Kent stories which also sees the hurling of the Millstone Grit from Tidenham Common (see Legend 4) and the version of Pigs (see Legend 14) which is traditionally told at Chepstow, a town which alongside Tidenham and Rogiet also lies on the Severn estaury.

Secondly, regarding Jack's traditional depiction in the grey habit of a Franciscan cleric, it may well be significant that the Devil's Quoit is said to have have been hurled from a place called Grey Hill, and that a few miles further north at a place called Gaer Llwyd (Grey Fort), are the stones of an ancient cromlech on the Chepstow–Usk road which are traditionally known as Siôn Cent's Quoits.

LEGEND 4 : THE MILLSTONE GRIT

On a visit to Thornbury I was pleasantly surprised to find that many people on the English side of the Severn still knew of Jack of Kent, although no one seemed to remember where the stone thrown by Jack from Tidenham was supposed to lie. In fact, a number of ancient stones litter the fields lining the eastern bank of the Severn near Thornbury, and I am told that there were once several others which stood upon the shore but which have since vanished under the water. Nevertheless, I have evolved a theory regarding the two stones hurled by Jack and the Devil from Tidenham Common, which is as follows:

Judging by the position of sandbanks in the Severn estuary, it appears likely that an old crossing point may well have existed between Stroat (near Chepstow) on the western bank, and Shepperdine (near Thornbury) on the eastern bank. As the name Shepperdine implies, this would have been a crossing popular with the local sheep industry, and so we might imagine sheep and other animals being driven from Thornbury to Shepperdine, before being ferried across the Severn to land at Stroat. Once at Stroat, the farmer then had the option of either turning left and driving his flock via Tidenham towards Chepstow market, or turning right and driving his flock via

Woolaston towards the well-known sheep market at Lydney. Therefore, I suggest that the stone thrown by Jack which apparently landed near Thornbury on the eastern bank, may in fact have landed in the general region of Shepperdine, and that the two stones standing on either side of the Severn were therefore associated with a convenient crossing point which took advantage of a northerly gap in the sandbank known as the Oldbury Sands.

While it is interesting to speculate that such an association with the sheep industry might imply an origin for this story consistent with the boom in the sheep industry which immediately preceded Glyndŵr's war and which also boosted the importance of the two 'Halfways' in south-west Wales, it is also noticeable that the Chepstow version of 'Pigs' (Legend 14) sees them crossing from Marlwood to Sedbury (adjacent to Chepstow) which is the alternative route passing south of the Oldbury Sands.

LEGEND 5 : WHITE ROCKS

The carrying of boulders in leathern aprons by giants with an interest in stone masonry, is behaviour typical of second-generation Scandinavian trolls, and these exploits were frequently shared with the British Celts who were also of the opinion that their ancestors had been of superhuman proportions. At Llanhilleth Church (originally St Ithel's) just west of Pontypool, two mysterious Welsh giants known as Phyllis and Ithel engaged in a performance virtually identical to that carried out by Jack of Kent and the Devil at White Rocks on Garway Hill, and I have sometimes wondered whether Phyllis and Ithel have somehow been confused with Idel and Kenedin who once led the Welsh of Archenfield across the River Wye in raids upon the area of Ross-on-Wye during the reign of King Stephen (1135–54).

The River Monnow runs into the Wye, and towering above it near Kentchurch is Garway Hill and White Rocks, which is thus high ground above a border stream and therefore a classic burial site for a Celtic tribal leader. Meanwhile, it is also interesting that adjacent to Kentchurch on the Monnow, Kenderchurch was once an important Celtic Christian site dedicated to St Kenedrus (Cynidr), and that 'Cenedl' is Welsh for a tribe or clan.

Regarding the whiteness of the rocks in question, this refers in Celtic terms to their (pagan) sacredness and is the root of an assertion (applied to many such ancient stones) that one must not touch or disturb the White Rocks for fear of disturbing the earth-spirits and invoking dire consequences. Meanwhile the idea of canescence is also reflected in the folk belief that painting one's doorstep white will keep out the Devil. According to Palmer (*Folklore Of Old Monmouthshire*) the Devil must have been flying when the rocks fell out of his apron at White Rocks, for some of the stones are apparently sometimes said to have landed at places some miles to the east, thus also accounting for the rocks on Garway Common, the Devil's Lappit near Tintern, and the Seven Sisters at Symonds Yat. This at any rate returns us to the river Wye not only in the region of Whitchurch (White church) but within a few miles of the Kent's Stone at Huntsham near Goodrich, which is also known as the Quin Stone (from 'Gwyn' or 'White' Stone). Thus, there seems to be a trail of Celtic White Stones which have later been demonised as Devil's Stones, leading from White Rocks to the River Wye around Symonds Yat and Ross-on-Wye (Idel and Kenedin territory), and the two sites at either end of this trail (White Rocks and the Quin Stone) are both associated with Jack of Kent. In folklore, such stones invariably could not, would not, and should not be disturbed by mere mortals, and the fact that this was particularly the case with Kent's Stones was recorded by L.M. Eyre (*Folklore* 16, 1905, p. 164).

At White Rocks, Jack of Kent and the Devil were intent upon building a dam, or a weir, or a fishpond, and are sometimes said to have been heading for the Monnow either to dam the river, or as in one account (H. Thornhill Timmins, *Nooks and Corners of Herefordshire*) so as to build the bridge at Kentchurch (see Legend 1). Sometimes however, Jack and the Devil are heading in the opposite direction towards Orcop Hill, on a journey which may relate to Orcop weir and to a flood-valley fishpool which once existed between Orcop and Garway. Meanwhile, there is one more detail in the White Rocks legend which might possibly be worth considering in the light of Owain Glyndŵr.

We are told that the Devil was forced to cease work when a cock crowed, and while this may be a precursor of the later local custom of 'waking up the Devil' early on Christmas morning ('plygain') so that he would be driven away by the crow of the cock, we are not specifically told that this was in order to herald the dawn. The cock is of course another representative of the crow (raven), and since another well-known Welsh superstition stated that if a cock crowed at odd times or during the night it heralded or predicted a death, this tale suddenly becomes a prediction-of-death story akin to the story of Jack of France at Dorstone (Legend 24). Furthermore, in view of the fact that in some versions the stones were dropped not by the Devil, but by his colleague, we are therefore entitled to wonder if the death predicted was that of Jack of Kent.

LEGEND 6 : JACK STONES

At Trellech, the three standing stones are said to have been hurled, not from the Skirrid, but by the Devil and Jack of Kent from nearby Trellech Beacon, and they are made of a limestone conglomerate known as puddingstone, which according to a popular folk belief is able to grow in size (in contrast with Arthur's Stone on Dorstone Hill which is said to have been shrinking for many years) and which is also noted at Garway Hill, where it is called plum-puddingstone. At Trellech, however, it may or may not be coincidence that pieces of puddingstone incorporated into the walls of local buildings are locally referred to as Jack-Stones, possibly in commemoration of Jack of Kent's famous burial 'within' the wall of a church, or of Jack's connection with the three standing stones nearby which are composed of the same substance.

There is an allegation, however (despite their similarity to the three Devil's Arrows in Yorkshire), that by whichever route the stones arrived, they had once numbered not three but *five*. This seems to have resulted from an association of Jack of Kent with another stone known as the Pecked Stone (meaning 'thrown'), which lies near the roadside at the other end of Trellech village where it celebrates the meeting point of five parish boundaries at a location also marked by an array of five trees, which have since been reduced to three. In the Middle Ages, Trellech, like Grosmont, was an important town, and somewhat further along the same road is Craig-y-dorth, where in 1404 Glydwr's forces achieved a spectacular victory over the English before chasing them all the way to the gates of Monmouth.

LEGEND 7 : TOPS AND BOTTOMS

This popular exploit of Jack of Kent is in fact another Scandinavian escapade, well known to folkloricists as 'A Farmer Tricks a Troll'. As usual, the British Celts have adopted the story and inserted various local characters into the leading role, and Christianisation has subsequently replaced the troll with the Devil. The same tale also appears at Little Comberton near Worcester, where the protagonist is called 'the Farmer of Comberton', and it is also perhaps of mild interest that the leader of the Peasants' Revolt, John (Ball) 'Mad Priest' of Kent, famously complained of the poor receiving 'only the refuse of the straw'.

LEGEND 8 : BURDOCKS

Like 'Tops and Bottoms' (Legend 7) this is probably another Scandinavian story in the vein of 'A Farmer Tricks A Troll', and accordingly it is also told in Worcestershire of 'The Farmer of Comberton'. Once adopted by the border Welsh, such 'tricking' stories were ideal for application to the clerical Jack of Kent, whose main early function was to make a fool of his colleague the Devil, who also came from Canterbury.

Appendix 1

LEGEND 9 : CROWS

Crows being the same as ravens makes this story of exceptionally Morriganesque interest, and since jackdaws are also included, and have a particular reputation as 'small thievish crows with a habit of haunting derelict buildings', this may not be unrelated to the English perception that 'Taffy was a thief', the origins of which lie in the past activities of Welsh raiding parties who traditionally harrassed the English borders at every opportunity.

The folkloric ability to 'confine or release' the crows (ravens), however, was not unique to Jack of Kent, for the story is very Celtic, very old, and with variations was also told of others such as St David, St Catwg of Llancarfan, Samson, and St Iltyd. Meanwhile crow stories of other kinds are widespread and occur for example at Longtown near Abbey Dore, and also in Shropshire. In the case of the latest and greatest Jack of Kent, however, the story becomes exceptionally suitable for application to Owain Glyndŵr who had claimed a corvine decent from Rheged via the Lord Rhys, and whose diehard outlaw supporters (Owain's Folk) were implied by the bards to have been 'crows in the dark dens of the forests'.

As a raider of the Marches, it may well be that Owain's men would have made use, not only of mountain heights and forest cover, but also of derelict buildings during such operations, and as a 'confiner and releaser' of Morriganesque spirits it is easy to imagine the Welsh leader giving the order which would 'release' his 'Ravens' upon the homes and crops of unsuspecting English settlements in the valleys below. In doing so we are inevitably reminded once again, as the Morrigan descends, that 'all corn is flesh' as per the natural cycle, and that Glyndŵr did indeed wield power over life and death, and as the Ravens finally swoop towards the fields, we might also note with interest that a term sometimes applied to scarecrows (as well as to other things) was a Jack-a-Lent.

During his war, Owain Glyndŵr is also said to have attacked Caerphilly Castle, where Siôn Cent is alleged to have confined crows in the keep as an alternative to the traditional venue of a 'roofless barn'. However, Caerphilly Castle had previously been attacked by Llywelyn Bren, and suggestions that it was still partially derelict at the time of Glyndŵr's attack, might therefore have made it an amusing alternative to a roofless barn. Meanwhile, perhaps underlying the idea of roofless barns is the possibility that in some respects and circumstances cromlechs might be considered in the same way.

Finally, it is also interesting that the traditionally rebellious Welsh of the Caerphilly area who doubtless supported Glyndŵr at the time were traditionally nicknamed Cawcis (crows), and this may explain a bizarre story reproduced by Julian Cope (*The Modern Antiquarian*), which he apparently heard at Trellech, in which Jack of Kent was a swineherd who allegedly placed all the *cows* in the trees, so as to keep them from trampling the crops. This unique compound of Pigs (see Legend 14) and Crows (see Legend 9), in which the crows are replaced by cows, looks like an error or a case of Chinese whispers, until one considers that cawcis is actually pronounced 'cow-cis', and therefore it might actually be a macaronic pun.

LEGEND 10 : SPADEFULS

A similar story told near Kidderminster just north of Worcester, has the Devil trying to dam the boundary River Severn with 'The Devil's Spittleful', this being the amount of earth contained by a small shovel once referred to as a spittle. From Burton Hill in Herefordshire however, Jack of Kent and the Devil hurl their spadefuls eastward to where Jack's spadeful is alleged to have formed the Canon Pyon Butt. The sides of small hills referred to as 'butts' were venues traditionally used for archery practice (so as to make it easier to retrieve one's arrows) and so it is interesting to find the following story also regarding the formation of Canon Pyon Butt which is told of the outlaws Robin Hood (the archer) and his great friend Little John.

'Robin Hood and Little John had a wager. Robin bet Little John that he could jump right over Wormesley Hill and clear the Raven's Causeway, monastery and all. They stood somewhere near Brinsop. Robin jumped and kicked a piece out of the hill with his heel; that's Butt-house knapp. Then Little John tried. He took a much longer run and jumped better, but his foot caught the hill too, and kicked out the piece which is now Canon Pyon Butt. It is further on than the other: he kicked harder. You can see the hole in the hillsides made by their heels now.' (E.M. Leather: *The Folklore of Herefordshire*)

Having noted that we are once again discussing heelmarks (see Legend 2), and that Robin Hood is also alleged to have fired arrows from the pigeon house at Wormesley a full mile across to Canon Pyon Butt (H. Thornhill Timmins, *Nooks and Corners of Herefordshire*, 1892), it is interesting to recall our earlier suspicion that the role-model for the outlaw Jack of (the) Kent in Cumbria, might have been Robin Hood's equal partner Little John (see Preface). In view of this, it is certainly tempting to wonder if it is entirely coincidental that the formation of Canon Pyon Butt in Herefordshire is actually ascribed to the efforts of both Jack of Kent and Little John (i.e. Little Jack), especially since the addition of a 'y', as in Jacky Kent, traditionally implies 'little' as a term of endearment, as does an 'i' in Welsh, as per 'little Sioni bach' (see Legend 15). Furthermore, in another version of the Robin Hood tale, he and Little John create Canon Pyon Butt while carrying spadefuls of earth with the intention of burying the monks at Wormsley.

LEGEND 11 : MAGICAL THRESHING

An interesting feature of this story is the fly, which Christianisation has demonised here as usual (the Devil was called 'The God of Flies'), but which as a blood-sucking insect is likely to have had its ancient origins in the field of bulls. Bull-sacrifice was practised both by the Druids and by devotees of the cult of Mithras, which had been early Christianity's main rival for the affections of Rome, and it is thus interesting to hear of a story told at Llanfair Careinion in Montgomeryshire of a bull being reduced to the size of a fly and thrown into a well in what appears to have been a piece of early Christian propaganda.

It is also interesting to note that the episode in the *Mabinogion* tale of 'The Dream of Rhonabwy' in which prophetic dreams were received as a result of sleeping upon a magical yellow (lunar) oxskin, reflects a similar effect achieved by sleeping upon the skin of a white (lunar) hart (stag), such as that adopted by Richard II as his emblem. Brutus of Troy, who was believed by the Welsh to be their ancestor, was indeed said to have received the visions of the moon-oracle while sleeping upon the skin of just such a white hart, and the fact that either an oxskin or a stag's skin would serve the purpose may well be due to the observation made by Graves (*The White Goddess*, Faber & Faber, London, 1961) that the cults of the bull and the stag were connected in parallel to the Moon-Goddess.[21]

Regarding the magical threshing of Jack of Kent, meanwhile, here he behaves very much in the tradition of a hobgoblin or a 'Robin Goodfellow', a Puckish spirit known to the Welsh as the Pwcca (from which comes 'hocus pocus') who was well known for helping about the house, doing odd jobs, and playing the fiddle. However, if upset, this useful character would either wreak havoc or simply leave the house in search of a new home.

Finally, regarding Jack of Kent as personified by Owain Glyndŵr, it is interesting regarding the business of corn, threshing, and 'St Matthew's Day in Harvest', that the Welsh of Glyndŵr's homeland were evidently very aware of the symbology of such matters, and of the fact that 'corn is flesh', since at Llansilin the vitality of the corn-spirit is still preserved by mixing grain from the last sheaf of the previous year's harvest with the corn of the current year.

LEGEND 12 : THE SCOTTISH ARMY

Guto'r Glyn, the bard of the late 1400s who sang of how the 'ravens' of Sir Rhys ap Thomas had prepared the victory of Henry Tudur at Bosworth, also wrote a heartfelt lament upon the death of a fellow poet, Llywelyn ap y Moel, who had been outlawed in the wake of Glyndŵr's war. In this, Guto'r portrays Llywelyn as waiting to meet a girl in a birchgrove where the branches were straight as arrows and the trees stood in order, 'like the spears of Owain's best men'. Such imagery recalls the alleged ability of the

Druids to turn trees into soldiers (as reflected in a well-known bardic work called 'The Battle of the Trees', and also in the Battle of Dunsinane Woods as described by Shakespeare).

It also of course reminds us of the occasion when Owain Glyndŵr is said to have ambushed Lord Ruthin by placing helmets on poles amid the trees in north Wales, and considering that 'corn is flesh', it is also strongly reminiscent of the occasion when Jack of Kent is said to have entered a field of corn in the Monnow Valley and turned the cornstalks into soldiers who then repelled the Scottish army. Despite the anachronism of the Civil War, which is explained by the fact that 'Jack' never dies, we thus have another legend of the Monnow Valley which relates very well to Owain Glyndŵr, seeming once again to invoke the corvine Welsh leader as 'Jack' as he exercises his power over corn, and thus over life and death.

LEGEND 13 : STOLEN CATTLE

This story, which is also told of St David, is yet another fine example of the principle of Cheating the Devil in which good is done with the aid of evil, and thus Jack is once again engaged in his original task of placing 'theological banana-skins' in the path of the orthodox medieval Church and its harshly polarised cosmology of absolute Heaven and Hell.

LEGEND 14 : PIGS

The Welsh Assembly first summoned by Hywel Dda is said to have been the model for Owain Glyndŵr's parliaments, and so one cannot help but wonder whether the story of 'Pigs' reflects the Welsh legal system put in place by Hywel Dda, which stipulated that when a piece of property was to be divided between two claimants, one party was to do the dividing and the other the choosing.

Leaving such whimsy aside however, pigs are noted for having much in common with corn in the Celtic tradition, and also for being important symbols of fertility and reincarnation, and so they return us very swiftly to the principle of 'corn is flesh' (man consumes corn, which becomes flesh, which returns to the earth, springs forth again as corn, is consumed, etc.). Pigs are therefore also connected with the Celtic Underworld ('Annwn') and are frequently acquired as the result of a swindle, though I have no idea whether the word 'swindle' was ever associated with 'swine', or even with 'a pig in a poke' (as per Poke's Hole, a place in a field near Kentchurch which is Puck's Hole inhabited by the Pwcca and their 'hocus pocus'), especially since swindle is supposed to come from the German *schwindeln* (i.e. a 'totter' rather than a 'trotter').

In Herefordshire, meanwhile, it is interesting that only one Celtic saint survived into the Middle Ages, namely St Dubricius, who established his cult where a mystical White Sow was found at a place called Moccas, the Welsh word for pig. It is also interesting, therefore, that Moccas is but 2 miles from Dorstone, where Glyndŵr seems to have ended his days, and it is also just a swineherd's drive from Hereford Market where the deal between Jack and the Devil is often said to have taken place. With all of this in mind, one is naturally entitled to wonder if the late Glyndŵr might have been herding pigs as well as sheep, although in any case the story of pigs in Celtic terms is once again entirely suitable for peasant application to Owain Glyndŵr in the role of Jack of Kent.

Finally, the tale of pigs has sometimes been told of Dickey Kent (Norton Collection III, p. 62), and this may be the result either of invention and evolution, Jack of Kent's association with John de Went (d. 1348) and who may have been confused with one Ricardus Went (fl. 1353), a monk of Tintern Abbey who achieved prominence in south Wales, or by the interchangeability in folk terminology demonstrated by the fact that the Jackass we know today was originally referred to as a Dickass.

LEGEND 15 : SIÔN CENT'S HOUSE

> *Mae'n bwrw glaw, a wthi gwynt*
> *A tŷ Siôn Cent yn shiglo*
> *A Sioni bach yn rhedeg mas*
> *Rhag ofon i'r tŷ gwmpo.*

This song was also sung of a west-Walian outlaw known as Twm Siôn Cati, and it also resonates with a well-known passage in the Bible (Matthew 7: 24–7). However, when it is found in the Welsh tradition regarding little Sioni Cent we are reminded not only of our suspicions regarding the outlaw Little John (see Legend 10), but also of the applicability of this stanza to the life of Owain Glyndŵr.

Owain was surely famed among the peasantry for two things, his ability to control the weather, and his failure which was signalled by the fall of Harlech Castle, an event at which he was probably not present, but from which he was rumoured to have escaped at the last moment. Is this therefore a wry observation that Jack had ultimately *failed* to control the weather, with the inevitable results?

LEGEND 16 : HIDDEN TREASURE

This story may relate to a medieval belief that the most common explanation of ghosts was that they were spirits who had returned because they had left treasure hidden somewhere in the world, in which case it was said that they could be helped by throwing the wealth in question into a river, lake, well, or other body of water. It is also interesting that Merlin was said to have hidden King Arthur's treasure in Arthur's Cave at the Celtic site overlooking the loop in the Wye near Goodrich, in the middle of which stands the Quin Stone, which was recorded in 1840 as a Jack of Kent's Stone. While it is amusing to wonder whether this was therefore the cave to which Jack of Kent was supposed to have taken the 'truan bach', whether Jack or the monk was the ghost in this case, we can only speculate.

LEGEND 17 : HORSES

It seems that the knightly Scudamores, like Sir John Scudamore himself, had always been chevaliers, and since we have already suggested their interest in the real (Welsh) Arthurian tradition, it seems pertinent to observe that just prior to the rise of the

Lord Rhys, one of the Wiltshire Scudamores had purchased Upton Scudamore from Robert of Ewyas with the offer of a white war horse reminiscient of the legendary white war horse required to complete the sleeping army of King Arthur.

At Kentchurch Court however, Jack of Kent's horses were black demonic steeds, and were duly referred to as the 'fiery coursers' which in the Welsh tradition of Siôn Cent are identified as 'the Horses of Annwn', the Celtic Underworld (subterranean 'deep') which had existed long before the invention of Hell. These horses were said to have been kept by Jack in the cellars under Kentchurch Court, however, since it is unknown whether or not these were actually ever used as stables, this may simply be a device designed to confirm their infernal origins.

The connection between Siôn Cent and horses is strongly made in the Welsh tradition, and as usual, many have therefore made the error of assuming that it refers to Siôn Cent the bard, but there is no evidence connecting Siôn Cent the bard with either Kentchurch or the Scudamores, nor is there anything linking him with horses, and no evidence of any such obsession in his poetry. Siôn Cent the bard may, however, have been accidentally implicated when another Welsh bard, a eulogist with whom he was famously in dispute, not only observed that Sion was abysmally poor, had nits and stank, but also enquired, 'Why are you attacking me, stable lad?'. However, far from referring to Sion's equine expertise, this was simply a macaronic pun on *gwas ystabl* a term meaning a low order or amateur poet, and so it certainly does not imply that the Welsh bard was likely to have been in charge of flying steeds at Kentchurch Court.

For this reason I suggest that the Siôn Cent who rode 'the Horses of Annwn' was no impoverished bard, but was in fact the Siôn Cent of Kentchurch, Owain Glyndŵr, a man who in his violent youth had been widely renowned for his mastery of horses, and of whom Iolo Goch wrote at the time:

he was a fierce mighty slasher, he did nothing but ride horses . . .
Great renown for knocking down a horseman did he win . . .

felling him splendidly to the ground, with his shield in fragments
. . . 'Candle of Battle' . . . his spear shattered from fury . . .
everyone indeed for fear of him shouting like wild goats, he
caused terror . . . neither grass nor dock grew, nor corn where he
had been.

Glyndŵr was described as tall and fair, and was mentioned only
once by Siôn Cent the bard (c. 1430) who called him 'graceful
and slender', but his strength must have been immense, for we
are also told that:

cased in armour he would practise leaping onto the back of a
horse . . . would walk and run long distances on foot, or he
would practise striking numerous and forcible blows with a
battleaxe or mallet. In order to accustom himself to the
weight of his armour he would turn somersaults while clad
in a complete suit of mail, with the exception of his helmet,
or would dance vigorously in a shirt of steel; he would place
one hand on the saddlebow of a tall charger and the other on
its neck and vault over him . . . He would climb up between
two perpendicular walls that stood four or five feet asunder
by the mere pressure of his arms and legs, and would thus
reach the top, even if it were as high as a tower without
resting in either the ascent or the descent. When he was at
home he would practise with other esquires at lance-
throwing and other warlike exercises, and this continually.

Such had been Glyndŵr's preparations for a weird outlandish
life spent largely on horseback, and which caught the last rays
of the sun at Kentchurch. Here, as Jack of Kent, he is said to
have ridden his last horses into the sky, and perhaps in this
instance we should picture him as a grey-bearded old man
whose face was hidden by a hood or a hat, for this was the
traditional appearance of the Nordic/ Scandinavian god called
Odin, whose cult had reached Britain long before the Vikings.
As a god of battle, Odin was an inspirer of warriors to such
frenzy that they hurled themselves naked into battle, fearing
neither death nor pain, just as the Dark Age Celts had done; he

was also a noted instigator of strife and discord upon a whim, and above all it was *Odin* who was famous for leading wild hunts on horseback across the heavens in precisely the manner practised by Jack of Kent at Kentchurch, his hooves bringing thunder to the firmament. Later, Odin underwent a voluntary death, and was resurrected, thus acquiring vast wisdom, and was well known for the two ravens, *Thought* and *Memory*, which sat upon his shoulders and which whispered in his ears.

Meanwhile, as Siôn Cent flew by, at the head of his Otherworldly hunt, the Welsh tradition tells us that a horse which he had confined within a barn some three weeks earlier, and which no one else had dared to move, burst out to join the throng, and as in the case of 'Crows' (Legend 9), we therefore note that Jack was ever a 'confiner and releaser' of spirits. Furthermore, as the spectral hunt flew on into the sky, it is interesting to speculate at what altitude they might have flown, for there was a traditional choice of 'High Wind, Middle Wind, or Low Wind' which was well known to airborne witches, wizards, and the fairies (fates), but which later may have been diluted by the superimposition of the Biblical (Hebrew) concept of the three heavens (air, stars, and God's domain).

It was surely just as difficult to follow Jack of Kent upon his equine escapades as it was to follow Owain Glyndŵr, for it was said of both Jack at Kentchurch and of Owain in north Wales, that they had deceived pursuers by putting their horse's shoes on backwards. Although the same story has also been applied to Llywelyn the Last (d. 1282), it has also been noted that the family of the Lollard Walter Bryt (who later joined the rebels of Maredudd Glyndŵr) were related to the Scudamores (see Table IV), and that they were also the owners of strange horseshoes (cast in such shapes as a child's foot and a cow's hoof), and it has even been suggested (W.S. Symonds, *The Malvern Chase*, Tewkesbury, 1881) that the Bryts might also have sheltered the outlawed Glyndŵr at their manor east of Ledbury (Revd R. Hyatt-Warner, *Birtsmorton Court*, Woolhope Naturalist's Field Club Report, 1906).

It is well known that at Glyndŵr's birth, his father's horses were said to have been found in their stables variously up to their knees, fetlocks, or bellies in blood, an image which doubtless appeared prophetic when it was reported of Glyndŵr's victory at Stalling Down[37] that after eighteen hours fighting the blood was up to the horses' fetlocks at nearby Pant-y-wennol. Once again this reminds us of Odin, who famously created a conflict between two kings so that their armies would wade through blood upon the battlefield, meanwhile it may be that Glyndŵr's acquisition of this motif was also inspired by his embrace of the legacy of Owain Lawgoch, who in the late 1300s had been urged by the bards of Anglesey to return from France to fight the English in the following terms: 'and once you have come, blood up to the knees'.

A more popular substance in which to wade, rather than blood, is of course water, and this invites the possibility of an analogy between the two. In this respect it may well be significant that we should come across a folk tale of an Owain (traditionally assumed to be Glyndŵr) which is found in Carmarthenshire at Mynydd Mawr, just south of Llandeilo beside a lake named Llŷn Lech Owain ('The Lake of Owain's Stone'), which forms the source of the River Gwendraeth Fawr, which issues southward into Carmarthen Bay (see Map 3).

Here we are told that this Owain had a well which he covered with a large stone, but that one day he forgot to replace the stone after watering his horse. As he rode home, he looked back, and was amazed to see that the well had consequently overflowed and was threatening to drown the entire district, but he rode back and circled the waters with his horse, and by doing so he contained the flow.

The result of course, was the lake we see today, but I suggest that for 'water' we should read 'blood'. Not only is the location of this site just south of Llandeilo tailor-made to commemorate the bloody cascade of Glyndŵr's 1403 campaign down the parallel valley of the adjacent River Tywi, but the Gwendraeth Fawr which issues from the lake even merges directly with the estuary of the Tywi as it flows into Carmarthen Bay, which if we are correct, is precisely where Owain's essence flows forever from Llanwrda into Môr, the 'deep' of the sea.

Stories of overflowing wells are common in Celtic folklore,

a Scottish example having caused Loch Ness, however, they are normally portrayed as disasters or punishments, and so this would appear to be a pro-Glyndŵr story, since the crucial point made here is that he succeeded in stemming the flood. In other words, I suggest that as per the position adopted by the Welsh chroniclers, this story essentially says 'Glyndŵr knew what he was doing, he cannot be blamed, he was in control'.

However, if we return to the stables at Kentchurch Court in south Herefordshire, where Baron Scudamore was said to have kept a hundred horses in the charge of a certain Jack of Kent, we might well find evidence that not everyone agreed, for as this ribald tale relates, these horses were producing manure at a rate that Jack clearly could not contain. 'Yes', the sceptical Welsh Border peasantry were saying, 'Owain and his horses were up to their knees in it alright, right up to their knees in it, we all were, and he *wasn't* in control.', and so, no doubt because the traditional bleeding of horses on St Stephen's Day (thought to increase their stamina) was especially popular in Herefordshire, dung was a natural analogy for blood.

LEGEND 18 : SPREADING DUNG

This may well be another Scandinavian troll story of the agricultural variety; however, when applied to Jack of Kent in south Herefordshire and Kentchurch, it may have become a logical extension of the relationship between dung and blood as per our theory of Horses (see Legend 17).

LEGEND 19 : THE DUNGEON

This tale of Jack of Kent has never previously been written down, but it was told to me in 2003 by a lady at Kingston in south Herefordshire who remembered it from her childhood, whereafter its authenticity was confirmed by the local historian Doreen Ruck.

All the local Marcher lords had their own dungeons into which miscreants were hurled before receiving justice at their lordship's discretion, and Sir John Scudamore was more experienced than most in the practice of imprisonment since he had formerly been responsible for the main dungeon in Archenfield, which belonged to the Talbots at Goodrich. However, in the dungeon under Glyndŵr's Tower at Kentchurch Court, beneath the bedroom known variously as Owain Glyndŵr's or Jack of Kent's, Jack seems to have been an outlaw who slipped through Scudamore's fingers with remarkable ease, and who even had the audacity to visit Grosmont, and I have been told that when the dungeon was excavated many years ago, some sawn-off iron bars were duly seen amidst the debris.

LEGEND 20 : THE CHRISTMAS BLOCK

The tradition of Yule logs, noted as particularly strong in Shropshire, Radnorshire and Herefordshire, involved dragging the log into the kitchen on Christmas Eve, placing it on the hearth and lighting it with a fragment of the previous year's log. However, this story (which once again seems to highlight Jack of Kent's general mastery of birds) may not be as innocent as it appears, and like many of these things (including the original village plays of Robin Hood) its task may have been to preserve pre-Christian or pagan wisdom in a coded form during the oppressive era of the medieval Christian state.

In this case, the key may be the fact that geese are birds which follow the sun by flying south for the winter, and that in this story they are engaged in *hauling* in a Yule log, Yule being the festival of the sun ruled by the Yule father, who was none other than Odin again (see Legend 17).

The Christmas Block is thus another macaronic pun, since the Breton word for the sun is 'heol' and the closely related Welsh equivalent is 'haul', and so the geese are really 'hauling in the sun', this being the very purpose of Yule, which was a pagan midwinter ritual designed to guarantee the sun's return, and thus to ensure the next year's harvest. Like the question of corn, this story therefore relates to the natural cycle, and to reincarnation, and in the case of Jack of Kent perhaps implies that he will never die, but will return like the sun to ensure the harvest.

LEGEND 21 : THE MINCE-PIE

This peculiar tale, which has the feeling of having come from a subsequent era, is somewhat reminiscent of the story of Jack Horner, a story based on Henry VIII's indignation at the wealth accrued by the abbot of Glastonbury, and in response to which the abbot is said to have sent the king a bribe in the form of a pie containing the deeds of twelve manors. However, the transporter of the pie, Jack Horner, is said in the nursery rhyme to have been eyeing this Christmas pie when he 'put in his thumb, and pulled out a plum, and said "What brave boy am I!"'. The plum was of course the deed for the manor of Wells, whereafter Jack is reported to have told the abbot that he had been given it by the king.

LEGEND 22 : THE DOVE AND THE RAVEN

Much analysis of this legend, and of doves and ravens in general, has already been dealt with in this book under the auspices of St Columba and Urien of Rheged, and while it is worth noting that Simpson (*The Folk-Lore of the Welsh Border*, Batsford, London, 1976) records a variant wherein the impaling of Jack's entrails on the beams of a roofless barn directly links this episode with crows (see Legend 9), we might also note that doves were released in churches at Pentecost, and that the variant predicting a good harvest if the dove should win has a certain Celtic poignancy. However, with everything else already discussed, our remaining interest lies mainly in the oven variant which has been preserved in the Welsh tradition.

Once again Siôn Cent the bard may have inadvertently been implicated here by virtue of the fact that one of his phrases struck such a chord that it later became the hook-line in many a popular song, namely, 'the oven of hellish nature'. However, the medieval stone oven was a well-known and inevitable metaphor for the old Celtic Underworld (Annwn) which had long since been identified by the medieval Christian Church with the flames of Hell, an observation which was doubtless confirmed by the fact that the deeper into the mines one went, the warmer it got, and the more likely it was that one would encounter one of the old earth spirits (goblins) which were now officially the 'Devil's imps'. Siôn Cent the bard was nothing if not an ardent follower of Christ, who was the only authority he respected, and it was therefore natural that he should find 'the oven of hellish nature' an invaluable receptacle for anything that smacked of either pre-Christian or Romano-Celtic-Christian ideas (such as the reincarnation of Dark Age leaders), of which he disapproved every bit as much as he disapproved of baronial and material wealth.

So, if it is not connected to the Welsh bard Siôn Cent, the oven variant is consequently left to compete with the bake-oven related activities of the Scottish army (see Legend 12) for any possible connection with the interesting site on the side of the Graig Mountain known as Jacky Kent's Oven. This small stone enclave might therefore conceivably reflect one of two things: either it is indeed a memorial to the raiding activities of the Scottish army in 1645 which occurred long after the actual lifetime of the latest and greatest Jack of Kent, or just possibly it is a typical outlaw's hiding-hole, just big enough to contain a man, which might actually have been used at some stage by the late Owain Glyndŵr.

Meanwhile, with regard to the oven variant as folklore, it is worth noting with regard to St Columba and Urien in north-west England and Scotland, that the Welsh account of Siôn Cent having feared the preparation of a place for him in Hell is reflected in a Scottish tale of doves and ravens which involves a similar cremation and the preparation of a 'bed' in Hell (School of Scottish Studies: Sound Archive: SA1971.111.A-B1).

Furthermore, it is also interesting that the original story of 'Jack the Giant-Killer' prominently featured both ovens and a hero who like Glyndŵr was pitched against an immeasurably greater foe in a manner reminiscent of 'David and Goliath', which in turn invokes the patron saint of Wales. Finally, as the ravens condemned by Leviticus (11:15) circle perennially above the corn, they know that all will burn like chaff, when as St Matthew (6: 30) observes, 'the grass of the field, which today is, tomorrow is cast into the oven'.

LEGEND 23 : HALF-IN AND HALF-OUT

As in the case of 'The Dove and the Raven' (see Legend 22) the question of 'Half-in and Half-out' as it relates to Limbo and the delicate position of the Celtic ancestors has already been discussed within the main text of this book. Nevertheless, it is worth acknowledging the existence of some minor aberrations, such as a note made by Simpson (*Folklore of the Welsh Border*, Batsford, London, 1976) that at some point it was apparently suggested that Jack of Kent might have been buried under the wall of neither Grosmont church nor Kentchurch, but instead under the wall of St Brigit's church at Skenfrith, although this is an innovation which seems to have gathered no moss ever since. More interesting perhaps is a little-known claim related to me by a resident of south Herefordshire, that Jack of Kent was buried under the ecclesiastical wall of Little Dewchurch some miles north-east of Kentchurch.

In a similar vein one occasionally hears of subtly different interpretations of the concept of 'Half-in and Half-out', such as a version from the Welsh tradition which explains that the Devil was to have any part of Jack which was either 'in' or 'out', and so he was therefore buried very carefully within the thickness of the wall, or a version reproduced in the *Atheneum* (26 July 1851, p. 808), which asserts that Jack had promised the Devil that he would not be buried 'in' the church where he could not be reached, and so he was therefore buried under the wall so as not to be outside either. However, the vast bulk of this tradition as applied to both Jack of Kent and to other such burials in folklore, concerns the idea of being 'Half-in and Half-out', and it is upon this interpretation that our thesis, like Owain Glyndŵr, rests at Llanwrda.

It is also interesting, in light of the fact that the famous Franciscan wizard-priest Friar Roger Bacon (d. 1294) was also buried 'Half-in and Half-out', that not only was burial in the Franciscan habit the standard medieval method of evading the posthumous attentions of Beelzebub, but also that its 'grey' colour (notwithstanding a tinge of 'dove-pink') rendered it 'Half-in and Half-out' of the realms of Light and Darkness, and that this might perhaps reflect the original mission of the friars to immerse themselves in worldly affairs while retaining their spiritual integrity, which within a century so many of them were failing to do.

The demise of Roger Bacon came only a decade or so after the 'Half-in and Half-out', burial of Roger de Clifford beneath the church wall at Aconbury in south Herefordshire (which his dark shade haunts to this day), and as we know, the 'Half-in and Half-out' burial of Jack of Kent seems to have occurred in early 1415. However, the tradition clearly continued to function into the Elizabethan era when the wizard Nostradamus was said to have received a similar burial in 1566, and no doubt it continued to be the fate of various wizards and witches throughout the persecutions of the 1600s, and beyond.

LEGEND 24 : JACK OF FRANCE

This in many ways is the most macabre and poignant story of them all. As we have already explained, there were excellent reasons, stemming not least from Owain Lawgoch (Yvain de Galles), why Owain Glyndŵr might have been referred to as Jack of France, and we *know* that as an outlaw he was referred to as Jack (see Chapter 12). Furthermore, the fact that this legend (which is the only recorded exploit of this character) lies so deep in Jack of Kent territory, and so close to Monnington Straddel and Kentchurch, concurs in suggesting that Jack of Kent and Jack of France are one and the same. Finally, these suspicions in south Herefordshire are confirmed when we hear from the Welsh tradition in Glamorgan that 'Siôn Cent was a terror to all folk', which is almost precisely the description given of Jack of France at Dorstone, and as we have also seen, the story of Jack of

France, like the story of Jack of Kent's demise, also relates to the village of Llanwrda in south-west Wales.

For a man who was described as 'the candle of battle', it is perhaps not inappropriate that the flickering tale of Jack of France is integrally concerned with candlelight, and this relates in turn to an ancient and long-standing belief in the appearance of strange lights which were believed to predict the imminence of a death. In many cases, while fireflies and glowworms may have played a role, these were caused by the ignition of methane or 'marsh gas' in watery areas where people frequently disappeared, and which in any case were areas viewed with particular 'superstition' due to the (pagan) Celtic belief that water was the medium which conveyed the spirits. These circumstances therefore gave rise to a belief in the existence of a particularly mischievious spirit of the marshes closely related to Will O' The Wisp (also known as as Jack O' The Wad), who while bearing the 'fool-fire' or *ignis fatuus* like the light of a distant inn, lured travellers to their deaths and rejoiced in the name of Jack O' Lantern. These misleading entities were of course themselves disembodied spirits who rose from the 'deep' and were associated with death, and so the appearance of any such strange light was duly dreaded and referred to as a 'corpse-candle'.

Finally, before the lights go out we should also note that the Devil, who had recently developed a habit of appearing in churches, was also known in terms harking back to pre-Christian times as the god of the Waning Year, which may well be why the Welsh chroniclers had been so anxious to imply that Owain Glyndŵr had died on 'St Matthew's Day in Harvest', the last day on which the daylight lasted longer than the night.

LEGEND 25 : THE WIZARD OF GROSMONT

There is little that one can say about the Wizard of Grosmont, and that is largely his appeal, for he is a lonely figure whose function is simply to walk the route from Grosmont to Kentchurch Court, and thus to serve as a reminder that the Scudamores were once familiar with a withered magician whom some called 'Jack of Kent', but many (eg. Evans & Britton 'Topographical & Historical Tour of the County of Monmouth' 1810) thought was Owain Glyndŵr.

LEGEND 26 : TO SIP AN APPLE

In a sense this story is another case of Siôn Cent making a fool out of his colleague the medieval Devil by virtue of an older knowledge of apples, which included the fact that they had not originally featured in the Garden of Eden, that the apple was a good thing, and that while Siôn could use one to good effect, the Devil had no power over them at all. Furthermore, the fact that the Devil (like the danger of apples) was in any case also a recent invention, is subtly implied by the presence of the fruit-bearing tree, which shows that the Devil is again being cast in his earlier (pagan) capacity as the god of the Waning Year (see Legend 24).

The Devil's plan to carry Siôn Cent away meanwhile refers in the same way to a widespread medieval belief that at the moment when the orchards were ripe and yielded their apples, the harvest beckoned the reaper across the fields and the year waned, the Devil would suddenly appear as a nightmare vision at the bedside of some vagrantly dreaming soul. Often in the form of a tall, gaunt, cadaverous and ashen-faced man, he would then attempt to carry his intended victim out through the window, whereupon it was said that the hapless sleeper would turn in horror to see his own body lying abandoned upon the sheets.

This is of course the same phenomenon which is these days medically researched under the general title of 'night terrors', which typically involve awakening, or seeming to awaken, during the night with a powerful sense of a foreign presence in the room, or even of a person actually sitting upon one's chest and making it impossible to breathe. This phenomenon is remarkably consistent in its manifestations across the world and is apparently due to a malfunction of the temporal lobes in the brain. Meanwhile it is also said to be so appallingly vivid and disturbing that its victims are terrified to sleep, and cannot separate the experience from reality, and of course the fact that it is nowadays the subject of what we call medical research makes it no less strange a fact of many lives. As for the experience of looking down upon one's body from a position in mid-air this too now has a medical name, i.e. the out-of-body or near-death experience, which is of course related to what some call astral projection.

Finally upon a lighter note, and fortunately for Jack of Kent, despite being carried out of the window by the 'god of the Waning Year', we still have time to prevaricate over a discussion of apples, and the trees upon which they grow. All across the world since time immemorial, and therefore long before the invention of the Garden of Eden, apples have represented life, love and immortality, and among the cultures in which they have featured thus are those of Greece, Scandinavia, and the British Celts. So it was that apples belonged to the goddess Aphrodite, that they grew golden and were guarded by three sisters in the garden of the Hesperides, and that they were received by Hercules from the three daughters of the West (Greek), also that Idun owned the apples of perpetual youth (Norse), and that Lugh demanded the golden apples which hung in the garden of the light in the East (British Celtic). In Britain, the Druids also held the apple-tree sacred, and later Arthurian Avalon took its name from the Welsh word for apple, and even at the very last, when Merlin finally went mad and lived in the forests, he took comfort from the apple-trees, and then came Christianity and the anonymous Tree of Knowledge which was later identified as an apple-tree, and so the apple was cast for ever, along with the female creative principle, into 'the oven of hellish nature'.

Nevertheless, the Scudamores liked apples. At their original seat of Upton Scudamore in Wiltshire near Norrington, it is recorded that the Scudamores 'anciently planted orchards' of the 'Scudamore Crab' variety which later became the celebrated 'Red Streak' apples of Herefordshire, and in c. 1690 Aubrey recorded that the Red Streak was already established there, and offered 'Mr Gwillim and Lord Scudamore' as worthwhile experts on the subject of cider-apples, and even today, adjacent to Kentchurch at Kaueros (Corras) where the foundations of

Lady Ysenda's chapel can still be found, the muddy remains are surrounded by Barn Orchard.

Finally, the story of 'To Sip an Apple' is also attributed to Virgil, but its roots may be much older, lying perhaps in Syria in a version of the Eden story which once featured a garden ruled by a goddess of fruitfulness and fertility, and later arriving in Cyprus, where desperately hoping for her favour was an angst-driven giant named Amphidexious, forever in two minds, whose right hand knew nothing of his left and so each hand strove endlessly to vanquish the other in the contest for the prize. The dual aspects of this tormented being were 'the god of the Waxing Year' and 'the god of the Waning Year', who would one day become Yahweh and the Devil, and they were the opposite aspects of a single nature whose violent battle was the comedy and tragedy of life spent in the search for lasting joy. In the far future, the goddess would be trampled beneath their whirling boots, Yahweh would win the garden, the Devil would gain power over apple-trees and orchards, and although the search for lasting joy would last forever, at last our search is over:

* * *

I am Taliesin, I sing perfect metre
My original country is the Land of the Summer Stars
I was with my Lord in the highest sphere
When Lucifer fell to the depths of Hell
I have borne a standard before Alexander
I know the names of the stars from north to south.
I have been a blue salmon
A dog, a stag, a buck on the mountain
A stock, a spade, an axe in the hand
A stallion, a bull, a roebuck
A grain which grew on the hill
I was reaped and cast in an oven
I am old, I am new
I have been dead, I have been alive
I am Taliesin.

(Taliesin, bard of the house of Rheged)

APPENDIX 2:
ADDENDA

In the course of my research I have developed over 400
ongoing theories regarding various aspects of the Jack of
Kent phenomenon. Those which proved strong or
interesting enough have been presented, but there remain
some other matters which are worth recording . . .

IOLO MORGANWG AND ST CAWRDAF

As we have seen (see p. 248), Iolo Morganwg (1747–1826) was
the leading scholar of his day in the matter of Wales and its
ancient traditions; he was highly intelligent and had access to
documents which have since been lost – but he also had an
agenda, which was to establish the importance of south Wales,
especially his beloved Glamorgan, and he was considerably
deranged. So it was that with this in mind he fabricated his
own material and inserted it into the existing tradition,
frequently with such skill that the results were seamless, and
for this reason there is a major project under way at the
University of Wales which is aimed at sifting the truth from the
tantalising mass of material that Iolo left behind.

One of the most important of the early Welsh sources which
Iolo Morganwg saw fit to modify was the 'Triads', a bardic
history of Wales in which items were grouped into threes for
mnemonic convenience, but by far the most interesting to
ourselves, is what the Triads have to say about St Cawrdaf.

The original Triads refer to Cawrdaf as one of 'The Three
Chief Officers of Britain', a military title implying a status
consistent with his established role as the Dark Age defender
of Brycheiniog against the Saxons. However, in view of the

theory which we have outlined in this book, it is a very curious thing that out of the entire Welsh pantheon of the Dark Ages, Iolo Morganwg chose St Cawrdaf to cite as having been one of 'The Three Prime Ministers of Britain' – a title which he said was earned by calling all Wales to arms.

THE OIL-PAINTING (SEE FRONT COVER)

In the last few months (courtesy of the contemporary John Scudamore) the staff of the National Museum of Wales have kindly agreed at short notice to undertake an examination of the portrait before this book goes to press, and based upon their analysis, they have made the following initial observations.

Although it has not been possible to provide an accurate date for the work, it appears likely that the landscape background and the clothed body of the subject were produced at a period earlier than the head and face of the subject, and since no substantial evidence survives of a previous portrait having underlain the current subject of the painting, the implication is that for an unknown period during its career, the painting featured a blank space which awaited the subsequent installment of a head and face, as seen today. Much evidence shows that for some reason the portrait itself was never properly finished, meanwhile two tiny background details are worth noting which are only discernible upon very close examination – namely a spectral figure making its way from left to right along the road in the middle-distance, and a very delicate pointed spire behind the manor house which Nikolaus Pevsner (*Herefordshire*: Harmondsworth, 1963) accepted as medieval Kentchurch Court.

In my opinion however, Pevsner was mistaken. The background to the building is clearly wrong as seen from this angle; other Flemish paintings in the *St Jerome* format have similar buildings in the middle distance (eg. the St Jerome in the Tate Panel at All Hallows-by-the-Tower, London, and its adjacent panel of St Ambrose), and while the portrait may or may not have been made at Kentchurch, I therefore suggest that the landscape was either painted elsewhere, or was invented.

If painted elsewhere, it is relevant that analysis shows the hill originally continuing to descend on the right-hand side instead of levelling out, and in this light one might examine the landscapes surrounding the Scudamore's other seats, such as Holme Lacy where many of the paintings at Kentchurch Court were said to have originally been kept, or even some of Owain Glyndŵr's other late haunts, such as Hergest, Croft, Monnington and Dorstone.

However, while it has recently been observed that the background is reminiscent of the Malverns, where the Bryt family once dwelt at Birtsmorten Court (see below), in my opinion it is more likely that the idealised landscape is an invention, and it may therefore be more significant that the painting was also once said to have hung in the Scudamore's chapel of Sancta Keyna where it would have functioned as a religious icon depicting St Jerome – which brings us to the subject of the portrait.

Having already dispensed with the Rector of Kentchurch in the 1380s, and with the Welsh bard Siôn Cent, the idea persists that this might yet be a portrait of Owain Glyndŵr (c. 1354–1415) aged sixty, after an extremely hard life. However, since the art experts maintain that the format of St Jerome only became generally popular from 1500 onwards (and the National Museum of Wales concurs), only one way remains in which this could still be the case, namely that the portrait was made during the 1500s but was based upon an earlier line-drawing of Glyndŵr which was once owned by the Scudamores.

While it would not be entirely inappropriate to depict Owain Glyndŵr in the guise of St Jerome (see p. 173), there is little evidence weighing either for or against this hypothesis. For example, the under-drawing of the portrait seems to reflect an ongoing process, and so it has been suggested that this might indicate an artist engaged in sketching a live subject rather than in copying a previous image – but this is not conclusive, and it is easy to imagine an artist being asked to copy an image which may have been too small, at the wrong angle, or too poorly drawn to copy directly, in which case sketching a general likeness would have been easier than attempting to directly trace or copy.

The alternative is of course that this is simply an unusual and unfinished picture featuring an unknown cleric in the role of St Jerome, which was indeed acquired by the Scudamores in *c.* 1500. As we have suggested (see Epilogue), in the late 1500s the phenomenon of Jack of Kent was at a popular high, which peaked with the release of Munday's play in 1595, and if we are correct, the Scudamores of Kentchurch were then well known to have been associated with a certain Jack of Kent, and were under pressure to admit that they had sheltered Owain Glyndŵr. Resigned to the fact that the rumours would never go away, and wishing to obscure what had really become of Glyndŵr, they may well have adopted a policy of promoting such available decoys as the Rector of the 1380s, the Welsh bard Siôn Cent, and the oil-painting, so as to fuel and focus the debate upon Kentchurch. Thus, the Scudamores have always been closely associated with Jack of Kent, and in all probability the oil-painting has become associated with Jack of Kent simply because it belongs to the Scudamores.

This, I suggest, is the most likely explanation, and yet, as M. Paul Bryant-Quinn has remarked, Jack of Kent is like 'velcro' in the way that he causes individuals and imagery to stick to him, and so whoever the man in the painting may have been, he has long-since become a Jack of Kent – and as Steve Blake has observed regarding Owain Glyndŵr, 'Whenever I see that painting, my head says "No", and my heart says "Yes"'.

THE BRYT (BRUT) FAMILY

An attempt seems to have been made to link the Welsh and Lollard causes, and so it is interesting that the arms of the Scudamores were prominently displayed by their friends the Bryts (the family of the Lollard Walter Brut) at their seat of Birtsmorten Court in the Malverns just east of Ledbury, where rumours also exist of an outlawed Glyndŵr in hiding (see p. 286). In 1423, Sir John Scudamore was engaged in trying to obtain an inheritance for his son John Scudamore 'Esquire' from the Bryts, and the erroneous assumption that John Scudamore Esquire was the child of Alice Glyndŵr has thus led to an otherwise unfounded claim that Alice had previously been married to one of the Bryts. In fact, as we have seen, there is good reason to believe that John Scudamore Esquire was the son of Sir John Scudamore's *first* wife, and she may well have been a member of the Bryt family, since this would explain both the matter of John Scudamore Esquire's inheritance from the Bryts, and the keeping of the Scudamore's arms at Birtsmorten Court.

THE '120' THEORY

A well regarded date for Glyndŵr's birth is the year 1354, and since we have reason to believe that he died during the winter of 1414/15, this would mean that he lived to be exactly 60 years of age. At the battle of Hyddgen (Pumlumon), Glyndŵr is said to have won an improbable victory armed with 120 men (2 x 60), whereafter he delivered a speech from two blocks of white quartz called 'Owain Glyndŵr's Covenant Stones' which stand exactly 60 feet apart. Jack of Kent meanwhile, is said in folklore to have lived to be 120, and so I shall leave the reader to wonder what significance, if any, such numerology might have.

TABLES

Table I: The Evolution of the Place-name 'Kentchurch'.

Location: Monnow Valley, South Herefordshire.
Evolution:

Chapel of St Kaene (1100) / Lann Cein (1130) / Eccl. Sancte Keyna (1205) /
Ecc. de Sancta Kayna (1277) / Sancta Keyna (1291) / Kenschirch (1300) /
Penchirche (*c.* 1310?) / Lyngeyn (1335) / Llangain (*c.* 1335?) / Keynchirche
(1341) / Kencherge (1386) / Keynchurch (1390) / Llankeyne (1504) /
Keynchurch (1584) / Kenchurch cum Llanhidog (1695) / Kentchurch (1840)

* * *

Table II: Other Suspects

JOHN OF KENT 'Cancellarius' (fl. 1213)

Chancellor of St Paul's Cathedral in 1213 who may have fled to Angers in
France as a result of the persecution of the clergy by the demonic King
John. John of Kent's network of ecclesiastical associations, and his possible
acquaintance with Hubert de Burgh (Earl of Kent), who spent much time
in the Monnow Valley area, add further to his credibility as an intriguing
pre-1321 candidate.
Verdict: Viable.

JOHN OF GAUNT (1340–99)

Fourth son of Edward III and father of Henry IV. He is suggested as a
candidate by his Lordship of Monmouth and the Three Castles (Grosmont,
Skenfrith and Whitecastle) which he visited briefly once, and doubtless
also by the fact that from his place of birth he was properly 'John of Ghent'
(Belgium). Embden (*A Biographical Register of the University of Oxford*) also
records a variant of his name as John Cante.
Verdict: Spurious.

SIR JOHN OLDCASTLE (d. 1417)

Leader of the Lollard Revolt which followed Owain Glyndŵr's war. Both
his rebel credentials and his ecclesiastical associations stand him in good
stead as a candidate. Under the pseudonym Falstaff, he was nonetheless

called 'Old Jack' by Shakespeare in *Henry IV*; he was based just north of Kentchurch at Almeley in south Herefordshire, where a field upon his lands was called 'Old Jakkesmedewe'; and he was also Lord Cobham of Kent, by virtue of his marriage.
Verdict: Viable.

JOHN KEMPE (Cardinal) (fl. 1419; d. 1454)
Occasionally suggested as a result of references made (*c.* 1600) to the main candidate Siôn Cent as 'John Kemp (Kempt or Cemp)', and confirmed by Paul M. Bryant-Quinn's discovery of poetry written by Siôn Cent but attributed to John Kempe. However, as per the Outlaw theory presented in this book, the occasional appearance of 'Kemp' in the Jack of Kent tradition is readily explainable at source, by the identification of Kendal (Kents-dale) with the weaver John Kempe of Flanders (fl. 1331) (see also Rymer's *Foedera*, 3, p. 238). 'Jack of Kemp' was once a character in the village Mumming plays of Kempsford in Gloucestershire.
Verdict: Spurious.

DOCTOR JOHN KENT OF CAERLEON (fl. 1482)
An interesting necromancer, wizard and writer of books on astrology. However, John of Kent was a very common medieval name. Moreover, this man lived later than any other candidate, and he lacks any demonstrable link either to the Monnow Valley area or to other regions where the legends of Jack of Kent are prominent.
Verdict: Marginal.

JOHN A KENT, OUTLAW (fl. 1483)
A border marauder who in 1483 (Court Rolls, 18 March) was indicted regarding 'treasons, felonies, trespasses etcetera, committed by John Kent and Bill Clifton in the county of Hereford and the Marches of Wales adjacent'. However, the reference to this miscreant as 'John Kent' may echo an earlier court document in which a defendant's name was crossed out and replaced with the insertion 'Robin Hood' – in which case this would confirm that both names came to imply a felon whose real name was not known to the authorities.
Verdict: Peripheral.

JOHN VAUGHAN (fl. 1535)
Abbot of the Cistercian Abbey of Grace Dieu near Grosmont, he is suggested only as a result of confusion with the main candidates John de Went and John of Kent (Rector of Kentchurch).
Verdict: Spurious.

* * *

Tables

Table III: The Rectors of Kentchurch, 1300–90

1300	Reginaldum de Schiptome/John Worth
1323	Roger Tilie
1334	John de Henle
1340	William Balle
1349	William de Foye
1349	Richard de Ewias
1351	Johannes Chandos
1351	Henry de Fowhope
1370	John Morsed
1381	Johannes Chandos/**John of Kent**
1390	Reginald Love

A list of the rectors of Kentchurch was given by Seaton in his *History of the Deanery of Archenfield*, which we have amended as follows:

Reginaldum de Schiptome, who had been in office since 1297, was granted seven years' leave of absence from Kentchurch on 4 April 1301 for purposes of study, and this is doubtless the reason that John Worth took over, although no date for his inception is given. The scenario is instructive, insofar as it demonstrates that in practice the listed rector would frequently be absent for one reason or another, his duties being performed by one or more understudies or lower-order clergy. In many cases this was due to pluralism, the lucrative holding of more than one benefice at a time. Seaton omits Johannes Chandos's brief tenure in 1351 (2 April–22 December); his second tenure in 1381 is likely to have been equally brief. Reginald Love is listed by Seaton as Reginald Lane, but he is almost certainly the Reginald Love who was presented to the benefice of Kentchurch on 17 April 1390 by a certain John Trefnant, Bishop of Hereford. Seaton states that the official patron of Sancta Keyna until 1334 was the Abbot and Monastery of St Peter's in Gloucester, but it is evident that the arrangement did not terminate at this date. St Peter's is also cited in the Registers of the Bishops as having been the patron in the cases of the appointments of John de Henle (1334), John Chandos (1351) and Reginald Love (1390) – and there exists circumstantial evidence that William de Foye (1349) was appointed under the same patronage. The implication is that the system of supplying priests to Kentchurch remained unchanged throughout the 1300s, devolving in practice to the diocese of Hereford, which presented each candidate for approval. This formality was traditionally performed in the case of Kentchurch by the Franciscan family of de Pembrugge.

* * *

Table IV: The Career of John Scudamore (Jnr) 'Esquire'

There has been some confusion between the careers of Sir John Scudamore of Kentchurch (Knight), and that of his son, John Scudamore 'Esquire', which has led to erroneous suggestions that the latter was Owain's Glyndŵr's grandson as a result of his father's marriage to Alice Glyndŵr. However, as we have seen, Sir John Scudamore (Knight) of Kentchurch, had a previous wife, who probably perished during the siege of Carreg Cennen Castle in 1403. Furthermore, the documents referring to John Scudamore 'Esquire', are consistent in indicating that he was born in *c.* 1398, and was therefore the son of his father's first marriage. The career of John Scudamore 'Esquire', thus appears to have been as follows:

1398	born
1403	his mother's death at Carreg Cennen.
1404	his father's marriage to Alice Glyndŵr.
1415	his father left for France (Agincourt/Harfleur).
1417	he witnessed a deed involving the Abrahalls.
1418	he witnessed another deed involving the Abrahalls.
1423	he was named as 'Esquire' in court action following his involvement in violence between the factions of Abrahall and Talbot. At this point, the identity of his stepmother (Alice Glyndŵr) had become known and had been identified by the hostile barony as the reason for the prolonged absence of his father, whom many now regarded as a traitor. Meanwhile, now aged twenty-five and doubtless keen to marry, John Scudamore 'Esquire's career was being obstructed by the baronial establishment, and this may well have inspired his involvement in violence against the Talbots.
1423	his father (now returned) was instantly embroiled in court actions, which began as he experienced difficulty in obtaining his son's inheritance from the Bryt family (see Appendix 2)
1430	his father made an attempt to claim Owain Glyndŵr's former lands in north Wales 'in right of his wife'.
1433	his father finally lost his legal battles against the hostile barony, was stripped of all his titles, and heavily fined by Henry VI.
1435	his father died.
1449	aged fifty-one, John Scudamore 'Esquire' was finally allowed to become a Knight, and as 'Sir' John Scudamore may then have married Mawd, a daughter of the 'craftie', corvine, and irrepressible Gruffydd ap Nicholas who was the current descendant of the Lord Rhys. If so, this

marriage in *c.* 1450 would have conjoined two key families, – the Scudamores, and the 'Ravens' of Dinefwr. Both parties would then have known the location of Owain Glyndŵr's grave, and the significance of the famous joke later made by Gruffydd ap Nicholas's descendant Sir Rhys ap Thomas in 1485, would be increased (see Epilogue). (Coxe, *Herefordshire*; Duncumb, *History & Antiquities of The County of Hereford*; Elizabeth Taylor, *King's Caple in Archenfield*; Ralph A. Griffiths, *Sir Rhys ap Thomas & His Family*, Part 1) .

* * *

Table V: The Evolution of the Place-name 'Corras'

Location: Monnow Valley (adjacent to Kentchurch)
Evolution:

Caueros (1100) / Kaueros (1135) / Kaueros (*c.* 1150) / Kaueros (1242) / Cauros (1247) / Caueros (1302) / Kaueros (1310) / Caueros (1334) / Kaueros (1422) / Kaueras (1424) / Corras (1504) / Cawros (*c.* 1525) / Cawros (*c.* 1550) / Corras (1584) / Cawres (1639) / Corras (2006).

Origin: 'Corras' or 'Corris' is quite a common place-name for which the usual explanation is that it derives from the Scottish 'Carossie' meaning a piece of land enclosed on three sides. However, while this is doubtless the case with another nearby 'Corras' at Orcop, which in 1600 was actually recorded as 'Carossie', it is quite evident from the above that the 'Corras' at Kentchurch is differently derived. It is also interesting that having remained remarkably consistent (essentially as 'Caueros') in the period 1100–1334, either the Black Death in 1348 or Glyndŵr's War in 1400 seem to have affected matters, since thereafter (1424) an 'a' appears as if to facilitate the incongruous 'Corras', which then establishes itself as the name despite receiving competition from the interesting form 'Cawros'.

Since about 1100, long before their acquisition of adjacent Kentchurch and its chapel in *c.* 1310, the Scudamores had lived at the manor of Kaueros (Corras), until in *c.* 1242 it passed from Lady Ysenda Scudamore, briefly to the Tregoyls (see Chapter 14), and thence into the hands of the Knights Templar of Garway Hill by 1247. However, it is likely that at some point following the suppression of the Knights Templar for Gnostic heresies in 1308, the Scudamores regained possession of Kaueros, since it emerges in their hands from the aftermath of the Black Death in 1348 – whereafter the chapel at Kaueros was demolished as a result of the death of the congregation.

For these reasons, together with others givien in the text, I suggest that the Scudamore's chapel at Caur-os (which they had held in the 1100s both before and throughout the days of the Lord Rhys) may originally have been dedicated to St Cawrdaf – whose name was originally spelt 'Caur-tam'.

* * *

Table VI: 1400–1430

1400s	Jack of Kent's Oak (in Kentchurch deerpark) referred to as already 'ancient' in a manuscript of this period.
1415–1421	Carreg Cennen Castle undergoing major repairs.
1415	Sir John Scudamore of Kentchurch stands down as Steward of Cantref Mawr – Owain Glyndŵr is dead.
1417	John Oldcastle the Lollard caught hiding in a secluded spot overlooking the Vyrnwy near Meifod in mid-Wales by Lord Powys, and is subsequently executed.
1417	John Scudamore (Jnr) 'Esquire' witnesses a deed involving the Abrahalls.
1419	John Kemp, who was twice a Cardinal, becomes Bishop of Rochester.
1420	Grosmont Castle allegedly 'no longer fortified after this date'.
1421	John Kemp (see Table II) becomes Bishop of Chichester and London.
1421	rumours circulating of a new Mortimer Revolt.
1421	Maredudd Glyndŵr finally accepts a pardon.
c. 1421	Joanne Scudamore, granddaughter of Owain Glyndŵr, marries Gruffydd Dwn and thus resolves the rift between the two families.
1422	Welsh chroniclers record of Glydwr's disappearance in the guise of a reaper.
1423	Scudamores and Abrahalls engage in a violent conflict with the Talbots.
1423	John Scudamore Senior has difficulty in obtaining his son's inheritance from the Bryt family.
1423	Neath Abbey still being looted.
1425	sudden death of Edmund Mortimer the Younger.
1425	Richard Duke of York inherits the estates of his uncle Edmund Mortimer but is made to wait for seven years before receiving them.
1425	Gruffydd ap Nicholas (a descendant of the Lord Rhys) adopts the symbol of the 'Raven' and rises to prominence in south-west Wales.
1426	John Talbot returns from Ireland and attacks the Beauchamps of Abergavenny.

1426	John Kemp becomes Archbishop of York.
1428	Kilpeck Priory closes (some sources say 1422).
1428	Lordship of Ogmore still assessing damage done by Owain Glyndŵr.
1430	Gruffydd Dwn is asked by Henry V to investigate Talley Abbey.

* * *

Table VII: 1430 – 1500

1430–1445	fl. Siôn Cent who wrote the majority of his poetry during this period towards the end of his life, when Sir John Scudamore was being pressurised and then punished for having married Alice Glyndŵr, and when suspicions may have been renewed that the Scudamores had at some stage sheltered Owain. While there is no evidence at all that the bard 'Siôn Cent' and the Scudamores ever coincided in space, the unsubstantiated suggestion has been made repeatedly in the form of hearsay, and therefore it may be that in later times the Scudamores were pleased to encourage the idea that they had patronised this Welsh bard, since he thus offered yet another 'decoy' in the debate regarding the identity of the Jack of Kent who had once haunted Kentchurch. In reality however, Siôn Cent was no friend of the barony, and would have been a most unlikely beneficiary of the Scudamores.
1430s	Rhys Gethin (one of Glyndŵr's former chieftains) is serving in France and lending money to Richard Duke of York, the nephew of Edmund Mortimer.
1432	Richard Duke of York finally receives the estates of his uncle Edmund Mortimer after being made to wait seven years.
1432	8 August Sir John Scudamore is disqualified as Steward of Kidwelly, Is-cennen and Carnwyllion, and as Steward of Monmouth, Grosmont and Whitecastle, and is replaced by the king's cousin Edmund Beaufort.
1433	Sir John Scudamore is stripped of all titles by the baronial scrum which is running the country during the minority of Henry VI, and he receives a fine so heavy that it could only have been paid with the aid of a network of friends and supporters. He is also replaced by Edmund Beaufort as Constable of Carmarthen.
1433	the possessions of Talley Abbey are described as 'wasted by misrule'.

1433	'John Monyngton' listed as an 'Esquire' in the county of Herefordshire.
c. 1435	Caerphilly area still suffering from dereliction caused by Owain Glyndŵr.
1435	Sir John Scudamore dies.
1436	political pamphlets in England warn 'Beware of Wales!' due to Welsh conciousness renewed by Glyndŵr's war.
1437	Henry VI declares his minority at an end.
1438	Henry VI writes to the Pope, describing the Welshry of the Hereford diocese as 'wild and untameable by nature'.
1442	Henry VI singles out the Welshry of Herefordshire for harsh punishments.
1442	Eleanor Duchess of Gloucester finally accused of witchcraft as a result of rumours spread by the baronial scrum.
1443	John Abrahall dies.
1443	a Charter of Kidwelly bans Welshmen from the town.
1444	the sons of Henry Dwn obtain cancellation of his debts.
1445	Gruffydd Dwn is captured in France having seen little of his wife (Glyndŵr's granddaughter).
1447	John Scudamore (Jnr) finally becomes a knight, and may subsequently have married 'Mawd' daughter of Gruffyd ap Nicholas, the current descendant of the Lord Rhys and thus a 'Raven' of Dinefwr.
c. 1450?	Ieuan Ddu, a bard of Brycheiniog, writes in the style of Siôn Cent.
1450	fl. Jack Cade who led a rebellion in Kent.
1452	'John Kemp' becomes Archbishop of Canterbury.
1453	John Talbot dies serving in France.
1453	Henry VI suffers first bout of insanity.
1454	John Kemp Archbishop of Canterbury dies.
1455	'The Wars of the Roses' begin (battle of St Albans).
1460	Gruffyd ap Nicholas (grandfather of Sir Rhys ap Thomas) whose arms were 'Three Black Ravens' is killed at the battle of Mortimer's Cross
1461–1483	Grosmont and Skenfrith Castles dismantled by the Yorkists.
1461–1506	the bard 'Hywel Rheinallt' writes wistfully of Cawrdaf's spiritual fortress.
1461	a Sir John Skidmore (Scudamore) surrenders Pembroke Castle to the Yorkists.
1482	Dr John (Kent) of Caerleon dies, and his writings are published.
1483	(18 March) 'John Kent' a Border marauder appears in court for offences committed in Herefordshire.
1485	Sir Rhys ap Thomas alleged to have slain Richard III at the

	battle of Bosworth, thus putting Henry Tudur on the throne.
1485	'The Wars of the Roses' end.
1492	Llantwit Major and Cardiff still claiming damage done by Owain Glyndŵr as the cause of revenue shortfalls.

* * *

Table VIII: 1500–1570

1500s	paintings of St Jerome popular at this time.
1500–1530	a map of this period shows the castles of Grosmont and Whitecastle in ruins, but the castle of Skenfrith roofed.
1500–1530	the bard Llywelyn ap Hywel writes in the style of Siôn Cent.
c. 1506	John Kent of Little Garway Farm at White Rocks acquires the building from the Knights Hospitallers.
1506	'The Embrace of the Saints' (George and David) is displayed at Carew castle by Sir Rhys ap Thomas.
1513	an edition of Tito Livio's work asserts Glyndŵr's death on Lawton's Hope Hill.
1531	Sir Rhys ap Thomas and his grandson persecuted by the Crown for making claims of descent from, and prophesies regarding, the Ravens of Rheged.
1536	Grosmont Castle in ruins.
1535/6	Dr John Vaughan is Cistercian Abbot of Grace Dieu.
1536–1538	Dissolution of The Monasteries initiated by Henry VIII.
1538	Bishop Latimer demonises and prepares to burn the effigy of the 'Virgin' at Pen-rhys.
1545	Grace Dieu is finally dissolved.
c. 1560	it is written that 'John Kent died at Llangain (Kentchurch) Herefordshire, and is buried there, Mr Scudamore was his master'.
1567	'Siôn Cent' is confused with 'John de Went' by reference to him as 'Dr Sion Guent'.
c. 1570	'The Mirror for Magistrates' talks of Glyndŵr having been 'seduced by false prophesies' and dying miserably in the mountains for lack of food.

* * *

Table IX: 1570–1680

c. 1570	Lady Scudamore promotes reconciliation symbolised by pax cakes.
1577	Hollinshed assumes that Jack of Kent was Dr John ('Kent')

	of Caerleon (fl. 1482), while just twenty years later Anthony Munday shows a much better understanding and calls him 'anciaunt of fame'.
c. 1590	Welshmen meet on mountaintops to hear stories of Wales's struggle against the English, and to listen to the lives of Taliesin, Merlin, and others. This, however, was a revival of interest in the Merlinic prophecies which would fade and die away over the next 200 years.
c. 1590	the Scudamore's adopt new motto 'Scutum Amoris Divini' (Shield of Divine Love) as Spenser's *Faerie Queene* appears.
1594	*The Wise Man of West Chester* foreshadows Anthony Munday's play *Jack a Kent, Jack a Cumber* which appears the following year.
1595	Anthony Munday produces his play *Jack a Kent, Jack a Cumber*.
1596	an inscription is carved on the beams of 'Jacky Kent's Barn' near Kentchurch, saying 'I.O.' Kent' and giving the year.
1600–1800	Merlinic 'prophecy' steadily losing its grip upon the popular imagination.
c. 1600	'Cent' (Kent) is confused with 'Kemp'.
1634	John 1st Viscount Scudamore 'the good lord Scudamore' restores the chancel and crossing of Dore Abbey and thereby saves the building.
1642	Civil War begins between Oliver Cromwell and Charles I.
c. 1645	*The Life of Sir Rhys ap Thomas* is written and includes the story of him lying under Mullock Bridge.
1645	(30 July) Richard Symonds draws a tombstone in Grosmont churchyard showing Jack of Kent and the Devil in embrace.
1645	(August) a Scottish Army besieges Hereford on behalf of Oliver Cromwell, and stages a raid on the Monnow Valley from which, in folklore, they are magically expelled by Jack of Kent.
1659	first recorded reference to Kent's Cavern adjacent to Kent's Hole Field near Torquay, which may or may not indicate outlaws known as Jacks of Kent in Devon.
1677	a family named 'De Kent' is prominent at Eardisley, north-west of Hereford (between Dorstone and Hergest) where plaques commemorating the family are embedded in the floor of Eardisley church. As with John Kent of Little Garway Farm, the possibility arises that this might be the same local family who had supplied the rector of Kentchurch in the 1380s.
1680	alleged excavation of Owain Glyndŵr's grave at Monnington.

* * *

Tables

Table X: 1680–2004

c. 1718   the Monnow Valley is still considered one of the safest areas for recusants and outlaws in Britain.

1721   Browne-Willis records that the grave of John of Kent (possibly the bard Siôn Cent) has been found in Glamorgan, containing his leather shroud and his pewter chalice.

1727   Dominam Viscomitissam Scudamore researches and writes concerning the Premonstratensian abbey of 'Hamm' which stood upon the Scudamore lands at Holme Lacy near Hereford.

c. 1800   the erratic Iolo Morganwg (see p. 248) curiously chooses to assert that St Cawrdaf summoned all Wales to arms).

1840   the 't' is inserted into Kenchurch by Col Scudamore, for postal reasons, while doubtless mindful of 'Jack of Kent'.

1859   the Scudamore's private chapel at Kentchurch (once 'Sancta Keyna') is largely rebuilt.

1881   Col Scudamore calls the oil-painting of Jack of Kent a picture of 'Owain Glyndŵr'.

c. 1900   Merthyr schoolchildren sing songs and tell stories of 'Jack of Kent'.

1978   (October) *The Legends of Jack O' Kent*, a limited edition art-book by P.C. Fencott, is published by Gronk Press in Toronto, Canada.

1996   'Jack of Kent', a ballad, is written and performed in the southern Marches by the Welsh minstrels Huw and Tony Williams.

2004   *The Mystery of Jack of Kent and the Fate of Owain Glyndŵr* is published by Sutton Publishing.

NOTES

1. 'KENT'. A remarkable amount of controversy surrounds the word Kent and its association with the Welsh term 'Ceint' meaning 'cornerland', which can also be applied within a Welsh context to 'Gwent', and which Steve Blake and Scott Lloyd (*The Keys to Avalon*) discuss in the context of a restructured version of British history which may well be substantially correct. However, it has fortunately proved unnecessary to add the 'Ceint' conundrum to the cauldron which this book already represents, since in practical terms it affects the argument neither in historical nor folkloric terms.

2. OPEN RELATIONSHIPS. In the interests of sexual equality and equal opportunities one should note that women were also allowed to consort with numerous suitors.

3. ECHO-CHAMBERS AND SARCOPHAGI. Some research has suggested that burial chambers were designed with acoustic resonance in mind, so it may have been to vocal and/or musical bardic accompaniment that a fallen king was dispatched to, or summoned from, the Otherworld. Meanwhile, regarding tombs in general and the mystical substance of stone, it is also interesting that according to Pliny a 'sarcophagus' was a stone which excelled at consuming flesh, and was therefore used by the ancients for entombment – doubtless so as to facilitate the passage of the deceased into the subterranean 'deep' or Underworld.

4. SKY-BURIAL. Of the relationship between the raven and various aspects of the corpse, an instance is found upon the summit of Hambledon Hill in Dorset, which was once ringed by a gruesome display of skulls, upon which the following report was made: 'It appears that when a member of one of the communities near the hill died, the body was exposed to the elements in a special area. . . . After the flesh had fallen off the bones, some corpses may have been selected for burial in another place with further ceremonies.' (*Scientific American*, March 1985, 252 (3)). As the report later admits, the flesh was likely to be torn off the bones by scavengers, which in a fenced-off area or in the case of a display of skulls on poles, would inevitably have been ravens.

   Having thus indulged in its customary communion with the head, particularly the eyeballs, the raven would then extend its interest to more difficult entrails, especially the liver, which it would inspect with exaggerated care, perhaps in order to ascertain its victim's state of

314

health. As representatives of the 'deep', and specifically of the Morrigan (the Celtic Trinity of Fate), ravens knew the occasion and outcome of future battles, and so an ancient belief developed which persisted into Druidic times, namely that by inspecting the liver of a sacrificed animal or human, the outcome of a battle could be predetermined. If the liver was healthy and blood-red, the omen was favourable, but if it was pale it augured defeat. From this practice (which was also engaged in by a biblical King of Babylon) we obtain the expression 'lily-livered', which has come to mean cowardly. Meanwhile, it is also interesting to note that in Merlin's prophecy of a battle between two dragons representing the Celtic and Anglo-Saxon races the Welsh are represented by the Red Dragon of Cadwaladr, while the Anglo-Saxon dragon was white.

5. RHEGED LOCATED. The location of the ancient kingdom of Rheged has long been the subject of vague assertions which have placed it variously in Cumbria, in Dumfries & Galloway in Scotland, in Morayshire and even in Strathclyde. However, while the Morayshire claim apparently derives from an error made by the scribe Geoffrey of Monmouth, the Strathclyde claim is based upon a simple mistranslation of 'Ystrad-Clywyd' in north-east Wales, which is indeed the general area long-since identified by folklore as Urien's domain. Steve Blake and Scott Lloyd (*The Keys to Avalon*) also identify Rheged as having enfolded the areas subsequently occupied by Owain Glyndŵr's medieval estates in north-east Wales, i.e. Glyndyfrdwy and Sycharth.

Nevertheless, Dumfries and Galloway aside, the claim that Urien of Rheged was also king of nearby Cumbria (from 'Cymri') is considerably more credible, especially in view of the fact that Urien was an exceptionally powerful Dark Age leader of 'The Men of the North', who had placed himself at the forefront of a Celtic alliance in the north and west. Considering that Cumbria was always a region of strategic concern culminating at Carlisle and Penrith (with which Urien and his son Owein are traditionally connected), it is therefore not unreasonable to assert that, emanating from the kingdom of Rheged in north-east Wales, Urien was at least highly influential in Cumbria.

6. WATER-OFFERINGS. It is well known from excavation that as the Roman army bore down upon the sacred island of Anglesey the Druids threw weapons, parts of chariots, tools, chains, musical instruments and cauldrons into the lake at Llŷn Cerrig Bach in their desperate attempts to summon aid from the Otherworld. Notwithstanding their obvious sincerity in this, it must be said that there is something exquisitely 'Monty-Pythonesque' about the religiously inspired behaviour of a people whose reaction, when terminally threatened, is to hurl all their best equipment into a lake.

Also well known from more recent excavations are the Celtic causeways researched by Pearson and Fields, which consist of dual rows of wooden posts extending from marshlands into areas of standing water. Along these are found the rusted remains of countless swords and other votive offerings which have been placed in the water as part of a religious ritual. Some of these sites, near which Norman churches were often later built, appear to have remained important and functional into the Middle Ages, and are thought to have been originally constructed in conjunction with the timing of lunar eclipses. A survey of their astronomical alignment would reveal whether or not such rituals were performed when moonlight created shimmering avenues of reflection down the causeways, thus offering an attractive wading-ritual along a reflected lunar path or white track.

7. THE ROMANISATION OF DEHEUBARTH. In 1881 Wirt Sykes noted: 'There is a Roman type, too, among the Welsh women. Many inhabitants of Cynwil Gayo parish, Carmarthenshire, are said to pride themselves on their Roman descent, and Roman names prevail among them. I have heard of two families in Wales of the name of Aurelius, and another of the name of Cornelius, whose features in both cases closely resemble the ancient Roman type. The resemblance holds good in both the men and the women.'

8. THE TORQUE OF ST CYNOG. A Celtic torque was a heavy split-circlet, usually made from twisted strands of iron, and traditionally worn around the neck. The ancestral pre-Christian custom of wearing torques accordingly dates from the Iron Age, and the torque of St Cynog (d. 492) was later described by the Lord Rhys's friend, the scribe Giraldus Cambrensis.

Meanwhile it might also be observed regarding the Lord Rhys's appropriation of this artefact, that in doing so he was once again exercising Deheubarth's traditional and proprietorial relationship towards the buffer-state of Breconshire (Brycheiniog), St Cynog having been an alleged son of Brychan (c. AD 390–450), the prolific Irish-Welsh ruler of Brycheiniog who preceded Cawrdaf.

9. THE IRISH IN WALES. Regarding 'The Forehead of the Two Lakes' – 'Tallach', 'Tallesch', 'Tallaghan', 'Talyllychau' or 'Talley' is thought to derive from the Irish (Goidelic/Gaelic) word for forehead, and thus reflects the influx of Irish terms into Welsh which accompanied the countless waves of Irish pirates, sea-traders, invaders and settlers who have visited Wales since time immemorial. Like other such guests, the Irish found south Wales most accessible, in their case naturally via Deheubarth, and while the Anglo-Saxons remained unwelcome the Irish (like the Romans) succeeded to some extent in becoming positively entwined with Welsh history.

St Patrick (c. 390–461), before his ministry in Ireland established him as Ireland's patron saint, is believed to have come from the village of Banwen (near Neath) in south Wales, where local place-names still evoke Ireland, and where the nearby Hirfynydd Stone shows an early Christian at prayer, surrounded by Irish symbology. Meanwhile, the prominent St Brychan (*c.* 390–450) was not only a prolific king of Brycheiniog – a kingdom traditionally engaged in an alliance of necessity with Deheubarth – but was also the son of an Irish prince. Furthermore St Brigit, who was well known to the Lord Rhys of Deheubarth, was an Irish triple-goddess closely associated with the overarching Morrigan, a pan-Celtic entity shared by the Irish with the Welsh and Scots.

10. GIANT BRÂN WADES IRISH SEA. If the region of Talley Abbey as 'The Forehead of the Two Lakes' does indeed signify the head of a subterranean Brân (raven), whose eyes are represented by the two lakes and whose nose is a nearby ridge, then it is interesting to note that the (oracular) head of Brân (the archetype) features in the *Mabinogion* tale of 'Branwen, Daughter of Llyr', which contains a description of Brân in the days before his decapitation as a 'giant' who was seen wading across the Irish Sea from Wales, and whose approach to the Irish shore was described as follows: 'We saw a huge mountain . . . a high ridge on the mountain, and a lake on each side of the ridge . . . and the mountain and everything were moving.' The text goes on to explain that the ridge was his nose and the two lakes his eyes. This tale may therefore commemorate an occasion when the men of Deheubarth crossed the sea to Ireland.

11. THE LADY OF THE LAKE. The Lord Rhys was presumably familiar with the ancient (Neolithic) link between women and water (see Chapter 1) long before he founded the nunnery of Llanllŷr, especially since there seems to have been a major tradition concerning 'The Lady of the Lake' just across the Tywi at Llŷn y Fan Fach, north of Llanddeusant. Here, a well-known water-goddess (who was one of three sisters) allegedly married a local mortal and thus became the mother of three sons who became doctors. Known as the 'Physicians of Myddfai', these doctors actually existed and were employed by Rhys Gryg, one of the sons of the Lord Rhys.

12. THE SONS OF THE 'DEEP' were surely indispensable when it came to accounting for the mysterious origins of illegitimate children, and the Lord Rhys, in later founding a nunnery in the midst of a sea-marsh, was undoubtedly aware that any sons later inadvertently conceived by the devout ladies of Llanllŷr could therefore only be the miraculous reincarnations of some ancient Celtic leader. Countless spirits of the 'deep' were said to arise from wells, rivers, lakes and marshes, and having thus evaporated possessed the ability to become airborne and to change shape. As such they had long since been defined by the church as 'demonic', and thus the visits of male spirits to ladies during the night made them the very model of a medieval incubus.

13. THE MORRIGAN. The dark-lunar aspect of the Triple-Goddess sometimes known as the Morrigan (pan-Celtic in her activities and also well-known to the Scandinavians) is ultimately associated in Britain with

the 'deep' of the sea (Môr), with her favourite guise of the Raven, and with Ireland, from whose shores a Prince of Leinster once drifted into her dark embrace, as described in the *Annals of Tigernach*: 'The deep clear depths of the sea and the sand on the sea bed have covered them. They have hurled themselves over Conaing in his frail little curach. The woman has flung her white mane against Conaing in his curach. Hateful is the laugh which she laughs today.'

In contrast to the positive full-lunar aspect of the Goddess (i.e. Ana or Anu), whose child-nurturing breasts are two Irish hills in Kerry, the child-devouring Morrigan is thus often characterised in her capacity as a Raven as a death-dealing Irish 'battle-goddess' closely related to the sea-going Scandinavian 'battle-raven'. Meanwhile inland, and on the mainland, her connection with the watery 'deep' continues via the water-cycle, in countless traditions which tell of Morriganesque spirits arising from rivers, lakes and wells.

14. 'DEMONIC' SUPERNATURAL BRIDES. The suggestion that various kings had connections to the Otherworld as a result of their marriages to supernatural brides (goddesses) was once quite common, and was originally a Celtic status symbol. However, from the point of view of the Anglo-Norman medieval Church, it obviously constituted an allegation of paganism that was very convenient in demonising the pre-Christian or Romano-Celtic-Christian Celtic ancestors, such as Urien of Rheged. However, it was much less convenient when it was applied by others to the entire line of Plantagenet kings, including King John and Henry III, who were popularly referred to as 'Devils' as a consequence of their ancestor Henry of Anjou having allegedly married a supernatural bride called Melusine – a harpy whose gothic legend smacks of Hammer films.

15. URIEN IN FOLKLORE. In Ystrad Clwyd, on the banks of the River Alun, the tale was once told of Urien's coupling with the dark goddess. This local tradition was recorded in *c.* 1556 and while it forms part of the folkloric evidence confirming the location of Rheged in north-east Wales it also makes the claim that Urien was a Christian – and it is even possible that its popularity at the time was a relic of the propaganda efforts of Owain Glyndŵr and his advisers in the early 1400s. Meanwhile, the legend is as follows:

> In Denbighshire there is a parish which is called Llanferres, and there is there Rhyd y Gyfarthfa. In the old days the hounds of the countryside used to come together to the side of the ford to bark, and nobody dared go to find out what was there until Urien Rheged came. And when he came to the side of the ford he saw nothing there except a woman washing. And then the hounds ceased barking, and Urien seized the woman and had his will of her; and then she said, 'God's blessing on the feet which brought thee here!' 'Why?' said he. 'Because I have been fated to wash here until I

should conceive a son by a Christian. And I am daughter to the king of Annfwn, and come thou here at the end of the year and then thou shalt receive the boy.' And so he came and he received there a boy and a girl; that is Owein son of Urien, and Morfudd daughter of Urien.

The identity of the woman here as the pagan goddess is reflected by her associations with hounds (another occasional guise of the Morrigan) and with water (the aqueous 'deep'), and by the fact that she declared herself to be the daughter of the king of 'Annfwn' (or 'Annwn'), the Celtic Otherworld of the subterranean 'deep' (i.e. the Underworld).

In adopting a pro-Urien and pro-Christian stance, the story inherently accepts the negativity of the woman's former pagan condition, and by the association with hounds it identifies her essentially as the negative aspect of the goddess known as the Morrigan, and it therefore applauds Urien's forcing of himself upon her as a valuable Christian service to all concerned.

Thus converted, the woman duly exclaims 'God's blessing!' before producing twins, namely Owein of Rheged and his sister Morfudd, who are thus also implied to be Christians, and whose arrival in tandem is interestingly reminiscent of the line in Iolo's eulogy of Glyndŵr, which observes 'his children come in pairs, a fine nestful of chieftains'.

16. AMBIGUITY OF THE BARDS. In his poem to the Bishop of St Asaph, Iolo Goch observes 'good was Rhun himself, who was born of love'. Professor Dafydd Johnston suggests in his notes that this must be 'Rhun, son of Maelgwyn Gwynedd', who was an illegitimate child. However, in his 'Eulogy to Tudur Fychan's Sons' Iolo refers to them as 'Rhun's pride', and Dafydd Johnston qualifies this by saying 'there were several heroes of this name, but the son of Maelgwyn Gwynedd is probably meant here, and also in the other reference'. On the other hand, having established that Tudur Fychan's sons were 'Rhun's pride', the possibility that Iolo is actually referring to 'Rhun son of Urien' (Owein's brother) surely increases when he enthusiastically proceeds to describe the home of one of these sons as 'a re-creation of the hearth of Rheged'. However, in any case, Iolo, like all the bards, rejoiced in the ambiguity of such references, and in equivocation in general, as he demonstrated in his 'Strolling Tour'.

17. MAGIC STONES. Regarding the mystical substance of stone, it is interesting to note that the possession of certain magic stones, such as that allegedly owned by Owain Glyndŵr, was a time-honoured tradition. One example of this was the 'Precious Pebble' said to have belonged to Owain Gwynedd (the colleague of the Lord Rhys and the second of Iolo's 'Three Owains'). It was a globe of pure rock-crystal that was once kept in an ancient house at Rhiwlas in Merionethshire in

a green velvet bag with a note explaining its identity (*Bygones Journal*, October 1876). Another example is the magic stone which Hubert de Burgh (d. 1243), the Earl of Kent and Lord of the Three Castles (Grosmont, Skenfrith and Whitecastle) allegedly supplied to Llywelyn the Great, whereafter de Burgh was accused of witchcraft, perhaps in the company of a certain John of Kent 'Cancellarius' (see Table I).

18. 'GWLAW! GWLAW!' Regarding weather-control, it is interesting to note that Iolo Goch, having already identified Glyndŵr with crows, called his children a fine 'nestful' of chieftains, noted his collection of peacocks at Sycharth, and even referred to Glyndŵr himself as a peacock. Peacocks are traditionally affiliated (via Juno and Hera) to the ancient goddess who once controlled the weather with the aid of her birds, and they are thus credited with the power to predict rain, which they prophesy with their cry of 'gwlaw! gwlaw!'

19. THE HEAD OF BRÂN THE RAVEN. Evidently aware that 'all flesh is corn' (see Chapter 1), the intimate communion of ravens with corpses as they descended upon early displays of severed heads in the late Neolithic was later reflected in the *Mabinogion* tale of 'Branwen, Daughter of Llyr'. In this tale the tribal leader Brân (Raven) waded across the Irish Sea and later volunteered for death by ritual decapitation; his severed head was later said to have been buried under the White Hill where the Tower of London now stands. A population of ravens survives there to this day, and it is said that if this 'fierce bodyguard' should ever leave the tower then the Island of Britain will fall.

20. OWNERSHIP OF THE ARTHURIAN TRADITION. Geoffrey of Monmouth's *History of the Kings of Britain* was written in *c.* 1130 during the reign of Henry I, and was a rewriting of the traditional Dark Age history of Wales (the *Brut*), which was paid for and influenced by Geoffrey's powerful patron, the Anglo-Norman Marcher lord, Robert of Gloucester. In it, Norman descent from the traditional Welsh ancestor Brutus of Troy was purported. Arthur became an ideal of Christian chivalry and Arthurian sites were relocated for political purposes within territories owned by the new Anglo-Norman medieval regime.

21. THE WHITE (LUNAR) HART. At the root of the Welsh tradition (Brut) is a belief that as ancient Britons they are descended from Brutus the Trojan who arrived in Britain in about 1200 BC and named it after himself. He subsequently divided it between his three sons, Locrinus, Camber and Albanactus, who were duly mentioned by Glyndŵr in his letter to the King of Scotland (see Chapter 7).

Brutus was well known for having received the moon-oracle from the ubiquitous goddess (then known as Diana of the Hunter's Moon) as a result of sleeping in the newly flayed hide of a white hart, and it was also well known that the white hart and the ox were interchangeable in this respect since they were both sacred to the lunar goddess – the heritage of the ox being derived from the bull-cult of Mithras on the island of Crete, where the 'Mino-taur' (bull) was apparently once accompanied by a 'Min-elaphos' (stag), who was associated with the local Moon-Goddess Brito-mart.

In Wales it is thus no surprise to find in the *Mabinogion* tale 'The Dream of Rhonabwy' that the dream which revealed the squabbling activities of Owein of Rheged and King Arthur on the banks of the Severn (see Chapter 2) had occurred as the result of the dreamer sleeping upon a magical 'yellow ox-skin'. In this silvery light it seems even more reasonable to suggest that Richard II, whose symbol was the white hart, was a king who was moonstruck by the goddess-principle.

22. THE WISE MAN OF CHESTER. Richard II's apparent intention to ditch the existing Anglo-Norman establishment, and to found a new seat of monarchy bolstered by a new relationship with the Welsh at Chester, has some interesting implications which might not have been wasted upon King Harold (see pages 251–2) or consequently upon Jack of Kent (see Preface pages xiv–xv). Here, doubtless informed by the local network of 'Welsh nobility' via his favourite and appointed heir, the Welsh-supported Roger Mortimer, he found a Celtic counter-establishment already in waiting, with a pre-existing and historically based cultural and military stategy directed against the baronial establishment in London – and centered upon the estuary of the Dee at a place identified by Steve Blake and Scott Lloyd (*The Keys to Avalon*) as the true capital of King Arthur.

23. OWAIN'S FEUD WITH LORD GREY OF RUTHIN. Two explanations were offered at the time for the feud between Owain Glyndŵr and his powerful English neighbour Lord Grey, but neither was very convincing. The first explanation suggested that Grey had deliberately delayed passing on to Glyndŵr an order from the king to serve in the Scottish campaign of August 1400, thus causing Glyndŵr's failure to appear. However, this story entirely fails to satisfy. For example, perhaps Glyndŵr had *deliberately* failed to appear, thus allowing the king and his army to march northwards to be engaged by the Scots, whereafter Glyndŵr had taken full advantage of the king's distraction to launch a long-prepared strategy aimed at liberating Wales. Afterwards the story of Grey's malevolence would have been circulated by the Welsh so as to make Glyndŵr appear wronged rather than opportunistic, and thus maximise his support.

The second explanation suggested that Glyndŵr's attack on Ruthin was the culmination of a long-standing land dispute. Although the Welsh chroniclers were naturally sympathetic to Glyndŵr, it is typical of such disputes that we cannot ascertain who actually began such hostilities, or when, or why – and furthermore the outcome of such common domestic squabbles, even in medieval times, was not usually a millennial war declared at the very moment that the monarch turned his back.

24. THE FOUR LIONS RAMPANT. The practice of showing the four red lions of the northern kingdom of Gwynedd in the rampant position

was a device of Owain Lawgoch, whose innovation was emulated by Glyndŵr.

25. VIRGIN MARY BLUE. The name of the Blue Hill or Bryn-glas at Pilleth has puzzled some people, but blue ('azure') was the colour traditionally associated with the Virgin Mary, whose efforts to supplant all her predecessors had become increasingly celestial: 'And there appeared a great wonder in heaven; a woman clothed with the sun, and the moon under her feet, and upon her head a crown of twelve stars' (*Revelation* 12: 1). The church at Pilleth lay within the old Hereford diocese which extended well to the north and east (thus enfolding much of the Radnorshire territory once held by Cawrdaf in the Dark Ages), and the official robe worn by the priests of Hereford Cathedral was famously Virgin Mary Blue.

26. OWAIN IN THE SOUTH. The assertion that Owain reached as far south as Newport and Cardiff at this stage is made by Adam of Usk, a somewhat unreliable scribe who was not even in the country at the time. He is also likely to have been secretly pro-Glyndŵr. To drive so far south so early would almost certainly have overstretched Glyndŵr and risked his line of retreat being severed, and it is thus considered unlikely. Adam of Usk's confirmation that Glyndŵr reached his own home town of Usk is much more credible, and it was a more realistic target.

27. THE THREE MARYS TOUR. The first port of call on this campaign was the notable shrine to Our Lady at Pilleth. Originally a sacred well inhabited by a 'Goddess of the Waters', by Glyndŵr's day this had become a chapel of the Virgin Mary identified by the Welsh name for the site, Bryn-glas or Blue Hill. The second port of call was Usk, where the cult of Mary Magdalene has been researched by Dr Madeleine Grey (*The Cults of St Radegunde & St Mary Magdalene at Usk*, 2002). The third port of call was Pen-rhys, a site owned by the Cistercian abbey at Llantarnam in the Valley of the Crows (Cwmbrân), which was founded by the Lord Rhys and which owned a monastery dedicated to St Mary Magdalene, the seal of which portrayed a monk addressing three veiled women. Pen-rhys, meanwhile, would soon be renowned as a shrine to the Virgin Mary. Like that at Bryn Glas, it was built adjacent to a sacred well which had been rededicated to the Virgin, and during the 1500s it became an internationally famous place of pilgrimage celebrated by a plethora of poets. Although it has been noted (*Glamorgan County History*, 3, p. 153) that the shrine only came suddenly to prominence in *c.* 1450, we may nevertheless safely assume that such a spectacular performance on the part of the Lady almost certainly indicates that she had been attending the sacred well at Pen-rhys for some time.

In the esoteric terms outlined by the Coptic Church (see Chapter 4), it thus becomes possible to conceive of the Three Marys Tour as a military campaign based upon a lunar cycle. Pilleth is identified with Mary the Virgin by virtue of being at Bryn-glas or 'Blue-Hill', and in terms of the Celtic Lunar Triple-Goddess it thus corresponds to Ana (Good Mother, Child Nurturer, Full Moon); Usk is identified by the presence there of the cult of Mary Magdalene, who in terms of the Celtic lunar Triple-Goddess corresponds to Macha (identified in the *Book of Lecan* as Raven – i.e. the Morrigan, Child-Devourer, Darkness, No Moon); and Pen-rhys is consequently Mary of Bethany, who in terms of the Celtic lunar Triple-Goddess corresponds to Badb (meaning Boiling, which refers to the cauldron of the waters symbolised by the lunar crescent or New Moon). However, this is pure speculation.

28. THE IRISH. Had the Welsh-supported Roger Mortimer lived and continued to serve as Richard II's Royal Lieutenant in Ireland, it is possible that he would have created an Ireland capable of contributing to Richard's intended new order. However, despite precedents of Irish-Welsh collaboration, by the time of Glyndŵr's letter in the winter of 1401 the situation in Ireland was so chaotic that he was compelled to address the letter in the plural, and the response was accordingly nil.

29. URIEN'S HEAD. In *c.* AD 595 Urien of Rheged was killed while fighting the Northumbrians (see Chapter 2). It is also recorded that his body was subsequently decapitated by his cousin Llywarch Hen (the warrior-poet and colleague of Urien's bard Taliesin), and his head was thus rescued and subsequently hidden, thereby ensuring the safe passage of his soul into the Otherworld, from which he would send aid and ultimately return (see Chapter 1).

30. PEN-RHYS. Now in Rhondda Cynon-Taf, was not only the site of the Cistercian grange dedicated to the Virgin, but it lay within forests as dense as those which surrounded Talley Abbey in Cantref Mawr, and in valleys which were even more inaccessible. As a result, it was also popular with outlaws.

31. THE UPPER TAF VALLEY. Despite the fact that Pen-rhys is now said to lie in the Rhondda, and thus a little west of what we would call the Upper Taf Valley today, Iolo would probably have regarded Pen-rhys itself as lying in the Upper Taf on the basis that it is situated in the midst of the network of streams which contribute to the river in its upper reaches – and indeed, since the word Rhondda means merely 'a babbling stream', in those days it may not have served to differentiate it from any of the other contributing streams in the area. This being so, Iolo is actually being quite specific in the 'Strolling Tour' and is indicating that he met the Abbot of Llantarnam *at* Pen-rhys.

32. THE THIRD BISHOP. Having identified 1404 as the probable year of John Scudamore's secret marriage to Alice Glyndŵr, it seems possible that, owing to the pressures of the time, the ceremony might have been combined with the marriages of two of Glyndŵr's other daughters (Janet and Margaret) to the Lords of Croft and Monnington, especially in view of the convenient proximity of the three grooms' residences in south Herefordshire. If so, while we have suggested Bishop Byford as a potentially presiding pontiff, it is also just possible

that this momentous ceremony might have been performed under the auspices of the local Bishop of Hereford, John Trefnant. Trefnant was probably still alive in the spring of 1404 and was not officially replaced as bishop as a result of his demise until 2 July, and therefore it cannot be ruled out that one of his last acts was the blessing of the clandestine triple-marriage of Owain's three daughters.

33. MORTIMER and PERCY. Edmund Mortimer's sister Elizabeth had married Henry Percy Jnr (Hotspur) and so the Earl of Northumberland, Henry Percy Snr was Mortimer's father-in-law.

34. MASS-GRAVE AT GROSMONT. The preaching-cross at Grosmont is also sometimes said to mark the mass burial site of local victims of the Black Death.

35. LOCATION OF THE YELLOW POOL. Raglan was established as a defensive structure in about 1070, but at some point before 1415 was developed by one William ap Thomas into a castle and a tower surrounded by walls, and standing within a moat or 'pool' which may have already existed, and it is said that the stone used in its construction led to it becoming known as the Yellow Tower. However, this latter assertion may well be as spurious as another which claims that Whitecastle derived its name from the limewash with which it was once coated (all castles were painted thus – but Whitecastle's name, came from the Welsh chieftain 'Gwyn the White', who once held it), and instead the moated site may simply have retained some association with the Yellow Plague (*Pla Melyn*) or Yellow Death (*Chron Chonaill*) which had assailed Wales in either AD 547 or AD 557. David Keys (*Catastrophe: An Investigation into the Origins of the Modern World*) argues that this Dark Age equivalent of the medieval Black Death may have seriously weakened the resistance of the Celtic west to the Anglo-Saxons, and in conjunction with internecine squabbling helped to precipitate the retreat of the Celts from the Severn to the borders of modern Wales – meanwhile it may also have propelled a wave of Celtic clerics and nobility towards Brittany.

36. ROBIN GOODFELLOW. The mischievous spirit known as Robin Goodfellow is traditionally associated with Puck (known to the Welsh as Pwcca), from whom we get the expression 'hocus pocus'. Also associated with 'Will o' the Wisp' and thus also with 'John (Jack) o' the Wad', Robin Goodfellow has also been linked with the Green Man (see Chapter 1), and was later noted by Shakespeare, who was clearly aware of the alliance between the peasantry and the outlaw spirits of the woods, and included it in *A Midsummer Night's Dream*:

> Either I mistake your shape and making quite
> Or else you are that shrewd and knavish sprite
> called Robin Goodfellow . . .
> Those that Hob-goblin call you, and sweet Puck
> You do their work, and they shall have good luck.

Like Puck therefore, Robin Goodfellow might well be described as a 'fairy, and merry wanderer of the night . . . rough knurly-limbed, faun-faced and shock-pated – a very Shetlander among the fairy-winged', insofar as he was in truth a rough outlaw, who, by virtue of having vanished into the forest in his Kentsdale Green had joined the ancient (Celtic) spirits of the woods – entities which by the Middle Ages had long-since been demonised by the state as supernatural powers which were 'not of God', but which were still regarded with credulity and affection by the peasantry. Meanwhile, the lives, deaths and identities of such men were by nature obscure, for they disappeared constantly and reappeared when they were rumoured to be dead, and so they never died.

37. STALLING DOWN. Following Glyndŵr's cataclysmic success in the Tywi Valley campaign of July 1403, it appears that he was thwarted by Lord Carew from returning to the north to attend the Battle of Shrewsbury (see Chapter 8). While his whereabouts in the immediate wake of this event are officially unknown, it may well be that he secretly remained in the south, since the following month he is said to have been in charge at the Battle of Stalling Down on the hill called Bryn Owen near Cowbridge, where the English were defeated. Here, according to folklore, the battle lasted for eighteen hours, 'after which the blood was so deep that it was up to the horses' fetlocks' – a story which has an interesting cadence with one of the legends told of Jack of Kent at Kentchurch (see Appendix, Legend 17). Meanwhile, it may also be significant that another piece of folklore (albeit transmitted by an unreliable source) relates that it was in the same area that Glyndŵr and a companion, having introduced themselves as a travelling minstrel and his assistant, once stayed for four days and three nights as the guests of a certain Lord Berkerolles of Coety Castle. Having thus taken advantage of the hospitality traditionally offered to travellers in troubled times, they were about to depart on the final evening when an anxious Lord Berkerolles warned them of a rumour that the terrible Glyndŵr was somewhere in the area. In the same vein he had just declared it his earnest hope that the Welsh leader would be captured soon, whereupon Glyndŵr is said to have extended his hand and revealed his identity. Such was the shock of this revelation that Sir Lawrence Berkerolles was struck dumb, and never spoke again.

38. THE SCUDAMORES AND FRANCISCANISM. While the Scudamores were evidently well acquainted with Premonstratensianism, not least via that Order's abbey on the Scudamore lands at Holme Lacy ('Hamm') near Hereford, evidence suggests that their domestic religious arrangements at Kentchurch were traditionally orientated towards Franciscanism. A detailed study of the priests supplied to the Scudamores' private chapel at Kentchurch indicates that they were consistently provided since the early 1300s by the Scudamores'

baronial friends and neighbours the de Pembrugges, who held high offices at Hereford Cathedral and who were the celebrated original sponsors of Franciscanism in the city. Furthermore, a certain Richard Scudamore (Mayor of Hereford from 1385 to 1387) is duly recorded as having been buried in the Grey Franciscan House at Hereford, as was a later Mayor of Hereford, John Mey, with whom young John Scudamore 'Esquire' was closely involved in the deeds regarding the demise of the de Pembrugge manor of Gillow prior to the violence between Scudamore, Abrahall and Talbot in 1423 (see Chapter 11). We may therefore conclude that visits by Grey Friars to Kentchurch Court were not considered unusual in the early 1400s.

39. LOCATION OF CELYDON. Steve Blake and Scott Lloyd (*The Keys to Avalon*) suggest that the Forest of Celyddon is more likely to have been in north-west Wales rather than in Scotland as other historians have suggested.

40. DOVE-PINK FRANCISCANS. In 1326 the Chapter-General of Benedict XII issued specific regulations regarding the design and colour of Franciscan habits, all of which were to be 'of the same colour, and not tending to either black or white'. In discussing the russet cloth of the early English Franciscans, Moorman, in his *History of the Franciscan Order*, therefore declares that 'this shows that the Franciscan habit of the 1300s was grey rather than brown', and maintains that in those days the term russet meant grey, rather than red-brown as it does nowadays – but this is a spurious argument.

Russet, regardless of its colour, is simply a coarse home-spun cloth worn by peasants, and thus indicates austerity. Meanwhile, the decree that Franciscan habits should tend neither to black nor white inevitably leaves open the door for introducing a delicate hint of colour – and it is known that blue was generally considered inappropriate by the Friars. However, as Moorman also relates, it had been told that Joachim of Fiore had famously prophesied, with regard to the Franciscans, of 'the rise of an Order dressed in the colour of doves', and Barthelmew of Pisa had described St Francis's own habit (when he chose to wear it) as 'ashy, pale and earth-coloured' – and here we shall rest our case, for while 'earth-coloured' suggests the possibility of a certain ruddiness, the concept of 'dove-colour' is still, as always, defined by the *Oxford English Dictionary* as '*warm* grey, with a tinge of *pink* or lavender'.

41. SHENMORE. Assuming that Owain Glyndŵr did indeed spend his last days at Dorstone, he would regularly have been obliged to cross the adjacent area of Shenmore when en route to Croft (or even Kentchurch) via the old Roman road which crossed the River Wye near Kenchester. In view of the fact that by now Owain was known as Jack or 'Sion', and considering that a well-known alternative spelling of 'Sion' was 'Shon', which is indeed found applied to 'Shon Kent' in various documents, one cannot help but wonder whether Shenmore is

simply a corruption of 'Sion's Moor' and was once a reference made to Glyndŵr's presence in the area. In view of what we have discovered, it seems a far more plausible explanation than the desperate attempt made by the normally authoritative Bannister (*Place-Names of Herefordshire*) to derive the name from 'Scearn-dung or Swin-morr' meaning 'nearby'.

42. GLYNDŴR AND LAWGOCH. Owain Glyndŵr may have been aided in adopting his late predecessor's mantle by his ownership of a piece of land three miles from Sycharth which had formerly belonged to Owain Lawgoch, and also perhaps by his reported ownership of a piece of cloth patterned with 'maidens with red hands' which might have referred to the blood-link in question.

Select Bibliography

Arber-Cooke, A.T., *Pages from the History of Llandovery* (Friends of Llandovery Civic Trust Association: Vol I, Llandovery, 1994)

Ashe, G., *Mythology of the British Isles* (Methuen, London, 1990)

Baker, *Baker's Chronicle: History of the Kings of England* (rev. edn 1733)

Bale, J., *Index Brittaniae Scriptorum* (1557)

Bannister, A.T., *The History of Ewias Harold, Castle, Priory and Church* (Bible & Crown Press, Hereford, 1902)

Baring, A. & Cashford J., *The Myth of the Goddess* (BCA, London, New York, Sydney, Toronto, 1991)

M.N.J., Late of Blackbrooke, *Bygone Days in the March Wall of Wales* (St Catherine Press, 1926)

Blake, S. & Lloyd, S., *The Keys to Avalon* (Element Books Ltd, Shaftesbury, 2000)

——, *Pendragon* (Rider, London, 2002)

Bord, J. & C., *Sacred Waters* (Paladin Grafton Books, London, rev. edn 1986)

Bradney, J.A., *A History of Monmouthshire*.

Brewer, E.C., *Dictionary of Phrase and Fable* (Cassell & Co Ltd, London, Paris, New York & Melbourne, 19th edn. n.d.)

Briggs, K., *Dictionary of British Folk Tales* (Routledge & Kegan Paul, London, 1971)

Bromwich, R., *The Arthurian Legend in Mediaeval Welsh Literature* (University of Wales Press, Cardiff, 1991)

Bryant, A., *The Age of Chivalry* (The Reprint Society Ltd, London, rev. edn 1965)

Buchanan-Brown, J. (ed), *Brief Lives: The Natural History of Herefordshire, John Aubrey's Projected Tract* (Penguin, Harmondsworth, 2000)

Coleman, D., *Orcop* (S.P.A. Ltd, Hanley Swan, 1992)

Compton Reade (Ed), *Memorials of Old Herefordshire* (Benrose & Sons, London, 1904)

Cook, G. H., *The English Mediaeval Parish Church* (Phoenix House Ltd, London, rev. edn 1961)

Cox, T., *Magna Britannia, or Topographical, Historical, Ecclesiastical, and Natural History of Herefordshire*, n.p., 1846)

Coxe, W., *An Historical Tour of Monmouthshire* (1801)

Curran, B., *The Dark Spirit* (Cassell & Co., London, 2001)

D'Alencon, U., *Les Frères Mineurs et L'Université D'Angers* (n.p., 1901)

Davies, J., *Folklore & Place-Names of Caerphilly District* (Caerphilly, 1920)

Davies, R.R., *The Revolt of Owain Glyndŵr* (Oxford University Press, Oxford, 1995)

Delaney, F., *The Celts* (Hodder & Stoughton, London, 1986)

Dillon, M. & Chadwick, N., *The Celtic Realms* (Sphere Books Ltd, London, rev. edn 1973)

Doble, G.H., *Lives of the Welsh Saints* (University of Wales Press, Cardiff, 1984)

Dugdale, W., *Monasticon Anglicanum* (James Bohn, London, 1846)

Duncumb, J., *History and Antiquities of the County of Hereford: Vol I* (Allen, Hereford, 1904)

Evans, J. & Britton, J., *Topgraphical and Historical Tour of the County of Monmouth* (Neely & Jones, London, 1810)

Embden, A.B., *Biographical Register of the University of Oxford* (Clarendon Press, Oxford, 1959)

——, *Biographical Register of the University of Cambridge* (Cambridge University Press, 1963)

Graves, R., *The White Goddess* (Faber & Faber, London, 1961)

Griffiths, R.A., *The Principality of Wales in the Later Middle Ages* (University of Wales Press, Cardiff, 1972)

——, *Sir Rhys ap Thomas and His Family* (University of Wales Press, Cardiff, 1993)

Gwyndaf, R., *Welsh Folk Tales* (National Museum of Wales, Cardiff, 1989)

Henken, E., *National Redeemer: Owain Glyndŵr in the Welsh Tradition* (University of Wales Press, Cardiff, 1996)

——, *Traditions of the Welsh Saints* (D.S. Brewer, Cambridge, 1987)

Hodges, G., *Owain Glyndŵr and the War of Independence in the Welsh Borders* (Logaston, Almeley, 1995)

Howell, R., *A History of Gwent* (Gomer Press, Llandysul, rev. edn 1989)

Jackson, M.N., *Bygone Days in the March Wall of Wales* (St Catherine Press, London, 1926)

James, P., *The Story of Carmarthenshire: Vol I* (Christopher Davies Ltd, n.p. 1959)

Jenkins, R.T. (ed), *Dictionary of Welsh Biography* (Honourable Society of Cymmrodorion, London, 1959)

Jarman, A.O.H. (ed), *A Guide to Welsh Literature: Vol.II* (University of Wales Press, Cardiff, 1997)

Johnston, D., *Iolo Goch: Poems* (Gomer Press, Llandysul, 1993)

——, *Guide to the Literature of Wales* (University of Wales Press, Cardiff, 1994)

Jones, G., *The Oxford Book of Welsh Verse in English* (Oxford University Press, Oxford, 1977)

Jones, T. (Tra) *Brut Y Tywysogyon* (University of Wales, n.p., 1955)

Leather, E.M., *The Folk-Lore of Herefordshire* (Jakeman & Carver, Hereford, 1912)

Lecky, W.E.H., *History of the Rise and Influence of the Spirit of Rationalism in Europe* (Loughmans Green & Co, London, Bombay & Calcutta, 1910)

Leland, J., *Itinerary of John Leland* (c. 1535–1543)

Levett, F.G., *The Story of Skenfrith, Grosmont, and St Maughans* (Monmouthshire, 1984)

Lloyd, J., *A History of Carmarthenshire* (William Lewis, Cardiff, 1935)

Lloyd, J.E., *Owain Glyndŵr* (Oxford University Press, Oxford, 1931)

Moorman, J., *A History of the Franciscan Order* (Clarendon Press, Oxford, 1968)

Munday, A., *John A Kent and John A Cumber* (Elibron Classics rev. edn n.d.)

Owen, T.M., *Welsh Folk Customs* (J.D. Lewis & Sons Ltd, Gomerian Press, Llandysul & National Museum of Wales, Cardiff, 1959)

Palmer, Roy, *The Folklore of (Old) Monmouthshire* (Logaston Press, 1998)

Page, W. (ed), *A History of the County of Worcester* (University of London, Institute of Historical Research, London rev. edn. 1971)

Parry, T., *A History of Welsh Literature* (Clarendon Press, Oxford, 1955)

Pennar, M. (Trans), *The Black Book of Carmarthen* (Llanerch Publishing, rev.edn. Lampeter, 1989)

Pevsner, N., *Herefordshire* (Penguin, Harmondsworth, 1963)

Pits, J., *De Illustribus Angliae Scriptoribus* (1619)

Rees, D., *The Son of Prophecy: Henry Tudor's Road to Bosworth* (Black Raven Press, London, 1985)

Rutherford, W., *Celtic Mythology* (Aquarian Press, Wellingborough 1987)

Seaton, D., *A History of the Deanery of Archenfield with a Description of the Churches in the Old Rural Deanery* (Jakeman & Carver, Hereford, 1903)

Sharpe, R., *A Handlist of the Latin Writers of Great Britain and Ireland Before 1540* (The Journal of Mediaeval Latin, Belgium, Brepols, 1997)

Simpson, J., *The Folklore of the Welsh Border* (B.T. Batsford Ltd, London, 1976)

Skidmore, W., *The Scudamores of Upton Scudamore, a Knightly Family in Mediaeval Wiltshire: 1086–1382* (Akron, Ohio & Winchester, Tennessee, 1982)

Stephen, L. (ed), *Dictionary of National Biography* (Smith Elder & Co, London, 1908)

Stephens, M., *The Oxford Companion to the Literature of Wales* (Oxford University Press, Oxford, 1986)

Strickland, A., *The Queens of England* (Chivers Press, Bath, 1972)

Symonds, W.S. (ed.), *Malvern Chase: an Episode of the Wars of the Roses and the Battle of Tewkesbury* (William North, Tewkesbury, 1881)

Taylor, E., *Kings Caple in Archenfield* (Logaston Press, Little Logaston Woonton Almeley 1997)

Thompson, E.M. (ed), *The Chronicle of Adam of Usk* (Llanerch Publishing, Lampeter, rev. edn 1991)

Thornhill Timmins, H., *Nooks and Corners of Herefordshire* (Elliott Stock, London, 1892)

Turvey, R., *The Lord Rhys: Prince of Deheubarth* (Gomer Press, Llandysul, 1997)

Waters, I., *Folklore & Dialect of the Lower Wye Valley* (Moss Rose Press, Chepstow, 1982)

Watkins, A., *The Old Straight Track* (Sphere Books Ltd, London, rev. edn 1978)

Webb, J., *Memorials of the Civil War between King Charles I and the Parliament of England as it Affected Herefordshire and the Adjacent Counties: Vol I* (Longmans Green & Co, 1879)

Westwood, J., *Albion: A Guide to Legendary Britain* (Granada, London, 1985)

Williams, G., *The Land Remembers* (Faber & Faber Ltd, London, 1977)

—— (ed) & Pugh, T.B. (ed), *Glamorgan County History: Vol III* (University of Wales Press, Cardiff, 1971)

Williams, G.J., *Iolo Morganwg* (University of Wales Press, Cardiff, 1940)

INDEX

Abbey Dore, 71, 171

Aberdyfi, 222

Abererch, 232–3

Abergavenny, 32, 68, 72, 87, 105, 110–1, 116

Abertridwr, 35

Aberystwyth, 71–4, 103, 106, 111 seige of, 134–7, 149, 229

Abrahall (John), 159–60, 250

Aconbury, 111, 160, 212

Adam of Usk, 60, 71, 96–7, 153–5, 239–40

Agincourt, 153, 155, 185

Aldworth, 211–12

Alexander (The Great), 31

Alice Glyndŵr, (see Preface), 94, 96, 109, 145–6, 151, 154–5, 158, 160–1, 164, 166, 168–9, 170–1, 181, 183, 185, 187, 192–4, 198, 229, 234–5

All Saints Day (All Hallows), 232

All Souls Day, 191, 218, 233

Almeley, 148, 156

Ana, 55

Anarawd, 19, 21

Anglesey (Mon), 6, 17, 39, 46, 51, 59, 65–6, 120, 128–9, 131, 144 submits, 132–3

Anglo-Saxons, (see Preface), 11–12, 16, 34, 47, 50, 92, 100, 113–14, 130, 179, 182, 200, 205, 206, 231, 239

Anne of Bohemia, 54–9

Anne St, 55

Annwn (Celtic Underworld), 180 (see also Appendix I)

Apples (symbolic fruit), 90, 176–8, 181, 185, 187, 236 (see also To Sip An Apple)

Archenfield, 33–4, 59, 62, 78, 80, 87, 111, 119–20, 123, 128, 145, 159–60, 164, 169, 182

Ark (see Noah)

Armes Prydein, 47, 77

Arthur, Arthurian tradition, 14, 16, 38, 44, 46, 48, 57, 74, 152, 178, 210, 224, 238,

Arundel (Earls of), 81, 108, 213,

Astronomy, Astrology, 46, 49, (see also Comet)

Audley (Lord), 134, 167

Augury, 6, 46, 90, 179–80, 213

Augustine St, (see Preface), 27, 179, 204–5

Augustinian Order, 28

Bacon (Roger), 212

Bala, 150, 210,

Ballards, Ballardy, (see Preface), 61, 67, (see also John Ball)

Bangor, 60, 66, 108, 110, 133, 192, 214

Bardolf (Lord), 120, 129, 131, 136–7

Baronial 'Scrum', (see Henry VI, Council)

Beaumaris, 66, 81, 86, 106, 111, 120

Benedictine Order, 28, 50, 158

Berkerolles (Lord), 104, 113

Bernard of Clairvaux, 28–9

Berwyn Mountains, 23, 164

Bishop's Castle, 71, 112

Black Death, 33, 226–7, 237

Black Mountains, 234

Bleddfa, 77

Bramham Moor, 137

Brân (Raven), 30

Brecon, 80, 88, 95, 108, 112, 124, 146, 230, 234

Breconshire, (see Brycheiniog),

Bretons (Britanny), 75, 81, 84, 103, 105, 110, 112, 121–2, 207–8

Bridge (The), xv, 171, 201, 267

Bridgnorth, 116

Bridget (Brigit) St, 29

Brittany, (see Bretons)

Bromfield, 134

Browne-Willis, 192, 193

Brut family, (see Bryt)

Brut (The), 7, 88, 100, 102, 114

Brutus, 7, 56, 75

Brychan, 183

Brycheiniog (Breconshire), 12–14, 18, 40, 183, 206, 223, 233, 237

Bryn-glas, (see Pilleth)

Bryn Owen, 168

Bryt family, 301, (see also Epilogue)

Bryt (Walter), 61, 159

Builth, 40, 71, 73, 87–9, 102, 116

Burdocks, 26, 276

Burton Hill, 52

Byford, 110, 117

Byford (Lewis, Bishop), 108, 110, 115, 117, 133, 136–7

Cadair Idris, 69

Cadell, 19, 21

Cadwaladr, 22, 47, 75, 99, 116, 177

Cadwallon, 116

Cadwgan (of Glynrhondda), 92–3

Caeo, 19–20, 40–1, 48, 73, 90

Caerleon, 116, 121, 123

Caernarfon, 66, 74, 81, 86, 105, 128

Caernarfonshire, 133–4, 157

Caerphilly, 32, 34, 80, 105, 111, 126

Cai (Kai), 38, 210

Caldicot, 33

Camber (Kamber), 31, 75

Cambrian Mountains, 40, 43

Campstone Hill, 111

Candles, Candlelight, 185, 189, 191, 218, 233

Canon Pyon, 52, 188

Canterbury, (see Preface), 28, 204

Cantref Bychan, 19, 21, 93, 105,

Cantref Mawr, 12, 17, 19–22, 25, 29, 39–40, 43, 48, 61–2, 73, 93, 105, 206, 210, 215–16, 223–4, 226–30, 234–5

Cardiff, 41, 80, 105, 111, 113, 116

Cardigan, 19, 24, 71, 73–4, 124, 129

Cardiganshire, 134, 144, 148

Carew (Lord), 100–05, 115, 134, 168

Carmarthen, 17, 25, 41, 61–2, 73, 93, 95, 99–106, 112, 117, 122–3, 145, 226–7, 229, 234, 239

    Black Book of, 47, 177

Carmarthenshire, 12, 17, 70–4, 95, 145

Carnwyllion, 95, submits, 131

Carreg Cennen Castle, 13, 22, 32, 77, 94–6, 98, 109, 159, 206, 223–4

Carrog, 22–4, 36, 39

Cathar Church, 27, 57

Catharine Glyndŵr, 84, 86, 138–40, 147, 154

Cawrdaf, 12–14, 18, 24, 206, 217, 223, 231–3, 237–9

Ceneu St, 183–5, 238

Ceredigion, 18–22, 24, 29, 41, 68–70, 101, 103, 146, support ebbing in 131

Ceri, (see Kerry)

Chapel Cottage, 166, 170

Charlton (Bishop), 50

Charlton (Lord), 69–71, 131, 134, 156

Charles I, 64

Charles VI (of France), 75, 110, 112

Chepstow, 14, 33, 107, 184, 213

Cheshire, 13–14, 205

Chester, 17, 58–60, 70, 86, 103

Chivalry, 57, 124

Christianity, Christian Church, 7, 10–11, 27–9, 33, 45–6, 49–50, 55–6, 61, 68, 152, 173, 176, 178–9, 200–03, 208–11, 214, 221

Christmas, 174–5

Christmas Block (The), 174, 289

Cistercian Order, 28–31, 41–2, 59, 62, 71–3, 91–3, 103, 114, 171, 222, 226

Civil War, 64

Clwyd, 39, 131, submits, 133, (see also Dyffryn Clwyd)

Coed Shon Farm, 168

Coel (king), 22, 183

Coety, 104, 113, 123, 125

Collen St, (see also Llangollen), 239

Columba St, 179, 200–05

Comet (of 1402), 76

Conwy, 66, 68, Conwy Valley, 137, 140

Coptic Church, 27, 55

Corn, as harvest 3–4, 6–7, 11, 15, 26, 53, 64, 111, 152, 190 as flesh, 11, 38, 152, 157, 200, 208

Cornwall, Cornish, 16, 47

Corras (Kaueros), 113, 160, 176, 178, 181, 237 (see also Scudamore, Ysenda)

Corwen, 22–4, 39, 63, 66

Cowbridge, 104, 168

Crach Ffinant, 88, 90, 184

Craig-y-Dorth, 113

Cremation, 193, 197, 208

Cricieth, 66

Croft, 109, 165–67, 188, 192, 193, 229, 235

Croft (Lord), 109, 117, 164–7, 170–1, 187–8, 193

Crows, 34–5, 277, (see also Ravens)

Cumbria, (see Preface), 13–14, 16, 23, 29, 179, 183, 205

Cunedda, 12, 16, 21–2, 99, 176

Cŵmbran, 92

Cwm-hir, 29, 71–2

Cymry, 12–13, 33, 152

Cynog St, 29

David St, 47, 176

Deathbed Stanzas (The), 186

De Clifford (Roger), 111, 212

De Clifford (Walter), 19, 21, 65

De Lancaster (Henry), 32–3

De Lancaster (Robert), 145

De Lancaster (Thomas), (see Preface) 97

Dee River, 12–13, 23, 48, 65, 80, 82, 238
Deheubarth, 12–14, 16–25, 28, 30–2, 39–44, 47, 66, 68, 72–5, 89–90, 99, 104, 119, 130, 205, 215, 217, 223–4, 228, 231, 233
Denbigh, 65–6
  submits, 133
Denbighshire, 131
  submits, 135
Despenser family, 32
Despenser (Lady), 115
Devil (The), (see Preface), 27, 204, 207, 211–13, 221
  and Jack of Kent, 8–9, 15, 26, 34–5, 52–3, 85, 107, 142–3, 180, 184, 189, 191, 195–7, 208–9, 236
  and Owain Glyndwr, 44, 48–50, 81, 83–4, 166, 169–70, 180
Devil's Imps, xv, 53, 85, 91, 201
Devil's Heelmark, xvi, 26
Devil's Quoit (The), xxxiv, 271
Devon, 16
Dinefwr, 17, 20–5, 29, 31, 62, 73, 93, 206, 215, 223–4, 228
Dore, (see Abbey Dore)
Dore River, Valley, 167, 170, 188, 194
Dorstone, 109, 167, 170, 185, 187, 189, 191–4, 198, 218, 229, 233–4
Doves (symbolic birds), 11, 178–80, 187, 196–223
  as Angels, 202, (see also Columba)
Dove and Raven (The), 196–7, 290
  principle of, 179, 198–208, 221
Dragons, 74, 177, 221

Druids, Druidic, 6, 10, 27, 29, 34, 45–8, 51, 178, 203, 208, 213
Dryslwyn, 94–5
Dungeon (The), 162, 288
Dwn family, 158
Dwn (Gruffydd), 153, 158
Dwn (Henry), 41, 59, 68–9, 90, 93, 104, 113, 131, 145–6, 148, 153, 156
Dyfed (Pembrokeshire), 18–19, 24, 41, 47, 68–9, 75, 92–3, 95, 99, 100–2, 113, 232
Dyffryn Clwyd, 39, 65, 76, 86, submits, 133

Eaton Bishop, 188
Edward I, 17, 31–2, 57
Edward II, 31–2
Edward III, 32, 50, 61, 173, 226–7
Eglwys Ilan, 35
Eifionydd, 67
Elfael, 40, 89, 102, 165
Elffin, 102
Elidir Ddu, 224
Everyman-Theory, (see Preface), 168,
Ewias Harold, 50, 105, 160, 211

Fates, 30, 90, 192
Flint, 59, 65, 87, 104
Flintshire, 13, 86, 104, 134
  support ebbing in 131
  submits, 133
Flood, 10–11, 179, 222, (see also Noah)
France, 32, 75, 81, 110, 112, 121–3, 130–31, 135–7, 147–151, 153, 155–7, 185, 190–1
French, 62, 84, 105–6, 110,

112–13, 121–4, 129–31, 140, 190–1, 238

French retreat, 129

French defeated, 131

Francis St, 181

Franciscan Order (Grey Friars), (*see* Preface), 32, 62, 65–6, 77, 111, 165, 168, 171, 176, 180–1, 198, 212, (*see also* Green-to-Grey)

Gam (Dafydd), 118, 132, 146–7

Garway, Garway Hill, 8, 35, 97, 178–9, 184, 222, 237

Geoffrey of Monmouth, 57

Geomancy, 58, 90

Giants, (*see* Preface), 3, 88, 184, 212–13, 224

Gilbert (John, Bishop), 60, 62

Gillow, 159–61

Glam Dicin, 47, 91

Glamorgan, (*see* Morgannwg)

Gloucester (Duke of), 158, 166

Glyndŵr (*see* Owain)

Glyndyfrdwy, 36, 39, 63, 66, 80, 87, 114

Glynrhondda, 80, 92

Gnosticism, 27–8, 55, 57, 97, 222, 237

Golden Valley, 171, 187–9

Goodrich, 159, 184

Gower, 24, 95, 101–2, 149, support ebbing in, 131

Grace Dieu, 50

Graig Hill, 117

Green Man, 6

Green-to-Grey (principle of), (*see* Preface), 164

Grey (Lord of Ruthin), 65, 76–7, 84, 105

Grey Friars, (*see* Franciscan Order)

Greyndour (Sir John), 118, 134

Grosmont, (*see* Preface), 33, 35, 50, 60, 64, 72, 107–8, 111, 121, 123, 162, 171–2, 194–5, 219, 227
  Henry of 33
  battle of, 116–20, 195
  church of, 195–7, 199, 207, 209, 227

Gruffydd Glyndŵr, 119, 138, 146

Gruffydd ap Nicholas, 224, 245, 251

Gruffydd ap Rhys ap Tewdwr, 18–19, 21, 48

Gruffudd Young, 156

Gwenllian, 39

Gwenllian (wife of Gruffydd ap Rhys ap Tewdwr), 19, 21–22, 48

Gwent (Monmouthshire),18, 29, 80, 105, 108, 111, 116, 118–20, 123, 128, 146, 151, 169, 198, 214
  submits, 125

Gwynedd, 16–17, 19–20, 22–4, 31, 41, 66, 120

Hal (Prince), (*see* Henry V)

Half-in & Half-out, 197, 292
  principle of 195, 208–214, 216, 221–2, 225–7

Halfway, 216, 225–7

Halkyn Mountain, 129, 132

Hamm, (*see* Holm Lacey)

Hanmer family, 110, 112, 134

Hanmer (John), 120

Hanmer (Sir David), 190

Hanmer (Margaret), 96, 138, 140

Harlech, 66, 71–2, 81, 86–7, 106, 111, 113–15, 118–19, 121, 128, 133–5 147, 163, 170, 174, 183, 215

seige of, 137–40
fall of, 138–4
Harold (King), (see Preface), 18,
    237, 259
Haverford West, 93, 113, 122
Hawarden, 65, 104
Hay-on-Wye, 72–3, 112, 23,
Head-Cult (decapitation) 4–5, 28,
    51, 58, 71–2, 90, 202–3,
    222
Hearkening Rocks, 1
Heart, 197, 207, 211
Hell, Hades, 50, 197, 199, 201–2,
    204, 209, 222, 236, 247,
    290–2
Henry I, 18–20, 28, 41, 217
Henry II, 20–4, 217
Henry III, 40, 60
Henry IV (Bolingbroke), 49, 51,
    59, 63, 65–6, 68–70, 72–5,
    79, 81–4, 86, 93, 96–9, 103,
    105–6, 108, 109–10,
    114–15, 117–18, 120,
    124–5, 128, 130, 136, 144,
    146, 149, 154, 187
  coronation of 59, 96, 97
  death of, 147, 187
Henry V (Prince Hal), 69–71, 81,
    86–7, 108, 112, 117, 120,
    129, 134, 144–5, 149–51,
    153–7, 166, 185
  ascends throne, 147
  death of, 158
Henry VI, 158, Council of, 158–9
Hereford, 17, 32, 35, 60–2, 64,
    87, 91, 97, 105, 107–8, 111,
    112–15, 117, 120, 149, 154,
    188, 214
Herefordshire, 12, 34–5, 52,
    78–80, 87, 94, 105, 110–12,
    115, 131, 145, 149–50,
    157–8, 161, 164–7, 169–70,

178, 182–3, 187, 191–2,
    194, 198, 211–12, 214, 239
Hergest, Hergest Ridge, 166–7,
    170, 187–8
Hidden Treasure, 127, 283
Holme Lacey (Hamm), 97–8, 160,
    229
Hope (near Chester), 86, 104
Hope-under-Dinmore, 166
Hopcyn ap Thomas, 101–2
Horses (see also Jack of Kent's
    Horses), 142, 174–5, 283
  and Glyndŵr, 49
Hotspur, (see Percy)
Hyddgen, 69–70
Hywel Dda, 16–17, 22, 24, 28, 32,
    41, 99, 112
Hywel Sele, 132

Iolo Goch, 37–42, 44–6, 48, 51,
    55, 58, 60, 63, 71, 80–1,
    88–91, 93, 96, 99, 101–3,
    113, 147, 179, 181, 184,
    215–6, 227–9
  death of, 114
Iolo Morganwg, 248, 298, (see also
    Epilogue, Appendix II)
Iona, (see Preface), 27, 46, 179,
    201, 207
Invisibility, 48, 90
Ireland, Irish, 16, 18, 24, 45,
    47–9, 55, 58, 63, 75, 81, 84,
    120, 159, 200, 203
Is-cennen, 13, 22, 94–5
Ishtar, 10, 55–6, 179

Jack-daws, as Ravens, (see
    ravens),
Jack Goodfellow, (see Robin
    Goodfellow)
Jack of France, 218, 233, 293,
    principle of, 189–91

Index

Jack of Kent (Siôn Cent), (see Preface), 95, 156, 173, 188, 207–9, 212, 239

Legends of, xv, xvi, xxxiv, xxxv, 8, 9, 15, 26, 34–5, 52–3, 64, 85, 107, 126¬7, 142–3, 162, 174–5, 196–7, 218, 219, 236, (see also Appendix I)

as Owain Glyndŵr, 49, 83, 94–5, 117, 164, 168–70, 180–2, 186, 189–90, 194–5, 198–9, 214–17, 227, 229, 269

as Dickey Kent, 107

embraces the Devil, (see Symonds)

Jack of Kent's Bake-Oven, 262–3, (see also Epilogue, photograps)

Jack of Kent's Barn, 35, 262

Jack of Kent's Bedroom, 94, 169

Jack of Kent's Ghost, 94, 169

Jack of Kent's Grave, 194, 195, 196, 197, 209, 219

Jack of Kent's Horses, 94, 142, 175, 180, 181

Jack of Kent's Oak, 94, 132, 169, 171, 176, 178, 186

Jack of Kent's Portrait, 94, 169, 171–3, 299, (see also Epilogue, Appendix II)

Jack of Kent Sayings (see Preface)

Jack of Kent Stones (see Kent's Stones)

Jack Stones, 9, 275, (see also Kent's Stones)

Jacques de Bourbon, 113, 121,

Janet Glyndŵr, 109, 164–5, 167, 170, 187–8, 192

John (king), 31

John A Kent (Outlaw), 254, 304

John ap Hywel (Abbot), 92–3, 118

John Ball (Mad Priest) of Kent, (see Preface) 33–4, 51, 116 (see also "Ballards")

John Ever-Afraid, 212

John Kent (Doctor, of Caerleon), 252–4, 304, (see also Epilogue)

John of Gaunt, 32, 59, 149, 303

John of Kent (Cancellarius), (see Preface), 289, 303

John of Kent (Rector of Kentchurch), (see Preface), 93, 198, 305

John de Went, (see Preface), 253

John the Baptist, 58

John the Little, (see Little John)

John the Spaniard, 106, 111

Kaueros, (see Corras)

Kemp (Jack of), 173

Kempe, (John, Cardinal), 173, 244, 304

Kempe, (John, The Weaver), (see Preface), 173, 226–7

Kempsford (Wilts.), 173, 214

Kenchester, 166, 188

Kendal (Kendal-Green), (see Preface), 163, 173

Kenderchurch, 176

Kent, (see Preface), 34, 204, 205

Kentchurch (Kentchurch Court), (see Preface), 35, 64, 94–7, 108, 113, 116–17, 123, 132, 142, 149, 155–6, 158–61, 164, 166–73, 176, 178, 180, 183–7, 193–4, 198, 211, 219, 222, 229, 235, 237

chapel at (Sancta Keyna), 178, 183–5, 195, 196, 209, 227, 238

dungeon at, 94, 162

Kentigern St, 182–3

Kent River, Valley, (*see* Preface) 183

Kentsdale, (*see* Kendal)

Kent's Stones, 184, (*see also* Jack of Kent Legends, Jack Stones, photographs)

Kerry (Ceri), 40, 89, 102

Kidwelly, 19, 41, 59, 63, 68, 71, 77, 95, 99–102, 104–5, 113, 131, 145, 148, 151, 229

Kilpeck, 50, 158, 160, 176

Kington, 188

Knighton, 78

Knights Hospitaller, 97, 178

Knights Templar, 27–8, 58, 97, 178, 184, 212, 222, 237

Knucklaas, 77

Lailoken, 183

Lancaster (House of), (*see* Preface), 60, 116, 216, 225–6, (*see also* De Lancaster)

Langland (William), 33–4

Laugharne, 101–2

Lawton's Hope Hill, 165, 187, 188

Ledbury, 63

Leominster, 108–9

Limbo, 209

Lincoln's Inn, 166, 169

Lingen, 166

Little John, (*see* Preface), 52

Liver, 5–6, 196, 199, 207–8

Llandaf (Cathedral), 105, 111

Llandeilo, 17, 73, 93, 215–16, 221, 223–4, 226, (*see also* Dinefwr)

Llandovery, 73, 91, 93, 109, 167–8, 215–16, 221–2, 225–7, 230, 234

Llandybie, 81, 190

Llanfor, 210

Llangadog, 168

Llangollen, 239

Llanllyr, 30

Llanrhaeadr-ym-Mochnant, 164, 240

Llanrwst, 82

Llansadwrn, 39, 210, 228

Llansilin, 37, 228

Llantarnam, 29, 92, 118

Llantrisant, 105

Llanwrda, 215, 229–35, 239–40

Llew Llaw, 176

Llwyn Jack Farm, 168

Llyn Peninsular, 67, 86, 135, 232

Llywarch Hen, 203, 210

Llywelyn ap Gruffydd Fychan, 41, 73, 93

Llywelyn Bren, 31–2, 38, 41, 43–4, 80, 111, 179

Llywelyn The Great, 31–2, 58, 60, 66

Llywelyn The Last, 31, 72

Locrinus, 31, 75

Lollardy, 57, 61, 149–50, 156–60, 170, (*see also* Wycliffe)

Lord Rhys (ap Gruffydd ap Rhys ap Tewdwr), 19–25, 27–32, 38–40, 42–4, 47–8, 62–3, 65–6, 71, 73, 92–4, 99, 130, 136, 180, 190, 206, 217, 223–4, 228

Ludlow, 12, 14, 78

Lugg River, 78

Mab Darogan, 11, 131, 151, 189, 192, 203, 215, 227, 239

Mabinogion, 14, 30, 48–9

Mabon St, 152

Machynlleth, 40, 69, 72, 121, Welsh Parliament at, 111–12, 114

Mawddwy (Red Rebels of), 155
Madog Fychan, 38
Maelor Saesneg, submits, 134
Magical Threshing, 53, 279
Magpies (symbolic birds), 203
Malcolm (king of Scots), 22
Maelienydd, 40, 89, 102
Maredudd ap Gruffydd (ap Rhys
    ap Tewdwr), 19, 21
Maredudd ap Rhys, 23
Maredudd Glyndwr, 147–8, 150,
    154, 156–8, 161, 163, 167,
    170, 187, 192, 234–5
Margaret Glyndwr, 109, 164, 167,
    192
Mary (of Bethany), 27
Mary Magdalene, 27–9
Mary (The Virgin), 27–9, 45,
    55–6, 78, 80–1, 179
Mascall (Robert, Bishop), 114
Medrod, 16
Menai Straits, 134–5
Merionethshire, 67, 132, 134,
    144, 146, 148, 150, 155–7
Merlin (Myrddin), 39, 46–7, 75,
    113, 171, 203
Merthyr Tydfil, 126
Milford Haven, 121–2, 124,
    225
Millstone Grit (The), xxxv, 272
Mince-Pie (The), 175, 290
Mitchell Troy, 96–7, 109, 113,
    154
Mithras, 10
Monmouth, 1, 14, 32–3, 47, 77,
    97, 105, 108, 113, 154
Monmouthshire, (see Gwent)
Monnington family, 109–10, 167,
    193
Monnington (Ralph), 109, 167
Monnington (Roger), 109, 117,
    167, 192

Monnington-on-Wye, 109, 167,
    171, 188, 192, 235
Monnington Straddel, 109, 149,
    164, 167, 188–9, 192–4,
    234–5
Monnow River, Valley, (see Preface),
    8, 50–1, 59–60, 64, 94, 111,
    116, 132, 162, 169, 171, 176,
    178, 184, 194–5, 198, 208,
    215, 224, 230
Montgomery, 71, 87
Moon, lunar, 2, 4–7, 10, 14, 27,
    47, 54, 56–8, 60, 63, 83,
    179, 199
Môr (sea), 4, 49, 183–4, 201, 239
Môr (ap Coel), 183
Morfa Bychan, 135
Morgannwg (Glamorgan), 18, 34,
    80, 92, 95, 105, 108, 113,
    115–16, 119–20, 123, 128,
    151, 169, 179
  submits, 125
Morrigan, 5, 13, 29, 44–5, 49–50,
    54–5, 91, 135, 200, 203–4,
    221, 223
Mortimer family, 59, 153–4, 156
Mortimer (Edmund the Elder),
    77–9, 84, 86–7, 101, 109,
    115–16, 121, 138–40, 147,
    154, 156, 161
Mortimer (Edmund the Younger),
    58, 77, 115, 150
Mortimer (Roger), 58–9, 62
Morvran, 49, 206
Munday (Anthony), (see Preface),
    49, 259–262, 264 (see also
    Epilogue)
Mynydd Myrddin, 171, (see also
    Merlin)

Nantconwy, 70
Neolithic era, 2, 46, 48, 55–6, 83,

91, 178–9, 199, 204, 210
Newcastle (Monnow), 132
Newcastle Emlyn, 20, 248
Newport, 80, 105, 116
New Quay, 103
Newtown, 40, 89, 102
Noah, 11, 179, 201, (see also
    Flood)
Norbert St, 29
Normans, 17–19, 24, 60, 179,
    206, 224, 237
Northumberland, (see Percy),
Northumbria, Northumbrians,
    13–14, 16, 46, 116, 200,
    204, 206
Nudd (Nodens), 45

Offa's Dyke, 40, 115, 165–6, 206
Oak king (see Green Man)
Odin, 51, (see also Appendix I),
Oil Painting (The), (see Jack of
    Kent's Portrait)
Oldcastle (Sir John), 118, 134,
    148–9, 303–4
  as Lollard, 149–50, 156–7, 166,
    170
  death of, 156
Oracles, 4, 46, 58, 90, 202
Oran St, 201–4, 207, 212
Orcop Hill, 8
Orleans (Duke of), 110
Osla Big Knife, 14
Oswald (king), 205
Oswestry, 65, 112, 134, 205
Otherworld, 1–7, 13–14, 16, 28,
    30, 51, 88, 90, 184, 199,
    201–2, 204, 209, 214, 239
Outlaws, Outlaw–Theory, (see
    Preface), 168, 173, 186, 205
Ovens, 197, 247, 290–2, (see also
    Jack of Kent's Bake-Oven)
Owain, 47, 190

Owain Glyndŵr, (see Preface), (see
    also Mab Darogan,
    Prophecy)
early days of, 36–51, 58–60,
    62–3
revolt of, 65ff,
success of, 86–94, 99, 102–12,
    115
coronation of, 112
attempted assassination of,
    132, 146
fall of, 140, 147
outlawry of, 144ff, 163–4
disappearance of, 147, 150–3,
    164
as Jack of Fance, 190–1, (see
    also Jack of France)
as Jack of Kent, 49, 83, 94–5,
    117, 164, 168–70, 180–2,
    186, 189–90, 194–5, 198–9,
    214–17, 227, 229, 269
as poet, 185–7
Owain Glyndŵr's Bedroom, 94,
    169
Owain Glyndŵr's Covenant
    Stones, 70
Owain Glyndŵr's Oak, 94, 132,
    169, 171, 176, 178, 186
Owain Glyndŵr's Portrait, 94,
    169, 171–3
Owain Glyndŵr's Tower, 94, 169
Owain Gwynedd, 46, 214
Owain Lawgoch (Yvain de
    Galles), 32, 36, 43–4, 75,
    81, 190–1
Owein of Rheged, 13–14, 22, 39,
    44–6, 48, 94, 99, 152, 179,
    182–3, 190, 200, 203–6,
    210, 217, 223

Painscastle, 25, 73
Paleolithic era, 1

Patrick St, 45
Peasantry (of Welsh borders), 44,
        50–1, 59, 67, 116, 119, 128,
        156, 158, 169, 181–2
Peasant's Revolt, (*see* Preface), 34,
        51, 56, 141
Pembrokeshire, (*see* Dyfed)
Penallt, 113
Penda (king), 205
Pennal Letter, 130
Pennines, 11–13, 179, 200
Pen-rhys, 80–1, 92
Penrith, 29
Percy family, 84, 103–4, 115, 156,
Percy (Henry, Earl of
        Northumberland), 115–16,
        120–1, 129, 131, 135–7,
        140, 156
Percy (Hotspur), 77, 86, 103–4,
        115
Percy (Thomas, Earl of
        Worcester), 77, 103–4
Petrus Christus, 171
Piers Shonks, 213, 221
Picton, 122
Picts, 47
Pigs, 107, 199, 281
Pilleth (Bryn–glas), 78–81, 84
Pluripresence, 69, 83, 90, 240
Pontrilas (Heliston), 35, 171
Powys, 16–17, 25, 41, 68, 131,
        156
Premontre, 29
Premonstratensian Order, 29–30,
        42, 61–62, 97–98, 109,
        226–9, 234, 235
Prophecy, 4–7, 14, 39, 80, 100–2,
        104, 114, 131, 189, 202,
        208, 239
    Son of Prophecy, 11, 34, 111,
        139, 151, 183, 189, 192,
        202–3, 228

Song of Prophecy, 34, 39, 203
Pumlumon, 69–70, 74
Pwll Melyn, 118–21, 120, 138

Quin Stone (Queen Stone), (*see*
        photographs), 184

Radnor, 25, 71, 77, 81, 84, 87–9,
        108, 112
    forest of, 165,
Radnorshire, 12–14, 17, 24, 71–2,
        75, 77, 79, 84, 89, 103, 165,
        206
Raglan, 118
Ravens (symbolic birds), 5–7, 11,
        14, 22–3, 30, 43–6, 51, 72,
        91, 104, 135, 152, 179, 182,
        198ff, 215, 221–2, (*see also*
        Morrigan)
    as crows, 5, 29, 34–5, 39, 92,
        197, 277
    as jack-daws, 5, 6, 51, 213
    as rooks, 5
    as sea–ravens, 49, 135, 206
    as Demons 202
    as descendants of line of
        Rheged, 13, 14, 21–2, 25,
        31, 44–5, 62, 90, 93–4, 179,
        203–206, 223–4
Raven's Cave, 13, 224
Raven's Seat, 176
Raven's Stone, 48
Rhayader (Rhaeadr Gwy), 24,
        28–9
Rheged, 13, 22, 39, 44, 183, 200,
        203, 205, 227
    line of, 39, 44–5, 94, 179, 204,
        251–2
Rhodri Mawr, 16, 22, 47, 99, 206
Rhuddlan, 65, 104, 121
    submits, 132
Rhun ap Urien, 39, 46, 203

Rhys ap Gruffydd (Sir), 39, 63, 223

Rhys ap Gruffydd (ap Llywelyn Foethus), 95

Rhys ap Gruffydd ap Rhys ap Tewdwr, (see Lord Rhys)

Rhys ap Tewdwr, 17–18, 206

Rhys ap Thomas ap Dafydd, 230, 235

Rhys ap Thomas (Sir), 251–2, 264

Rhys ap Tudur, 140–1

Rhys Ddu (The Black), 135–8, 140–1

Rhys Gethin, 116

Rhys (The Terrible), 78

Richard I, 24–5

Richard II, 36, 51, 54–63, 65, 68, 77, 83, 85, 115, 130, 154, 176, 189

Robert III (of Scotland), 75

Robin Goodfellow, 168

Robin Hood, (see Preface), 52, 163, 168, 188, 213, (see also Epilogue)

Romans, 10–11, 47, 57, 173, 183, 188, 200, 202–3, 207, 209, 225, 234

Ruthin, 65, 76, (see also Grey)

Sancta Keyna, (see Kentchurch, chapel at)

Schism (Great), 33, 130, 157

Scotland, Scots, 19, 22–3, 31, 36, 45, 47, 50, 65, 76, 81, 83, 111, 120–1, 129–30, 136–7, 140, 157, 201, 208

Scottish Army (The), 64, 280

Scrope (Archbishop of York), 120, 124

Scrying, 6, 46

Scudamore (Skidmore) family, (see Preface), 95, 97–8, 113, 117, 154(tm)5, 158–60, 167, 169, 171, 178, 183, 186–8, 193–5, 209, 211, 229, 237–9 (see also Epilogue)

Scudamore (Joanne), 158

Scudamore (John, Sir), (see Preface), 94–9, 108–10, 117, 123–6, 148–51, 154–5, 158–61, 168–9, 175, 180, 185–6, 189, 192–3, 194, 198, 227, 229–30, 234–5, (see also Epilogue)

    first wife of, 96, 98–9, 158–9, 164, 166, 171, 227, 234

    marriage to Alice Glyndŵr, (see Preface), 94, 145–6, 160, 164, 166, 168, 169, 171, 185, 192, 193, 194, 198, 229, (see also Epilogue)

Scudamore (John, 'Esquire'), 155, 158–9

Scudamore (Philpot), 97–8, 108–9, 141, 154, 161

Scudamore (Ysenda, Lady of Kaueros), 178

Senghennydd, 31

Sennybridge (Pontsenni), 234,

Severn River, 12, 14, 16, 70, 82–3, 115–16, 123–4, 165, 184, 205–6, 213, 223, 231, 238

Shakespeare, 48–9, 79, 82

Shap Fell, 29

Shenmore, 188

Shrewsbury, 17, 37, 42, 66, 103–4, 140, 154, 159

    battle of, 103–4, 115

Shropshire, 86, 103–4, 115, 131, 133, 141

Simon de Monteforte, 97

Index

Siôn Cent, (see Jack of Kent)
Siôn Cent (the bard), (see Preface), 173, 186, 199, (see also Epilogue)
Siôn Cent's Quoits, 184
Siôn Cent's House, 126, 282
Siôn Gwdffelow, (see Robin Goodfellow)
Skenfrith, (see Preface), 50, 113, 182
Skidmore, (see Scudamore)
Sky-Burial, 5, 199
Skye, 207
Snowdonia, 19, 66, 77, 144, 146,
Somerset (Earl of), 66, 105, 198,
Son of Prophecy, (see Prophecy)
Sophia, 11, 27, 55, 178, 202
Spadefuls, 52, 278
Spain, Spanish, 112, 121
Spreading Dung, 143, 288
Stag (symbolic animal), 89, 176
Stalling Down, 104, 168
St. Asaph, 60–2, 183
   bishop of, 45, 76, 103, 108, 145, 182
   submits, 132
St. Clears, 101, 122
St. David's, 28, 45, 60, 130
St. Jerome, 172–3, 299, (see also Jack of Kent's Portrait)
St. Matthew's Day, 152, 155
St. Swithin's (London), 138
Stolen Cattle, 85, 281
Strata Florida, 19, 29, 41–2, 73, 103, 210
Strathclyde, 16, 22–3, 47
Stroat, Kent's Stone at, (see photographs) 184
Suffolk (Earl Of), 158
Swansea, 71, 81,
Symonds (Richard), 211–12, (see also Epilogue)

Sycharth, 36–7, 39, 42, 66, 87, 103–4, 228

Taf River, Valley, 41–2, 91–3, 100
Talbot (Gilbert, Lord), 117–18, 129–31, 134, 138
Talbot (John, Lord Furnival), 138, 159–61, 185
Taliesin, 39, 46, 48, 102, 203, 212, 227
Talley (Tal-y-llychau), 29, 30, 42, 61–3, 97, 109, 114, 226–9, 235
Tenby, 12
Teme River, 12, 123, 231, 238–9
Thomas ap Gruffydd, 63
Thornbury, 184
Throwing Stones, (see Preface), xvi, 269
Tidenham, 184, 213
Tito Livio, 165–6, 187
Tolleshunt, 210
Tops & Bottoms, 15, 276
To Sip An Apple, 236, 295, (see also Apples)
Tower of London, 59, 96, 119, 138, 141, 146–7, 156, 182
Traeth Mawr, 70
Trefnant (John, Bishop), 60–3
   death of, 114
   burial of, 214
Trefor (John, Bishop), 108, 115, 145
Tregoyl family, 211
Trellech, 9, 33, 113
Tripartite Indenture, 88, 115–17, 121, 124
Triple-Death, 3, 6,
Trolls, (see Preface)
Tudor family, 39, 59, 65–6, 68
Tudur Glyndŵr, 118
Tudur Fychan, 228

Tywi River, Valley, 12–13, 17–22,
30, 40–1, 43, 70, 73, 77,
89–90, 105, 114, 122, 168,
177, 206, 216–17, 225–6,
230, 234, 239
invasion of, 91, 93–4, 99, 102,
104, 114, 168, 215–16
support ebbing in, 131

Underworld, (see Annwn)
Upton Scudamore (Wilts.), 154,
173, 211, 214, 221
Urien of Rheged, 13, 16, 21–2,
25, 29, 39, 44–6, 90, 99,
115, 179, 183, 200, 203–6,
217, 223–4, 227
Usk, 72, 80–1, 116, 118, 120–1,
123, 184
Uther Pendragon (Uthr
Bendragon), 74, 77

Van Eyck, 171, 299 (see also
Petrus Christus, Jack of
Kent's Portrait, Epilogue)
Valle Crucis, 114, 145
Valle Magdalene, 29
Vaughan family, 166, 188
Vaughan (Doctor, John), 304, (see
also Epilogue)
Vikings, 16, 49, 199, 206–7

Warwick (Earl of), 111, 134
Waterton (Sir Hugh), 95, 149

Watt Tyler, 34, 51
Weather-Control, 48, 82–3, 90,
121, 125, 136, 140, 211
Welshpool, 65, 71, 112, 134,
140
Whitby (Synod of), 27
Whitecastle, (see Preface), 108
White Hart, 58, 176, (see also
Stag)
White Rocks, 8, 179, 184, 273
White Sow (see Pigs)
Whitland, 17, 28, 41–2, 59, 92–3,
100, 112
Will O' The Wisp, 236
Witchcraft, 50, 158, 180, 212–13
Wizard of Grosmont, 194, 219,
294
Woodbury Hill, 124, 238
Woodstock (Council of), 22–3
Worcester, 12, 14, 69, 72, 74, 77,
80, 116, 147, 191, 238
battle of, 123–4, 128, 131,
238
Wycliffe (John), 33–4, 57, 149,
157, (see also Lollardy)
Wye River, Valley, 14, 70, 83, 167,
184, 188

Yarweh, 10, 27, 56, 200, 222
York (Duke of), 106, 108
Yorkshire (Sheriff of), 137
Yule Log, (see Christmas Block)